Adolescent Portraits

FIFTH EDITION

Adolescent Portraits

Identity, Relationships, and Challenges

Andrew C. Garrod

Dartmouth College

Lisa Smulyan

Swarthmore College

Sally I. Powers

University of Massachusetts, Amherst

Robert Kilkenny

Harvard University

PEARSON

Boston • New York • San Francisco
Mexico City • Montreal • Toronto • London • Madrid • Munich • Paris
Hong Kong • Singapore • Tokyo • Cape Town • Sydney

Executive Editor: *Karon Bowers*
Editorial Assistant: *Lara Torsky*
Senior Marketing Manager: *Wendy Gordon*
Editorial-Production Administrator: *Annette Joseph*
Editorial-Production Coordinator: *Holly Crawford*
Editorial-Production Service: *Denise Botelho*
Composition Buyer: *Linda Cox*
Electronic Composition: *Omegatype Typography, Inc.*
Manufacturing Buyer: *JoAnne Sweeney*
Cover Administrator: *Kristina Mose-Libon*

For related titles and support materials, visit our online catalogue at www.ablongman.com

Between the time website information is gathered and then published, it is not unusual for some sites to have closed. Also, the transcription of URLs can result in typographical errors. The publishers would appreciate notification where these errors occur so that they may be corrected in subsequent editions.

Library of Congress Cataloging-in-Publication Data

Adolescent portraits : identity, relationships, and challenges /
   Andrew C. Garrod ... [et al.].—5th ed.
     p. cm.
   Includes bibliographical references.
   ISBN 0-205-41800-7 (alk. paper)
   1. Adolescence—Case studies. 2. Adolescent psychology—United
States—Case studies. I. Garrod, Andrew.

HQ796.A3343 2005
305.235—dc22   2004046154

Printed in the United States of America

10 9 8 7 6 5 4 3 2 1 RRD-VA 09 08 07 06 05 04

CONTENTS

Peers

PART THREE   CHALLENGES   243

Cases Categorized by Theme

continued

Cases Categorized by Theme (*continued*)

PREFACE

The fifth edition of *Adolescent Portraits* includes five new cases and one reflection by an earlier contributor on his life since writing his story. In order to accommodate the new cases and maintain a reasonable page length for the book, we have withdrawn the expert analyses of three particular cases. In choosing new cases and removing others as well as the experts' discussions, we have considered feedback from faculty and students using the book and our own understanding of the important issues facing adolescents in the first decade of this century. We welcome further comments on the usefulness of particular cases and the varied ways in which you may use them in your courses. We particularly value suggestions about critical adolescent themes that are not yet addressed in our text.

This fifth edition is accompanied by an Instructor's Manual, which includes further suggestions of teaching strategies and assignments for using the cases. An expanded review of films also appears in the Instructor's Manual, along with a sample of cases from the first four editions, which we thought were important to keep available to instructors: "Working through My Adolescence," "Running Hurdles," "To Be the Best," "Guilt Was Everywhere around Me," "No 'Boring Little Friends,'" and "Love Me for Who I Am."

ACKNOWLEDGMENTS

In the preparation of the fifth edition of *Adolescent Portraits*, we are deeply grateful for the editorial and administrative skills of January Moult, a junior at Dartmouth College, and for the editorial suggestions of Dody Riggs and Michael Holmes.

The cases in this book are the words of college students who have taken our courses, individuals who were willing to share their life experiences with many outsiders. Although we cannot thank them by name, we wish to acknowledge their personal strength as well as the time and energy they invested in this project. In addition, we want to recognize the many students who worked with us on cases that have not been included in the book; they, too, gave tremendous amounts of themselves as we worked to shape the final manuscript.

We would also like to thank the following reviewers for their comments and suggestions for this edition: Donna Brent, Skidmore College; James H. Dalton, Bloomsburg University; Charlotte Markey, Rutgers University; Tonya Rondinone, St. Joseph College; and Paul D. Sanderson, Assumption College.

OVERVIEW

The Study of Adolescence

The way in which we view adolescence depends, to a large extent, on our perceptions of human nature and the relationship of the individual to society. Current researchers draw on past perceptions but also bring a new set of lenses to the field. Many have begun to realize the diversity that characterizes their individual subjects and the difficulty in generating a theory that captures the experiences of all adolescents. Using the lenses of class, ethnicity, race, gender, and sexual orientation, researchers work to describe and explain the complexity seen in adolescent thought, behavior, and relationships.

Twentieth-century understanding of adolescent development has some of its roots in earlier studies of human development (see Elder, 1980; Muuss, 1996; Sisson, Hersen, & Van Hasselt, 1987 for additional information on historical trends in the study of adolescence). The first consideration of adolescence as a separate stage of life is often attributed to Plato (1921) and Aristotle (1941), both of whom described the adolescent as unstable and impressionable. They advocated schooling for girls and boys that would shield them from society and help them develop the self-control and reason that characterize a mature individual. In the Middle Ages, the prevalence of Christian views of human depravity and of knowledge as external to the individual led to a less developmental perspective. Children and adolescents were seen as miniature adults who needed to be socialized into acceptance of adult roles, values, and beliefs (Muuss, 1996).

John Locke and Jean-Jacques Rousseau helped to restore society's belief in the qualitative difference between children and adults. Rousseau, in particular, emphasized a process of development during which innate knowledge and character unfold throughout childhood and youth. In *Emile*, Rousseau presented his view of this process and the role of society in nurturing and schooling young people as they develop into responsible citizens. Rousseau attributed different natural characteristics and social roles to males and females and suggested that, while the process of development is similar for both, schooling toward the end product should differ as a result of their divergent natures and responsibilities (Martin, 1981).

In the nineteenth century, several social and intellectual movements influenced perceptions of human nature and adolescence. Charles Darwin's *The Origin of Species* included humans as part of the natural world, providing a more biological and evolutionary view of human development and growth. The industrial revolution led to a gradual deemphasis on the family's role in socialization for work and relationships and a growing discontinuity in an individual's experience of home and work. Accompanying movements such as child labor laws and compulsory schooling contributed to society's perception of a phase of development between childhood and the assumption of an adult role in society, a phase which G. Stanley Hall named *adolescence* in 1904 (Bakan, 1972).

Hall (1904) described adolescence as a key stage of life in the evolution of the mature individual. Drawing on Darwin's work, he postulated a scientific theory of recapitulation in which the individual develops through stages that parallel those of human civilization. Like Rousseau, he saw development as a natural, largely innate process that could be guided and supported by society. Hall characterized preadolescence as the "savage" stage in the life of the individual. Adolescence followed, a transitional period to adulthood filled with contradictory emotions and behaviors: selfishness and altruism, sensitivity and cruelty, radicalism and conservatism. Through the struggle of adolescence, the individual is reborn and a new self is created, ready to assume a role in modern society.

Hall's work influenced the study of adolescence through the twentieth century, but it has also been modified and challenged over the years. While Freud and those whose ideas developed from his work (e.g., Blos, 1962; Erikson, 1968; A. Freud, 1946) continued to focus on biological imperatives and their influence on the individual's psyche in the process of development, others began to take a more sociological perspective on adolescence. The work of Margaret Mead (1958) and Ruth Benedict (1950) suggested that society determines the behaviors, roles, and values of its adolescents. Others focused on the effects of social disorganization, social class, and social institutions on the life of the adolescent, documenting the role of environment in the shaping of experience (e.g., Havighurst, Bosman, Liddle, Matthews, & Pierce, 1962; Hollingshead, 1949). In the 1950s, studies of adolescence tended to emphasize the role of the peer group and the uniqueness of the adolescent experience; adolescence was seen as discontinuous with both childhood and adulthood. Adolescents had their own culture, comprised of a unique language, patterns of interaction, and beliefs.

While the events of the 1960s contributed to this perception of an adolescent subculture, they also led those who study adolescence to focus on the intersection between the life course of the individual, the age cohort, and the historical context within which the individuals act (Elder, 1980). Some researchers and theorists, following Mead's emphasis on cultural influences on adolescence, focused on the social-historical context of adolescent development. They challenged Hall's view of adolescence as necessarily stressful by examining continuity and change in adolescent behavior over time (e.g., Modell & Goodman, 1990; Steinberg, 1990). Others began to reexamine the period of adolescence within the context of an individual's lifespan. Research in child and adult development and in ego, cognitive, and moral development led to an understanding of adolescence as one of a sequence of life stages during which the individual addresses key issues such as identity, autonomy, attachment, and separation. The emphasis in this work has been on phases or stages of development that cut across social, historical, and cultural boundaries (e.g., Erikson, 1968; Kohlberg & Gilligan, 1972; Piaget, 1972).

Some of the most recent work in the study of adolescence has challenged approaches that emphasize either sociocultural determinism or universal developmental theory, suggesting that understanding adolescence involves a consideration of how social categories such as race, ethnicity, class, and gender interaction with processes of individual development (e.g., Gonzales & Cauce, 1995; Leadbeater & Way, 1996; K. Martin, 1996; J. B. Miller, 1991; Sears, 1996). The historical and cultural context is important in understanding adolescent experience, but it may not be sufficient to explain an individual's behaviors, beliefs, and sense of self. Stage and phase theories of development tend to overgeneralize from small, nonrepresentative samples and often ignore key variables such as race, class, gender, and sexual orientation that have a profound impact on an individual's experience and identity. The study of adolescence, then, has become more inclusive in terms of who is studied, what questions are asked, and how experience is analyzed. It has also become more complex, as we take a range of variables and contexts into consideration when examining individual development.

Research in the past thirty years has also refuted the "storm and stress" model of adolescent development that grew out of Hall's work. This approach sees adolescence as a time of severe turbulence, during which relationships disintegrate as the individual rebels against internal and external value systems (e.g., Blos, 1962; A. Freud, 1946, 1958). In contrast, more current work in the field emphasizes continuity and renegotiation as processes that characterize adolescence. "Normal" adolescent development encompasses a wide range of experiences, including a variety of family structures, sexual experimentation and orientation, and ethnicity and racial exploration. Although some adolescents may experience more environmental stresses than others, these challenges occur within a meaningful personal and social context for that individual. Researchers have come to accept many variations within their definitions of normality in adolescence.

Even as researchers and teachers try to understand the multiple aspects of each individual's identity, the context within which American adolescents develop continues to change, further complicating the picture. Adolescents in the late twentieth and early twenty-first centuries are growing up in a society that takes technology and global communication as givens. On a large scale, this adolescent cohort's historical and cultural context is one in which international shifts and conflicts mean changing relationships between the United States and other countries. Increased international communication continues to change our knowledge of relationships with others around the world. Closer to home, these adolescents experience a society that is working toward greater acceptance of diversity—one in which women and minorities strive to defend and work toward their goals while simultaneously trying to change society. Although they are growing up in decades of change and progress, today's adolescents also face persistent political and social problems: educational systems struggling with declining enrollments and shrinking resources; urban, suburban, and rural communities focusing on teenage drug use, school violence and the spread of AIDS; and continuing racial and ethnic questioning and occasional conflict. The social questions and issues that surround them demonstrate to today's adolescents that society does not have all of the answers and that it often seems to lack the direction and commitment needed to find them.

The Case Study Approach

Those of us who teach courses in adolescent development continue to search for materials that address our students' lives and illuminate emerging approaches in the study of adolescence. Such materials help students learn what past and present theorists and current research have to say about the adolescent experience and engage students in asking questions about those theories and approaches as well as their own lives. We want our students to be thoughtful and critical participants in the study of adolescence, contributors to our growing understanding of how this phase of life relates to the larger life cycle.

The authors of this book first found this kind of material in a book called *Experiencing Youth,* first published in 1970 by George W. Goethals and Dennis S. Klos. We all used this book in our own study of adolescence and initially incorporated it into the courses we taught. *Experiencing Youth* (1976) is a set of first-person accounts written by undergraduate and graduate students (the latter appear primarily in the second edition) that highlight key issues in adolescent development: autonomy, identity, and intimacy. These cases demonstrate how powerful narrative can be as a way of examining individual lives within a framework of theory and research on adolescence.

By listening to the voices of individual adolescents, students and teachers of adolescent development can gain a greater understanding of the issues facing some of today's adolescents. Case studies illustrate the complexity of the individual experience and the interactions among an individual's needs, ideas, relationships, and context. Each case, taken alone, helps us begin to know one more adolescent and his or her experience; taken together, the cases provide a rich overview of the field of adolescence. Through them, we come to a greater understanding of key theories and current research findings in the field of adolescence as we examine patterns in their lives and the lives of others. We are indebted to Goethals and Klos for helping us and our students learn the value of the case study.

Despite the strengths of *Experiencing Youth,* we felt a need for cases that reflected the experiences of today's adolescents—their social and historical context, their diversity, their concerns—and for the theoretical frames that reflected more recent work in adolescent research. In this book, we build on the model provided by Goethals and Klos, bringing together the voices of students in our own classes and some key theories and approaches used in the study of adolescence. Each case in this book was written and revised by an undergraduate or very recent graduate, most of whom have taken a course in adolescent development.

Although it is never possible to be completely representative, we chose students and cases with the goal of achieving a cross-section of ethnicities, class backgrounds, and experiences. The book includes cases written by first-year college students who reflect primarily on their early adolescent experience and by students who have recently graduated from college and look back on those years as well. The nineteen case writers include adolescents who are white, African American, Native American, Latino, Asian American, and several who are biracial. The writers include men and women who are gay and straight, and those who are questioning their sexuality. Case writers come from around the United States as well as the Caribbean, India and Vietnam; from urban, suburban, and rural environments; from more and less privileged backgrounds; from single- and two-parent homes; from situations that have stimulated reflection and those that have allowed the writer to develop without thinking deeply about the implications and meanings of his or her actions and ideas. Although we have included each case under a major topic (as listed in the Contents), each case addresses a number of issues. The chart at the front of the book provides a guide to the themes present in each case, as do the abstracts at the beginning of each case. See the Instructor's Manual for further suggestion for using the cases in this book in a variety of classroom settings.

PART ONE

Identity

Theoretical Overview

The seven cases in the Identity section of this book show a pattern of a struggle for meaning and a quest for wholeness. Within the categories of values and ideology, ethnicity/race, and sexuality, the adolescent writers wrestle with important choices—who they want to be, how to relate to others, what values should guide them, and what their place is in various spheres of their lives. Though the content of the autobiographies may differ from case to case, the reader will see that the writers share common explorations and preoccupations with the self: the self in relation to others and the self in relation to the broader society. We offer here a framework for approaching the cases in this section.

Erik Erikson (1968), who has helped shape our understanding of identity, proposed a detailed and widely applied psychosocial theory of identity development. Convinced that the study of identity is as crucial to our time as the study of childhood sexuality was to Freud's, Erikson forged a radical rethinking among psychoanalytic theorists about ego structure and the role of culture and environment in personality development. As is inevitable, his writings have, over the last decades, been expanded (e.g., Marcia, 1967) and debated (e.g., Gilligan, 1982) by a succession of theorists, some of whom have significantly broadened his theory's applicability. Its general acceptance, however, remains widespread, and his ideas form the foundation of the psychological approach we take to the cases of this section.

When asked to describe his adolescence, one of our students recently wrote: "I don't know where it started and have no more idea if it's ended. Something inside of me tells me I'm in transition between something and something else, but I don't know what." In transition between two "somethings," this young man is not at all sure where he has come from and even less sure of his destination; he is Kurt Lewin's (1939) "marginal man," uncertain of his position and group belongingness. As an adolescent, he is in a stage of his life in which pressures, both internal and external, to define himself become simultaneously impossible to ignore and impossible to satisfy. He is working to establish a self-concept while at the same time realizing that this concept is changing as rapidly as he can pinpoint it. Like Lewis Carroll's Alice, he may well reply to the question: "Who are you?" posed by the Caterpillar, by saying "I, I hardly know Sir, just at present—at least I know who I was when I got up this morning, but I must have changed several times since then." In Erikson's terms, the adolescent has entered a psychological moratorium—a hiatus between childhood security and adult independence.

Adolescence is a critical stage in the individual's development. Adolescents are intensely aware of how they are seen by others—aware, as V. S. Pritchett (1971) observes, that "other egos with their own court of adherents invade one's privacy with theirs." It is a time in which the values and perspectives of others become clearer to the developing mind. The adolescent must first attempt to evaluate his or her different options—different ethical positions or religious beliefs, acceptance or rejection of societal norms, attitudes toward sexuality, ideological stance in relation to family and friends—before he or she can choose among them. In this sense, the search for identity is not only the process of molding an image of oneself—it is also the attempt to understand the fundamental components of the clay that will be used.

The ego of childhood, strengthened by identifications with significant others and by growing mastery of the tasks of school and family life, will no longer hold; the challenge now for the adolescent is a creative synthesis of past identifications, current skills and abilities, and future hopes—all within the context of the opportunities the society offers. This challenge is made immeasurably harder because of the technological society we live in, in which multiple roles and careers tantalize us with choice. Mead (1958) suggests it might be easier to live in a society in which roles are inherited through birth or decided by gender! Yet the autonomous creation of identity, the redefinition of one's relationship, the crystallization in various domains of a sense of who one is, what one stands for, and how one relates to the world, is the critical task of the developing adolescent.

Erikson's theory of ego identity formation focuses on the concepts of ego identity, the identity stage, and the identity crisis. He defines identity as "the capacity to see oneself as having continuity and sameness and to act accordingly. It is the consistent organization of experience." As Côté and Levine (1987, p. 275) point out, there are two dominant characteristics defining the concept of ego identity: (1) the sense of temporal-spatial continuity of the ego, a requisite indicator of ego identity (Erikson, 1964, pp. 95–96), and (2) the self-concepts (the configuration of negative identity elements) that unify individuals' experiences of themselves during interaction with the social world. "The development and maintenance of the sense of ego identity is dependent upon the quality of recognition and support the ego receives from its social environment" (Côté & Levine, 1987, p. 275). In contrast, those who have challenged psychosocial notions of identity have suggested that we should think of defining identity in terms of the individual's connections/relationships in the world and see the individual as embedded in rather than outside the social context.

The concept of the identity stage introduces us to the notion of ego identity formation and the process by which identity is transformed throughout the life cycle. Erikson held to the epigenetic principle of development in which "anything that grows has a ground plan, and that out of this ground plan the parts arise, each part having its time of special ascendancy until all parts have risen to form a functional whole" (Erikson, 1968, p. 92). The stages are not merely passed through but instead add cumulatively to the whole personality; Erikson saw the quest for identity and the crises that it often produces as the defining characteristics of adolescence. His psychosocial stage theory is founded on the belief that life is composed of a series of conflicts that must be partially resolved before the developing individual can move to the next stage. He proposes eight general stages of conflict: trust versus mistrust, autonomy versus shame, initiative versus guilt, industry versus inferiority, identity versus identity confusion, intimacy versus isolation, generativity versus stagnation, and integrity versus despair (Erikson, 1968). Following psychoanalytic theory, these stages appear in sequential order but are never completely resolved. The formation of ego identity does not then take place only in the identity stage; the degree to which one satisfactorily resolves the identity crisis is heavily dependent on the resolutions to the challenges of the first four stages in Erikson's eight-stage life cycle theory. Each item exists "in some form," Erikson tells us, before its decisive and critical time normally arrives (Erikson, 1968, pp. 93, 95). That is, there are identity elements in all preceding stages just as there are in the succeeding stages, and if the conflicts in these earlier stages are concluded satisfactorily, the healthy development of the ego is more probable. If the conflicts are resolved unsatisfactorily, negative qualities are crystallized in the personality structure and may impede further development.

The psychosocial moratorium—a time of deferred choice—is the period in an adolescent or young adult's life for resolving the identity crisis. It is a time when role experimentation is encouraged and where there is little expectation that the individual will commit to permanent responsibilities or roles. The identity crisis "is precipitated both by the individual's readiness and by society's pressure" (Erikson, 1980, p. 130). The age at which the identity crisis occurs may vary "according to such social structure factors as class, subculture, ethnic background, and gender" (Côté & Levine, 1987) or socialization factors such as child-rearing practices and identification with parents (Jordan, 1971). The moratorium must end, with the experience of role experimentation complete and the achievement of a resynthesis of positive identifications. These achievements enable the individual to find "a niche in some section of society, a niche which is firmly defined yet seems to be uniquely made for him" (Erikson, 1968, p. 156). The niche is dependent on the adolescent's feeling that commitment in the areas of values, vocation, religious beliefs, political ideology, sex, gender role, and family lifestyle are accepted, settled, and expressions of personal choice. Other more critical theorists, Jackson, McCullough, and Gurin (1981) for example, have suggested that the option of having a moratorium and being in a position to choose in the area of commitment are limited by social, political, and economic structures and dominant ideologies.

Allied with Erikson's faith in ego identity is his understanding of the difficulty involved for adolescents in creating and maintaining this identity. Identity confusion, and the resulting identity crisis, results from the individual's inability to understand the "mutual fit of himself and the environment—that is, of his capacity to relate to an ever-expanding life space of people and institutions on the one hand, and, on the other, the readiness of these people and institution to make him a part of an ongoing cultural concern" (Erikson, 1975, p. 102). Feeling pressured by society and his or her own maturation to choose between possible roles even as personal perspectives are rapidly changing, the identity-confused adolescent experiences a confusion that challenges his or her ability to form a stable identity.

Erikson believes that the success with which the adolescent resolves these crises is extremely important for the eventual achievement of intimacy with others. It is only through the commitment to sexual direction, vocational direction, and a system of values that "intimacy of sexual and affectionate love, deep friendship and personal abandon without fear of loss of ego identity can take place" (Muuss, 1996, p. 54). Identity achievement, as opposed to identity confusion, allows the individual to move smoothly from preoccupation with the inner core of identity to exploration of the potential roles this self will play in intimate relationships with others.

Erikson's construct of identity versus identity confusion has been expanded by James Marcia (1966, 1980). Marcia, whose work on the ego and identity development began with his dissertation "Development and Validation of Ego—Identity Status" (1966), establishes two concepts already mentioned by Erikson—crisis and commitment—as the determining variables in identity achievement. "Crisis refers to times during adolescence when the individual seems to be actively involved in choosing among alternative occupations and beliefs. Commitment refers to the degree of personal investment the individual expresses in an occupation or belief" (Marcia, 1967, p. 119). Using these variables as the determining standards, Marcia breaks Erikson's fifth stage down into four substages: identity diffusion, identify foreclosure, moratorium, and identity achievement.

The identity-diffused individual is characterized by having neither an active involvement in the search for identity roles nor a commitment to any of these roles. He or she is not questioning alternatives. At this point, the adolescent is like James Joyce's Stephen Daedalus, "drifting amid life like the barren shell of the moon." Identity foreclosure is characterized by commitment without crisis; that is, the individual has chosen a set of values or ideological stance, most often that of his or her parents or valued others, without examining this value or searching out alternatives. In moratorium, on the other hand, the individual is in the midst of a crisis, actively questioning and searching among alternatives, without any commitment to one option. In achievement, the individual has experienced the crises of moratorium, and has successfully made a commitment. Identity achievement is most often attained in the college years, with moratorium and diffusion characteristic of earlier adolescence (Santrock, 1990). It should be pointed out that differences exist between societies and between groups and individuals within societies in the length of the sanctioned intermediary period, the psychosocial moratorium (Manaster, 1989). Also, those not afforded the time or opportunity to engage in identity seeking may well not undergo an identity crisis in adolescence or young adulthood.

Some theorists, among them Miller (1991) and Surrey (1984), have suggested that theories of identity development have been theories of separation and autonomy rather than connection and relationship. They believe that whereas adolescent boys seem concerned with separation and individuation, adolescent girls create identity more in connection to peers and members of their families. Carol Gilligan (1982) writes of her reservations about Erikson's theory in *In a Different*

Voice. Gilligan points out that Erikson recognized sex differences in identity development and discussed how for men identity precedes intimacy and generativity in the optimal cycle of human separation and attachment, but for women these tasks instead seem to be fused—the woman comes to know herself through relationships with others. Erikson nevertheless retained the sequence of identity preceding intimacy. The sequencing of Erikson's second, third, fourth, and fifth stages, Gilligan suggests, little prepares the individual for the intimacy of the first adult stage. "Development itself comes to be identified with separation, and attachments appear to be developmental impediments, as is repeatedly the case in the assessment of women" (Gilligan, 1982, pp. 12–13).

The process of adolescent identity formation may also vary in accordance with the ethnic and racial background of the individual. A number of theorists have presented stage theories of ethnic or racial identity development (e.g., Cross, 1991; Kim, in Ponterotto & Pederson, 1993). These frameworks of analysis suggest that nonwhite adolescents tend to begin the process in a stage in which they either identify with the white majority or are unaware of the role of race or ethnicity in their experience. They move, often as the result of a series of events or encounters in which their race or ethnicity becomes salient, into a stage of awareness. In this stage, individuals become more conscious of their position in the society and begin to question who they are in relation to their own racial or ethnic group and in relation to the dominant culture. In a third general stage, adolescents identify with their racial or ethnic group and often immerse themselves in an exploration of that group's historical, cultural, political, and social position in the society. The final stage in most of these theories is a stage of integration and internalization, in which the individual incorporates his or her identification with a racial or ethnic group into a more comprehensive identity. This more inclusive identity may allow individuals to identify with their group and interact successfully in the dominant (white) culture.

Ponterotto and Pederson (1993) provide a similar framework for examining white racial identity development. The stages they posit parallel those previously described and include preexposure, conflict, prominority/antiracism, retreat into white culture, and redefinition and integration. Other authors have explored the interactions among the multiple identities adolescents actually contend with during the process of identity formation. James Sears (1996), for example, has examined the experiences of adolescents who are both gay and African American, and Alex Wilson (1996) probes the lives of those who are gay and Native American. In Leadbeater and Way's book, *Urban Girls* (1996), researchers report on studies that investigate the experiences of male and female adolescents juggling issues of gender, race, ethnicity, and class as they figure out who they are. And Maria Root (1996) and others have begun to explore the lives of multiracial adolescents and adults and the complications involved in developing multiracial identities.

In her examination of black identity formation, Fordham (1988) considers the phenomenon of "racelessness." She explores the relationship between group (black) identity and academic success, and concludes that black adolescents follow one of two paths. Some respect an "individualistic ethos," disregarding their mandatory membership in the black group—a path that may lead to academic success.

Others consider this to be "selling out" and espouse the "collectivistic ethos" of their minority group in order to avoid becoming "nonblack," although they sacrifice academic success in the process. Ward (1989) examines identity formation in academically successful black female adolescents and discovers that racial identity formation is compatible with academic accomplishment. Considering not only the factors of beliefs, values, attitudes, and patterns of family socialization, but also "the girls' own subjective understanding of the role that race plays in their lives" (p. 217), she concludes that racial identity must be considered in order to gain a complete understanding of identity formation.

Alternative perspectives on the process of identity development in adolescence, then, focus on the examination of the individual in context. Development is seen as a process of renegotiating relationships, redefining oneself in relation to individuals and social groups (family, racial or ethnic group, class, and gender) of which one is a part. In the seven cases that make up the Identity section of this book, we include cases that address several aspects of identity development—values and ideology, ethnicity/race, and sexuality. In most cases, the writers are, themselves, engaged in exploring multiple identities. We encourage the reader to examine these autobiographies through a consideration of the following questions. What roles do issues of trust, autonomy, initiative, competence, and identity play in each person's case? Within what contexts does the author define himself or herself? What relationships and connections contribute to his or her sense of self, and how are they changing? Advisable, too, is an exploration of identity status—the evidence of crisis and/or commitment—in relation to each case, an approach similar to that followed by Ruthellen Josselson (1987) in *Finding Herself: Pathways to Identity Development in Women.*

Whatever theoretical perspective one adopts, and we suggest an eclectic approach, the essential components are a simultaneous discovery and creation of self leading to a deepening self-understanding. We believe the cases in this section capture that process in both tone and substance. In each case there is a greater sense of understanding and acceptance of oneself at the end than at the beginning. Each author makes clear that the process continues, but they seem here to have reached at last a plateau from which they can look back and survey their progress. Readers may do well to suspend somewhat their theoretical assumptions while reading a case, lest they miss the sheer spectacle of lives unfolding. Though different identity theorists provide a useful framework for interpretation of these cases, the best of them are but a scaffolding for understanding. We should try to listen first to each author in his or her own terms, to see the authors' evolution through their own eyes. In the unique and intimate details of their individual lives we can discern the outline of a universal struggle to identify our true selves. Your readings here should influence your understanding of theory at least as much as theory influences your reading.

1 The Struggle of a Lifetime

Born into small-town life, this college senior describes a lifelong confusion about who he is and what purpose his life serves. The kind of teenager pious adults point to as a "fine young man" who will "make us all proud," Jon conforms to expectations while longing to be a "regular kid." Lacking the ease and self-confidence to develop close friends, he experiences loneliness and isolation from his peer world. A religion of good and evil choices gives comfort and affirms his self-sacrifice and avoidance of typical adolescent pleasures. Beginning college away from home offers Jon an opportunity to re-create himself, but he repeats the lonely pattern of social and sexual avoidance. Through a change in academic focus to theology and involvement in campus ministry, he questions the moral certainties of his Christian beliefs, including its condemnation of homosexuality. He sees his future framed by the struggle of balancing service to others through a religious vocation with the need to be comfortable within himself and accepting of his human needs and imperfections.

My early childhood revolved around a close family, and Sunday dinner after church at my grandparents' house was a weekly ritual. Until I left for college, Nana and Gramps—my mom's parents—hosted a huge homecooked meal for our extended family. There was never enough room on the table for all the different dishes Nana made. Everyone had multiple helpings of mashed potatoes, ham, carrots, and strange things like turnips and parsnips. We would spend the afternoon talking, playing outside, and taking care of their two horses. My dad's parents would join us all on holidays, and since all four of my grandparents grew up in the same town, they loved to sit around the table telling stories about Bedford when they were young—and poor. "We didn't know we were poor," Nana would say. "We thought we had it good."

I grew up in Bedford, too, in the same green duplex as my mom. One of the many little towns in the so-called Coal Country of Pennsylvania, Bedford came into existence around the anthracite mines. All of the mines have been closed for years now, and things are not looking up for Bedford, which is the poorest of the nine towns in our school district. The population is almost entirely blue-collar, working-class families, elderly on social security, or various arrangements of people on welfare.

My family always pointed out the drunks walking up and down the main street, making sure I saw them falling over and looking dumb. I fully got the message when I was ten, when Gramps gave up alcohol for good after years as a borderline alcoholic. He owns a fuel delivery business, which was his father's before him. Now well over seventy, Gramps still works six days a week, more than eight hours a day, with no vacations, ever. His business is his life, and I know he'll work until he dies . . . probably behind the wheel of an oil truck.

Gramps started driving trucks when he was twelve years old, and at eighteen he borrowed $1,500 from his mother to buy his own coal truck. Now the business is worth more than two million dollars, and he worries about what will happen when he dies. He lives modestly, shares his profits with my mother and her sister, and makes special trips in the winter to deliver oil to people whose tanks are empty, even if they cannot pay. Though not a religious man, he is a kind of pastor to the community. He knows literally everyone and their family histories, and he spends time visiting with people when making deliveries. He buys their homemade pasties and pierogies, lends them money when they need it, and is an advocate for the working people with business and governmental bureaucracies. While growing up, I spent every Saturday working with Gramps, managing his office, riding on the oil truck, filling bags of coal and tanks of kerosene. His mother said he grew up too fast, and I realize more every day how much like him I am.

My own family is a strange one, inheriting from my dad's side the characteristic of not talking to each other. We stopped doing things as a family by the time I was in middle school, and since then my parents, my younger brother and sister, and I have each had independent lives. Trained as a nurse, my mom cannot work anymore because of severe joint problems that keep her in almost constant pain. For a while she was a teacher's aide in special education classes for children with emotional and behavioral problems. What I remember best about mom is her taking food and clothes into school for her kids, who often came to school hungry and without winter coats. I remember how frustrated she got at the administration's apathy. My father is a hospital administrator who hates his job. Work causes him huge amounts of stress, and he usually spends all his time at home watching television, which does not help the fact that he is overweight with heart problems and diabetes. I think he feels locked in a self-defeating cycle.

Though I remember family vacations and playing ball in my backyard, I was never really close with my brother, Luke, who is one year younger than I. Now a junior in college, Luke always felt that he was living in my shadow—he was "Jon's brother." Trying hard to be visibly different, for a while he wore only black clothes, and he still has long, unkempt hair. Now an accomplished musician and very happy with his life, Luke was always the outsider of our family. My sister, Rachel, is five years younger than I, and I remember helping take care of her as she grew up. Rachel is very different from Luke and me, an outgoing social butterfly who is constantly on the phone or chatting on-line with her friends to arrange trips to the mall or lament a boyfriend lost.

I was dubbed "the smart one" in my family early on. In elementary school, I loved learning and was excited to go to school. Education was important to my family, but the rest of the town saw it differently. Sports reigned supreme, and the other boys had been on mini-football teams, which their parents coached, since they could walk. My parents never got me involved with them, and though I was on a YMCA swim team for a while, I was awful at sports. Not able to throw a football to save my life, I hated recess and was always the last one picked in gym.

By fourth grade, I was bored to death with school, and my teachers persuaded my parents to transfer me to Bridge Street School for the "academically gifted" located three towns away in a community of upper-middle-class professionals. Students were bussed there from all over our district, but I was the only one from Bedford. At Bridge Street the classes were harder, and for a while I was lost. I got a C on a test for the first time ever, and I didn't win the spelling bees anymore. I was determined to excel again, and by fifth grade I had risen to the top of the class and regained the reputation as the one who always got the highest grade—and who was picked last in gym. Besides my natural shyness, I had a hard time fitting in because I lived in a different town from everyone else, and my parents weren't about to drive me all over. The other kids came from wealthier families, too, and I never had the right brand of clothes or backpack. But life was good, as my parents would remind me. I had a loving family, clothes on my back, food on the table—"some people don't even have that, you know."

For middle school and high school, everyone in the district came to centralized buildings, with heavily tracked classes to keep the "good" doctors' and lawyers' kids in the honors classes with the "good" teachers, and everyone else in the "regular" ones. Entry into that coveted honors group had taken a lot of work for me, and it took even more to stay at the top. I was thankful for making it and felt responsible to do my best. That's all my parents ever asked for, but my best kept getting better and requiring more from me. I felt guilty if I gave less than 100 percent and wondered how other people in my honors classes could totally blow off work.

For me, academics always came first, but in high school I took on a string of activities and leadership roles in school. Student council, newspaper, literary magazine, and chorus filled up my days, and then there were more and more positions in Boy Scouts, church, and community organizations. I worked constantly, and I was sure it would all pay off. I pressed on, earning the praise of adults and the certificates and plaques that covered the walls of my room. My résumé was growing at a frantic pace, and I envisioned that someday I would be valedictorian, get into a good college—maybe even Harvard—and be "successful." *Then it would all be worth it.*

Toward the end of the summer before my junior year, the choral director from a private school asked me to join his select choir for a concert tour in France. Jumping at the chance, I ended up singing in Notre Dame, Chartres, and Orléans Cathedrals. The music was spiritually moving, but the people were the most wonderful. Though I avoided going drinking every night with the junior and senior guys in the choir, it was okay. Everyone truly liked me for who I was, and I finally found a group of people that *I* liked. I finally fit in.

That experience made me disgusted with my high school, where no one, including the teachers, cared much about anything. Far from loving learning as I once had, I was now doing the minimum amount of work to get the highest grade, which took less and less effort as teachers and students became more and more apathetic. Overseas, I saw for the first time a whole world beyond my little town. I realized that life could be different from what I saw in high school, and I wanted to know and see and do more, to break out. I was convinced that I would go to college far, far away, probably never to return. Most of all, though, I wanted real school friends like I had found in the choir in France. I finally knew it was possible. When the choir director invited me to transfer to his private school, with a full scholarship, I *really* wanted to transfer, but my parents resisted until I just gave up.

When school started in the fall of my junior year, I felt that I had made the wrong decision and had forever lost the chance to change my life. By that winter, everything came crashing down; the stress I was feeling overwhelmed me. I felt unfulfilled by my work outside of school and hated being in class. More than that, my reputation had taken on a life of its own, and I hated the "Jon Davies" I saw in the mirror. I was supposed to be this responsible, honest young man full of integrity and honor, who would "make us all proud." I spoke at fundraisers, got put on boards of directors as the token youth, and was paraded around as Scouting's poster child. I didn't drink or party, have sex, or smoke pot. I was "trustworthy, loyal, helpful, friendly, courteous, kind . . ." just like a good Boy Scout. I did what adults think kids should do, but I was torn between the life I was living and an intense desire to "be normal." Why did I care so much what everyone thought of me? Why was this reputation so important to me? Why did I cling to it?

Because it was all I had to cling to. It embodied all my successes and the praise of adults. It was the source of my self-worth and pride. Now it was falling apart underneath me, and I was alone. For the next few months, I spent hours crying and talking to myself in my room, agonizing over my desire to go to that new school and start over sans reputation. I lamented my inability to tell my parents forcefully, "This is what I want." But I still am not sure I knew what I wanted—I was running around in circles and had to do something. I realized that I could not live up to that "Jon Davies" image that everyone had for me. For a while I thought I should say, "to hell with it all" and go be "regular" like everyone else—get drunk, go on dates, not do any homework, hang out, and just love living life without a care in the world. Forget the stress, forget the responsibility, forget being a leader. I wanted to be a teenager. I wanted my childhood back. I wanted to experience all these things for myself. But a nagging part of me said something different. The sacrifice would have been so high and would have cut off *everything* that made me who I was, however out of control it had become. My experience in France gave me hope that there might be some other choice, and there the story of my faith truly begins.

For most of my life, my family attended Second United Methodist Church, a quaint little place just a block from home. My mom taught Sunday school and my dad was on the board of trustees. There were lots of nice people who cared about each other, especially the children, and I did the typical Protestant things: Sunday school, youth group, Christmas pageants, and church suppers, in addition to the service on Sunday mornings. It was a great place to grow up, but by high school I was dissatisfied. The forty-five-minute sermons were boring and totally irrelevant to my life. By senior year, all the kids I grew up with stopped coming, and it was weird to lose all my church friends to jobs, girlfriends and boyfriends, and general apathy. I wondered whether church for most of the congregation was not just a social ritual that made them feel good about themselves. And I wondered about me. What drew me back week after week? Had church, too, become part of my so-called good-person image?

My *own* faith became important after it intersected with that stressful winter of my junior year. For the first time, I questioned the faith I was taught. I did what the adults said to do: I was a good person, I went to church. And look where it landed me: miserable. I somehow knew that turning into a wild and crazy teenager would not work for me, so I turned instead to examining Christianity *for myself*. I thought it might be the way out of my confusion. I began to listen to Christian radio and read free books from evangelical preachers like Billy Graham and Chuck Swindoll. I found a new message of sin and grace, pain and renewal, death and life spoken to people living in sadness and confusion, who did not always succeed, and who were not perfect—something I could identify with.

There was no one time when I was "born again," but that winter saw an important change. I found Bible verses that spoke to my need, especially "Come to me all you who are weary and heavy-laden, and I will give you rest" (Matthew 11:28). I had always had my church, but I had never learned to *be* a Christian. Now I heard a passionate promise of reward for the struggle and ultimate meaning far more significant than anything I worried about. I prayed those "asking-Jesus-into your-life" prayers, and I felt changed. The radio preachers and book authors were so clear and perceptive, pointing—it seemed—right at me. Most important, I found a sense of peace as a real gift of God. My life was mostly the same; I just had a new outlook. Faith was my way out of confusion, the source of ultimate meaning for my life, and a way to deal with failure.

As much as I used faith to get back on track, I still lacked friends. Evangelical talk about purity and walking the narrow path of righteousness made me judgmental of my peers at school. But by the senior awards ceremony, my achievements and ostensible success could not make up for what I was feeling inside. I got more prizes than anyone else, and new plaques joined the collection already covering my bedroom walls: National Merit Scholar, AP Scholar with Distinction, and my Ivy League admissions certificate topping them off. For a long time these honors were a confirmation from the adult community that I was on the right track, that I was the model to follow. But if loneliness was the cost of this kind of affirmation, I felt I had made the wrong choice.

At graduation, I was named valedictorian of my class—the ultimate prize toward which I had worked since sixth grade. But first the principal gave a long speech—to thunderous applause—about the baseball players who had won the state championship earlier that day. Then he quickly announced the valedictorian and salutatorian, offered his congratulations, and had us stand in our place amid the sea of 250 navy and silver gowns just long enough for the yearbook photographer to snap our picture. It was the ultimate hollow victory.

Coming to college, I had huge expectations. The wood-paneled library seemed the essence of the intellectual life I hoped to find. Here would be a place in so many ways far from home, where learning would finally be valued and where I would fit in because I was smart. More than anything, I wanted friends. In the basketball arena with the thousand other new students at our first class meeting, someone gave a speech saying, "Now's your chance to make a new start, to create yourself again, to be the kind of person you want to be." My parents were gone, no one knew me, and I could be just like everybody else. I would stop being shy and just go up and meet people. I would go to fraternity parties and drink, maybe even join a frat. I would get the girlfriend I never had in high school, be involved in sports for the first time ever, maybe try out for crew. I would see movies, take road trips, and hang around. But I never did any of those things. My freshman English professor called me one of the college's "closet intellectuals," and inside I hoped that there were others like me.

Freshman year was a replay of high school. I spent all my time studying, convinced that I had to get an A in every class. I followed college rules meticulously, so thankful to be at a great college. A near 4.0 GPA and two academic citations proved that I could make it, that I was good enough. I planned to double major in Russian and government and then work for the State Department. I decided to spend sophomore fall on a foreign study program in St. Petersburg, Russia, which was supposed to confirm my plans to enter the foreign service. But I was in for a big surprise.

Any illusion of self-sufficiency was gone after ten weeks in Russia. It was a totally different world. Fourteen students lived in little four-person apartments on the eighth floor of a broken-down dormitory whose stairwells smelled of trash and vomit. Sometimes we had hot water; most of the time we did not. The heat seldom worked right, the windows never closed all the way, our stove caught on fire, and the bathrooms smelled like sewage.

And for the first time I lived close up with people who acted my image of *normal*. My three roommates spent most of their time drinking, drinking, and drinking. They went to bars, clubs, or room parties more nights than not. It baffled me how they could do no work, sleep through class, and never study. How could they waste this opportunity? Most of all, I saw them drunk and hated it. I could never imagine being so *out of control*. Sure, I saw drunk students bumbling around campus, and heard stories of random hookups and "booting" in the bathroom. Even though I thought they looked dumb and immature, I had felt I needed to try all this out in order to be like everyone else. Now that I was seeing face to face the hangovers, vomiting, and vulgar drunken conversations, I wondered if I had to do it for myself to avoid feeling regret. I wondered if this was really the prerequisite for having fun and friends.

But it was also in Russia that I began to appreciate simple blessings of life. Beggars were everywhere—on the sidewalk, in the subway, in churches. On a cold November afternoon I will never forget, I was walking into a store to buy postcards, and an old woman in a wool coat and head scarf was standing in the entranceway. Her eyes were cast down, her hand outstretched, and she said *"Pomogitye!"* I knew the Russian word: "Help." Never before had someone cried out for help, right to me. More than a little shocked, I rushed inside but felt horrible the whole time I was shopping. It was the best kind of guilt. My ten postcards cost 22,000 rubles, a little over three dollars then, and though most people give beggars spare change, I handed her a twenty-thousand ruble note on the way out. She looked at it, put it into her pocket, and began to cry. "*Spasibo vam bolshoe.*" Thank you, she said, and she began to pray out loud. She thanked God for me, and prayed that I might have every blessing, love, and happiness. She reached out, and I let her hold my hand. I remember the warmth of her skin so clearly, the tears in her eyes and mine. Over the next month I had many old Russian women pray for me, holding my hand as I looked into their eyes, and I know God heard them all. Their prayers truly changed my life, and all it took was to stop and look them in the eye, to see not a miserable beggar but Christ Himself.

As powerful as my time in Russia was, the routine of college life took over soon after returning to campus sophomore winter. One big change, though, was the resolution of my search for a church home. I spent all of freshman year "church shopping," often attending the United Church of Christ (UCC) in the morning and St. Andrew's Episcopal Church's student eucharist in the evening. The UCC was a lot like my church in Bedford, but I eventually chose St. Andrew's.

Entering college, I had a very evangelical understanding of Christianity: God created the world, sin came into the world by Adam, all are guilty of sin and should be damned, Jesus died to save us from hell, and if you believe in Jesus you will be saved, otherwise you go to hell. That was it: plain and simple absolute truth. Right was right, wrong was wrong, nothing in between. But I also had a passion to learn more about Christianity, especially Roman Catholicism, which was demonized among Protestants back home: "They worship statues, you know." I took religion classes, studied the Bible for myself, read the church fathers and contemporary theologians, only to find a Christianity I never knew before. Truth was hardly as simple as I thought.

At St. Andrew's, I found a church focused on Holy Eucharist and rooted in the historic Creeds. With a new appreciation for tradition and the work of the Holy Spirit, the Church in all its human frailty replaced a literal reading of the Bible as my source of theological understanding. In the parish there are feminist liberals, family-values conservatives, and everything in between. Side by side we share one bread and one cup around the Lord's table. Anglicanism has become my foundation for learning more about God, and I appreciate its freedom of ambiguity.

Soon after settling in at St. Andrew's, I realized that its college ministry, minimal my freshman year, was now gone altogether. Honestly looking for Christian friends for myself, I suggested to the priests that we start something up again, and found myself appointed as the student minister with the task of rebuilding from scratch a campus ministry. With no idea how to do that, I tried hosting dinners, getting speakers, organizing worship services, and a hundred other things, but hardly anyone came. I was working hard, praying hard, but nothing happened. The clergy talked about how I was planting seeds, but I was looking for some fruit.

At the same time, I very much felt the need to be "successful" in other ways: to make a lot of money and/or become famous. Preparing to be an important diplomat who would make a difference in the world, I received a Rotary Ambassadorial Scholarship to spend a year at Moscow State University in Russia. But deep down I knew this was the wrong path. For so long I had lived according to the expectations of others, and being ambassador or international businessman was never something I actually wanted to do. I remember how my father always talked about hating his job and my mother about wishing she had gone to a music conservatory instead of nursing school. "Do something you'll enjoy," they always said, "don't make the same mistake." So when some typically Russian logistical snags gave me the chance to back out, I chose not to go to Moscow. Though my parents and mentors still are dumbfounded, it was a key decision that set the rest of my life into motion.

During that sophomore spring I had no idea where I was heading, but not going to Russia became the surprising first step toward exploring a call to the Episcopal priesthood. My first taste of ministry came in Scouting, where I led chapel services at summer camp. I loved studying the Bible, selecting songs, and writing prayers. Soon I was asked to do more than chapel services, though. When campers were homesick, they got sent my way. Staff with real problems ended up at my tent. The same happened in high school, when I heard about devastating breakups, arguments with parents, and complaints about teachers. There was nothing I could do to help, but I guess people found me a safe person who would take time to listen to them.

Though being a clergyman has always been on my mind, I never spoke about it to anyone. I was afraid of what people would think of me. I was afraid my parents would think they were wasting their money on my first-class education, afraid that my high school teachers would be disappointed, afraid that my hard-earned status as an intellectual would be in question, afraid that other students would think I was crazy. In this training ground for investment bankers, a future priest was definitely "sketchy."

But my choice of the Anglican church and a call to the priesthood were strengthened in the aftermath of the brutal murder of Matthew Shepard, a gay college student from Wyoming. Since Matthew was a devout Episcopalian, I impulsively contacted my college campus' homosexual advocacy organization about helping with the vigil they were organizing. When asked to make spiritual remarks, I spent hours in front of the computer trying to figure out what to say—how could I offer something meaningful that would touch the souls of people I knew little about?

When it was my turn to speak, I was petrified of offending someone and making the tense situation worse. There were already people planning, in the name of Christianity, to protest Matthew's funeral with "God Hates Fags" signs—and here I was the guy from the Episcopal Church. Midway through my remarks, which were vague because of the Anglican Communion's conflict over homosexuality and my own confusion about its morality, I knew I was merely making myself feel good that we bothered to show up. So I skipped to the prayer I wrote, and after a moment of very holy silence, began: "Eternal God, unsearchable and unknowable mystery, our refuge from one generation to another. To you we turn with sighs too deep for words."

When I finished, I sat down, and I listened. For the next two hours, students told painful stories about their victimization that to me were unimaginable. I could not empathize, *only listen*. A Native American student, beaten up in a town parking lot for confronting someone about a sexually offensive homecoming T-shirt, a gay student who received death threats, African Americans, Jews, Latinos, all saying that life at this campus was not nearly as comfortable as people made it out to be. And I wondered what responsibility the Church had in causing their pain and the hate and fear that led to it. Do we in our rush to grab hold of and proclaim the truth end up causing evil, sin, and death? In that night of holy tears, I learned a great deal, most of all that God's people are not all like me, and that I have a lot more to learn.

In a Christmas card from my rector, he wrote that that night confirmed in his mind my "true priestly calling." But as I became more of a presence at St. Andrew's and prepared to take the first official steps of the ordination process, I realized the need to deal more directly with the most difficult questions in my life.

Living for so long as a loner, I value the freedom of independence. But my lack of good friends for the last twenty years has taken its toll. At school I was never close with anyone: I never went on dates, never had a girlfriend, and did not go to any of the proms. I came up with lame excuses, maybe because it was easier to make them up than to learn the social skills I lacked but everyone else seemed to have perfected. In high school, the stories of other people's sexual encounters became cafeteria and locker room conversation.

With my Boy Scout values and evangelical Christian sense of right and wrong, everything sexual seemed pretty wrong. The whole issue went unspoken in my family. And as much as I stuck to my beliefs, I began to wonder if I was the abnormal one. At Scout camp, one staff member my age, Doug—a vulgar guy who chewed tobacco—constantly asked me, "You get laid yet?" knowing full well the answer was "No." After a while, Doug made a little addendum to his comments: "If you don't get laid soon, I'll know you're a fag." Was I?

Without real-world experience of romantic relationships, I often sought release from my sexual tension through Internet pornography. High-tech versions of newsstand magazines, what I saw on the computer screen in a dark room by myself was all I knew of sex. Partly *because* it was so detached from reality, it became my reliable outlet. I could distance my public self from my private desires and let them wander and explore, without risking my image. This was better and safer than really having sex, or so I told myself. All along it felt strange, though, and fake.

Sometimes I felt like a hypocrite, masquerading as someone righteous but with a clear sense of the sinful habit I allowed to entangle me. Pornography kept me trapped in a cycle of disappointment with myself, and I wanted for a long time to break out of it by force of will. At other times, I realized that sexuality would not magically go away and that creating another prohibition for myself, or another benchmark for personal moral achievement, was equally self-defeating and missing the point.

For the longest time, sexuality was bound up in my image of the wild and crazy teenager, and later with the "work hard, play hard" frat guy. At first fraternities were a secret world of carnal pleasure that appealed to me as a way to be normal for a change. Later I thought fraternities were the only way I could make friends. Maybe playing beer pong, the college's favorite drinking game, was a necessary rite of passage. So many times on a Saturday night, I resolved to finally go to my first fraternity party. I would get dressed and walk almost up to the house, see the line of people outside, and every single time I turned around and went back home. The yelling and loud music, kegs of beer, people dressed up and flirting, all seemed to say "This isn't for you." "But what is for me?" I wondered. "Is there another way that won't leave me full of regret or set me up for a midlife crisis?"

I always was a person outside of every group but with a foot in them all, and most of my relationships were one-sided: me helping people. I felt like I was their counselor or mentor, never a friend, but I also wondered how I could help people when I didn't share their experiences: bad relationships, divorces, single parents, drugs, suicidal thoughts, bad grades, and the list goes on. From what people tell me, they talk to me because I am a patient listener, actually care about them, and am a stable person they can rely on or use as an example.

That last part is the trick. In high school I took pride in being that example. As much as I hated my reputation as a "fine young man," I wanted people to believe that I could *really* help them get their lives straightened out, so they would be good, just like me. I constantly wavered between questioning my own normalcy and trying to get the people I was supposedly helping to follow my Scouting ideals and Christian morals, ones that I then believed to be universally true and good.

Giving up that need to make people be like me, admitting that I really need to learn a lot of social skills, and making time to spend with people instead of just working have helped a lot. But there still is more. Dan's questions, "Did you get laid yet?" and the implicit one, "Are you gay?" would replay themselves in my mind. So many girls in high school and college told me, "You'd make a great husband," but because girls have always been my closest friends, I could never conceive of them as a "hookup" or a "chick" or someone I'd "get with," like the more popular guys did.

But the longer I remained a virgin, the more suspect I became as a closeted gay. And I secretly wondered myself. I never met an openly gay person before college, and even then homosexuality was categorically condemned by evangelical Christianity and Boy Scouting, still my two main sources of moral authority. But my sexual fantasies were about both men and women, and bisexuality was an even more foreign notion to me. I wondered if I was deluding myself by offhandedly excluding a possibility far more dangerous to my reputation than I could imagine.

I got to know a lot of homosexual people in college, and that real-life exposure made me question the outright moral condemnation I had been quick to apply to them—and to myself. I felt locked in between the pressure of those who said "repent" and the ones who said "come out." But both seemed too like a prepackaged solution. When I was honest with myself, I realized that my homosexual feelings, directed toward heterosexual guys, were essentially envy masked by lust; I most wanted to *have* what they *had*: the muscular body, the popular girlfriend, and physical intimacy.

And so I set about exercising more, taking care of my body and appearance, becoming more emotionally self-confident, and asking myself what I truly imagined for my future. Part of me really longs for a family, but more often I wonder if I am called to a more radical service in a life of celibate singleness. Even within my religious tradition, that option is uncommon and strange. And though the mystique of "getting laid" has faded from its earlier importance to me, to others I still appear as a closet gay: a suspicion which has become more problematic as I encounter homophobic attitudes in my church and Boy Scouting. When I came to college I was offended by the term *homophobia*, but I realize now how much the fear of being called gay has interfered with my own life and the lives of other young people.

There is an Ojibway saying that I carry inside my appointment book: "Sometimes I go about pitying myself while all along a great wind is bearing me across the sky." The great wind in my life has been Boy Scout camp, where I have spent every summer since I was fourteen. There, away from my parents and school, the woods provided an alternative reality, a break from the discouragement and stress of the rest of my life. When I think I have no friends, I remember all of my close relationships on camp staff. We have shared late nights around campfires, deep conversations about the important things of life, the sweat of hard work, and days that never seem to end.

For the last two years, I served as program director of the camp, and my main goal was to create an environment in which the teenage boys who were campers there could be themselves. It would be a place that pushed their limits but supported them when they failed, where people cared about each other and could reveal their weaknesses, where approval was not conditional on fitting into images, and masculinity not dependent on performing physically, smoking and drinking, or making fun of people. It seemed a near-impossible challenge, but it has begun to work. And all the while I became more free, more confident, more at ease. I became my own true self.

I had just begun to curb the widespread practice of using "faggot" as a put-down, when midway through the season the Supreme Court ruled that the Boy Scouts of America was free to exclude homosexual Scouts and leaders from the organization. So when a camper said to me, "Boy Scouts hate gays, right?" I was at a loss to give him a good explanation without disagreeing with official policy and risking my job.

Can I be true to myself and still be a Boy Scout leader? Can I best advocate for change from the inside or the outside? Those same questions face me as I consider more seriously a call to ordination, which would place me squarely within the institution of a church which has lost its former appeal to me. Hypocritical, irrelevant to daily life, and bound up in bureaucratic infighting, the church seems very distant from the radical way of Jesus as self-sacrificing servant and liberator of the oppressed, which is now the core of my personal faith. Even the sermons of my priests at St. Andrew's, once moving and intellectually challenging to me, now seem like empty words. So what if "Jesus died for you and would do it all over again if you were the only one"? What does that mean? I want to know what *difference* being a Christian makes.

One day a Jewish student asked me, "Do we see God?" I answered with a presentation of the differences between the mystics and the scholars, but he interrupted and asked, "What do *you* say?" I never thought about that before. What *do* I say?

This year, I have begun to spend much of my free time at Royalton Heights, a low-income housing development just a ten-minute drive and yet worlds away from campus. As I come to know the children there by name, I see them living in the midst of sexual abuse, alcoholism, illiteracy and poverty, hunger, neglect, and violence. Looking them each in the eye, touching their lives, and allowing their lives to touch mine, I find the moral conflicts of my time in Russia coming back again. How can I spend three dollars on an ice cream cone, when children ten minutes away are going hungry? How can I worry about a perfect GPA when adults there can barely read?

It is a daily struggle as I think about my future. People who are poor, hungry, in prison, suffering from the captivity of abuse and neglect, these are the ones the homeless Jesus I claim to follow called "blessed." These are the ones in whose lives I find God, yet I know that my comfortable lifestyle depends at least in part on their suffering. I still want to preserve myself, to feel fulfilled, to somehow recapture that part of me that got lost in my growing up. But Jesus says that the only way to find one's life is to give it away for the sake of the world. What will I say?

I don't know. I still struggle with my simultaneous desire for close friends and the freedom to love everyone and avoid any exclusive group. I enjoy being independent but realize that I need a source of stability for myself. I have been working on the social skills I never learned growing up, and I am less shy and afraid of self-disclosure. I have some close friends, male and female, with whom I can freely talk about my life, both the good and the bad parts. I struggle with sexuality, but now it is symbolic of the larger question of how to live out my vocation, as a married or celibate person. Liberated from the burdens of adult expectations and my own academic and moral perfectionism, I am beginning to discover my true self. And while I believe deeply that the Kingdom of God is our true human destiny and that no one will be truly free until all are free from oppression, I struggle to let go of my need for security and live a life of service, with no guarantees. This will be the struggle of a lifetime.

2 Someday My Elders Will Be Proud

This Native American woman recounts her experience of living in two worlds. Jean describes how her mother raised her and her three brothers after her father abandoned the family when she was quite young. These circumstances, along with abuse at the hands of her uncle, leave lasting emotional wounds she will not address until much later. While firmly rooted in and proud of her Native American culture, Jean becomes a scholarship student at an elite secondary school. Her family's relative poverty and the condescending attitudes of her classmates further feelings of self-doubt, low self-esteem, and ethnic inferiority. Her transition to college does not succeed; she turns to heavy drinking, fails academically, and returns home. She gets a job working with troubled Native American adolescents, and through helping the self she sees in them, she finds a purpose in returning to college.

I grew up in Bismarck, North Dakota. My parents met through a relocation program. Relocation attempted to assimilate Native Americans into urban life from their reservation or tribal communities. The goal of the program was for an individual to gain economic self-sufficiency by means of a vocation or technical school education. My parents were in just such a program in Denver, Colorado, where they met and married. That is where my three brothers and I were born. My mother, a Cheyenne, was 22, and my father, a Blackfoot, was 21 when they had me. I am the oldest.

My father ran back to his reservation in Montana before my youngest brother was born. I must have been almost 4 years old. I have no concrete memories of him. My mom says that he taught her how to take care of me, because she didn't know that much about babies. He began drinking when I was born, and he was a womanizer. Soon his drinking got out of control. Despite her problems with our dad, Mom would always tell us how he loved my brothers and me and that he was a good father to us. Whenever he came home we would run and crawl all over him. We never saw him again after he left Mom and us behind. Dad died on the reservation when I was 7 years old, from alcoholism. He was only 28. I don't remember exactly when Mom told us, but it held no meaning. It seemed that he had already died when he left.

By the time I was 6, my mother had moved to Bismarck, where many of her relatives and immediate family lived. We did this because family was important to her tribe and they would help us as much as they could. Initially we lived off welfare and the help that our relatives could give us. My mother decided she didn't want us to live like that forever. She wanted to be a good example for the four of us, so she worked during the day and went to school at night to get her bachelor's degree in social work at the state university. We grew up in a single-parent family with the benefits of an extended family.

Mom worked through temporary services at factories and we got some monetary help from our father's social security benefits after he died, food stamps, and AFDC. We were very poor. We went to garage sales, Salvation Armies, and Goodwills for most of our clothes, furniture, and toys.

During those years when my mother pushed herself, my brothers and I were watched by one of my mom's younger brothers. She had no choice; he needed a place to live, and we needed a baby-sitter. I think he was in his twenties. He stayed with us from the time I was in first grade until I was in the sixth grade. He was always there after school when we came home. He taught us good things, like to stick up for each other when we used to get chased home from school by the white kids and not to be afraid of fighting for ourselves.

However, our uncle was alcoholic and had a violent streak in him. We became convenient scapegoats for him when he was sober or drunk. Even though my mom forbade him to drink in her home, he still did. There are lots of stories about how we couldn't wear shorts because the belt or switch marks were too vivid. He never hit us when Mom was home. When he did whip us, he'd say to us after he was finished, "You'd better keep your mouths shut and not tell your mother." And we stayed silent.

It was for stupid reasons that we got whipped. Who moved his magazine, who messed up the kitchen, who lost his sock and where was it? Who did it? Guilt, innocence, truth, right, wrong, what did any of that matter? It meant nothing. We could have been perfect children but that wouldn't have changed anything. We learned to clean the house as soon as we got home, and maybe it was good enough, maybe it wasn't. We learned to hide in our rooms until Mom got home. We used to be mean to our dogs and sometimes to each other. He made everything seem our fault.

Why didn't we say anything? I don't know. I remember one time how our uncle picked up my brother Lance by the hair and Lance was screaming. I never felt so helpless. I was mad, but I was afraid too. I knew it was all wrong, but I was glad in a way too, because it wasn't me. Mom kicked him out finally when I was in the sixth grade. All that mattered to us then was that he was gone. I still remember the relief I felt.

Why so long to get him out? Mom had to know. All I can think of is how her tribe is strongly patriarchal; men rule the home, and women must listen to and abide by what their brothers say. You never tell them that they're wrong; it would be disrespectful. In the traditional way, uncles are a second father to their nieces and nephews. Alcoholism ran through her side of the family and our dad's. I know that our two uncles had a violent father and uncle too. Those behaviors were probably passed on, and were allowed to continue because men have so much power to do what they want. Mom hadn't quite broken out of that mind-set when our uncle was living with us, and she tried so hard to make our lives better at a cost to hers. I couldn't really be angry at her because I remember how she tried to make us happy.

When I first started actively remembering everything that our uncle did to us, I hated him. I was glad that he couldn't hold a job, that he had a rotten marriage, that his own kids were uncontrollable and spoiled, that his drinking gave him critical liver and heart problems. But I tell you, it's strange. He loves us. I'm not going to live fueled by hate, and so I tried to understand what there was in him and his life that let him beat four little kids. He never had it easy himself, and he is the one who has to live with what he's done. He doesn't need another person who hates him or another part of his life to make him more bitter.

Many of our relatives on my mother's side lived in Omaha. Lots of these relatives were members of the newer religion, Native American Church. NAC integrates Christianity, adapting to urban life by getting an education or keeping a job, and being aware of what's good and beautiful in life, in other people, and in yourself. At least that's what it means to me.

An NAC meeting lasts throughout a night; you pray for whoever the meeting is for, including your family. You get no sleep, people sing "hymns" that are in the native language, and you eat a bitter-tasting cactus called peyote. The old school relates the Bible to life, and others talk about what their elders told them about being good people. People talk about how to cope with problems, talk about why things are the way they are, how you can look at your misfortunes, and how we must appreciate and recognize the good that we have. They talk about humbleness and realizing that so much of what we deal with will pass in time. It was there that I felt awe for wisdom and reasoning.

We drove back to Nebraska frequently for NAC meetings and for traditional religious ceremonies, where we prayed and made offerings to the gods and spirits, holding feasts and dances to honor what was being done for the people. We used to travel around the surrounding states for powwows—intertribal gatherings where dancers and singers from different tribes got together to dance and visit with one another. We also stayed with close relatives with whom my mother's generation had grown up. They told us stories from long ago and they fed us and took us along with them in their areas. The four of us liked going out of town; our world was not defined by the city.

When I finished sixth grade at the public school, Mom had me tested for a private school that an uncle's wife highly recommended. They wanted me to go to a school better than the public junior high. I was accepted and given a scholarship, and when seventh grade came around I went there. At the time, I didn't want to go. I wanted to go on with my friends to the public junior high.

I remember feeling that I didn't fit in and being apprehensive. It was an affluent Episcopalian college preparatory school, grades K–12. It wasn't race that made me an outsider, though there were undercurrents of it. If anything, it seemed to be worse in grade school, where my brothers and I had come home crying, until they told us to fight and stick up for each other. I'd say that poverty made me an outsider.

The first day an English teacher had us write essays on the furthest place in the world we had been. After we finished, we placed them up on the bulletin board. I wrote about Nebraska, and when I looked at the other essays, I saw people saying, "I've been around the world on a cruise ship." A larger majority than I could have imagined said countries in Europe, California, all over. Showing off seemed to occupy a great deal of time at school.

Kids were mean there, not physically, but with their words. "*Who* does your shopping for you? You've *never* been to the Calhoun Club? *Where* do you get your clothes from? You mean you *haven't* been out of the U.S.? You *rent* your home? You mean you don't get an *allowance?*" I couldn't have what they had or really understand the importance of it all, and I felt it acutely. There were the times when I would be talking with someone and instead of listening to whatever it was I was saying, they'd be staring at my clothes.

It wasn't anything that my family or relatives understood. We all knew that it was a good thing for me to go to school there. They wanted us younger kids to be able to work at the jobs we wanted and not struggle like they had. Being poor was awful, the bills were too many and too much. I knew all of that in a vague sense way down and I suppose that's why I stuck it out. But still, it didn't help me in dealing with the daily questionings or scornful looks from my peers. When they did that, I just looked away or down, shoulders slumped, because I felt self-conscious.

Learning the stuff from the books wasn't ever really hard; it was just memorizing most of the time. So I'd memorize and forget everything later. Mom made sure that I did homework when I was home. She always used to say to us how important school was, because if we had it, life wouldn't be as hard for us as it was for her generation. If anything, the material was boring. I noticed that the kids were highly conscientious about doing their work. Grades mattered to them in a way I never really understood. Mom never said to me, "Jean, I want you to get As," and she never acted disappointed when I didn't get an A. All Mom ever said was, "Did you try?" and that was enough. The other kids did their work because they wanted a good grade. For me, it was a way out.

The only way I could figure out to make things better was to bug Mom incessantly about clothes. She tried her best, but it wasn't good enough in my eyes to catch up to the other kids. So I started stealing from stores and from unlocked lockers at school. And then it happened; I got caught. I felt hunted, and I knew the other kids would really talk. "Can you believe what she did?" Most of all, I knew that I would hurt Mom. That's what mattered the most to me. I got suspended for a couple of days. When my mom and I came in to talk to the middle school director and I was asked "how come?" I ended up crying and talking about how people called me names, looked at me funny, and that I couldn't take feeling bad about myself anymore. I hadn't realized that those things preyed on my mind, that they hurt, and that's why I was stealing.

So Mom and I went home and she talked with me. She said that it was wrong to steal, and that it reflected on myself and the kind of upbringing I had. She said how it was easy to steal, it was cheating, and that it was hard to tell the truth and live by it. She said that we all make mistakes and that it was all right. "Just learn something good from this." And then she talked to me about the things that I had been called. "They're wrong and cruel and do not know you or your strengths. They're just a bunch of kids." I knew what I had done and felt ashamed about myself, but she made me believe in her love and in myself. From Mom, I learned to be compassionate.

I think I learned that I couldn't be myself at that school. I had to be like the other students to be happy there; I had to be rich and snobby. Because of my family's poverty and our tribal gatherings, I couldn't be like them. Not really anyway. Most of the time I was bored, or distracted by home. So what if the football team lost? So what if you're pissed off because you can't talk on the phone past 8:00? What kind of problems are those?

I felt that I had to put on airs, or have a dramatic life that people would be interested in, otherwise I was a lonely person. I needed to find a niche somehow, somewhere. So for about two years, somewhere between eighth and ninth grade, I became a liar. I made up the death of a relative, talked about things like drinking, or weed. I told people that I was part Greek. I quit when someone asked about my Greek grandmother. I knew what a lie it was, and I thought to myself, what about your real grandmother? Why can't you be proud of her and everything back home? It was like I had erased her life, said it was nothing by making up another woman who never even existed. I knew something was really wrong with me then. I cringe at the pitiful person I was. I see why I did what I did, but still . . . I decided that never again would I lie like that because it takes away from the truth of my life. It's "cheating." Parts of my life were ugly, and not understood, but it was mine. My life was no less important than my schoolmates'. Life can't be for everyone what it is to the affluent or sheltered, and none of that makes them better than those less fortunate or different.

By this time I realized how hard it was for my mom to support the four of us on her own. I know the bills and our teenage wants that got more and more expensive were getting to her. She would lash out at us about "never being satisfied" or about not helping enough around the house. She used to point out our faults to us, not in a nice way, during those times. For myself, I cowered during those times when she lost her temper. I couldn't help it. But it wasn't anything like those times with our uncle when we were kids—I understood why she was frustrated and yelling. Even so, Mom always came through for the four of us. She would tell us how smart we were, and how strong we could be. If we did something wrong, she would understand what drove us, but always tell us to learn from it all.

There were other times when we went to an NAC meeting, powwow, lodge feast, or a meal with the relatives. I loved all those things. I didn't think about why I felt that way, all I did was feel good. I remember being back at school in the ninth grade after one weekend when we'd been to a powwow. I was in math class, looking around and listening, but my attention kept fading. I kept staring out the window, remembering. We had been to Canada, and the powwow was by a huge network of lakes. During one of the breaks, my brother and I had gone out onto the lake on a motorboat. He killed the engine in the middle of the lake and we were drifting; we could see the powwow ground, all the campers, smell the fires, hear the singing, see dancers walking around in bright colors, shawls and bustles, people laughing.

We tried to start the engine, but it wouldn't, and we had forgotten to bring oars along. We were drifting farther and farther away to the opposite shore, and right before we got tangled in the reeds by the shore, we tried one last time to start the engine. It started, and we were laughing, and the wind whipped our hair back as he gunned the engine. We sped around for awhile like that, and when we got back, we had a good story to tell.

People were always teasing each other about something. That's what I liked, laughter. At night you could see all the stars; coffee tasted the best when it got chilly after the sun went down. The smell of a wood fire was always around too, and you were up late and probably tired, but you were having a good time, so it didn't matter. Out of the four of us, I liked to dance the most. When I was small, I used to dance until I had blisters and they would make me rest for a while.

No one at school, though, would know what in the world I felt good about, or why. I felt caged. What did I care about a logarithm? I was disgusted when I kept hearing three girls across the aisle talking about the teacher, how nerdy she looked, and wasn't John hot, he just broke up with his girlfriend.

Reconciling school, our trips, and home life was hard. Keeping up with us and the bills was hard on Mom, and she was alone. Even though she finished up at college and got her degree, $18,000 a year didn't go far enough for the five of us. Mom was always stressed, and then there were the four of us being adolescents going through all of our stages. Sometimes I wasn't the nicest person, and got mad or upset when I couldn't do something because we didn't have the money. I would act like it was all Mom's fault. My brothers Rick and Lance were starting to hang out with the crowd at school that smoked weed, skipped school, and acted tough. Lance tried to run away one time when our uncle who used to live with us threatened to beat him up if he kept on smoking cigarettes.

My youngest brother, Bill, went to school with me. My other two brothers went to the public high school. They also tested for our school when they finished sixth grade, but there weren't any scholarships for them. By the time they were offered one, Mom couldn't swing it. As it was, the school was always hounding her to pay up. If she had paid on time, we would have gone without food, and probably heat and electricity too. Most of me wishes that my other two brothers could have gone to school with us, but part of me feels so glad they didn't. Basically, I didn't want them to feel bad about themselves. I know life would have been "easier" for them, but do years of ridicule have to go along with it?

By the middle of the ninth grade I developed some friendships. I found it easier to talk to other new students. For the first time in two years, I had friends. Most of the time our talks revolved around classes, boys, how hard track practice was. I liked it.

I think that high school for Bill and me was a time where we numbed ourselves to being poor and to forgetting the Cheyenne and Blackfoot ways. It was easier that way. It seemed that we had to learn to be one way at school, and another at home; but it was hard, how are kids supposed to do that? I went unwillingly to family functions. My family didn't see that much of me the last two years of high school. I was involved in sports, stayed over at friends', or talked with them on the phone incessantly. I didn't want to hear about how far we were behind in bills anymore. School was easier because it was shallow. I could handle talking about classes, but I couldn't do anything to help Mom or not make us poor.

By the time I was a junior, my brother Bill was in the upper school, too. Only thing is, I didn't like him that much because I saw things about myself from his behavior. He looked down on our family for being poor; he was ashamed. School and the people in it were the most important to him. I saw it in him when he brushed my mom aside. She was trying to tell him something, and he answered in a condescending voice to her. I was angry at him for not respecting everything she had done for us. He paid more attention to his friends than family. He said derogatory things to my other two brothers like, "Oh, what do you know?" and after a while they'd say things about our "rich private school." He looked down on them, and I thought, my God, it was only luck that got Bill and me in; it wasn't Lance's or Rick's fault they had to go to public school.

By the time it came around to applying for schools I had a sneaking suspicion that I had neglected something really essential by ignoring as best I could home and the tribes for so long. I applied to colleges because it was what everyone else did. I did fairly well on the entrance tests, had a good grade average, and got recommendations from teachers who liked me. When I applied to school, I applied to out-of-state schools because I wanted to see what it was like elsewhere. The whole process was funny, because I had all these Ivy League schools interested in me. I didn't really care about going to a top school, but most of the other kids did, and a lot of them did double takes when one of my friends teased me loudly about Harvard calling for me. I liked the school I'm at now the most because it had a Native American Society. I knew that I would need some connection to my background to help me out in school without my family or relatives.

Again, my relatives and mother were encouraging. I'll amend that. Everyone but the traditionals were glad for me. As a young woman, I should have been starting a family, not running across the country for four years. They never actually said anything, but when Grandma told them, they'd look away, or talk about something else. In my eyes, going to college wasn't going to make me less Indian, or forget where I came from. If anything it would enhance it.

It used to bug me sometimes when Grandma would say where I was going, because the way she said it would make other people jealous of me. Lots of people she told this to had kids in state schools or community colleges, and I felt bad because they were just as good as me. I didn't want people to be envious, or think that I was snotty. There were a lot of relatives like that, who were proud of me, but I hated it when they would announce where I was going; they didn't always mention that Sue was doing something really good for herself by going into the Marines, or that Bob was a supervisor in a plastics factory. They weren't any less than I was; in fact, the things they did demanded so much more.

Graduation was boring, and I wasn't crying like most of the other students were. I just remember being glad that school was finally all over with. I wouldn't yearn for my years in high school, and I wouldn't miss most of the people there.

My family brought me to the airport. Mom, Grandma, Grandpa, two uncles, two cousins, and my brothers were there. They took all kinds of pictures of me and my brothers, me and my cousins, me and Mom. I said goodbye to my brothers, and Mom was crying. She tried not to, but I knew she would miss me. And all of a sudden, I knew that I would miss her, too. It startled me. I had tears in my eyes and was biting my lips, and Grandma said, "You're going away to do a good thing. Nothing bad has happened. We don't have to cry." They called my name as I boarded, and I turned as they snapped a picture. I sat in my seat and looked out the window, crying. This man tried to make small talk with me, until he saw me crying, then he let me alone. The plane started to go towards the runway, and I looked at the terminal, and there they all were, standing and waving. I could still see Mom crying. Love. I was leaving love.

I was excited about going to school, partly to be on my own, but I thought because it was college, people would be wise and mature, that there wouldn't be the cliques like in high school. I was wrong. It was freshman week, and most of the people were *just like* my high school peers. I was horrified. I couldn't get into the class spirit, I didn't like my roommate, I didn't like most of the bubbleheads I met. I didn't really feel my purpose in being there—except possibly to meet all the self-important people and party as much as I could. It was a time when I had to stand on my own and rely on my strengths. The only thing was, I didn't know what my strengths were. It didn't feel like I had any.

I was sitting alone one night that first week looking at the stars, like I used to at powwows or in Nebraska. All of a sudden I had a tight feeling in my chest, and I said aloud, "Why am I here?" I felt like walking into the woods and crying, because I didn't want to go through a repeat of being new, like when I started private school.

This is what I did my first term at school: I went to math class for the first week, I went to English for the first half of the term, and to my third class maybe once a week. I drank whenever I could. I remember being three or four papers behind in my English class. I read the books I had to; I just couldn't sit down and say something about the topic questions. I sat in front of a computer, and for the life of me, couldn't think of a damned thing to say about Conrad's imagery in *Heart of Darkness* and its effect on the reader. I went to math for the first three classes and it was all review, from like the eighth grade. The thing is, I always hated math. It was my earliest class, and I didn't feel a compelling need to wake up and go to it.

When I drank too much, I would end up crying and babbling. One time I was at a fraternity, looking at the mob of people dancing, watching people weave in and out through the tightly packed basement to get a beer, and I saw people jumping up and down and crowing with triumph about a beer pong game when a cup got knocked over. I was supposed to be having a good time. I ran out and stood under a pine tree, fists bunched up, crying for my relatives. I was always embarrassed about crying or babbling like that, and would act like I had never done it the next day. I was homesick, more than I had thought possible, but I didn't know it. I felt empty and knew something was wrong with me because I should have been having the time of my life. After all, I was young and at college.

People tried to help me. Friends would ask if I'd gone to class, if I'd caught up in math and English. I'd say no, and they'd say, "Jean, you've got to or you're going to be in trouble." I'd laugh, or say nothing. I got called in by my freshmen dean, and he asked how come I was having trouble. I said I didn't know. I was nervous and afraid of what he'd say to me. He said, "You went to a private school, you did well there, you are more than capable of doing well here. You're messing up. Why aren't you doing well?" I didn't say anything. He asked if I was homesick, and almost sobbing, I said yes. He told me that I had to go to classes, and that I could do it. I walked out of there, and composed myself. Crying, what good did it do anyway?

I used to talk with my mom about once every week. She always asked about the people who I was meeting. So I'd tell her about the people I hung out with, what we did or talked about—except the drinking parts. Mom hated to see any of us ending up alcoholic. She asked about classes, and I'd say that they weren't going so well. She'd ask about how I was doing, and I'd say, "I don't know, Mom, not so good." She always said "You can come home if you want to, Jean. You know that. We want you to be happy."

Somehow I imagined that if I had a boyfriend, everything would be okay. I had met this Native American guy my freshman week. I went looking outside of myself for what I lacked. I liked it that he still had close ties to his tribe, that that was where he drew his strength from. I had spent the night with him a couple of times after parties during the weekend. Platonically, I mean. We spent most of our days together. People were always wondering if we were ever going to get together. I wondered too.

John came up and said he wanted to talk. I had had a knot of anxiety and yearning in me, and it loosened up. He said something about wanting to wake me up with a kiss when I had slept in his room, taking it slow, how he had fun when we were together, and that he respected me. But it was almost like he was dictating a letter to me or something. Maybe I should have gotten up and gone to him when he finished talking. Instead, I said that I needed to go to the bathroom, because I really did.

When I came out, he had gone downstairs, and I felt disappointed. He ended up drinking until he passed out, and then I knew that we didn't have anything. I felt immensely alone, and sad. The next day we studied together, and that was it. He wasn't very talkative. We went back to his room, and he said I would probably hate him, because he had decided to get back together with an old girlfriend, and that he didn't want to date someone who wasn't Navajo. I told him I hoped it worked out for him, and felt surprised that I meant it. But that was the last straw for me, and I set myself on the path of self-destruction. I just drank whenever I could, tortured myself with dreams of getting him back, and forgot completely about classes.

With the end of the first term came finals. I wouldn't get up to go to my math final. Why go? I was going to fail anyway. I still needed to finish three or four papers, and I hadn't done my term paper for my third class.

I got a call over break, and my dean said that I had been suspended. So when I went back to school it was to pack. Dimly, I regretted it. I had been on my own out there, and I was just beginning to see that there was a lot I could have done, such as pulling my act together, being independent, and maybe learning to loosen up with people my age and have fun.

Mom was supportive of me, as were most of my relatives when I got home. I didn't really know what to do with myself in terms of getting a job, or going to the state university. I didn't really feel like doing anything. For about three months I stayed home a lot, cleaned, cooked, hung out with Mom and my brothers. I tried to escape from thinking about myself and what I would do. The only things I made an effort for were to go to Nebraska with my grandmother and to go to as many NAC meetings and powwows as I could.

I started to drink on the sly. I'd drink when there wasn't anything for me to do, or just to liven things up. One time, I had been slipping into the bathroom to take a shot of vodka every now and then, and I got carried away. My brother Rick told Mom that I was acting weird, and I remember sobbing as she rubbed my back. The next morning I woke up, and I thought, "Oh my God, what have you done?" I felt apprehensive, I couldn't remember anything, and I couldn't really believe that I had gotten stinking drunk like that.

Mom came home, and this is what she said: "Jean, you can't do this to me. This happened to your dad. If something happens to you because of drinking, I'm going to feel really bad. What's the matter? Why are you doing this?" And I didn't know what to say. But I realized that the parents are supposed to die first, not the kids. I saw in her face that Mom knew that she couldn't help me. I had to help myself, and drinking like there was no tomorrow wasn't going to do it. I saw how my not thinking had led me to so many things, and that somehow I needed to make sense of what was bothering me. I said how sorry I was, and for the first time in my life, I meant it.

So I enrolled in a religion and psychology class during the evenings and I got a job tutoring math and English at an inner-city alternative high school for Indians. Most of these students were from the reservation and had come from North and South Dakota, Nebraska, and Montana. Indians flock to Bismarck for jobs or for excitement. Most of us are poor, lots are alcoholic, and many come from dysfunctional families. What smacked me in the face was seeing that abuse was a way of life, the only way of life they knew and accepted. Their education: poverty; alcohol; drugs; emotional, physical, and sexual abuse.

There was a girl named Sharon who did her work and was quiet. When people picked on her she would cower. When she was called on in class her voice shook and she wouldn't look up. If I told her she was smart or looked pretty that day, she'd say, "No I'm not." If she had to ask me for some help with some problem she'd say, "I'm so stupid, I can't do this." I heard Sharon's boyfriend sneering, "Why am I even with you, I could have any woman I want." Sharon said, "I'm sorry, please don't be mad. I'll be how you want me to be." When I heard that I winced and ran into the bathroom. I tried to block out the echoes of her beseeching him. Those were my words whenever anyone was mad or displeased with me. I knew how that felt in your gut.

They had nothing. So those that still had any fight left in them latched on to being tough, independent, and reckless, all for pride. Everyone needs something. I don't know why the kids talked to me and told me about their lives so much. I don't know why they picked on almost all the other teachers and aides (to their faces most of the time) and left me out of their ridicule. Maybe it was because at 19 I wasn't that much older than them. Or because I was Indian. I liked to laugh with them or tease them when I could. And when they talked to me, I listened, because what they were telling me about was their lives.

All I could say to them was, "It doesn't have to be that way, you know." Those kids are the trapped, the bereft, the haunted. They are the reason I came back to college. I have to find a way to open up a life and world outside of their childhood so that they can at least get through high school and get an adequate education, one that prepares them for college. I have to find a way that doesn't make them feel ashamed about their pasts. I want to change the schools somehow. Schools and your success in them determine what kind of life and career you're going to have. I see so many kids weeded out, and it has nothing to do with their intelligence. Why is the path through high school to college so narrow?

Working helped me decide what to do with myself in terms of college. Since my return, I have done fairly well in classes. I still have problems in making myself go to classes on a regular basis and doing all the reading that I'm assigned. I'm more caught up in my family life and what goes on there than in my studies or the issues at school.

I don't aim for straight As, but for learning what I can that will be useful to me when I go into education, or what will help me understand people in general. I also try to learn as much as I can about the culture here, what kinds of ideals and standards motivate the students and professors. It's still a pain a lot of the time, because for all the advantages that most students have here while growing up, and for all their intelligence, there's an incredible lack of compassion or understanding that there are people who live hard, hard lives. Their worlds and lives are closed, too, and it disheartens me lots of times. Sometimes I think that academic knowledge is how they gauge the wisdom and respect of one another. It's something I don't understand, because what does academic knowledge have to do with who we are as people? As far as I can see, wisdom has nothing to do with books and theories.

For a while when I first came back, I joined a coed house, but I found that I still drank a lot to pass the time. I was hungover at least three times a week. I drank so much that I ruined something in my body. Now, when I have more than three beers or mixed drinks, I'm hungover really badly the next day. Luckily, I only get carried away once or twice a year like that. Now, I'll have a beer with dinner once or twice a month, and that's about it. I don't really miss it because I finally figured out that drinking solves none of my problems. It only wastes my time.

Since I have been back I have been an active member of the Native American Society and have lived at the Society's house whenever possible. It feels like a home. Most of my friends are Native American, not because I'm prejudiced, but because I'm much more at ease with them. I am still really quiet and shy when I first meet people, and I avoid at almost any cost participating in class. Just this past year I decided that I couldn't always be like that, and for now that's enough. I also fell in love for the first time. We were together for two years but broke up three months ago. It was so hard—it still is.

Peter accepted me for who I was, faults and all. He used to say that he wanted the two of us to be able to do what we both wanted, and then be able to tell each other about it all. But I didn't know how to accept myself, and I demanded so much from him. It was as if I expected him to make up for things lacking within myself, within my life. Now I know that there's no one in the world that can do that for me but myself. Until I met Peter I was always lonely. With him I learned how to actually reach out to another person instead of being someone who just dreamed about love. He reached out to me and I learned to trust.

One time I went out with a high school friend, and she was talking about how her father went to meetings for abused children and children of alcoholics. She named off all the symptoms that these children have. And you know, as she listed off the characteristics, she described me. I sat there with my mouth open, and it felt like I had been punched in the stomach.

I saw a lot of the abused child behaviors in myself throughout the whole time Peter and I were together. It's like there was a lightness in me after I realized it. Even when I was with Peter I often felt hopeless and depressed. I was always afraid he would leave me. I never understood what he saw in me, so I would try to be what he wanted. I couldn't stand getting into fights with him, and if I was ever mad at him, I'd sulk around and keep it in because I was afraid to express it. I was so insecure with myself. Things would build up, and when we finally got it out in the open, I wouldn't even know myself what I was mad about. Somehow I felt inarticulate and that I didn't even have the right to be mad. I still have some of these tendencies.

I see how I turned him into a kind of addiction and couldn't give him what he gave me, love and acceptance. When I told Peter about the fact that my brothers and I had been abused, and that I wanted to do something about it, he held me. My voice was shaking, and I could barely get across what I had found out. Peter asked if I felt like crying, and when I said yes, he said, "come here" and hugged me. But I couldn't cry. And when he asked how I felt, I said I felt ashamed. He said, "Oh babe, you don't have anything to be ashamed about. It wasn't your fault." And then I cried.

As time went on, when we were apart I became more and more insecure. I demanded that he put me at ease and hounded him to keep me a part of his life. I smothered him. Slowly, I lost confidence in myself and in him. Then I knew that I had a long, slow battle to feel good about myself and to not revert to my victim reaction. Oh God, I just wish we had met years from now when I was normal. I wish I had not been abused. But that is not going to change the past. I need to deal with how things are now, and slowly get rid of the things from my childhood. At least now I am aware, unlike many people who never have an inkling about what beneath it all is really bothering them.

Graduation is finally in sight. I plan to go on to graduate school for Indian education. I want to work in curriculum and administration, but I will probably teach first so that I can get some practical experience. I find that because of my experiences away from home I've gotten a lot of perspective that has, in the end, allowed me to appreciate my heritage. I will always do my utmost to keep family ties, NAC, traditions, and powwows in my life. I want all that, or something like it, for my children.

I've learned to think about myself as important and to know that I have strengths. I'm finally starting to be at ease with myself and with other people, and I look forward to the person that I'm becoming. It's been a long, slow haul. When I walk down that aisle for graduation I want my relatives to be there with me, and I'll walk proudly. I would do everything over again. I wrote this poem that speaks for me and for others:

I wear a coat. I wear tennis shoes.
I play a game and I am winning.
I go to school. I feel the worth
in the knowledge of my relatives.
I play the game, I do not live it.
Knowledge from all areas . . .
My thought, my hope:
someday that all my elders will be proud
respectful of the little ones who follow them.
I dream . . . to make a way for the small ones not yet here.
The younger ones to play the game in a skillful manner.
In a way that I never could.
It is our wish, it is our wish.

3 The Hatred Within

This writer wrestles with issues of family, ethnicity, and self-esteem. José, a twenty-year-old Latino junior, whose parents emigrated to the United States from Central America, explores his early experiences at school and his growing belief that his academic success made him not only "different" from other Latino/Latina students, but "better." Only when he reaches college does he come to understand this attitude and his disdain for his parents' relatively humble origins as a form of internalized racism. Drawn into the major Latino organization at his college and assuming a leadership role in student government, he comes painfully to name and eschew his self-hatred and embrace his developing Latino identity.

We were always horrible to the poor old man, Mr. Connors. He was the stereotypical high school substitute teacher—scolding us in a voice that echoed off the back wall and putting us to work with boring written exercises. We would respond by acting up, throwing papers, talking back, and pulling practical jokes—tormenting him in any way we could.

"Poor old guy," I thought. No more than five feet tall, he was bald except for the fringe of white hair that circled his bare dome. He wore rectangular eyeglasses and always came decked out in a full gray suit. I think it was the only suit he owned because he seemed to wear it whenever he substituted.

One morning, only a few minutes into the tormenting, the national anthem began over the P. A. system. As always, we stood up while the music played. Usually we did a good job of being quiet, but this time my friend Andrew and I kept joking and chatting as the music played.

When the song was over, Mr. Connors did exactly what I expected the typical "old-timer" would do. He began to yell at us for showing disrespect to the nation, but instead of focusing his obvious anger at both of us, he looked dead at me.

"Why don't you try that in your own country?" he barked.

Silence. I was in absolute shock. Did he really just say that? Without a second's pause I responded, "Why don't you try that in yours?" I took a step forward.

There was no mirror there, so I have no sure idea what I looked like. But knowing how I get, I'm sure my face turned a bright red, my eyes became narrow and angry, my eyebrows crouched down. When I'm enraged, I make it very obvious. And it usually has the desired effect of intimidation because it's such a contrast to my usual jovial expression.

"This *is* my country," he answered back without a pause.

I took a few more steps forward. Not rushing to him, but with a slow threatening pace. "Well, this is *my* country, too."

"Well, how about your parents' country?" he asked, seeming not to realize that he was pushing me more and more, and that with every comment he uttered he was becoming more and more offensive.

"How about *your* parents' country?" I snapped back in the same mocking tone.

"My parents are indigenous," he said smugly.

The word at the time was unfamiliar to me. Although I was mad at myself for not knowing it (I wanted to step above this man as his intellectual and physical superior), I shot back, "What the fuck does that mean?" I didn't know what had come over me. I didn't swear at teachers, even substitute teachers. I joked, I kidded around, but I was always as respectful as my sense of humor allowed me to be.

He answered back by saying that the word meant his family had always lived here. Since he didn't look Native American, I had to assume he meant his ancestors came aboard the Mayflower or a similar absurdity. At that point I was at the foot of his desk, an arm's length away from his gleaming dome. I had no idea what I was doing. How can you ever be prepared for a confrontation like that? What did I hope to do when I reached him? Hit him? Spit in his face? I stood there barely a second before Andrew and my other pal Dave came from behind me and pulled me away, yelling, "Come on, José, back off! He's not worth it." And I knew he wasn't worth it. But what was it? What had happened to me? What did I think I was going to do? Why was I so enraged?

I wasn't the kind of student who turned violent so quickly, not with students and especially not with teachers. But something had come over me. My shock and disbelief at his words had drawn me magnetically toward him. Did he really say that? To this day, it remains the first situation that comes to mind whenever someone asks me if I have ever encountered outright racism. It was a slap in the face. But in hindsight the incident reveals more about me than it does about Mr. Connors.

Why did he look at me and not see a student like any other, or even an annoying teenager who had little respect for his country? Why did he appear to view me as a brown-skinned foreigner who didn't belong and deserved to have his identity questioned by a high school substitute teacher? That day in my sophomore year I felt like a minority. I felt like a Latino student. I felt like I didn't belong. Every other day, however, I took pride when my friends told me, "José, you're so white."

I'm surprised that it isn't harder to admit. As I see it now, I was a sellout in high school. I was a box-checker. I was a coconut. Name the insult and I was the epitome of it. In college, a friend referred to Latino students who didn't recognize their background or culture as "those who didn't associate." That was me. I didn't associate.

My high school was pretty diverse. The students in the Honors and Advanced Placement courses I took, however, were almost entirely white. I was lost, along with a handful of other students of color, in a sea of white faces. Given the fact that my classes were full of white students, it's no surprise that my friends were all white as well. I occasionally hung out with the one other Latino student whom I had known since kindergarten, but he, too, didn't "associate." He dressed in khakis and corduroys, polo shirts and button-ups, clothes that most people considered "preppie." And in my high school, preppie was synonymous with smart, and smart was, with a few exceptions, white.

Daniel, my good friend from the fourth grade on, was white with blond hair and blue eyes. My two best friends at the time, Nelson and Sara, both had dirty blond hair and piercing blue eyes. The pack of a dozen or so girls I hung out with junior and senior year were, with few exceptions, white. All of them were upper middle class. Most of them owned cars when they turned sixteen. These were my friends and I was proud of them.

But it was more than just the fact that they were white. I don't think there's a problem with having a lot of white friends, and I don't think I sought them out because of their skin color. They were just the people I saw every day. But what *did* matter was the attitude and thoughts that grew from this valuing of whiteness. Why did Mr. Connors's comments hit me so hard? Precisely because I was in denial of the fact that I was any different from my friends. I was like them. They were like me. It hurt me to be singled out as a Latino because, deep down, I really did believe that I was better then most Latinos. I was smart. I was hard working. I was ambitious. I was successful. I was funny. These traits, I thought, were uncharacteristic of most Latinos. Mr. Connors brought me down, and I'm sad to say that that was the biggest reason he upset me so much all those years ago. He tore me away from my misconception that I was accepted and belonged in the white world, which I saw as the embodiment of the good, happy, and successful life. He forced me to confront my own racism.

I talked to my mom about this late in my senior year of high school. I actually complimented her on her parenting skills. I pondered how she had managed to raise us in a way that made us better than most Latinos. It never occurred to me how wrong this thinking was. I would never have dared to repeat my racist thoughts out loud. But at the time, I thought them. I saw other Latinos and would often assume the worst. It was easy to convince me that one was a drug dealer or a criminal, as I was already biased against them. And I always made that distinction clear: I, and for the most part my nuclear family, was not a part of *them*.

But these were all thoughts I kept buried deep down inside. I continued to check off "Hispanic" whenever forms asked for the optional race/ethnicity classification. I took pride in it then. With so few Latinos who aren't wastes, I figured I was helping myself. They would see me as an anomaly, I told myself. I was unique and that made me very happy.

So, besides the little box that I would check off from time to time, my culture and background meant nothing. In fact, I would treat it as a joke:

"Quit stealing my money, spic."
"Hey, don't look at me, I'm just a spic."
"Ah, those spics just don't get it."
"You're such a grubby, grubby spic."

These were words I spoke, phrases that sprung out of my mouth and the mouths of my closest friends. They were always said in jest and I always approved. I found it funny, because I thought being called a spic was pretty damned ironic. I recall a white friend telling me I was more white than he: I acted white, I dressed white, I talked white. In essence, to him I was normal, and normal was white. You're not part of a gang? You must be normal, you must be white. You don't shoot up every morning or carry a gun? You must be normal, you must be white. You don't speak Spanish in school, you don't know how to Latin dance? You must be normal, you must be white. And I laughed when he said I was a spic. How funny, I told myself, me . . . a spic? I thought I was anything and everything but that.

Besides these occasional insults, which I then thought were perfectly fine, my days at school had nothing to do with being Latino. I was normal, I told myself, therefore my ethnicity couldn't be my prime characteristic. I considered it a contradiction. This kind of thinking—this utter disdain for who I was—is something most people will never be able to understand. I think it's natural for adolescents to question their identity, but I did more than just question: I denied everything that was natural to me.

I would avoid the sun as much as possible late in high school. Why? Because I tan pretty easily and I didn't want to get too much darker than other students. A slight tan was okay, but I didn't want to get carried away. I didn't want to stick out. Sometimes I would actually fret over my darkening summer tan. How can I remain as white as possible? I would look in the mirror each morning and wish not just that my skin and features were different, but that my whole ethnicity could be washed away. My self-hatred lay at the core of my being. And that's where I kept it.

When I brought my friends home, I would be ashamed when my mom and dad, whose English was so bad, spoke to them. I would cringe when my dad tried to crack jokes because his thick accent made him sound like some teenager in a man's body. I would be embarrassed when my dad swore without pause and told them some anecdote. I would never bring my parents to school as other children did for events or programs. Worst of all, the superiority I felt over Latinos I also felt over my parents. They were older, and more experienced, but because they couldn't communicate on the phone with their mortgage bank as well as I could, or because I understood the seven o'clock news better than they did, I felt like I stood on a higher plane. I used to look at my best qualities as traits that were somehow incompatible with the language I spoke at home, the color of my skin, and the values my parents taught me.

My story, my struggle as a Latino student in a white community, is also the story of my parents. The two cannot be separated. I now realize that much of my journey is a continuation of what they began so many years ago. They immigrated illegally from Honduras to the United States several years before I was born. In

Honduras my father was on his way to becoming an engineer; my mother was a teacher in the school system. When they came here, they lost everything and were forced to take menial jobs in a country where the language confused them. Within months they were caught and sent back by la migra. When they came to the United States the second time, they struggled constantly but they also thrived. My oldest brother Armando, who is nine years older than me, immigrated with my parents. My other brother Steve, five years older than I, was their first-born in America and therefore was given the most American name they could think of.

Until I was 7 years old we lived in the "poor" section of our city. Surrounded by black and Latino kids, the feeling I can most recall is fear. I was scared of riding the bus to school. I was scared of the other kids. I was much like the scared white boy in a black neighborhood. I was scared of the others because I saw myself as inherently different. Even in elementary school, I had begun to develop the self-hatred and racism I would carry with me throughout my adolescence. All I knew was that while I was home, I had to cover my head with my pillow to drown out the police sirens and gun shots. But when I went to school and sat with the "smart kids" in the reading and math courses, I was nestled in a peaceful, white community. When my parents were finally able to save enough money, we moved out of the poor section and into the white community I had held so dear.

My father was, and still is, a drunk. Drinking was more than just something he did; through the years it had become a part of the man. I cannot imagine him without a beer in his hand, just as I cannot separate the man from the violence he inflicted. I respected and looked up to my father when I was young, but perhaps most of that came from my fear of him; fear of what he would do if I misbehaved. He was a pretty intimidating man, with a big round beer belly and huge biceps and calves. Some of my earliest memories are of me hanging off his extended arms, like a skillful monkey swinging along the trees. He had a loud, booming voice. His Spanish was always rough and convoluted. It wasn't that he spoke poorly, it was just the slang or expressions he picked up and used like Standard English: "So I told him, 'Hey guy, fuck you, okay? Fuck you.'" He seemed always to be telling a story, always swearing, and, of course, always drinking. He was in his forties, but to me he sounded like a teenager trying to be cool. But as I grew up, I came to see him as a meaner, darker character. He wasn't just big anymore, he was scary. His resonant voice, which sounded like he was yelling even when he was in a good mood, often brought me to tears.

The last time my father hit me is still vivid in my mind. I was in seventh grade. I had a paper route all through middle school, and I usually delivered the papers right after school. One weekday after school I went to a friend's house instead of delivering my papers. We hung out the whole afternoon, playing cards and telling stories. I didn't get home until a little after five o'clock. I froze when I saw my dad standing on our front steps as I rode my bike into the driveway. He stared at me, clearly angry. My dad didn't even wait until I was inside the house to start yelling. "Que hora es esta para llegar?" He asked why I was late. Living in front of the high school, I was aware of the crowd of students staring at me as my father scolded me. I went inside, angry that my father would embarrass me like that. As soon as I was inside he slammed the door and continued his abuse: "Donde estabas, babosada?" In Spanish he called me a little shit, irresponsible, no good for not calling and telling him where I was. His face was bright red as his words tore through me.

As he stormed upstairs, I knew where he was going and what he was getting. The door to my brother Steve's room, which is down the hall from the kitchen, opened up and I saw his face pop out. I clung to Steve as little brothers tend to do. "If he hits me, I'm running away." I whispered, "If he hits me, I swear, I don't care, I'm running away." Tears were already streaming down my face and I braced myself for what I knew was coming. I heard my father pound down the stairs. He swung a belt and I foolishly tried to block the blows with my hands as he screamed to me to put my hands down. Again and again he brought the belt down across my thighs. The pain spurted in quick stings. There's no pain worse to me, at least in my memory, than the feel of a belt against my skin. I just wanted him to stop. I screamed louder, begging him to stop.

Eventually he stopped, probably tired of my screaming and tears; he turned abruptly and went upstairs. I remained crying, curled up in a little ball on the kitchen floor. I wished that I had the guts to actually stand up, grab my things, and leave the house forever. I had imagined and planned it so many times before—what things I would take with me, where I would go. But it was never meant to be anything more than a product of my imagination. Instead of making my plan a reality, I cried, just as I had done so many times before.

I'm not sure if he had been drinking that day or if it was just a bad mood. I mean, why hit your son for being late? My father, and the way he made me feel that day, became the personification of Honduras and my cultural roots. He was exactly what I wanted to avoid becoming. When he drank, I saw him as a stupid, pitiful fool. And it didn't take long for me to project those feelings on to all minorities around me. Except my mother—who I saw as different.

My mother is the sweetest woman in the world. She would do anything for me, including staying married to my father. She did it for me because she knew a divorce would hurt me. She did it for me because she didn't want us to have to move out of our nice home in front of my high school. She did it for me because she needed my father to help pay for college. I guess I take it for granted that it really was all for *me*. But there's no doubt in my mind that it was.

I was born with a heart murmur, which made me vulnerable as a child. My family took extra care of me, but more than anyone my mother was anxious for my safety. It was partially because of her personality, but also due to the circumstances. The combination of my sickness at a very young age and the fact that I was her last child—forever her baby—meant I was bound to be treated differently. She poured the last of her motherly instincts and care into me. Well into high school she would tuck me in at night and wake me up in the morning. Some nights I asked her to rub my back and, though she jokingly complained, she always did it. My closeness with my mother was a contrast to my father, whom I saw as the enemy.

As I grew up, my importance in the family and in her eyes grew. Armando never finished high school and failed my parents' dream of being the first son to graduate college in America. Steve failed similarly after only two terms away at the state university. I became their last chance. Out of thirty-two cousins on my father's side, I am the fourth youngest yet only the second to go to college. When Armando got into trouble, my dad unloaded on him in the only way he knew how. My father's mother had supposedly whipped my father into submission many years ago. A rope would have been a welcome change to some of the instruments he was beaten with as a boy in Honduras. Yet somehow he grew up loving and thanking his mother for every bit of punishment she handed to him. Similarly, my brother Armando has consistently defended my father for the pain he has inflicted on us. He, out of all of us, has stood by as my father's sole defender. For that reason, among others, my brother Armando and I did not often get along. Even though he knew my dad beat me, Armando felt he had gotten it much worse and viewed me as a spoiled brat.

My mother did not defend my father for most of their marriage, nor did she fight back. She quietly withstood his verbal abuse whenever he drank too much. Over time, however, whether it was the freedom she felt now that she was in the United States or her own personal growth, she began to speak up and assert herself. When he yelled, she would yell back. Usually, though, she was the voice of reason to his temper tantrums. Most of the time he didn't listen and kept on shouting, stalking off in anger and sleeping for the next few weeks in the basement, where he had a bed. Eventually, when I was in high school, my father moved most of his clothes down there and for months at a time would not sleep in his own bed with my mother. Through it all they stayed together . . . although *together* is a strange word to use for two people who never spoke, never stayed in the same room together for more than a moment, and were married, it seemed to me, in name only.

When they argued, my dad would say anything to interrupt her, to keep her quiet, to regain the peaceful life he remembered from Honduras. Her spirit took him by surprise. This wasn't the way it was in Honduras, he must have thought to himself. This wasn't the way it should be. The wife, he felt, was supposed to cook his food, serve him his drinks and meals, clean the house, stand by him always, and never talk back. But my mom, the wonderful woman that she is, would not stand for that. She knew that she was an American woman now and that things would have to change. Sometimes, crying to myself, I would hope that my mom would just give up and stop arguing back. I respect her now for being strong, but as a little boy I just wanted the shouting to stop. But no matter what, I always blamed my father. He was exactly what I didn't want to become and yet he was also the biggest male presence in my life. In my mind he represented Latino males, therefore I had no desire to grow up and become one.

As easy as it is to blame my father, another side of him, a gentler one, surfaces in my memory. He isn't always the man who beat me and yelled at my mother; sometimes he's the man who sacrificed so much for his family. During my sophomore year in college I was profiled in the college newspaper as a campus activist. The article described everything I'm involved in and all of my accomplishments. I referred to my mother as the "force in my life." A few days after it was published, I sent the clipping home. I was worried how my father would take it. When I finally spoke to my mom about it, she said they had read it together and they both had cried. He was not angry or jealous, as I would have expected him to be. She told me that my family had had a barbecue and invited all my family members. Sometime during the party, my father pulled out the article, which he had already taken to work to show his friends, and translated the article into Spanish for my relatives. My mom told me that everyone was so proud of me, but my thoughts were with my father. This is the man I call my dad, this is the man who, along with my mother, I strive to prove myself to each day in spite of his harshness to me. When I look back on my life, I won't see it as a success unless both of my parents see it that way as well. In the back of my mind is the knowledge that if things had gone differently twenty-odd years ago—if my parents had made just a slightly different decision, or if my father hadn't worked half as hard—my life would be completely different. I owe something to them, whether I like it or not, and that knowledge drives me to achieve, even when I feel that "I have too much to do."

That's why my narrative can't be separated from my parents' story. Their journey to the United States didn't end when they arrived for good, or even when they finally became citizens. The two stories continue in tandem, and just as important is the extended family they left in Honduras and the extended family that traveled with them. Growing up, I was often surrounded by my many aunts and uncles, cousins and second cousins. Just as my father became the embodiment of the Latino man—everything I didn't want to grow to be—my extended family also represented my ethnicity, my culture, and the target of my racism.

I saw my nuclear family as different from their little clans, and as I grew up, *different* also meant *better*. We Garcias were somehow special. My aunts were either single, divorced, or remarried. My cousins were constantly being arrested, having children out of wedlock, causing their parents grief. My cousins were the only Latinos I had any close connection to, so, to me their behavior exemplified all Latinos. They got into trouble, broke the law, stole, cheated, lied, and were disobedient. Although my brothers and I occasionally exhibited some of these behaviors, I nevertheless saw us as above it all. My female cousins got pregnant, moved in with boyfriends, married and divorced early—all the kind of behavior that I considered "subwhite." To do the wrong thing, then, as I saw my cousins do the wrong things, was to be less than white, to be *not* succeeding in America.

It is true that my brothers and I were generally better behaved, and better educated, and better mannered than many of my cousins. But instead of leaving the comparison there, I took it a step further and said that this was because they were Latino and were acting it, while we were Latino but we had somehow overcome our heritage. Overcome our heritage! This idea disgusts me now, and yet there was a time I didn't even question it. I didn't think of my family as successful because we were Latino or in addition to being Latino, but *in spite* of that fact.

The notion of overcoming my heritage recalls a poignant incident that occurred during a family vacation to Honduras. On the road, a small child around my age came up to our van and asked for a ride. We told him we didn't have any room, but as we started to drive we noticed that he had climbed on the back of the van and was prepared to ride with us, at fifty or sixty miles per hour, holding onto a ladder. At the time I disliked the little brat; I couldn't believe he had the nerve to try and hitch a ride from us. A dozen years later I think of that kid and can't help but see myself. If circumstances had been different, I could have been him. That notion would occur to me again and again, but at the time, and even as I packed bags for college, I still looked at that boy—at so much of my identity—with disdain.

My parents didn't pressure me much to succeed; I put the pressure on myself: I was the one who had to bring respect to my family after Armando dropped out of high school and Steve dropped out of college. Armando and I constantly argued, and he refused to come to my high school graduation. I think my success only highlighted his failure. My parents' pride in me was a sharp stab at him. He had been expected to be the first one to do so many things that I was now doing. Steve was more complacent, always assuming he would return to school and catch up with me. And that's how I left for college—angry with most of my family, convinced that I was better than my family and my heritage, and bearing the burden of bringing home what my parents wanted to see: a good report card and a college diploma.

For the most part, college was everything it was supposed to be: I was having the time of my life and meeting so many amazing people. It wasn't until my first meeting of La Unidad, the Latino student organization, that I had my first confrontation with the hate inside me. I had gone to the meeting because I felt an obligation to go. Despite my belief that I was better than my background, I was also confronted by the feeling that my status as a so-called box-checking Latino was what got me into college. Why else would I have identified myself as such? *Associate, identify*—words like these meant the difference between being seen as an outsider to the Latino community or a link within it. If you identified, that basically meant you acknowledged your heritage, you went beyond your box-checking status.

I went to that first Unidad meeting because I felt an obligation, not because I felt I would gain anything from it. I didn't want to be seen as a Latino student by the mainstream but I also didn't want to be seen as a sellout by the Latino students. My self-hatred and hatred of my ethnicity was deeply buried, and I had no intention of making it known. I barely thought about it, and that's the way I liked it. But my first weeks at college were characterized by a sense of exclusion, a sense that I didn't fit in anymore. Dressed in Abercrombie and Fitch, attending their parents' alma mater, most students seemed so different from me. I was afraid someone would suddenly discover that I didn't really belong. I had an overwhelming feeling that I had to start my life over again, build myself back up, yet I didn't know who I was or how to go about it.

That first Unidad meeting we all sat in a stuffy room, the Latino students on display for one another. I was immediately hit by the feeling that I was very *unLatino*. The others somehow exuded more Latinoness. It was in their accents, the speed of their speech, the Spanish words they mixed into their English. They all talked about home cooking and dishes that they loved, and although I loved my mom's home cooking, I didn't know the correct names of the foods she prepared. But most important, they all seemed to know more about their individual cultures. They were more culturally, socially, and politically aware than I ever thought I could be. What did I know about Honduras? I couldn't even tell you what kind of government they have there, let alone how "my people" are doing. What did I know about Latino culture besides what I learned in school, which was nothing? My cultural ignorance had never even occurred to me as a problem; suddenly it became a very big one.

The worst moment was when we went around the room and introduced ourselves. One by one they spoke, pronouncing their names with a full Spanish accent. Some people I knew always did so, but a few caught me off guard. *Drew* became *Andres, John* became *Juan*; the speed at which people said their names increased, and as we quickly went around the circle, I didn't know what to do. Of course, I could easily have used an accent, but I never did and I didn't want to do so just to fit in. I even had a fear about doing that. What if it came out badly? What if I couldn't even say my own name right? I didn't want their eyes on me, them to snicker and know that I was only a fake. I just wanted to come to the meeting, sit back, and feel like I had made up for the fact that I checked *Hispanic/Latino* instead of *white*, which is what I wished I were, or *Other*, which is what I felt like.

When the introductions finally came around to me, I blurted out my name, *José García*, with a full accent. I felt like a sellout, not because I didn't want to be Latino, but because I was willing to hide my true self in order to be accepted as Latino. I was more confused than ever. Inside I knew that I thought poorly of Latinos and that my racism was deeply rooted, yet I was willing to act unlike myself in order to be accepted by my Latino peers. I didn't know who I was or what I wanted. I only knew that I wanted to be accepted. I wanted to please everyone, and was finding I couldn't please anyone.

My confusion got worse before it got better. I had gotten involved early freshman fall in my college's student government. Representing the student body, the organization constantly worried about whether or not they were truly being representative. So they would literally take a count based on gender and race/ethnicity. I wasn't just a normal involved student, I was the token Latino, or so it seemed to me.

The word *token* was one that I would get to know well as time went on. Token Latino, token minority, people of color versus minority, ignorance versus racism, the relationship of power in racism, prejudice, institutional racism . . . these were all terms and phrases that I had never been acquainted with before my first year at college. I had a crash course in being nonwhite. I'm convinced that if you asked a white person, half of those terms would draw a blank response. It's not simply because they're white, but because they have had no contact with these issues. I'm a great example. I had never considered any of these issues, yet I was that person of color, I was that token minority. I was *supposed* to know. That lesson came to me during a student government meeting when I was asked to give my opinion as a Latino. I wasn't asked to give it as a student who happens to be Latino, but to give the official Latino opinion, as if all we Latinos got together one day and took a straw poll on a number of issues, all of which came out unanimous. There is diversity among races, but there is also diversity within races. I wanted my friends to be color-blind. I didn't want to be seen as Latino or ethnic or other. In a short time I went from hating my ethnicity to not minding it, but still being grateful when people could ignore it. The inner hatred I had grown up with was gone, but something rotten remained. I still had a way to go before I would embrace and actually be proud of my culture, rather than just tolerating it.

I continued going to Unidad meetings, continued struggling through my ignorance. I heard other students of color talk about the racial issues they had confronted growing up. I began to find more and more aspects of my childhood that related to their childhoods—similarities in being the children of immigrants. Most of all, I was surrounded for the first time by students who shared my skin color and also shared my academic success. I was no longer the exception in a sea of white faces. The wall I had built up between myself and my ethnicity began to break down. Despite being 70 percent white, my college introduced me to diversity. So before I realized it was happening, that lifelong correlation between *white* and *successful* stopped making sense to me.

I recall a late-night conversation with my friend Jake who is half Latino and half white. He casually mentioned that he was against affirmative action, that he saw it as reverse discrimination against white students, and felt that it only served to emphasize racial lines more. As he put it, "Why should white people today have to suffer for what white people in the past have done?" This comment led to a passionate debate. I argued that, despite what he believed, there was a racial divide in this country. It was social, as evidenced by my high school substitute's behavior years before. It was economic, as evidenced by the poor section of my hometown that bussed me in and out when I was younger. It was educational, as shown by all the white faces in my upper-level classes from elementary school through high school. It was cultural, as witnessed by the isolation I felt at my first Unidad meeting. "You're right," I argued. "Most white people of today have nothing to do with what happened years before. But that doesn't erase the problem. That doesn't change the fact that minorities are still suffering because of what happened years before. Furthermore, whether whites are directly at fault or not, it doesn't change the fact that whites have benefited. Because others have lost, whites have gained. It's not a question of right or wrong—it's just the way things are. But that doesn't mean we shouldn't try to change things." Jake kept arguing that minorities just needed to "stop feeling sorry for themselves."

That night I developed my own theory on this subject: "Look Jake, it's like life is this one big long-distance race. Ever since the race began, the minority runners have been oppressed, kept back, slowed by slavery, by conquest, and so on. And all this time the white runners have been getting ahead. Suddenly, all restrictions are dropped. No more slavery. No more segregation. Everything is made equal. But is it really equal, Jake? All that equalization under the law doesn't change the fact that all these white runners have had centuries' long head start. How does that translate to real life? In economics, in education, in social attitudes? These are all big problems and they call for big solutions. I don't think affirmative action is the best long-term solution, but it is a temporary one until people are willing to make the bigger commitment."

Jake said that he used his Latino background to get him into college, just as he used his running talent (he was recruited by the college for cross-country). That was all his identity as a Latino meant to him. With my mind entrenched in issues of race and ethnicity, I was outraged at him for saying something like that. And yet just a few months before I could have said the same thing.

At college, once I began to deal with the long-suppressed issues of my ethnic identity the floodgates opened. Sometimes I got in serious arguments and found myself saying things I couldn't believe I was saying. In those moments I claimed all white people were racists or the United States border should be completely open all the time. But that was part of my learning process, of pushing forward. I was in the process of testing, trying things out, seeing where thoughts would go and then evaluating whether I still believed them or not. I was trying to find myself under years of buried ignorance, self-hate, and prejudice toward my own culture.

In another late-night conversation with friends, I recalled that small boy who had wanted to hitch a ride with us in Honduras, who I had disliked so much. "What's so different from me and so many of the naked kids I see running around in Honduras, begging on the streets? Sure, I think my drive and my work ethic have been important, but I think the key difference has been the opportunities I have had—attending schools that are leaps and bounds above anything in Honduras and pursuing so many things that my parents never had the chance to. And yet it might have been completely different. It could be another kid sitting here today and me in Honduras. That's why I don't think I'll be happy in life unless I'm helping them realize their own potential. I want to give others all the opportunities that I had." And the minute I said it, I knew I believed it with all my being—I knew I would never look at my role or purpose in life in the same light again. I was never religious, and yet I felt I had found my calling. I knew then I could never be an investment banker or businessman. My place was in service, in education, in any field where I could use my skills to improve the lives of others and help them open doors.

In spite of my new insights, the same demons remained inside of me. When you look at yourself in the mirror for years and see someone who is unattractive because of his skin color, hair color, speech, and other characteristics, those negative feelings don't go away easily. I felt I had a big nose, that it was too round and not slim enough. I hated the fact that I would always be a good four inches below average height. I even came to dislike my boring brown eyes and black hair. My own insecurities about how I looked and fit in remained. Even though I was growing intellectually and emotionally, I had not yet purged many of the old thoughts that haunted me.

My self-hatred was also hatred of my background and my relatives. My perception of myself and others had been altered by all the new people I met at college. Generalizations I had held to—that all Latinos are lazy, all students of color are inferior to whites—were shattered while I was at school. My relationships with members of my family and their relationships with each other had also been forced to change as a result of my absence. My leaving home was exactly what my family needed.

Just how far the healing had progressed is evident in a radiant photo taken at Armando's new apartment, which he shared with his fiancée, Molly. In the photo, we're embracing each other tightly. My father has one arm extending far to his right to reach my brother and the other hand is tightly grasping my mother's shoulder. My mother is smiling beautifully; it's a genuine smile. She seems truly happy—happy to have her family all around her. You can almost read her thoughts: she has her family together again, different than before, but together. Caught in that photo is me kissing my brother. For no other reason than because I was feeling happy and wanted a funny picture, I embraced Armando's face and kissed him on his right cheek. He remained smiling while looking at the camera, his arm tightly around me. After the photo was taken, Armando wrapped his arms around me and pulled me in for a full hug. Steve came over as well. And right there, in the kitchen of my brother's new house, with my parents and his fiancée watching, Armando began to apologize to me for mistreating me for years and years. As we embraced, Armando sobbed, "I'm so sorry, José, I'm so sorry for everything I put you through. But you know I did it because I loved you and wanted only the best from you. You're my little brother, there's nothing I wouldn't do for you." He then opened his arms to Steve, and with the three of us wrapped in each other's arms, forming a little circle, Armando continued, with tears in his eyes, "You guys are my brothers, my little men. I love you two so much. So fucking much! I'm always going to be there for you guys, whatever you might need. You fucking come to me, all right? There's nothing I won't do for my brothers." The tears were coming down my cheeks now, and Steve, usually calm and reserved, also began to cry. Our coming together in love and reconciliation was the climax to what I had slowly been developing the whole year—my acceptance by and of my brothers after years of alienation. While we hugged, I remember hearing my mother tell my father to look over at us. I sensed her deep inner happiness. She was so proud to see her sons finally come together.

Several months later I took another step forward in my journey. I interned in Washington, D.C., working as a research assistant for a nonprofit organization focused on strengthening the Latino community. I found myself surrounded by people who had centered their lives around making a difference in the Latino community. Two men in particular, leaders in the organization, further altered my views on Latinos. Both had gone to Ivy League schools and their résumés were packed with incredible experiences. They could have done anything they wanted to in life, but they chose to give back to their respective communities. I met many prominent Latinos through them and my perceptions of Latinos, which had expanded exponentially since high school, was further improved. Any significant prejudices I had were eliminated by the success of these two men. I admired them *and* they were Latino. In the past, I would have joined these two facts by thinking, *in spite of* their being Latino. It's such a small detail and yet reveals so much about how I thought.

I was still working in D.C. when I flew home for the weekend to see the production of a musical in my high school. I saw the show with Dan, my friend since the fourth grade. I told him about my involvement in student government, my increased activism, and life in general at my small liberal arts college. But since I was in D.C. at the time, I also mentioned my internship and the great time I was having. With pride, I pulled out my business card. "Empowering the Latino community?" He read off the card, smiling at me and waving the card to a mutual friend from high school. "Look Chris, José is Latino now. Look at the card. Our little brown friend's creating community!" His tone was mocking and they both began to laugh as they gazed at the card. "This is the biggest load of PC bullshit. I can't believe you're a part of this crap!" He laughed louder, staring at the card in disbelief.

I felt crushed. This had been my childhood friend? This had been the life that I had enjoyed so much? I was ashamed of who I had been and what I had believed, but I didn't think the shame ran so deep. Was there anything I could turn back to? Was there anything that didn't stink of my racism? It had been a while since I felt so uncomfortable, fidgeting in place, wanting to be anywhere but there. And right then I was struck with a realization that came just before I would have begun feeling sorry for myself. "Hey Dan, fuck you," I said. His mouth opened in disbelief, his laugh stopped in midbreath. I continued, "Just because you haven't grown up in the last two years, doesn't mean that I haven't."

"Hey Mr. Latino, don't take it personally. I just think that doing this sort of thing is very unlike the José I knew in high school," Dan said, handing the card back to me.

"A lot about me is unlike the José you once knew. People change, Dan, and ya know what? I'm happy with the changes I've made." I gave both of them one last look in the eye and then returned to my seat in the theater. I don't think I was particularly articulate or eloquent, but I got across what I wanted. I didn't back off.

As the show continued, I recalled that late-night conversation with Jake and the passion with which I spoke of privilege and racism. An image of that boy from Honduras came to mind and I again imagined myself living his life. I then remembered Mr. Connors, the substitute teacher, and the anger he had made me feel. I reflected on the dozens of conversations in which I called myself a spic and spat on my culture. Finally, I thought of my mother and father and all they had given me and continue to give me. Dan, who silently took his seat next to me, had accused me of being "very unlike the José he knew in school." I smiled, happy that he was right, proud that I didn't joke along with him and deny what I had spent two years forming, what is still forming, what I hope never stops forming.

4   Color-Blind

The daughter of an African American father and white Austrian mother, this college senior has a childhood blissfully unaware of racial identity questions. As she entered college, however, she began to realize that there has been a powerful racial subtext to her relationships with white men. Realizing for the first time that some white men desire her because of her color and some exclude her for the same reason she began to question many aspects of what it means to be biracial in American society. Likewise, she experienced the condemnation of black students at college for her interracial dating. Caught in the middle, and now believing her parents' "color-blind" upbringing of her to have been naïve and unhelpful, Christine engaged in a painful process of questioning her basic assumptions about race and identity.

My parents talk little about their interracial marriage and the difficulties they have encountered as a couple. My father grew up in Alabama, my mother in a small town in Austria. My father never shared with me his mother and sister's disapproval of his marriage to my mother. I am only aware of this because on one or two occasions, my mother had made a reference to their hostility toward her and me during the first two years we were in the United States. After being told of my father's intention of marrying my mother, my grandmother strongly opposed it and refused to welcome "white trash" into her family. And for a long time, I was not welcome in her home either, because I was the child of such a sinful marriage. Once, at about age 2, when I was visiting my father's stepsister, my grandmother allowed me into her home, though she still rejected my mother, her "white" daughter-in-law.

My memory of the visit escapes me, but according to my mother, all of the grandchildren were visiting my grandmother at the time. A cheerful and bubbly child, I had arrived at her house in good spirits, but when my mother had returned, I was extremely quiet and sad. My mother says that my grandmother had given gifts to all of her visiting grandchildren except for me—the granddaughter of a condemned marriage. That was the last time I visited my grandmother until I was much older. I visited her in a retirement home when she had Alzheimer's disease several months before she passed away. Despite my grandmother's inexcusable actions, I never hated her, nor did either of my parents ever speak negatively about her. My parents attributed her dislike for their marriage to her age and the cultural attitudes of the South.

My paternal grandfather, however, adored my mother. Though I was not extremely close to him, I did see more of him than I did my grandmother from whom he was divorced. He had visited us occasionally while I was growing up and my family had once gone to see him in Alabama when I was 16 years old. During our short visit to the South, my family noticed that people stared at us a little longer, both because we were strangers in the segregated town and we were an interracial family. Despite the stares and scrutiny we experienced we dismissed the stares as the stupidity of the South. We did comment on the silliness of it all, but we did not discuss the social implications or the challenges we as children of a biracial marriage might experience as we got older.

Race was not an awkward topic for my family to discuss; we were comfortable with being members of an interracial family. It just did not make sense to dislike someone based on skin color. As difficult as it is to comprehend I never looked at my parents as a black father and a white mother; they were simply my parents. I grew up "color-blind." I knew that they were black and white respectively, but I did not understand what that meant. I was unaware of the difficulties both the black and white communities could have with an interracial couple. I had not yet been personally touched by the hostilities and disapproval of the outside world.

My mother's family was not thrilled about my parents' marriage either, but for different reasons. They did not want their daughter to move to the United States. As a result of the distance and language barrier, I was not close to my mother's parents. Despite their disapproval, my parents were married. I know that my parents had gone through a difficult period during the beginning of their relationship as a result of family members and strangers disagreeing with their choice to marry each other, but my parents were able to weather the difficult times and, overall, they have had a successful marriage.

The eldest of three, I am a child of this Austrian and African American union. My sister is three years younger, and my brother is five years younger. My parents married in Austria while my father was in the service. Soon after I was born, we returned to the United States. Four states and two children later, my family settled in a small, predominantly white community near Portland, Oregon, when I was in the second grade. My father had left the army and had taken a job in law enforcement, and my mother began a career in teaching. For the most part, my community was not ethnically diverse. There were very few African Americans in my public schools as I was growing up, and I was not good friends with any. Overall, my closest friends were white.

Before people knew me or my family in my new town, I sometimes had to answer questions about adoption and why my mother was white. I vividly remember in the second grade, a friend asking me if my mother was my real mom. Even after answering yes, it was still unclear to her how it could be that I had dark skin and my mother had light skin. I had to explain to her that my mother was white and that my father was black. Sometimes classmates would look at my mother with her white skin and blonde hair, then look at me with my black hair and dark brown skin, and in a somewhat surprised and confused voice ask, "That's your mom?" Occasionally, children (and adults) would ask me where my mother was as she stood next to me. Someone had once asked me, "If your father had been white and your mother black, would you also be white?" I never took offense at the questions; I simply answered and tried to explain, though there were times when I wished I didn't have to. The one offensive comment I remember, which I did not think of as offensive at the time, came from a friend in high school. She had previously lived in San Diego and one day said to me, "You don't act like the black people I knew in San Diego." It did not occur to me to respond back, "Well, you don't act like the white people I knew in Boston."

My first discussion about race and ethnicity took place during an intense program the summer before my senior year in high school. In the midst of the emotional and mental stimuli during the program's week of "racism and oppression," I was forced to ask myself questions about my background and beliefs. The issue of race hit close to home when Greg, a student in the program and a child of a biracial marriage, shared his personal struggles of growing up in Portland, Oregon, and the difficulty he sometimes faced as being neither black nor white. As he spoke about his background, Greg had prompted questions I had never been faced with before. I found myself partly relating to some of his frustrations and not relating to others. For the first time, I wanted to examine my experience as a biracial child. However, in spite of my interest, I was hesitant and did not seize the moment. The social implications of being a biracial child was a new topic for me. I was confused and uncertain about my feelings. For the most part, I had always had a good sense of who I was, but that afternoon as I listened to Greg speak, I wondered. I was 17 years old and I asked myself why my identity was now being questioned. Planning to leave home for college after my senior year in high school, I could not afford to *not* know who I was. I sat there in silence. That summer, the door on race had been opened, but I had soon returned to my placidly comfortable home. It would not be until I entered college that the conversation would begin again, and I would be forced to explore the issues surrounding my biracial identity.

The issue of race was never really discussed in my home. Sometimes, we discussed it on a political level, referring to others, but it was never seriously discussed on a personal level in reference to my family. Only once, when I was in the tenth or eleventh grade, did my mother raise the topic seriously. After she had watched a news program on biracial families the night before, she asked us at dinner if we ever had problems being children of a mixed marriage. We all answered no, and we moved on to another topic. I believe my parents had thought it better to wait until we brought up the issue of race, but after seeing the TV show, my mom thought perhaps she better finally raise the topic herself. Since none of us said we had any difficulty, she left it alone. I honestly do not believe that either of my parents were aware of the special challenges we were to face when we got older.

Overall, I was well liked and successful in school; I was ranked fifteenth in my high school class. I was an athlete on the state track and gymnastics teams, and as the junior-class president, I was very active in student government. I was also president of our honor society, was homecoming princess, and was voted "most likely to succeed" my senior year. I spent most of my time with a small group of close friends, but I also had other friends from many different cliques: the jocks, the stoners, the brains, and so on. Although I was well liked, I never dated nor even kissed anyone in high school. In fact, when I was homecoming princess, I had to ask a male friend from out of town to accompany me to the dance. Though I was delighted and surprised to be given the title, I was also embarrassed and confused for not having a date.

While in high school, I never considered the possible effect race could have had on my relationships with boys. I guess I didn't consider skin color to be an issue because there were two interracial couples in my school, and my sister had also dated a white guy. I also wasn't really interested in dating, so I didn't give it much thought. The few times I did think about it, like most girls, I was more insecure and self-conscious about my body weight and appearance than my racial identity. However, I did not know what was in store for me after leaving my hometown.

The door of racial consciousness that had been opened a little the summer before my senior year was to be opened wide when I entered college. Before I left for college, my parents did not warn me of the difficulty I would encounter as a result of my ethnic identity. Whether because they themselves did not know what I would encounter, or did not know how to broach the topic, or were trying to protect me, I cannot say. Perhaps as a white person, my mother could not relate, and therefore could not know what I would experience. As a black child of the South, perhaps my father found the issue of race too painful to discuss. I do not know. In any event, the two extremes of their respective colors meant they would not be able to understand my experience as a mixture of them both.

During the first week of freshman fall, I met Vanessa and Shawna, who were to become two of my closest friends. It would be the first time in my life that I was to be good friends with anyone African American. I do not remember our first conversation about race, but I clearly remember debating and even arguing about the implications of being an African American in the United States. We argued about "imposed definition"—the way outsiders perceive each person—and "self-definition"—the way one perceives oneself. I argued that since I was only half black, I could not align myself with one race or the other and, more importantly, that race was not significant. I frequently got the response that we live in a racist society that will never be color-blind. In shock and frustration, friends tried to tell me of the historical backdrop still affecting many blacks today. However, I did not care about ancestors from years ago. In my mind, my background was limited to knowing that my mother was born in Austria and my father in the United States. It was that simple. Even though it struck me as very interesting that so many African American students at my college thought their roots were very important and felt it crucial to strive to obtain more facts, I lacked the desire to do the same. I believe this attitude was linked to my parents' lack of encouragement during my earlier years to discover my heritage, though now they are very encouraging. My black friends seemed to have parents who strongly encouraged them to explore their past.

I was frequently told by friends and acquaintances that society will always label me as a black woman regardless of my mixed background. Sometimes mistaking my desire to claim my European background as wishing to identify with the dominant culture, I was questioned about my allegiance to the black community. In response, I argued that by identifying myself solely as black I was denying a part of me. In addition, I found it unfair that blacks were given the right to claim their mixed ethnic-racial heritage, whether it be Cuban-African-American or Haitian-African-American, but as an Austrian-African-American I was challenged. My friends tried to reassure me that they were not trying to deny my Austrian heritage. They questioned why I didn't know more about my black ancestors. Sometimes I felt I had to recognize only my African American heritage in order to avoid being accused of succumbing to the dominant culture's pressures and beliefs. Regardless of others' definitions and explanations, I could never quite comprehend the importance of defining oneself by race or ethnicity. As a product of a family that did not stress race, it seemed odd to me for such emphasis to be placed upon one's racial background. I was criticized as being too idealistic for stressing the primary importance of regarding people as human rather than as members of a racial group.

Another point of tension was the role of ethnic affinity houses on campus. Confused and uncertain about the intent and purpose of these organizations, I often debated with Vanessa and Shawna about the purpose of these groups. Though I now understand the need for the African American organization and other affinity houses, at the time I could not comprehend the need for such groups. Why was it that a WASP-only organization would be considered racist, yet the college African American organization was not? I felt that these organizations negatively accentuated the differences between races and further secluded themselves from the rest of the college community. It was explained to me that the college African American organization was needed for some students because the college campus was not a diverse environment and the organization helped minority students adjust. In my opinion, the opposite was true. There were many people of color at my college, and I found the campus to be diverse.

The African American organization was a very uncomfortable place for me. I did not understand the slang being used, nor the hairstyles and products members referred to, or in some instances, even the food they were discussing. Needless to say, I was not active in the African American organization. The only organization presentation that I attended was on the topic of interracial relationships, or "Jungle Fever." The guest speaker was an actor in the movie Jungle Fever, directed by Spike Lee. He shared his positive experience of having dated a white woman, but his sincerity and love for her was challenged by some members of the audience. Theories on why this successful black man was dating a white woman ranged from his insecurities and self-hatred as a black man to his desire to have the "great prize" or "trophy" at his side. Although not everyone spoke negatively about interracial relationships, I left saddened, angry, and frustrated. I was upset with one audience member in particular. He criticized the black male who marries a white woman, concluding that such a man possesses many insecurities, and that a "true black man" marries his "strong black queen." This statement was made after I shared my experience as a child of an interracial marriage. I couldn't help but feel that his comment was directed at me.

Even at the time of the Rodney King incident when, ironically, I was enrolled in my first black history course, I was not active in "race politics" at my school. I remember gazing out of the classroom window and watching the protests and speeches on the quad, as my history professor spoke of the injustices and struggles of the past. I did not participate in any of the protests and marches; I was still determining my new identity as a minority and what it all meant. My sister, on the other hand, was very involved in the forums and speeches at her conservative college. Like many of the minority students at my school, she felt frustrated with her student body's general lack of concern and understanding of the sensitive issues surrounding the Rodney King case. She told me about her frustrations in trying to educate others on race, while also concentrating on her studies. She felt it should not be her job to enlighten the rest of the campus and that she might be happier at a historically black college. My sister came to feel so strongly about this that she left school to take time off. She is currently applying to schools and hopes to find a more intellectual campus with a strong black student body.

I cannot explain why my sister was able to find and cultivate a stronger tie to the black community than I did. During college, she and I have discussed the issue of race several times, and though we have similar opinions and viewpoints, we inevitably end up arguing and abruptly ending our discussion in frustration. I tell her I do not understand how she can feel a connection with the black slaves and experience their suffering any more than I can understand how young Jewish people relate to the pain and suffering of their ancestors in the Holocaust. I can sympathize as a human being, but I can't understand how skin color can create a stronger link and greater understanding of other's suffering. I also do not understand her new belief that, except for our mother, she no longer has anything in common with white people. Our conversations usually end with her accusing me of being influenced by the dominant white forces. Ironically, of the three children in my family, she is the lightest skinned, yet she is the most "militant" in advancing the "black cause." I think her new attitudes are the result of her experience at her small conservative college and the influence of her African American boyfriend and other black friends.

My brother is a junior in high school and is coming to terms with his biracial identity two years earlier than I did. In general, we share some of the same experiences and feelings, though he is more enlightened than I ever was during my early stages of discovery. He has been confronted with race issues and has discussed the implications with my parents. At his predominantly white, well-to-do prep school, he has been challenged by a few of the black students. They question his allegiance to the black community and, on occasion, remind him of his skin color. In spite of our similar experiences, unlike me, my brother has become involved in his school's African American club. Always struggling to keep a foot in both communities, he sometimes finds the fight exhausting.

My most upsetting brush with racial conflict occurred one Friday night in a fraternity basement. I was hanging out and having a good time with a friend who happened to be a white male, when I noticed a black male across the room giving me disapproving looks. Uncertain as to what would warrant such stares, I ignored him and continued talking and laughing with my friend. Eventually the stranger approached me as I went to the bar to get a drink. Taking the liberty to judge my behavior, he informed me that it was wrong for a black woman to date a white man, that we need to stick together and keep the race strong; we cannot dilute it by mixing with other races. With his light brown skin, he looked like a product of a biracial marriage himself. Overcome with complete disbelief, I stood there numb. I was first overcome with shock and anger, which was followed by sadness, and then I was angry again. No one had ever told me personally that interracial relationships were wrong, and I had never been condemned for associating with white males. I was outraged at the stranger. First of all, the male to whom I was talking was just a friend, and second, race should not dictate with whom I will be intimate. Furthermore, I felt he was unfairly judging me and my family.

My friend took me outside to calm me down. He tried to comfort me, but neither he nor anyone could understand the anger and frustration I felt. I left the fraternity alone; I needed to reflect on what had just happened. After calming down, I thought about my parents' marriage and thought about the hardships they must have endured to make their marriage a success. I also wondered if they ever conceived of the hardships their children were to experience as products of their marriage. A few days later, I saw the same guy on campus, and he apologized. I later learned that he came from a very wealthy family and attended a predominantly white prep school. I also found out that his sister was to marry a white man in a few weeks.

Despite that very upsetting incident, I did subsequently have a five-month romantic relationship with a nonblack male at school. His name was John and he was Jewish American. During the time we were together, I never felt judged by the college community nor did I question the community's feelings on interracial dating. That is, not until I saw a fellow student's documentary film on interracial dating on my campus. I went to see the film with one of John's best friends and a friend of mine. After seeing the film, I was disappointed that John had missed it. I believed that the film would have prompted us to discuss our interracial relationship on a personal level that we had not done before. Now I wanted to know how his friends and fraternity brothers felt about him dating someone of a different race. Was he ever confronted by others with the issue of dating a black woman? Before the film, I would have definitely said no, but after the shocking testimonies in the film, I wasn't so sure. Although I ultimately knew that dating across color lines was not a concern for him and that what other people thought did not dictate whom he would date, I was still curious to know if, as an individual in an interracial relationship, he ever felt judged by others.

John and I had talked about race early on in our relationship. I was aware from the very beginning that he wanted to marry someone Jewish. On one of the first nights we went out, we talked into the early hours of the morning about his desire to marry someone Jewish. However, our discussion was not on a personal level; it had been a philosophical-sociological discussion, and we did not examine our potential interracial relationship. He tried to explain and justify to me his conscious choice to marry someone within his own cultural group. As someone who was struggling with self-definition and imposed definition and having never felt any strong feelings for one race or another, I found it was difficult to understand why and how at the age of 21 he could eliminate all women of races and cultures other than his own as potential partners in marriage. Although John himself had a strong sense of his Jewish culture and had strong ties with his background, his parents were certainly a powerful influence in his decision. I wondered if they were aware that their son was dating a black woman and what their reaction would be. I never asked him because I didn't want to put him in the awkward position of having to defend his parents. Also, I did not want him to get the idea that because I was interested in his parents' potential opinion of me, that I was therefore thinking about marrying him.

The following summer I spoke with a black woman who had a strong desire to marry an African American, and for the first time I had an understanding of why someone would prefer to marry within their own race and cultural group. She said that she would not rule out marrying someone of another race or background but believed that there were many things she experienced as a result of her race which could not be explained to someone who had not experienced it. Her potential husband would have to belong to the same group in order to understand this important aspect of her life.

I had many questions about race and relationships, and the documentary only provoked more. John was my first real boyfriend, and we had been dating for four months. I wanted to share with him my uncertainties about our dating. I feared being viewed as a mere "college toy" since, in his eyes, as an African American woman, I was not marriage material. I wondered why he believed he could only marry a Jewish woman, yet he dated women from other ethnic groups. His previous girlfriend was white. Though I was not in any way interested in marriage, after the film and the discussions I had with others about the issue of interracial dating, I was curious about the role I played for him. I never believed that John would date someone based strictly on skin color, and I never thought that he had an ulterior motive for dating me, but after the film I learned that some people are fascinated with skin color and consider it all a game, while others consider crossing racial lines a sin.

I had always found someone attractive based on their looks and personality and I never thought about getting involved with someone based on their skin color. After seeing the film and having a number of discussions about interracial dating, I realized that some people actually do think that way. All the faces in the documentary were familiar; they were faces I had seen in the library, the student center, dining halls, and at parties. I was surprised at the number of people, both black and white, who were opposed to interracial dating, and I was disturbed by the film's story of a failed relationship largely due to the external pressures of disapproving outsiders. With it already so difficult to find that special someone, why did some people feel adamantly opposed to interracial couples?

In the film, there were two white students who admitted to having "jungle fever." A woman spoke of the black male anatomy and said she had once begun dating a black man based solely on the old myth that black men were better endowed sexually. A white male spoke of his attraction for black women because, according to him, they were better in bed. I sat there disgusted. I could not believe my ears as I listened to their ridiculous claims. I was particularly disgusted with that same white male who, the term before, had told a friend of mine that he found me attractive. I felt disgusting and dirty as I sat in the auditorium and listened to him openly express his racist feelings and desires for black women. What I once thought to be a compliment was nothing more than attraction for my skin color, a false association with great sex. I sat there quiet. I did not want anyone to know that I had been an object of those feelings, that I had once evoked such sick thoughts. I knew I wasn't to blame for his offensive sexual lusts, but I could not help feeling dirty and ashamed. This is the guy who had smiled and waved to me crossing the quad on the way to classes. The same guy who was so nice to me in the library, cafe, and in the gym. I could not believe my ears. I kept asking myself if he was acting or were these his true feelings. I had believed him to be a nice and sincere guy. I had guessed that the reason he was extremely nice to me was that he liked me, but I would have never imagined it was because of my skin color. As he continued to talk about how black women are great in bed, he made me feel like an animal. I asked myself how many other guys honestly believe in the myth. I never once considered that someone might be interested in me because they believed it would be "fun" to date a black woman. Was this guy's attitude the exception?

The documentary left me with a lot of unanswered questions. Following the film, I had an interesting conversation with a black student who was one of John's best friends. He desperately tried to describe his frustrations as one of only two black males in a predominantly white fraternity. He described feeling as if white women only wanted to be his friend. He attributed his lack of girlfriends to two things: Few black women came to hang out in his fraternity, and nonblack women were not interested in him since he was a black man. He asked, "You belong to a predominantly white sorority, don't you sometimes feel the same way?"

"It's not a white sorority. My house is ethnically mixed. There are women of many different backgrounds," I said.

"Whatever," he replied. "There are only what, three black women in your house?"

"To tell you the truth," I said, "I never thought about my skin color being an attraction or a turn-off for males. I understand the getting-a-date-for-house-function-blues, but I never attributed the difficulty to the color of my skin."

My thoughts on the issue continued to spin, particularly about the reasons and implications of crossing race lines. Why was it that I never blamed my skin color for not having a date, yet my friend did? Perhaps my European features "saved" me. The next week, after doing a lot of self-questioning and exploring, I brought the topic up at dinner with a group of black female friends: "Do you think some men are attracted to black women on the sole basis that the woman is black?" I asked. The question was greeted with a simultaneous "Yes!" I was surprised that without any hesitation or moment of discussion they all agreed. One woman stated, "I was told by a friend in a historically black Greek house that he has heard about a mainstream fraternity on campus that actually has a contest to see who can sleep with a woman of each ethnic/racial group. Each race is ranked, and depending upon the woman's background, the guy gains points. It's something like, if the woman is Korean, the guy gets 10 points, Puerto Rican 20 points, and so on. I don't know all the details, but that's what I heard," she said.

"Do you honestly believe that?" I asked in disbelief.

"Yes. It's definitely not something in which the entire house participates, but it's definitely believable. It's just a question of which house." I didn't know how to react. I was just shocked by the thought. I could feel chills down my spine and I was disturbed by the rumor.

It was nauseating to think that someone could become involved with someone else because of skin color and, worse yet, to win a contest. The male was considered the victor of a stupid and disgusting contest; the woman a mere victim. Was it possible that guys at school, supposedly intelligent males, would do such a thing? I called a friend, who is also a minority, and told her of the rumor. She didn't seem at all surprised.

"Do you think that story is true? Do you think there have been guys who have been attracted to me because of my skin color?" I asked.

"Yeah," she replied. "Not all guys, but I am sure that there have been some who liked you because of your skin. Not to say that no one has ever liked you for you, or that you are not attractive, but your combination of dark skin color and traces of European features are a combination of the forbidden and the embraced. Mike liked you for your skin color, and Billy once told me that it was obvious to him that you were not all black. He said he could tell by your nose, cheek bones and hair." I didn't understand her point.

"And what are you saying?" I asked her.

"Well, in Billy's case, I got the sense that your European features assured him that you are not black; therefore, it is okay for him to like you. And as for the guy in the film, your black skin appealed to him, as it does to others who have 'jungle fever.' In both cases, race is an issue—in a negative sense."

For a very brief moment after that discussion, I thought about questioning the motives of all guys interested in me. I could never, however, bring myself to confront any of them with this serious question. I eventually abandoned my shaky belief that race affected my relations with males because it was difficult for me to believe or comprehend that anyone would date someone from a different race or ethnic group out of curiosity or because they thought it would be fun. It just seemed so ridiculous to me. It was not until recently that I began to contemplate seriously the role race has played in my interpersonal relationships.

John had gone to Israel during the summer before our senior year, and during his stay, his ties to his Jewish culture were strengthened. It was a day after returning for our senior year of college that we broke up. I wasn't devastated by the split. During the summer, I had also been thinking about breaking it off; I wanted to be able to spend as much time as possible with friends before graduating. John stumbled through the words when he broke up with me. He mentioned how spending time in Israel really confused him, his parents were pressuring him, he just needed to work through the garbage, and he thought it best if we broke up. Later, when I asked him to please better explain what happened, he simply said that he didn't want to be tied down and didn't want to be in a relationship. Nine weeks later, he started dating someone else. She was Jewish.

Although my experience as a biracial child has at times been difficult, I do not disparage interracial relationships. As a result of my parents' marriage, I believe I hold a unique perspective on the world. I have realized that my skin color may be an attraction to some men and a turn-off to others. I need to confront this issue and ask the next person I become serious about whether I am being ruled-out or ruled-in because of my skin color. I sometimes feel that as a biracial woman I have one more doubt to add to the list of insecurities most women experience when dating. "Does he have 'jungle fever' and like me because I am black? Or does he consider it a sin to mix the races and dislike me because I am black?"

I am still exploring and defining who I am. During my senior year in college, my younger sister wrote me a letter encouraging me not to worry about the future and "life after college." She wrote, "Gather your strength and confidence from our ancestors." With the letter, she included a short family tree. It was then that I discovered my great-grandparents were Native American on my paternal grandmother's side and that my great-grandfather on my father's side was West Indian. It came as a surprise to learn I have even more "mixed blood" than I realized, but so, too, do many black Americans.

In retrospect, it is difficult for me to say whether I would have liked for my parents to broach the topic of race while I was growing up. I sometimes wish that they would have talked about the implications of being biracial. Other times, I am very thankful for the journey of self-discovery. I have come to terms with what it means for me to be a biracial child in this country and I am at peace with my self-definition. But I also realize that there is a continuous struggle between self-definition and the external perceptions and assumptions of others. People continue to make judgments and assumptions about my actions based on my skin color. It is usually very subtle, and I find it difficult to address. Recently, a colleague of mine at work told me she knew of a very attractive black man whom I should meet. After her comment, I questioned if she would have given the same offer to a white colleague. Did she assume that I would only date black men? Did she think I should only date black men? Would she have said to a white woman, "I know an attractive white man whom you should meet?"

I also have to cope with many of the same injustices from the white community as all minorities do. As a child of a black-white union, I carry a part of my white mother with me wherever I go, so it is sometimes difficult to feel aligned with the black cause when it requires taking sides between the white and black communities. I have come to define myself as neither black nor white, but as a union of the two. I am still exploring the definitions and implications of the terms black, brown, African American, mixed, mulatto, and so on. I am definitely more enlightened than I was when I began this journey of self-discovery and definition, but I have much more to learn and sort out. I've begun to research my background and have contacted my oldest living relative on my father's side to find out more about my heritage. My grandmother on my mother's side is also helping put the pieces together. I want to be able to give my children the gift of the past. I realize now that my family does not just consist of my parents and siblings. Regardless of the questions in my own mind and those of others regarding my biracial identity, I know who I am and I am proud.

5

What If I Don't Want to Whistle?

This is the story of a young black man who grew up living with his mother and half sister in modest circumstances in south central Los Angeles. In spite of economic hardships, his mother is determined that her children receive an excellent education. Orion attends a succession of mainly white private schools that prepare him well academically, even while they undermine his sense of racial pride. His struggle to achieve a sense of self, compounded by his battles with anxiety and his insecurities concerning relationships with women, makes for a very challenging adolescence. Only late in his college years does he open up in his relations with others, question his internalized racism, and align himself positively with the black community.

It was a bright California morning, but at 7:55 my classroom with its high ceilings was still cold, and I shuddered at the prospect of discussing race that day. In my senior English class at my boarding school outside of Los Angeles, I was the only black student in a class of eight. On most days the color of my skin was not an issue, but I dreaded the times when we talked about racial matters. Although no one voiced the thought, I knew that my comments on the subject would be assumed more valid than others'.

We had been assigned two essays to read the night before. The first was a paper explaining what the term *nigger* meant for black people, and the second was about the life experience of a black man in New York City. In the latter essay, the narrator had adopted a strategy of whistling classical music during his evening strolls in order to prevent whites from crossing to the other side of the street as he approached them. My muscles tightened as I anticipated the discussion, not wanting to hear ignorant remarks about race and then have to bear the weight of correcting them without appearing overly sensitive, angry, or condescending.

The class discussion began with the essay on the word *nigger*. Students searched desperately for a politically correct way to speak about the reading. "I thought it was interesting," said John tentatively and noncommittally. Brian added, "I guess it was good, but I just can't understand why black people would call themselves a name that is so insulting?"

I remember the look Mr. Manson gave as he shrugged his shoulders in response to Brian's question. It was as if he were struggling to keep a straight face—like he had selected this particular reading as a practical joke. With his knowing smile, he seemed to be pointing out the stupidity of "those niggers" who don't even have enough sense not to insult each other.

I didn't know how to tell them any more eloquently than the essay had that the term *nigger* was not insulting coming from one black to another; especially when spelled with an "a" and not an "er," it was completely dissociated from the way racist whites used it, as far as my black friend Carter and I were concerned. I felt like a person of a religious faith trying to explain to nonbelievers why it was that I believed: Some things just can't be explained logically.

Not wanting to enter the conversation, I averted my eyes. My anger built; if the teacher had not understood the article and could not even regurgitate the arguments provided by the author, then why was he teaching it? Feeling powerless, I wondered what would have happened if I hadn't been present. Would the discussion have become an open forum for everyone to voice his or her condescension for blacks?

"Well, do you understand it?" Mr. Manson, as expected, asked me. I nodded in return. "Do you mind trying to explain it to us?" Even though it was a lost cause, I tried to make it clearer. Attempting to explicate the various connotations of the word *nigger,* I tripped over my words in anger and confusion for five minutes before I finally gave up all together and we moved on to the next essay regarding whistling classical music to put white people at ease. Everyone agreed that it was unfair to be black in New York and get treated as a thug. Then my friend Jay added, "Yeah, it's too bad, but at least he found a good way to get around it." There were nods all around, and I felt blood rush to my face. "That is not a viable solution to his problem," I blurted out. "The guy wasn't free! To be treated civilly you have to whistle? That means you are assumed guilty until you prove your innocence." I likened the situation to having to show someone a list of credentials, or having to shuck and jive, whenever you wanted to be treated with respect. "Can you imagine a nation of 'free men' who have to sing and dance in order to show that they aren't dangerous and be treated fairly? What would happen if you couldn't whistle? Or God forbid, didn't feel like whistling?" But I was the only person who saw how this was problematic. Reading the facial expressions around me, I could tell people thought that I was causing unnecessary trouble by being "too sensitive" about the issues, so I silenced myself.

In many ways, I fit the demographics for the stereotypical black male. I grew up in the inner city raised by a single mother without ever knowing my father. Yet, in other important ways, I do not fit the profile. My mother was an attorney, and as children my sister and I attended elite private schools on 90 percent scholarships.

My sister is three years younger than I am. We have different fathers, neither of whom ever married my mother; she tells us that at a certain age she wanted two children and then she got them—by two different men. My sister has had more contact with her father than I have had with mine. He lives in the same large West coast city as we do, and my mom and sister run into him once every couple of years, often to my sister's embarrassment.

I do not know my father at all. I am told I met him once when I was 3. I'm not sure if I actually remember it or if I have constructed my memory of the incident: I just picture him lifting me up in the air in our front yard. The only photograph that survives of him is his driver's license. I know that he was 6' 2", weighed 201 pounds, and shares the same last name as me.

My mom used to drive me by an apartment building, pointing and saying, "That's where I met your father." That statement always left me uneasy, and I struggled to make sense of the motivations behind it. What exactly did it mean? Was it supposed to comfort me? Did it comfort her? From time to time, she would drop one-sentence descriptions of him into our conversations. "Your father was a salesman," she would say. Or, "Your father used to run track." But I never knew, for example, at what level he ran—was my father a champion? "Your father busted his leg open riding a motorcycle," she would tell me. But I didn't know if that meant he had a limp or any other physical, emotional, or psychological trauma because of the accident.

I don't think of my father too much, but as I write this I sometimes think that I might remind my mother of him, perhaps when she sees me from afar, walking toward her. At times, I reflect on which of my qualities, positive and negative, might resemble his. I wonder if my mom misses him, if she ever loved him, and how long they knew each other before they slept together. I wonder if my mother told my father and my sister's father about how she wanted children. If my father is anything like me, I can imagine him doing my mom a favor and supplying her with a child. But I can't imagine what was going through his head as he agreed. Did he even care that he was going to have a child?

In the end, all I could do was try to make the very little I did know about my father fill the great void where the images and memories of him should have been. When I was in third grade people would constantly ask me, "Don't you miss not having a father?" And eventually I was forced to liken it to not having a tail. "Do you miss not having a tail?" I would respond. How can you miss something that you never had?

My mom and I have always had a contentious relationship. I think now, at the age of 21, that a possible source of this friction was the dysfunctional relationships she had had with men—and her consequently negative attitudes toward them—which she projected onto me. My mom may not have properly dealt with her "issues" with the men in her life, including her children's fathers and her own father as well. Oftentimes when arguing with my mother I felt like the topic at hand had the emotional baggage of wrongs done to her years before my conception. Growing up, I could not communicate with her without her seeming to take everything as a personal attack. I think this lack of communication may have led her to sense that I wasn't appreciative of all she was doing for me—which may have been true.

My mom valued education and insisted that I go to private schools. She saw how much energy I had and knew that public school would be too trying on my patience, so she sent me to the Jordan School, an overwhelmingly white campus of five hundred students from kindergarten to eighth grade. I went to school with the sons and daughters of doctors, lawyers, business people, and movie stars. My family, however, lived in a one-bedroom house that was really a garage converted into a home. Above all, my mother was a single mother supporting her family on a single salary. Although she was an attorney, she was honest—and thus not rich. My mom, my sister, and I shared one bed, which I often wet as a child. Our home was a perpetual mess, and I hated not having my own room in which I could be neat and organized, like all of my wealthy, white academic peers. I didn't care how big or how nice our house was as long as it was clean and acceptable. I never wanted to show off: I just wanted to pass by unnoticed.

Our house was in south central Los Angeles—only three blocks away from where the Reginald Denny beatings took place—and I hated returning home to it. When we got out of the car and walked to our house, me carrying my sleeping sister over my shoulder, we would have to duck behind parked vehicles when cars drove by for fear of being shot. We were never the victims of such crimes, but I do remember going to sleep with the sounds of helicopters circling around the house as if we were in a war zone. Those helicopters, I thought, were undoubtedly hunting down a black man for some asinine crime. The noise of the propellers made me think of a plantation owner thundering on horseback through his fields just to instill fear in his slaves.

We drove one and a half hours each day to get to and from school. Our 1979 blue Toyota Corolla looked like a relic from World War II, recently hauled out of a junkyard destined to spend the remaining years of its life as an embarrassment to two black children going to an affluent white school. It was the single most potent symbol of the divide between our peers and us. I didn't care where I lived because the kids at school didn't have to see that; but they did see our car, and it was like a huge propaganda machine announcing the arrival and departure of the two poorest kids at Jordan. At the traffic circle where everyone stood waiting for friends, we would get out of the car and bowls of cereal and other junk would fall out, creating an embarrassing mess.

All through my time at Jordan I stole from my peers—things like electronic games and portable audio devices, not for the enjoyment of the goods themselves, but to wield some social clout. I wanted to walk around with an accessory like all the other kids who had Game Boys and Casio watches that functioned as calculators and stored phone numbers. After stealing, though, I'd usually feel so guilty that I tried to throw the stolen items away.

I was constantly comparing myself to the students of my school. I remember in kindergarten asking my mom questions about myself as we drove into Jordan. I once wondered, "Why can't I be white?" Somehow, I already felt like my identity was unsatisfactory. In fact, until I was 12, my experiences were such that I had concluded that all white people were rich and all black people poor. When I revealed this to my mom, she was shocked.

From an early age I was frustrated by our family's financial situation, which neither my mother nor I could change, and at school I felt isolated and cut off from any maternal protection. As a result, I felt as though my mom were the reason for all of the injustices in my life, and so I resented her. She in turn began to resent the situation she found herself in—a single mother working very hard to send two children to an elite private school, one of whom, a son, who would openly tell people that he disliked or hated her.

I remember being disappointed in kindergarten and first grade when at schoolwide recitals I would perform in front of an auditorium filled with nicely dressed parents and not see my mom. It became worse after the recital. "Perhaps I just missed her," I'd think to myself. "She'll come through in the end. She's my mother." I would rush out of the back doors of the auditorium and run toward the front with all of my peers expecting to see my mom walk out. But she didn't. I was introduced to a strange new world of being alone.

In third grade we had a Thanksgiving potluck at school, where everyone brought in a dish and the children dressed up. I remember the children laughing at me and the way I ate, saying I was making a mess. I felt so bad and embarrassed that I began to cry and didn't finish the meal. When my mom came and asked why I looked so down, I told her that I hadn't gotten to eat any of the pumpkin pie that I had brought in; one of the teachers explained what had happened and how the kids had made fun of me. After hearing the story my mom went out and bought me a pie, thinking it would solve the problem. But it didn't, and I had learned my lesson: When I needed my mom to be there she would not be. I knew that she cared, but I also felt that she knew nothing about and had no influence over the world I was living in at school.

In the mornings I would occasionally arrive late, which I thought was a situation to be worked out with my mother. Yet the teacher still chose to call me out and humiliate me in front of my peers, telling me to be on time. In the afternoons, sometimes my mom had to come late to pick me up, and members of the faculty would have to stay after school and wait until she arrived before they could leave. I felt guilty when this happened; the teachers' body language and curt sentences were as loud and powerful as any insults they could have said. I knew they were mad at me and my mother, but what could *I* do?

In the new environment of school, my connections to my family and homelife seemed to be severed and to serve no purpose; so I had to teach myself how to survive and adapt. My mom was like a god. She had created me and the situation I found myself in, but she was rarely present. To trust in her after experiencing the pain I felt in her absence would have required a faith so immense that I would have been crushed under its weight.

In light of the distance between my mother and myself, relationships with others became more and more relevant in my life. In south central Los Angeles I had only a handful of black companions; the Hispanics were all friendly and they were mainly who I hung out with. My most lasting impressions of black people were of the couple of black neighborhood bullies who had beaten me up and stolen my bikes multiple times. Meanwhile, the black kids at the Boys' and Girls' Club I belonged to made fun of me for the way I spoke, saying I sounded "white." I began to view young blacks as threatening and unaccepting of me. The problem wasn't that I myself did not feel I was black; a quick glance at my exposed arms and legs clarified that. It was more a question of how everyone else viewed me. In the black community there is always a concern that successful black people are trying to deny their "blackness." Certainly some blacks feel that once they are successful they have nothing to do with the black "struggle." But this was never how I felt.

In the sixth grade my mom signed me up for the Big Brother, Little Brother program in the hopes of providing me with a long overdue source of male guidance. A long period of time elapsed before I was officially assigned a Big Brother, so in the interim my mother located a co-worker who was willing to temporarily act as one. Sherwin was a very friendly older black male in his early fifties. We were both interested in computers, so we spent all of our time playing video games and building machines. He was probably the best black male role model I ever had: he was intelligent, patient, honest, and friendly. However, three years after we had applied I was finally officially matched with a Big Brother; when this happened— and when he started coming on to my mother—Sherwin was phased out of my life.

My new Big Brother, Jim, was a 30-year-old, white, Jewish male. Over the eleven years that we have been paired together, Jim has provided me with a considerable amount of financial aid and has always been there for me emotionally as well. However, there has been a lot of tension and little communication between Jim and my mother. On my mother's part, the conflict lies in the fact that Jim is a male and wealthy, which has led her to believe that I would immediately assume that whatever he says is of more worth than what she says.

I went to high school at Blair, a mostly white, affluent boarding school of 250 students, and my first year there was marked by an increasing sense of anxiety. I was tired of being pigeonholed as black and seeing the contributions of my "race" over the pages of history being limited to slaves and uppity freedom fighters. There seemed to be only three blacks worthy of study: Martin Luther King, Malcolm X, and Rosa Parks—as though blacks had made no contributions or changes outside of the civil rights movement. I felt that these heroes lived in a social and political climate far different from my own and I found it very difficult to incorporate their lessons into my daily life. I was also reluctant to accept any of the alternative black role models the teachers presented to me because they didn't speak to any of my personal interests; they were not meant for me specifically but for any black person, and they were not appreciated solely for their talents. Their first achievement was that they were black and whatever professional accomplishments they had made came second. I wanted the order of appreciation switched: I wished their professional talents to be appreciated first and foremost, with their race mentioned as a trivial afterthought.

Another source of the increasing sense of anxiety I felt upon entering Blair was the socially challenging environment. At boarding school, for the first time I spent protracted periods of time with my peers outside of an academic setting. During my freshman year I was bothered by a group of kids who seemed rebellious and claimed to be thuggish in spite of the fact that they were attending an elite boarding school. As a result, my style of dress changed from the tough boy gangster image, with big, baggy pants and basketball jerseys, to one of well-fitting khakis and polo T-shirts. This decision was of some importance to me because I felt that in rejecting that thuggish style of dress I was rejecting my culture. But dressing in a way that seemed through association to glorify drugs, money, violence, ignorance, and the mistreatment of women wasn't a true reflection of what my life was about. Similarly, in seventh grade I had stopped listening to the rap and hip-hop radio stations because the deejays presented themselves as ignorant. I wasn't rejecting black culture or music in general, but I was rejecting rap's nihilistic messages and what the deejays were choosing to define as black culture. I was not a "sell-out" or someone filled with self-hatred. Viscerally, I just could not accept negative images that harmed my sense of self-worth.

During my time at Blair, my only black friend was Carter. He had a short temper and an aggressive personality. His outlets were poetry and basketball. Although we were the only black males in our class, I did not feel closer to him as a result. In fact, our sociocultural differences made me feel somewhat estranged from him. I did worry sometimes that I gave blacks like Carter the impression that I wasn't proud of my heritage because I spoke so differently.

During one spring break, my mom invited Carter to visit our house. This was the first time a friend of mine had ever come to stay at my home and I did not know how he would react to our circumstances. Also, although we were of the same race and from similar economic backgrounds, it was difficult for to me decipher Carter's speech. With the language and cultural barrier between us I began to lose faith in the belief that all blacks could understand one another due to skin color. My skin color did not help me decode the strange words that permeated his vocabulary, like "yo," "B," "tap," "chill," and "bitch" (which was used to refer to all women).

On the first day of spring break we rented movies from the public library, and as we watched one around midnight, we began debating the movie's story line. Soon our debate escalated into a heated argument that moved beyond the movie's plot. Eventually Carter became enraged and screamed, "You don't even trust me!" He told me that earlier that day he had asked me what kind of music I listened to and I had told him rap, but when he looked through my CD collection he found that I also listened to classical and alternative rock. He seemed hurt by this, which shocked me, as I didn't think I had the ability to upset anyone at all—let alone Carter, who seemed so tough on the exterior.

I hadn't told him what other music I listened to because I still wasn't secure enough in my identity, racially or otherwise, to openly share who I was and what my interests were. Some of the music I listened to was made by white people, and I didn't want him to consider me a "sell-out." I didn't know how to tell him that I had been beaten up and made fun of as a kid for acting and talking "white." At the end of the conversation, he made me confident that he was not going to judge me based on the genre of music I enjoyed, and I felt comfortable opening up to him.

By the end of the vacation I was using his lingo nonstop. Once he referred to my mom as a bitch but then immediately apologized. "That's alright, I know what you mean," I said. But averting his eyes, he said, "Naw, that's not cool. I really do like her." And I believed him.

Throughout our time at Blair, Carter and I continued to grow closer, especially after I spent a week at his apartment. I felt I understood him better after seeing where he was from, yet I still wondered what he thought about my blackness, as race rarely came up as a topic between us.

Because of our close relationship, I asked Carter to write me a peer recommendation for college. It was at this point that he finally allayed some of my insecurities by telling me that he did not feel that I was a "sell-out." Still somewhat unsure, I asked him about the way I spoke. He considered for a moment and replied, "That's just the way you speak. You change when you are around me and when you speak to a Mexican and when you are in French class. You just have a knack with languages and you change accordingly. It's just about learning how to adapt." These words were some of the most comforting I have ever heard.

Besides Carter, my two other best friends in high school were Phillip and Jay. Jay and I were extremely similar. We both enjoyed math and were rather serious. We used to exchange stories about how we would both wake up on Saturday mornings during junior high and spend the first couple of hours in bed just thinking. We had similar conceptions about society and the same insecurities about what qualified as intelligence. Both procrastinators, we bonded over our consequentially sub-par performances on papers and final exams.

Regardless of grades, Jay was implicitly considered one of the smartest guys in our class and most everyone respected him. He was extremely logical and did everything for a reason, whereas I would act on instinct and impulse. Jay understood me better than anyone else and taught me a lot of lessons about what it means to be a friend. I had misguided ideas about the nature of friendships: I thought that the minute you got into an argument or a fight that you should call it off. It was hard for me to entertain the idea that you could be mad at someone you still liked. Jay realized that if I did something that appeared to be done out of malice it was probably because I didn't really know the source of my anger or that I was trying to get attention. He was a good listener and I could tell him about very personal things.

Phillip joined us during our sophomore year. The grandson of a famous playwright, Phillip was bright and good-humored and had impeccable taste in literature and music; and he would never lower his standards to suit the politics of skin color. When I stumbled upon a black hip-hop trio in his CD collection, my curiosity was piqued. I had not been impressed when I had heard one or two of their songs before, but seeing that Phillip owned their album led me to reconsider their merit.

When Phillip took a course on "Black Authors" while I opted for a class on "The Boarding School Experience," he approached me curious as to why I hadn't taken the course he was taking. I didn't know how to explain to him that I felt estranged from schools' representations of blacks. However, as the term progressed and he read books by Toni Morrison and Ralph Ellison and insisted on how good they were, I wished that I had taken the course. In these ways, Phillip helped me to find my way back into black culture, music, and literature.

One of Jay's most important contributions to our friendship was encouraging me when I decided to start seeing a counselor for my anxiety during my freshman year. In fact, to my surprise, all of my friends fully supported me in this. I saw the counselor once a week for half a year, and though she didn't cure me of my anxiety she did help me cope with it. One of her best suggestions was that I keep a journal. I began writing almost daily to loosen the grip of emotional paralysis through self-expression.

I remember the first day I began writing. It was a free period and rain was falling outside the library window. I was feeling anxious but started writing in my spiral-bound notebook anyway; and before long the words just flowed out of me. I felt like I was in the throes of mania. There was something magical but at the same time sort of sickening to me about the whole process—as though it were an unhealthy happiness. My thoughts were definitely me, but they were frightening. Excuse this comparison, but I related my journal writing to the work of Goya: beautifully dark and complicated pieces that reflect an intelligent but tortured mind.

Writing became my outlet; I wrote about everything. I let my friends read my journal until junior year of high school—it felt good to get things off my chest and share them with someone else. I felt that I was being my true and honest self in my journal entries, and I wanted everyone to know the part of me that never got a chance to surface in daily conversations. At one point, Phillip had stumbled across a passage where I admitted to feeling somehow incapacitated by my skin color. After reading the entry he approached me confused, wanting to talk about it more. He felt for me, not in a pitying way, but as a friend, and the way he approached me made a huge impact on the response he was given. Had I been approached in a condescending way, I would have been defensive about the inquiry. Although we never got around to fully addressing the issue, it was his concern that mattered most to me.

My close guy friends and my writings helped me to develop and further understand myself, but I still wasn't comfortable around girls. I never would have asked out Karen, my first girlfriend, left to my own devices. I hadn't much experience with girls and I didn't quite know what would be required of me and what role I was supposed to play. When Karen told me after dinner one night in tears that she liked me, I wasn't sure what to do. I either didn't believe it or didn't know how to take it; I think a lot of this had to do with the lack of love I had for myself.

Karen and I dated only for a short while freshman year (although I never told my mom about her, because she had said that I couldn't date until I was 30). Suffering from acute anxiety at the time, I ended up saying things like, "let's just go out on weekends," thinking that over the weekends, without the pressures of school, I could be a better boyfriend to her. But this suggestion made me seem shallow—and even sleazy. My behavior was sometimes aggressive and cruel, and I realize that this was, in part, a result of my frustration for feeling forced into the relationship. It wasn't just Karen; I couldn't cope with the idea of going out with anyone. I felt that it was another part that I would have to play that I didn't have the lines for.

I do not feel that my relationship with Karen, or with any other girl, was complicated by my race. Sometimes I wondered if girls were attracted to me because of my skin color, but I am fairly positive that no one dated me to live out any sort of fantasy about black men.

Although I didn't understand this at the time, I feel that my *own* insecurities about my race did permeate my relationships and other aspects of my life, however. It took my Asian American advisor to point out to me the importance of being aware of your own race. Sophomore year, he wrote on my report card that he was concerned that I had not begun to address the importance of race in my life. My mom agreed with him and brought the issue to my attention, as race had always been a vital component of her life and she wanted to make it important in my life as well. My mom made whites seem like the enemy, but in attending primarily white schools my whole life I did not see how being race conscious was going to help—especially when *I* was the one who would have to negotiate life amongst whites, without her there to support me as I treaded alone on enemy territory.

Instead of making enemies of whites, I tried to minimize my differences by ignoring the issues surrounding race. I was afraid that if I confronted them I would suffocate under the pressure of a problem I had no means of resolving. So when my mother and my advisor brought the matter up, I didn't know how to react.

I didn't *know* what it means to be black. I didn't feel *black.* I felt like me. I didn't think that I had any contributions to make to any discussions about "blackness" that would aid in a white person's understanding of the concept. I had always attended white schools and I had not thought that the people there were racist; I had white friends who seemed to like me. Looking back, I think the truth was that I thought we *were* somehow inferior; I hadn't yet learned what a black person had to be proud about. What I associated with black culture were dashikis and dreadlocks and other things that weren't a part of my daily life.

When I went back to school the day after my advisor had spoken to me, I ignored his suggestion. I didn't know what to do about my "problem," so I avoided confronting it. I did make advances on the relationship front, however. I began to realize that I didn't have to treat women the way I had treated Karen. The turnaround was mostly precipitated by my love for my sister, with whom I had an ideal relationship. I thought I should try to model a relationship with potential girlfriends after the one I had with her: one of mutual respect and understanding. My love for my sister became a mantra for the rest of my high school career. She earned my respect because she was always there for me, well-spoken, and able to get along well with my mother.

My next serious relationship occurred during my junior year in high school. Her name was Nicole, and she was a freshman and the youngest of three sisters, all of whom lived fairly troubled lives, dealing with the stigma of coming from a divorced household and the fact that their mother was dying of brain cancer. I probably would never have asked Nicole out, but she waited patiently and let me come around in my own way. Nicole was important to me and I was determined to learn from the lessons of my relationship with Karen. I decided that no matter what I felt, I would not allow myself to take out any undue aggressions on her. Throughout our time together, I felt that I was able to accomplish this, but we broke up nonetheless due to extenuating circumstances.

Nicole's mother died the summer after we broke up. We tried to get back together my senior fall, but it didn't work. She kept referring to jokes that we made during our last year of dating. It felt like she was trying to return to the period of our past when her mother was still living; until I told her, she hadn't noticed this. I explained to her how much I cared for her and that I didn't think it would be healthy for us to see each other under the circumstances. She agreed that it would probably be for the best to break up.

Overall, I enjoyed our relationship; it taught me how to identify and channel my feelings and to treat people appropriately. Although sad, I left Nicole feeling good about my ability to maintain a healthy relationship with a woman. With that in place, I moved on once again to the issue of race that I had been putting off confronting.

One day after sports practice, my friends and I went to visit Benson, a sophomore, in his dormitory. He had all sorts of expensive digital audio-visual equipment and told us how he had caught his friend Tony on tape falling off a couch and hitting his mouth against the coffee table, and that we should watch it. He added that Tony had said some pretty offensive stuff in the video and that he didn't want us to take offense, eyeing me warily. We assured him that it couldn't be that bad, so he began the film. When we saw our friend hit his head against the coffee table, we were left so amused that we asked eagerly what came next. Benson said that the following part was offensive and he didn't want to show us, but we pushed and he reluctantly played it.

In the video Benson had asked Tony, who was white, to say something, and he chose to say, "The Negro should go back to Africa." Given that Tony's style—his dress, musical tastes, and parlance were all strongly influenced by black culture—it was shocking that he purported to hold these racist beliefs. Once we had seen the clip, everyone turned to me, expecting me to be vehemently upset; but I didn't know what to be. I was surprised and speechless and tried to shrug it off. Was this racism, I wondered? Did this often happen when I wasn't in the room? And if it did, what was there to be done about it? I began to feel helpless. If this was racism, who was there that I could tell? And what would *they* do about it? This was one of the first experiences where I learned a harsh reality about the way others viewed my race.

I also learned a lesson about a condescending dimension of affirmative action during a school assembly my junior year for the highly selective National Merit Scholarships. The headmaster read the names of the winners, and to my surprise mine was called. I was wary; surely I had not done as well as the other people being called up. When I was handed my award, I immediately noticed that it was of a different size and color as the others: My award was for noteworthy achievement in the African American community. I was incensed and embarrassed. Why the special attention? No one else noticed this discrepancy, but I wanted to be treated fairly and not judged by a different measuring stick. It made me feel that society had decided that my race was inferior and that we should be rewarded for whatever work we could produce, regardless of its quality.

I graduated from high school without having resolved how I felt about race and what it meant to me to be black. When I arrived at college, I was still very unsure of my own identity. Conversely, my freshman-year roommate, who was a Native American, was very proud of his culture. He felt no shame about his heritage, and would tell me about going to the Native American Society and how he took part in a powwow. I admired the way he spoke confidently and respectfully about his people. I had thought that any society that was not completely in sync with mainstream white culture would feel ashamed of their differences. I was surprised that he didn't feel this way. I wanted to ask where he got his pride, hoping that it would rub off on me.

Inspired by my roommate, I joined the African American Society (the AAS) on campus. Although I had long felt distanced from the black community and feared that they might not accept me, I participated timidly in their events, and, in spite of the fact that I felt a little awkward, I never stopped. I had joined the AAS not in order to have fun, but out of a sense of responsibility. I felt like I owed it to the black community. Still, I didn't know how to "behave" with other members of the AAS. I was afraid that my awkwardness would once again evoke emotional abuse and that I would relive my childhood experiences at the Boys' and Girls' Club.

A turning point in the formation of my racial identity occurred my sophomore year during an off-campus program in Barcelona. There, I found out, much to my surprise, that I would be living with a black Spanish family with three brothers close to my age. I was shocked. Up until that point, the members of my biological family in the States had been the only black people that I knew of that spoke Spanish.

I do many things that most stereotypical black people would not—and every time I find others of my race doing the same thing I am shocked. It's as if doing something positive or unique makes me an outsider in the black community. It could be that there are lots of blacks who don't like violence, like to read, are fond of the idea of falling in love, and enjoy theological debates. I, however, have not met them. With the way mass media implies that the only way a black male can succeed is if he portrays himself as ignorant or violent, I don't think that many blacks believe that they can do otherwise: it wouldn't be black. Although aware of these messages, I was not impervious to them, and I felt that when I met my Spanish brothers I had to act rough to show that I was worthy of their camaraderie.

At one point when I was on the verge of proving my toughness, my younger brother stepped back with a surprised look that seemed to say, "What is this guy doing?" The looks on his older brothers' faces betrayed similar sentiments. Although they did seem sort of impressed with my bravado, they did not make generalizations about my being just another rough black American. Instead they said, "*Pues mira que fuerte Orion es*—Look how strong Orion is." It was like being looked at as if I were an individual human being. It made me realize that blacks in the States, or at least myself, tended to look at other blacks as if they are animals incapable of acting otherwise.

My journey to Spain was the first time since seventh grade that I attempted to formulate a different definition of "blackness." I decided that the concept of blackness was an illusion. I decided to free myself from any definitions of blackness and to simply live and be whomever I wanted. I decided to pursue whatever interests I had without fear of them not being the "black thing" to do. In Spain, I felt free to define myself, to learn to snowboard, to read, to write, to learn French, to skateboard, and to play guitar. When I returned from Spain, I told my family and friends how blessed I felt for having had the educational opportunity to travel to Europe.

Yet, while I had come much farther in comprehending myself, I was still having trouble understanding the opposite sex. By senior year, I had not yet had a steady girlfriend my entire time at college and I was still a virgin. I called Jim, my Big Brother, who insisted that finding a girlfriend was not as hard as I was making it out to be. He suggested that perhaps I should start considering that there might be a more serious issue at work. I started thinking seriously about all of my sexual and romantic experiences. I then told him how many of my baby-sitters and I had abusive sexual relationships when I was younger and that I was concerned that this might affect how I related to women. Although I had written about being sexualized by my twenty-something-year-old baby-sitters in my journal, I had never mentioned it to any adult. After a short silence, Jim replied that he felt this new information was beyond his training as an amateur psychologist and that I should seek professional help.

So in the fall of my senior year I went to see a counselor at school about my love life—because I was 21, in college, and a virgin. I was prepared to open up and talk about my baby-sitters, my mom, my sister, Nicole, and Karen. I wanted to be as candid as possible so that the counselor could see the situation as clearly as possible.

As it turned out the psychiatrist was a black man, which was helpful to a certain extent because I felt I could tell him openly about my recent concerns about dating someone black. He asked me if I thought it mattered or if I had any preference about dating one race or another, and I told him no. If I liked a girl, then I liked a girl; it just so happened that most of the girls I had an interest in were white. I did, however, think Hispanic, Indian, and from time to time black women were attractive, too. I thought that the relatively limited number of instances in which I had dated or had had interests in black women was due to the scarcity of blacks in my educational environments. For the greater part of my life, I have been surrounded by whites. And the blacks I did see tended to have different social backgrounds from me and so I didn't always get along with them.

I told my counselor how I felt uncomfortable pressure to date and marry a black woman. I had overheard my mother in an argument with one of my older cousins about interracial marriages. She was yelling in the kitchen that she would not even speak with my wife if she were nonblack. My cousin was asking her, "But what if your son met a nice Asian lady in college and wanted to marry her? Would you still disapprove?" My mother responded that she would not allow her to come over to the house. She began referring to my wife-to-be as my "decision." She said, "Well, he and his 'decision' can stay and live on one side of the city, but if he wants to come visit me, he'll just have to leave his 'decision' at home."

Although my counselor didn't really help me solve my insecurities about feeling pressure to date a black woman, a good Hispanic friend of mine, Ivan, told me not to worry about what others thought, because a relationship involves just two people. I asked him if he felt pressure from his parents to marry someone Hispanic, and he said no. He said that his mom would probably prefer it if he did, but she wanted him to be happy more than anything. He encouraged me to understand that my mom might be acting out of love because she thinks it would be easier for me to marry within my race.

I feel certain that, in general, the representation of my race in my school experience has had negative effects on my self-esteem. I hated discussions that singled me out as different, and perhaps inferior, to my peers. I have mingled in educational communities that are predominantly white, and this racial isolation led me to endure long periods of insecurity about my blackness. I eventually formed a sense of color-blindness, believing that race is irrelevant in human relations. The merits of blacks are so rarely praised by the dominant social group in America that it is often hard to be convinced of our self-worth. Up until my senior year at college, my education took me away from a culture where my ethnicity is seen as a source of pride.

Still, my private education was in many ways helpful in providing me with opportunities. I am currently a week away from graduating from an elite college that I may never have attended had it not been for the unbending will of my mother, who insisted that I attend a secondary institution of rigorous academic standards. I feel indebted for the many experiences my education has given me: running in the country, camping, rock climbing, horseback riding, deejaying for a radio station, and teaching and living abroad. I am grateful that I can read, write, and express myself eloquently; but most of all I appreciate the confidence my education has granted me in terms of my academic ability.

Now, one week before my college graduation, I look back and reflect on my journey from being a black child who wanted to live without race to becoming a person who is beginning to formulate a valid racial identity. I have come to realize that in the United States a black person cannot grow up healthily without reconciling himself with his race. Although my own reconciliation with my race is not yet complete, I want to share the conclusions I have reached so far on what it means to be black with the community around me; I believe I can do that by teaching elementary school students in public school in Atlanta, which I plan to do after I graduate.

My choice in going to Atlanta is partly based on my wish to finally connect with and be surrounded and affirmed by people of my race. A Hispanic friend of mine told me that it is silly to choose where I live according to skin color, but it makes sense to me. I feel that with my personal experiences and interests I would have a lot to offer no matter where I went, but I feel that it is particularly important to provide a positive role model for other black youth perhaps in the midst of negotiating their own racial identities. I wish to counterbalance the negative portrayals of blacks with positive, truthful ones—ones that aren't created and selected by someone for financial gain. I would like the children I teach to come to whatever conclusions they want, but I want them to have more than just one definition for being "black," one that is broader than the media's portrayal. After all these years, I believe black is not incompatible with peace and happiness. Blackness is what I want it to be.

6 Falling for Someone

In this case, Graham traces his personal journey from withdrawn and awkward young boy—interested in girls but not knowing the "rules"—to self-possessed young man who values honesty and communication in his relationships with women. In a middle and high school culture where sex is viewed as a goal-oriented activity, Graham insists that for him emotional connection is an essential part of physical intimacy. He describes the significant romantic relationships he has had in high school and college, assessing why the yearlong relationship with Sarah ultimately failed and why the burgeoning relationship with Nora holds more promise.

I wrote a poem about the first night we went to get coffee together. A couple of weeks later, on Valentine's Day, I printed the final copy and spent an hour making it into a card. We were in a play together at the time, so that night at rehearsal I set it slyly amidst the things on her dressing-room table after everyone had gone to warm up. When I saw her again, she was waiting out in the hall, smiling. "Thank you, Graham," she said breathlessly, eyes gleaming. "I'm almost in tears. I couldn't let everyone in there see me lose it."

"So you like it?"

"I love it." She threw her arms around my neck and gave me a fierce hug, and then she squeezed my hand again, smiling, before reluctantly slipping back down the hallway to finish costuming. We didn't know what to say to each other the rest of that evening, so backstage, we just smiled at each other and blushed.

A week later at senior cocktails, she pulled me aside. "I started writing this the same night you did," she said, placing an envelope into my hands, "but it's taken me longer to finish." She sat and watched me as I read it, the noisy crowd just around the corner. Both of our poems described the same feelings, the same lovely moments. She wrote more than I had dared to include in mine; it made me dizzy, reading and re-reading the lines, the subtext too strong to ignore but too good to be true. All I could do was blush and smile and giggle like a schoolboy; she started, too, and there we were—two college seniors on a couch around the corner from a large cocktail party, rocking and giggling like children.

Her name's Nora. She's pretty, she's funny, she's talented, and she's smart. We've got common interests, common viewpoints, common tastes in music and food, and the same sense of humor. We're attracted to each other, and you can tell by the shine we both get when we're around each other, the lovely little flirting that goes on. The kicker is that she has a boyfriend.

I'd come a long way from the shy boy I used to be. Throughout my childhood I was shy, quiet, and withdrawn. Most people find it significant that I'm an only child and that I am adopted. "Oh, really?" they murmur, with a click of their tongue. "That must be rough." Well, no, actually—it hasn't been rough. I can't remember a time not knowing I was adopted, and I can't remember a time when the concept has ever caused me any grief. My parents are my parents, and if you get to know them it becomes immediately apparent how like them I am. My parents treat me as an equal, and for that I respect them.

I've always felt as though I had a high degree of responsibility and freedom in my family. They never gave me the sex talk, though: I learned all I knew about sex from the kids at school between third and fifth grade. I was not one of those sexually precocious kids who leapt right into the act and got it out of the way. I saved myself for as long as I felt I could and still gave away my virginity at seventeen. That was pretty old by the standards in my town—there just wasn't much else to do. I hit an early growth spurt and was five-foot-ten going into junior high. I towered over everyone and was husky in build—not exactly fat, but pushing the limit. I was clumsy with my size. I slumped. The subtle ways of fashion were mysterious to me— what to wear, what to say, how to posture myself—and my attempts at conforming to them seemed immediately transparent to the popular kids, who ridiculed me.

I've liked girls for as far back as I can remember, but I missed learning the rules somehow. I remember one time, when I was in seventh grade, at someone's birthday party. The room was darkened, and everyone was being social. I was standing with my back against the wall, watching it all, when I caught my own gaze in a big portrait-sized mirror hanging on the opposite side of the room.

I vividly remember feeling as though I was seeing myself for the first time: I stood head and shoulders above the reflected people, my lank and longish hair parted sloppily down the middle, with my bangs tickling my eyebrows. My almost-too-small shirt was open at the collar, and I wore a thin gold chain around my throat. My expression was blank, noncommittal; the corner of my mouth kinked up slightly in an expression of universal dismissal, but I held my own gaze for a long time. Dismissal was a safe expression to assume. People who seemed not to care about anything were the least fun to ridicule.

It was still common at that time to talk about sexual intimacy in terms of baseball: Making out was "first base," intercourse a "home run." Everyone was eager to know how far someone had gotten the weekend before. The analogy of a game was perfect, because it neatly removed emotion from physical intimacy; it reflected a perfectly goal-oriented mentality. This was a game I wasn't playing, partly because I didn't know the rules and partly because all that my parents had told me about physical intimacy as far back as I could remember was that it was something that you only did with a person that you loved.

Enter Melissa Reynolds, someone I had placed on a pedestal all through seventh and eighth grade. It didn't dawn on me until after the fact that we had been considered "an item" for about two months, which was pretty cool to me in retrospect, considering she was a year older and a grade above me; older loosely equaled cooler. Nothing ever came of it physically: Had someone suggested that I kiss her, I would have laughed in that person's face.

I saw Mel as untouchable, all encompassing. I was physically attracted to her, yes, but at that point in my life physical affection was a symbol of love, and I was so certain that I was unworthy of her love that any desire to hold her or to kiss her was buried by self-doubt. It *never occurred* to me at that stage of my life that I could be desirable physically to a girl who was physically desirable to me.

This leads me to think that physical and emotional development are related but ultimately different processes. In many of my friends, the desire for sexual release seemed to develop before the desire for any interactive emotional context, but I recall my desire to feel loved as dominant over the urges of my flesh. What did I want from girls? I certainly experienced simple physical lust, but in another sense I longed for emotional support, personal validation. These physical and emotional desires felt somewhat disconnected in me. Physical affection from my early girlfriends became a reflection of my self-worth, showing that I was attractive enough or witty enough to merit their attention.

Anyway, Mel must have eventually gotten tired of me because the next thing I knew we weren't speaking—it was as if we'd never met. This didn't surprise me greatly, and since I had never felt as though we were bound together by anything mutual, all I felt was disappointment. The advantage of a pessimistic attitude toward something is that when it goes wrong, you've been anticipating it. I suppose I thought pretty little of myself; I had no confidence with my peers because I felt as though I didn't understand them, didn't belong. I spent a lot of time talking about these issues with my best friend, Jeff.

Jeff is an only child, as I am, and we've ended up being like brothers. I guess I call him my best friend because I feel as though he is the one person who understands me the most completely. There was very little that I didn't share with him emotionally throughout high school, and he never judged me. He just accepted me for who I was. I could be completely honest with him and not fear his scorn or reproval.

Until high school, the female mind remained largely mysterious to both of us, a combination lock to which the cool guys seemed to share a secret code. They treated girls like trash, but the girls seemed to eat it up. All I knew was how to be polite, honest, and friendly. Self-deprecatory. I was the "nicest" guy everybody knew. It was in this mind-frame that I met Missy, My First Girlfriend. I asked her out on Valentine's Day of my sophomore year; she was a junior, and it was with her that I abandoned virginity.

My introduction to intercourse was somewhat anticlimactic, so to speak. In the back of my car, almost nine months after we had been going steady, we decided to "just see what it's like." The October leaves swirled in the dark parking lot behind the public library. We had parked beneath the farthest lamppost, which some kid had shot out with a pellet gun some months before, and the light across her anxious brow was silvery and dim. She nervously brushed a strand of her long blonde hair out of her mouth. Her blue eyes were wide and fixed on me. I was fumbling with my belt. She was as tall as I was, and the tiny backseat was cramped and uncomfortable. We were already more frightened than curious, and the sensation of momentary insertion was so unbearably sweet that it pushed us immediately over the edge into panic.

We leapt apart, buckling and zipping furiously until we were safely tucked back into our pants, and then we held each other tightly for a few moments, panting, before jumping into the front seat and zooming out of the parking lot and onto the well-lit streets of town, windows down, the night breeze cooling our damp faces. The next day we were terrified that she was pregnant, even though our contact hadn't been but three or four seconds. The biological facts of the matter didn't seem relevant to us; no matter how brief, the mere pleasure of the touch seemed enough to doom us.

As our fear faded, however, our desire deepened, and within a week we couldn't get enough of each other and began having intercourse in earnest. At the time, I truly believed this was Love: "the real thing." I spent all of my free time with her, to the point where my parents began to suggest that maybe we were seeing too much of each other. This enraged me—I felt that they didn't understand our feelings for one another, didn't realize the depth of our connection. I began to feel as if I didn't need anyone else's affection or approval—I had all I needed emotionally in Missy.

Over the summer, I kissed another girl. I was disgusted with myself morally because my physical desire had gotten the better of my desire to remain faithful to my girlfriend. At the same time, though, I was overcome by the physical thrill of my bravado. Things between Missy and me deteriorated, and we broke up after she went off to college that fall.

I had a silly little relationship with a sophomore my senior year, but I was more concerned with college applications and with getting out of Dayton than I was with her. My first sexual encounter here at college, though, is worth mentioning: I was a bright-eyed, first-term freshman in this brave new world, and hence easy prey. A junior named Alice asked me to her sorority formal, and I accepted. We drank quite a bit and danced suggestively enough to earn catcalls from her sorority sisters. She came on to me very aggressively and brazenly, which I don't recall as particularly *arousing;* I was dizzy, and I remember a vague excitement of being in uncharted waters, the thrill of having someone come on to me like that. I didn't encourage her advances, but then I didn't discourage them, either.

When we got back to campus, Alice asked if I wanted to stay in her room that night rather than walk home. I was tired and drunk, so I went up with her into her room and collapsed on the bed. I lay there watching the ceiling slowly spin, and she suggested that I'd be more comfortable without all of my clothes on. This was undoubtedly true. She helped me undress and heap my clothes on a chair in the corner, and then we both crawled into the bed and pulled up the covers. Soon we were kissing and rolling around, and although we didn't have intercourse, things got awfully passionate. I remember vaguely the point at which it seemed to be over and I could drop off into an exhausted sleep.

I awoke the next morning around seven with mixed emotions. Alice was the first sexual predator I had ever dated, and I was realizing that it wasn't such a great experience. The complete lack of emotional substance to the whole affair depressed me, and I was angry at myself for having done such a thing. I got dressed and Alice walked downstairs in her nightshirt to the door with me. As I remember it, I never said a word the whole time; I just sort of looked at the floor and got out of there as quickly as I could. She made light comments, trying to start a conversation, I suppose, but all I really remember her saying was "give me a call" at the door as I stumbled out.

The irony of this, to me, is the gender reversal in this scenario. Isn't it supposed to be the older frat boy who asks the shy young freshman girl to the formal, gets her liquored up, and then convinces her to spend the night in his room? One difference is that I don't feel like I was taken advantage of; I never felt like any of the responsibility for my actions lay with anybody but myself. I didn't *have* to drink or stay in her room, I decided to. One thing I'll say to Alice's credit: She was clear about what she wanted, and maybe that kind of communication is better than none at all.

Communication is imperative. I think a major reason that my relationships at college have seemed different from the ones I had in high school is that people communicate more. For example, my buddies here are all important to me, yet there is no significant sense of hierarchy; no single one of them fulfills my every interpersonal need. That being said, my happiness still seems to some degree dependent upon my relationships with others. I get depressed when I feel unloved or unnoticed, which leads me to think that I *need* other people, I *need* friends around me. Is it possible to be completely self-sufficient? Is it desirable?

As a kid, I spent a good deal of time by myself. I guess I was lonely but then I never really remember being unhappy, as such. I often enjoy being alone; I *need* to be alone sometimes. Ideally, I have a balance of quality time with my friends, quality time by myself, and activities that combine social interaction with independent work.

For example, I like to act. I like to get up on stage and impress people. I like the attention and the freedom of my body on the stage—the freedom to expand my personal space until it encompasses an entire room. I unleash my voice and express my energy. I love the applause, washing over me in its thunderous *yes*. On stage, I can be graceful and funny and tragic; I control the dynamic. I can feel alone in a room full of people, letting them in and out of my life as I wish, and then enjoy their approval.

I am most exultant when I am living a scene moment by moment, never anticipating the next, not inhibited by the sequence of emotions I'm scripted to experience, but rather living a fictional story line as spontaneous, as now, as if I were the character. Acting is a strange mixture of awareness and spontaneity; I have the chance to figure out how my character will behave before the action takes place. When I walk onto the stage and into the world of the play, I'm living spontaneously in a self-controlled moment; there is nothing to be unsure of, so I can experience a range of passionate emotions without doubt, without unpredictable repercussions—everything's safely scripted beforehand.

I met Sarah the spring of our sophomore year. She was beautiful; she had dark, thick hair that fell to her jawline and big, brown doe eyes. When I looked at her, she'd smile and sometimes glance away and blush.

We began spending more and more time alone together. We'd go for a jog, grab a bite to eat, take in a movie, or just walk around and talk. At some point I realized we were sitting on her bed in her room one night, and the conversation had fallen into one of those comfortable silences. It occurred to me to kiss her, but then I thought I'd better ask, just to make sure. When I did, she smiled and blushed and said yes, and we kissed and it was bliss. It felt like chemistry; it felt right. "Why did this take us so long?" she smiled, as if she'd been thinking about it for a while. It occurred to me then that maybe I had, too. I suppose things happen at the pace they happen, and that's part of the beauty of courtship.

We saw more and more of each other. By the end of the term, we were going steady. I don't recall ever being that happy in my life, in the sense that *nothing* mattered. It was a mindless kind of happiness: The world could have ended and I would have been content to go down with it knowing that there was Sarah and me.

The romantic clichés are clichés for a reason—because they are indeed Fantastic, they are Magnificent, they are 100 percent true. It's bliss, it's beautiful—it's walking on air; it's as light as a feather. She was radiant, and when I looked at her I couldn't *stop* looking at her. I wanted to touch her and hold her and hug her close and melt right into her body, fuse like that, curl up like a kitten inside her and wrap around her and weave through her hair and fall into her eyes. I don't know if that's the healthiest phase of falling for someone, but it is certainly an exhilarating lack of perspective.

Every time I looked at her, I was struck anew. With other girlfriends, that sense of astonishment diminished over time. I'd "get used" to them, so to speak, in the sense that my aesthetic attraction to them became internalized, accepted, understood, not thought about consciously. But with Sarah, it was like seeing her for the first time every time I looked at her. She was also the most intelligent girl I'd ever dated; she thought in a wonderfully straightforward, logical way. We could discuss issues and never lose each other; our processes of deduction seemed to mirror each other's and work in exactly the same patterns. This is not to say that we never disagreed; rather, I mean it always seemed that we understood one another.

In her eyes I was funny, talented, intelligent, and diverse—"Is there anything that you *don't* do?" she asked early on—so different from the other boys she had dated before. She described me as passionate, inexplicable, dynamic, rational, emotional, ridiculous, sophisticated, sophomoric, artistic, communicative—unlike anyone she'd ever met. And my willingness to go head-over-heels, hopeless-romantic crazy for her was probably exactly what she was looking for at the time when a fling with another frat-boy, Econ-major, cookie-cutter, blue-blazer, third-generation-legacy stereotype had fallen through in her life. I fit. She fit. We were perfect for one another for impermanent reasons. We spent that summer together at school, and the whole term went by in a happy blur.

In the fall I went to study in London for two terms. Sarah took the winter off to go ski and work in Colorado. There was a general feeling of unease in me; I feared that she might get into an exciting new environment and fall for someone else. I also feared meeting some nice British girl and breaking my word to Sarah; I'd not yet been successful in a long-distance relationship. I came home to the U.S. over break and flew up to see her after Christmas; she was going to meet me in the airport. I wasn't sure what to expect—would she feel the same?

I was one of the last people out of the plane, and as I walked across the tarmac in the bitter night's wind, I felt a strange calm come over me. I was excited to see her, but perhaps I was steeling myself for a letdown. I walked through the door into the bright terminal.

She was sitting in a chair against the wall, leaning forward with her elbows on her knees when the crowd parted and we saw each other. Her hair was longer and I was again struck by how lovely she was. She rose and we embraced—it was wonderful; that sense of gently trying to pull the other person completely into oneself. For me, it was an ecstatically silent affirmation.

We drove home to her house in Albany, New York, and tried to catch up on what had happened in the time since our last letters, the last phone call, the whole term in general. There was so much I wanted to say, but somehow we just sort of sat smiling in silence as we drove through the dark. I could smell her favorite perfume, the scent of her hair, the fabric softener she used on her clothes. The sound of her voice was so much different in person than it had been on the telephone.

We ended up spending almost the whole time with her parents. They were all better skiers than me, and they all looked like one big, happy family. Her parents always seemed a *shade* distant toward me. I wasn't sure if it was just that I was their daughter's first "serious" boyfriend, the fact that I was a creative writing major, something specific about my personality, or a combination of these things that inspired this coolness. She was Daddy's Little Girl, and I suspect that part of the odd feeling originated in the psychiatrist's evaluative eye he always seemed to be examining me with.

I think from those four days, I wanted definite confirmation of her feelings for me. Sarah wasn't the best at articulating her emotions. "The more we try to pack everything into four days," she said, "the harder it will be to go without it again." I wasn't sure what that statement implied.

Sarah was uncomfortable with the idea of her parents seeing us in any physically intimate way. We were very comfortable with one another when nobody else was around, but with her parents it was an almost visible fear, a tension that lasted the whole four days. When the day came to have her take me back to the airport, I was still confused.

I went back to London; she went to Colorado. I enjoyed hearing how animated her voice became over the phone when she told me about the crazy high jinks she had gotten into while working on the mountain that week. I was having a better time myself, meeting people and traveling around Britain. All seemed well until that fateful day when I talked to her, perhaps two weeks before the end of the quarter. We talked for an hour, but I never felt like she was actually in the conversation.

"You know, Sarah," I suggested, "I've been wondering if maybe this relationship is going to be the same when we both get back to campus in the spring."

"You know, I have, too," she replied with audible relief. "I mean, it's been so long and we've both been through *so much*. It's strange, isn't it? I'm not really sure how to feel about you any more." All of this in a light, *thank goodness we agree!* sort of tone. Well, I had to sit down.

". . . Are you *serious?*" I asked, after a moment. "What exactly does that mean?" Silence on the line.

"I thought you wanted us to be honest with each other," she said.

"Well, yes—I do. I do. But Jesus, maybe not *this* honest." I was floored. It felt as though a deep hole had opened up somewhere inside my gut, and everything was getting sucked down into it. My center of gravity had suddenly become a black hole. I couldn't let myself believe what seemed to be happening, not after all this time, not this way.

"Well, we can talk about it when I meet you in France, right?" She seemed to want to wrap up this discussion.

"You still want to do that, then?" This gave me some kind of hope.

"Of course I do! I wouldn't miss that for the world." Sarah's family and another family had a tradition of going to Europe biannually to ski. Sarah and I had made plans to go to Paris before their trip was scheduled to begin.

I mumbled a few shaky good-byes, and the conversation was over. I went into my room and lay down on my bed and stared at my ceiling for about two hours. I couldn't get over that hollow emptiness inside myself. A strange detachment came over me, and I was sort of marveling at how interesting a sensation it was. *I haven't just been dumped, that's for sure. She never said we aren't going out anymore—after all, she's still going to meet me in Paris over break, like we planned. That must mean something. We'll talk about it. She'll see that she still cares about me when we meet again face to face. This is not a disaster.*

Cut to a wide-angle shot of me two weeks later, sitting alone in Gatwick, waiting for her to deplane. I'm having a coffee and reading *Bleak House*. The crowd parts and there she is, walking toward me, smiling. She is deeply tanned from the slopes of Colorado, and her teeth are brilliantly white. She carries a large duffel sack over her shoulder, which she swings to the floor as I stand up to greet her.

A grandmotherly embrace. A dry peck on the cheek. There could be no doubt anymore, but somehow I managed to convince myself otherwise. It's amazing what things we won't let ourselves believe when we don't want to believe them. The taxi ride back to my room was mostly silent, uneasy.

We spent a day and a night in London. It was immediately apparent that things were different between us, but I denied the signs of this. There was no physical affection beyond the casual or the accidental—the few times she made contact with me were sisterly, almost reluctant. When we got to Paris, it was worse: She didn't want to talk about it; she didn't want to acknowledge that there was anything to discuss. "Less not spoil our time here," she said a couple of times. It was terrible.

The city of romance was gray and wet. A cold wind blew through the streets. We slept in the same bed, but she would not be touched—if I brushed against her, she rolled away. This was not done in a cruel way, which somehow made it worse. Her absence of emotion was harder to handle than love, hate, or anger: Anything would have been better than her wistful distance. It was as if I was fading out like an old photograph, slowly losing cohesion until light itself began to bleed through me; I could almost feel myself becoming more and more translucent and ghostlike.

Even when I would grab her and pull her close to me, hug her fiercely as if to say "See me! See me!" she would look into my eyes and smile vaguely, sadly, until I thought my heart would literally crack. She never wanted to face it, to discuss it, to admit that this was happening. I felt like she was lost, but she was always there— I'd look up from the bed while she was gazing out the window and it was *her*, in the *flesh*, and that kept alive in me a strange kind of hope.

Her family and their friends arrived in the city; we all spent the day together, and they all looked knowingly at me. That evening I left alone for London, as planned.

I spent the spring term at school, where it finally ended, almost a year after we met. Ultimately, I had to do it myself. We both arrived back on campus and got in touch; a week or two went by during which we ate lunch, met for coffee, and did the usual sort of things together, but as in Paris there was no spark at all.

Finally, I went to her room one afternoon. She was lying on her bed reading. I sat down in a chair next to her and said, "I think it's really time we talked about this." She stared at her book. Her tension was palpable; I wanted to make it as painless as possible.

"What do you want to talk about?" she said.

"I get the feeling that you don't care about me anymore," I replied.

Pause.

"That's not true. . . ." She was struggling with the words. "I just don't think I care about you in the same way that I used to. I think things have changed." I explained to her why it was important for me to *hear* this from her, to actually have it *said* and *deal* with it once and for all. I told her that not knowing for sure was the worst thing and that it was wonderful at last to be communicating sincerely again.

Her relief was visible and immediate. From then on, I asked if she was still interested in being friends and she gushed that of course she was. I hoped we could still spend some time together, and she assured me that she wouldn't want it any other way. I was so happy that she seemed at last to be looking *at* me rather than *through* me, that I seemed to finally *exist* again in her eyes, that I forgot about what was really being *said* here: We were breaking up.

It was maybe a day and a half before it began to sink in that things weren't going to be like they had been before. When I'd suggest activities, she always had other plans. She told me that she was sorry, that if she could make herself feel the same way that she had before then she would. I asked her if she had fallen for one of the guys she was living with in Colorado, and she flew off the handle. *That's not important. That's none of your business. I can't believe you'd ask me that.* Panic. A week later she's dating Kevin, a guy from school she'd met while out West. She began avoiding me.

I began to see Sarah in new ways, began to hear the things my friends were saying (that perhaps they had been hinting at all along) about our incompatibility. Had our relationship been doomed from the get-go? I wondered just how much of my affection for her had been based upon my emotional needs at the time. It seemed in my life that I just bumped into these girls I was serious about and that fate dictated my relationships. Not my own emotional state, but the chance meeting of one special girl. For a while after Sarah, I looked at it as almost entirely dictated by my own emotional state: I thought that if I was emotionally ready to have another big relationship, I'd find the girl to have it with and convince myself that it was destiny. As I see it now, big relationships in my life have probably been just as dependent upon my emotional needs at the time as they have been upon who it was I happened to meet during that period—a combination of chance and internal readiness.

I loved to hold Sarah, I loved to be close to Sarah, but did I love *Sarah?* What exactly was I waiting six months for? Why did the lack of physical intimacy over both of our vacations strike so fundamental a chord in me? Was she purely a beautiful object with whom I sexually validated myself?

No. The lack of physical intimacy at vacation time was a problem because it was the way in which we communicated. Since she didn't discuss her feelings very much, I read them in her body language. An affectionate hug around the waist was one sign that she cared for me. Being apart had a preservative effect on our relationship, then: Without communication there could be no unified evolution, and a relationship in stasis eventually goes stale. I got used to not seeing Sarah for so long, but without the physical we didn't communicate. We spoke on the phone but very seldom about how we felt, about "us" or what was going on emotionally. When I saw her in person, then, I needed that physical communication. Not because I couldn't stand going without the sex—I had done fine without it for three months—but sex would have given me a document to analyze, a script from which to interpret her feelings. I could have found affirmation in her physical interaction with me, but our halfway vacation was stifled by her parents' constant presence.

We never said that we loved each other. It didn't make sense to; I had told other girls before that I loved them and then proven myself false by breaking up with them. Telling someone that you love them is all very well and good, but where do you go from there? It's a rut. Once you say it, it immediately begins to lose its meaning. It fades. There is no greater emotional profession, but there are many types of love. I told Missy that I loved her, and I still believe that I did—I was madly, hopelessly, Romeo-and-Juliet in love with her. I wanted to surrender myself completely to our love. It was ridiculous. Wonderful, but ridiculous in the way only first love can be, with its talk of forever and eternity, of magnitudes beyond the mortal.

Sarah never got that into it. I don't know how Sarah saw love, but my guess is that she was saving it for later. This was fine by me, since I'd said it too often to other girls and soured it in my mouth. Clichés don't mean much, so we used little body language haiku. It felt like love, but perhaps both of us knew deep down that there was something missing (an element of clear and fundamental communication?), that there was some kind of unwritten expiration date between us that made it "not love." Further, although I feared it might expire within me, I now believe that from the beginning it was doomed to expire within her. That didn't stop us, though, from falling happily into whatever it was for the time being.

Looking back, I don't regret a minute of it. The experience changed my perspective on relationships. For a while I dated around, hooking up with friends and acquaintances, fulfilling the desire that flesh is heir to, but emphasizing the transience, the lack of emotional substance to such behavior. My partners and I would talk beforehand, making sure that what was about to happen "didn't mean anything." It was fulfilling physically and convenient emotionally—a handy kind of disposable love, you might say—or like instant coffee, one cup at a time. But after a year of that lifestyle, I began to feel a little hollow and hunger for something more emotionally substantial.

I often need someone to remind me that there is a broader perspective from which to look at my life: a girlfriend, a buddy, a parent. Usually, there is an element of understanding that exists between myself and my male friends that I don't think exists between myself and my female friends or my parents. I feel as comfortable with a girlfriend as I do with a best friend—I freely share my inmost thoughts and feelings—but sometimes there is some doubt in my mind as to whether or not they truly understand where I'm coming from in the same way that, say, Jeff would.

With Nora and me, it seems like an entirely new experience. Three weeks have elapsed. She broke up with her boyfriend a few days ago, and we've been seeing even more of each other since then. Both of us are happily in that phase of exultant exploration with which relationships characteristically begin, but I'm approaching this with a mixture of skepticism and hope. Will it be possible to develop our ongoing physical attraction as well as our actively evolving emotional and intellectual relationship? She tells me I'm unlike anyone she's ever dated before, but I've heard those words before. Still, she can explain her thoughts and feelings in detail, and I do feel as though we connect in a unique way. I don't want to kid myself anymore—I don't want my actions to be dictated by my emotional needs.

I'd like to behave in complete accordance with my moral and rational convictions. I often catch myself doing otherwise, but I continue to make the effort. For example, there was a period of two days when the chemistry between Nora and me had become undeniable, but she had not yet formally ended her relationship with her boyfriend—"overlap," she calls it. I urged her to deal with that situation, even though I knew how difficult it must have been for her, remembering the pain and sadness I felt when Sarah was not straightforward with me. She discussed everything with him; she explained her feelings and why she felt the way she did. It wasn't easy for her to do, but he's an extremely mature and friendly guy, and she tells me that although he was hurt, he appreciated her honesty.

I hope that I'm better equipped to deal with this relationship because of what I've been through with Sarah. I'm very happy getting to know Nora, although I am wary of being hurt again. Communication is important to her, too, which is refreshing, and overall I feel good about the direction we've been taking. People may never meet Mr. or Ms. Right in their lives; the very concept of the perfect partner may be unrealistic in and of itself. If we all communicate, if we are willing to work at it, I do believe that any relationship can be an ultimately productive and therefore positive experience in our lives—and besides, isn't it almost more fun not knowing?

7 A Step in the Only Direction

This writer's central theme is coming to terms with being gay. The twenty-year-old autobiographer recounts the emergence of homosexual longings in junior high school amid all the peer pressure toward heterosexual involvement. Ben has his first gay experience as a first-year college student, and he realizes that these feelings represent where he wants to go with his sexual life and that he must somehow come to terms with being gay in a straight world. He describes an excruciating coming-out scene with his parents that begins a period of coming-out to friends, though he avoids being openly identified as gay at his college because he perceives an antigay environment. Ben blames his parents for his reluctance to be more active in his advocacy of gay issues at his college. This resentment of his parents for their lack of true acceptance of his sexual orientation remains a powerful source of anger and insecurity for him, and it reflects his struggle to maintain both a sense of belonging and self-respect in a homophobic society.

How can I study with *that* over there?" I asked myself over an open philosophy textbook. "Finals are coming so you'd better pay attention to your books and not to anything or *anybody* else," I warned myself. Still, I found myself rubbernecking awkwardly every time I heard one of the two doors at the west end of the study hall open. After reading the same paragraph about fifteen times due to my perpetual rubbernecking, *he* walked into the study room. Of course, I again awkwardly contorted myself in my chair in order to catch a glimpse of whoever may have entered the scene, and when I did this time, I found myself in a locked stare with a very attractive man. The stare, which seemed to last for minutes, could not have been more than a second and a half glance, but that was enough to make me forget about Mssrs. Kant, Hume, and Hegel.

Tim, as I later learned was his name, placed his things on the long wooden table right next to the door he had just passed through and sat down facing my back. I had to know if his glance was just casual or if it was more. I turned toward the clock and stole another glance at Tim. However, again, my attempt did not go unnoticed. Tim was waiting to meet my glance with his. My heart was racing! I was sure that everybody in the silent study hall could hear it pounding loudly in my throat. I could not keep myself from looking again, and I was greeted by an "inviting" glance. One time I was met by a rather forward raising of the eyebrows.

"Your attention, please. The library will be closing in thirty minutes. If you wish to check out books. . . ." What was I going to do?! The library was closing, so I headed for the door—the door farther from me and closer to Tim. He had begun to pack up when I did, and he *just happened* to be at the same door at the same time that I was. He held the door open for me (literally and figuratively, as I'll explain later), and I passed within inches of him and choked, "Thanks."

"What's up?" he asked in a friendly voice as we headed for the stairs.

"Not a lot," I stuttered. "And you?"

"Where are you headed?" he answered with a smile.

My God. It was really happening. This beautiful man was making a pass at me. By the time we reached this point in our "conversation" we had reached the first floor of the library on our way toward the doors that lead to the west end of campus.

"Where are *you* headed?" I answered meekly.

"Would you like to go somewhere and talk?" he asked.

"Sure," I answered, choking on my heart.

Since that evening, I have had no doubt whatsoever about my sexuality. I am gay. I have always been gay. I will most likely always be gay. I am happy being gay. It is true that the fact I am gay creates some barriers in life for me, particularly in the political world and other professions. Also, the possibility of having a family is considerably decreased by the biological incompatibility with homosexuality. Finally, being gay has caused me to distance myself from people, like my family, to whom I would like to be closer. However, these are things that mean very little in comparison to the life I imagine if I tried to live a straight life as a homosexual. I couldn't live a charade like that. My happiness stems from my being me, and my being the only one who knows what is best for me. Homosexuality is not the cause of my happiness. My acceptance of it is.

But what about the first eighteen years of my life? Was I happy then? I will answer yes and no to this question. I answer yes because I was truly happy before my mind understood what it was to be sexual at all. When I did not understand sexuality (heterosexuality or homosexuality), I was ignorantly blissful. My troubles began when my body began changing and when my intellect began understanding those changes and the feelings they caused. Before I get into the inner conflict of my adolescence, let me say something about my early childhood.

I was the most self-confident child I knew. I wasn't afraid to say or do anything to anybody. In elementary school and in middle school I was always the teacher's pet. Why shouldn't I have been? I was the model student: well-behaved, respectful, entertaining, and intelligent. It all came very easily and naturally. To behave in any other way would be to behave as I was not. As I look back on those years before high school, I see many things which I am now better able to understand.

In middle school I was very involved with the drama club. My singing voice is comparable to a cross between Elvis and Roger Rabbit, but I was always on stage in the school musicals. I was an attention "addict." My habit was more than adequately supported by the many attention "pushers" around me who were more than willing to give me a fix. I never had trouble dealing with people in the structured and regulated environment of school. However, out of the classroom I was out of my element and, therefore, a very different person. Still, I was very charismatic and self-confident until the subject of sex was brought up. I just couldn't participate in the "oogling" that my friends engaged in. I didn't find Danissa and her chest as inviting as everybody else did. John's conquest of Cindy wasn't the least bit interesting to me, particularly because I didn't yet have the sexual drive to engage in these behaviors myself. When I did develop this drive, I guess in eighth grade, I found myself equally disinterested in Danissa and her chest. Instead, I found myself very interested in Tony and his sharp features and muscular build.

Parties! I loved them then. I love them now. Soda and chips have been replaced by beer and more beer, but the idea of getting together with a group of friends (an audience) and sharing some stories and laughs is my favorite way to spend time. Well, maybe my second favorite way. Parties were great in middle school until I became sexual. An innocent game of spin-the-bottle among friends was a lot of fun. Actually, it seemed pretty inane to me. Why would anybody want to voluntarily enter a situation in which he or she would be forced to kiss somebody else? What was the big deal about kissing anyway? I must have played fifty games of spin-the-bottle, and not once did I get any pleasure from kissing. Kissing wasn't repulsive to me, but it wasn't attractive either, until I began to have sexual desires for men. I felt forced to play spin-the-bottle. If I didn't, I feared being labeled as gay. And I *wasn't* gay. That's what I told myself so often, in fact, that I actually believed it for a while.

Things got tougher, however, whenever one of my oversexed and underexperienced adolescent friends would suggest that we play a game of "French" spin-the-bottle. It sent a shiver up my spine and caused my stomach to contract to the size of a pea. They wanted me to put my very personal tongue into somebody else's equally personal mouth. No way! I wasn't even interested in putting my tongue in Tony's mouth. I don't know what I wanted to do with Tony. I think I just wanted to be with him, to admire him, to touch him. I put my foot down when it came to institutionalized French kissing, and this seemed odd to everybody else. "Why not?" my friends would ask. My answer was usually something like "I'll only do that with somebody special" and not "It's gross and I'm afraid to try it," which was the true answer. I laugh when I think of Susan (who later earned herself the reputation of being the class slut) trying to teach me how to kiss: "It's just like giving somebody a raspberry only into their mouth." Ick!!! More than four years would pass before I had my "first kiss." Needless to say, my attitude toward kissing is very different now.

Now, before I jump from middle school into high school, is the best time to say more about the relationship between my twin brother and me. First, I should note that I haven't told my brother Keith that I am gay. I do not feel that close to him, nor do I feel that he would react in a positive way to learning that his own twin brother, albeit fraternal twin brother, prefers intimacy with men over sex with women. Also, I have respected my parents' wish that I not tell my siblings about my homosexuality. Anyway, Keith and I always got along, and we always fought. We were best friends and worst enemies. In middle school we had different friends. He hung out with the tough Neanderthal jock crowd. I moved in more civil circles. My friends were students, actors, and other human beings.

Academically, I've always been a better student than Keith. I was enrolled in my school's Gifted and Talented Students program. Keith, on the other hand, excelled on the playing field, particularly the gridiron. I participated in athletics, as well, although I disliked most team sports and was equally as terrible at most of them. I even played full-contact football until the end of middle school when everybody got big and I didn't. I know that I only played in order to be "one of the guys." The pressure in my community to be this way was tremendous. I needed to be accepted by my peers, and the only way to do that was to appear to be like every other normal heterosexual young man. This pressure existed even before I became aware of my sexuality and was only exacerbated by my feelings of "abnormality," which I suffered when I began to have sexual feelings for men.

When we entered high school, the tables had turned. Keith was more relaxed and at ease than I was. I had a serious lack of self-confidence, especially in the social sense. I wasn't comfortable. I just couldn't bring myself to talk about girls and all of the other stuff that high school guys talked about. My friends loved to talk about all of the girls they wanted to sleep with, and I found it very difficult to feign interest all of the time. I did, however, more often than not, awkwardly participate in the talks about girls and sex. However, in the back of my mind was the ever-present feeling that I wasn't normal, and that I must change. This problem was exacerbated merely by being placed in the new physical surroundings of high school. Perhaps it is more accurate to call them "physique-ful" surroundings. My new, more physically developed age-mates of high school provided many more stimuli to remind me constantly of my feelings about men.

In high school our groups of friends changed. Keith and I started to hang out with the same people, most of whom were male and from the other middle school in town that we did not attend. Some played with me on the soccer team. Others swam with me during my one-season career on the swim team. I attribute my brief swimming career to the many distractions that the swim team offered. The only thing more brief than my career with the swim team was the "brevity" of the team's uniform. I barely made it all season without any very embarrassing moments.

My female friends were generally the same as those from middle school. In general, I never had any problems getting along with girls in school. I just never "got anywhere" with them sexually. Today, I am almost never intimidated by any woman, but I am often intimidated by handsome men. I don't know why this is, but I would venture to guess that it has something to do with my desire to be liked by men and my disinterest sexually in women. I am not sexist. This is not a sexist phenomenon; it is deeper and far more fundamental to my personality than any "ism" could be.

Keith and I are opposite in every way. He, as I've said, is a great athlete and a good student; I am a great student and a fair athlete. He loves the Grateful Dead; I love Beethoven. He is an engineering student; I am a liberal arts student. He is a registered Republican; I am a Democrat. He is a conservative thinker (an oxymoron if ever there was one); I am a liberal. He is heterosexual; I am gay. How do we get along? Honestly, I'd have to say that we don't get along. We were never very close except in proximity to each other. We don't agree on anything except that we never agree on anything.

I don't want to be like him in any way. Deep in my heart I feel that Keith is a fundamentally bad person, one who doesn't care about hurting others. I pride myself on my integrity, honesty, and open-mindedness. Keith, in my experience of nearly twenty-one years, lacks these elements of goodness. (He is very similar to my father, whom I will discuss later.) I must make it sound like Keith and I were and are constantly at each other's throats. That is not the case. It is true that we argue occasionally, but more frequently, I choose to avoid any argument by changing the subject at hand, particularly if it is one of the standard liberal versus conservative questions. I don't like to appear like a "flaming liberal," which in my home is equated with "flaming homosexual." As far as Keith is concerned, our relationship is a farce, a play in which one actor believes he is living his part and the other is simply humoring him. My sexuality, combined with my paranoia about discovery and then rejection, has caused me to isolate myself from my family and anybody else with whom I feel unable to be completely open. Nowhere were the fundamental differences between others and me greater than at home.

Keith and I are the youngest of six children. All together we are three men and three women. A regular Brady Bunch without the maid. There is a seven-year gap between my youngest sister and Keith and me. (Keith and I were not a product of Planned Parenthood. Instead, I believe that we were the product of the Catholic Church, or worse yet, my parents' ignorance about and inability to discuss sexual issues such as birth control.) Because of this dramatic age difference (thirteen years in the case of my oldest sister) I was never very close with my older siblings. The most time we spent together was when one of them (always one of my sisters) was forced to stay home and baby-sit. When I entered junior high school, my youngest sister was the last to leave home and go to college. Although I was never very close to any of my siblings, whenever we are together we always seem to have fun. Of course, all conversation revolves around very impersonal subjects, except for the standard "Do-you-have-a-girlfriend?" question which I have learned to dodge with great creativity and eloquence. I lie.

I lie because my family is very different than I am. I don't know how to explain this difference, but it has always existed, and I think it always will. It has to do with our fundamental natures, and mine was and never will be like theirs. They are racist. I am not. They care only about themselves and their families. I tend to look at life on a broader scale. This "bigger picture" has caused me to isolate myself from my siblings because I feel that they are unworthy of my attention. I am not going to agree with their racial slurs and homophobic remarks, and until I feel that I can tell them about my sexuality, I am unable to defend myself in the face of such remarks.

My brothers and sisters are fun people to whom I would like to be closer, but until I can be honest with them, I will continue to alienate myself from them.

My relationship with my parents is very similar to my relationship with my twin brother. I love my parents very much and I appreciate all that they have done for me. At the same time, I detest their very existence. They stand for everything that I oppose. My relationship with my parents can be divided into two periods: our relationship before I told them that I was gay, and my relationship with them since.

Before I went to college, things between my parents and me were stable and simple. I succeeded. They praised. I did not spend a lot of time with them. Sure, they were proud of me, but, upon reflection, I don't believe that they really know what I accomplished. They were always more concerned about whether or not I needed a car than what pieces the Wind Band, of which I was the president, was playing for the seasonal concert, which they only went to out of a sense of obligation. We never discussed my interest in girls. Granted, it would have been a very short discussion, but they never even showed any interest. My father never had "the talk" about sex with me. I doubt that he has even said the word "sex."

I am grateful that my parents have been such good providers. However, I resent them for filling me with prejudices and hate which I still have to work to combat even today. Blacks are no good. Jews are no good. Puerto Ricans are no good. The English are no good because of what's happening in Northern Ireland. (My mother is a full-blooded Irishwoman who blindly believes that only the English are to blame for all of the violence in Ireland. I've since learned that this is not necessarily true and that my mother knows very little about her "homeland.") Finally, homosexuals are no good. This is what they have taught me through their actions and words. They have taught me to hate myself. I have learned to love myself since I have left home for college.

My relationship with my parents has been more of a farce since I told them that I am gay. Imagine that: raised in a household where the word "sex" was not even uttered, and I've told them that I am gay. I admit that telling my parents when I did was a mistake *for me,* but it has also reinforced my belief that they are fundamentally ignorant people. (I have a perhaps unfair tendency to freely interchange the terms "ignorant" and "conservative.") That was a lonely summer. I had lost Tim in the spring. He was nearly the only person who knew about me. (He had introduced me to a few other gay men, and I had met a few others after we broke up.) Working, eating, and reading. That's how I spent my summer of 1988. I worked all day long at two jobs. I'd come home and make my dinner. I'd then retire to my room where I read books with homosexual themes, like Mary Renault's *The Persian Boy,* Christopher Bram's *Surprising Myself,* and AIDS nonfiction like *And the Band Played On.* I used to leave these books around the house, and although I doubt my parents knew the content of them, I guess I left them out subconsciously hoping that they would get the message I wanted to convey. At the time, I consciously thought nothing of leaving the books out; I didn't want to appear to be hiding anything.

Periodically, my parents would confront me about my self-isolation during that summer. My response was always, "Everything's fine. I'm just tired." Then it happened. I came home from work one night and I was confronted immediately by my father. He said, "We know something's bothering you, and we don't want you to tell us that there isn't. We can't help you unless you tell us what it is that's on your mind. We are your parents and you can tell us anything. What's the problem?"

"I don't have a problem," I answered in a very insincere tone, but I was feeling rather pressured. My dad was getting equally upset. It was more than obvious that I was keeping something from them and that I wanted to let them know, but from where would I muster the courage to do so? I could barely speak. My breathing seemed to stop. I had to consciously remind myself to inhale or else I would find myself passed out on the kitchen floor.

"I do want to talk to you and Mom, but I would like to talk to you tomorrow." I needed time to plan what I was going to say, although I had done just that hundreds of times in my head already.

"No. I want you to talk to us now. We are your parents and we don't like seeing you like this."

I was nearly in tears. This was the big one, and I knew it. I had let the cat out of the bag (my parents hate cats), and it was only a matter of time before I would have to let them know. I suggested that we all sit down in the den. My dad turned off the television right away and sat down on the couch. My mom lit a cigarette and settled down in her recliner. I sat uneasily on a futon opposite my mom and next to my father. (I can't believe how all of the uneasiness is coming back to me as I sit here and recall what happened that evening in August. My hands are shaking as I type.) There was an incredible tension in the air, one which created the loudest silence I have ever had to break.

"I don't have a problem really. I just want to talk to you about me. First, I want to say that I love you very much and that what I'm going to tell you will not change that at all. I want things to be the same after as they were before."

"Of course. We love you and always will. You can tell us anything."

"It's hard for me to do this because I know you so well and because I treasure your love so much. I think that you both would agree that I am a good person who has never done anything to embarrass or shame you."

"No, you haven't. What are you trying to say, Ben?"

"This isn't easy for me. I want you to understand that I need you and that I don't want this to change your love for me. I haven't always been completely honest with you. There's something about me which I have to deal with, and I want you to know about it too."

By this time tears were streaming down my face. My mother was sniffling as she puffed feverishly on her cigarette. My dad was noticeably shaken and struggling to maintain himself.

"I'm not everything that I appear to be. Er, rather, there's more to me than is apparent. I'm not . . . I'm not exactly what you think, and it bothers me that I haven't been completely honest with you. I'm the same person, but there's something you don't know about me. I'm . . . I'm not . . . I'm not exactly. . . . This is very difficult for me to do because I don't want to hurt you, but I also don't want to be dishonest. I'm not . . . I'm not exactly straight."

My God, I said it. It took me a while, but I came out to my parents. The silence was even more deafening than before. This time my father broke it by questioning me.

"What do you mean you're not exactly straight?"

I couldn't believe it. There weren't going to make this easy at all.

"I mean I'm gay." I barely choked that out through my throat, which had contracted to inoperable dimensions, and the tears flooded my face.

"How long have you known this for?"

"For a long time. Since the beginning of high school."

"Why didn't you tell us before?"

"Because I was afraid of being rejected. I don't want to hurt you, but I don't want to lie."

"Why are you telling us now?"

They were making this tough! "I want you to know about me. I don't want to be dishonest with you. I want some support in dealing with this. I don't want it to be something I have to hide or that we can't talk about."

"You say you are homosexual," (Did I actually hear my father say the "H-word"?) "but what do you mean by that?"

"I find other men attractive."

"Sexually?" (Wow! He just said the "S-word," too!)

"Yes, sexually."

"Why didn't you tell us before? We could have helped you."

"I wasn't sure before. Now I am, and I want your support."

Then it happened. For the first time in my life, I saw my father cry. He couldn't keep it inside any longer. He broke down in tears, jumped to his feet and hurried to the bathroom right next to the den. My mother and I sat and listened to him for a few minutes before I said, "This is what I didn't want to do. I didn't want to hurt you."

She choked through her own tears. Shaking, she said, "We're glad that you told us. We only wish you had told us sooner."

My dad returned after blowing his nose. He had pulled himself back together, but was still quite shaken. The inquisition recommenced.

"Have you told your brothers and sisters about this?"

"No, I haven't."

"Do you plan on telling them?"

"Yes, sometime."

"We don't think that's a good idea."

"Why not? I don't want to lie to them either."

"We don't think they will be very accepting of it."

"I'm not going to tell them right away."

"We hope that you don't ever tell them, but if you ever do, we'd like you to tell us that you are going to before you do."

"Okay." I wasn't about to make things worse by starting an argument. I haven't even considered telling my siblings after this fiasco, so this promise has been very easy to keep. After I graduate, I wonder if it will be as simple. We talked for a long time about me and how I feel and what they can do. My dad felt guilty and wanted to know if he did anything to cause this. I told him of course not, and that is not why anybody is gay. He needed to know why, but I couldn't answer that question myself. After about an hour spent discussing everything from AIDS to the destruction of the American family, my dad was again in tears. My mom had really never stopped. Instead of rushing from the room, this time he stood up and pulled me up to him and hugged me tightly.

"You're my son. We're always going to love you. We could never reject you. We only want you to be happy." This was the first time my father had hugged me in many years. He has only done so on one other occasion since, that being upon my return from my term abroad. My mother stood and joined our hug. All of us were crying. My father ended it and said, "I'm going to bed now." I don't think that anybody slept for about a week after that night.

Things were more than a little bit tense around the house for the next few weeks before I returned to school. We talked about my sexuality once more before I went back to school. They suggested that I not return to school for the fall term, and that I see someone professional in order to try to change my sexual preference. What preference? I told them that psychiatrists can't change people that way, and that I was going to go back to school. I was seeing a counselor there, and I would tell her all about what they wanted.

The theme of this second conversation was, "We're only happy if you are happy." I told them that I was happy and that I didn't know if I was going to ever change. They asked me to look into it by reading books and talking to a counselor. I said that I would, but I never did. I wouldn't know how to be anything else except gay. They told me that I had devastated them, but that they would never reject me as their son. They told me that they probably would never accept me as being gay, and that homosexual acts greatly repulsed them. I hate them for saying those things. The last thing I needed from them was guilt. I have to believe that they are not sincere in their claim of happiness in my own happiness, because they were making me very unhappy.

We have only discussed my sexuality on one other occasion during the next two years. It was in the car on the way up to school after my leave term abroad. They basically wanted a progress report on how my conversion to heterosexuality was going. I told them that there had been no progress, but that I had tried (another lie). They were terrified that their son was everything that the stereotypical "faggot" was. I did everything in my power to dispel these unfair and ignorant conceptions. I also told them that it wasn't something that anybody could change. That was the last time we have discussed my homosexuality.

If I had the opportunity again, I would never have told my parents about me. They have not been supportive at all of me and my inner conflict with my sexuality. In fact, it is an implicit understanding that unless I change, my sexuality will not be an acceptable topic of discussion. I am never to bring anybody home with me, as my brother would bring home a girlfriend. They have made it clear as well that unless I change, I will be unhappy and, therefore, they will be unhappy. What they don't understand is that when they ask me to be something which I cannot be, that is, heterosexual, they cause me to be unhappy. I am happy being gay, and I could not be happy pretending to be straight. I refuse to live a life of self-sacrifice for the sake of my pseudo-happiness and their peace of mind.

My relationship with my parents since I came out to them has been a comedy at which I am not permitted to laugh. They worry about ostracizing me, and for this I am grateful. They do sincerely love me. What I don't like is the extreme over-compensation which occurs when I am around. When we dine out, they never bring up a controversial topic of discussion in fear that their flaming liberal, that is, homosexual, son will embarrass them by dropping to his knees and performing fellatio on the cute waiter. Our conversations are very superficial, and tend to revolve around what I want to do after I graduate. I have cleverly come up with the interesting topic of law school in order to put their minds at ease. Basically, I am never told "no" anymore, which is nice, but not at all like the parents I had for the first eighteen years of my life.

One good thing has come from telling my parents about me, and from suffering the ensuing inquisition. It has forced me to examine myself and my sexual development in order to better understand why I am what I am today. I now understand why, when my father would take Keith and me to the racquetball club on Monday nights, I would be more interested in showering in the locker room and soaking in the whirlpool than I was in playing racquetball on the vacant courts. I also now understand why I could not help but have an erection when such showering and whirlpooling was accompanied, and please pardon the pun, by other club members. I understand now why I preferred to watch the men's gymnastics and swimming events in the Olympics instead of the women's basketball games.

The impetus for my first taste of sex was the men's gymnastics floor routine competition in the Olympics. (My first taste of sex was solo, so I should clarify myself by using the term "masturbation.") My parents, Keith, and I were watching the Olympics, which were on quite late as they were broadcasting live from Los Angeles. All three had fallen asleep, and I woke them to send them to bed. I, on the other hand, was not sleepy at all. I was glued to the set. In fact, I was mentally conjuring up some very interesting routines for two people. I decided to give one a try. I stripped down to my jockey shorts and watched the screen. Without making a lot of noise or breaking anything, I tried to imitate the more basic rolls and bends that were being performed three thousand miles away. I found myself with an erection. My tumbling was very pleasurable. Soon I discovered that my erection was leaking. As I had never masturbated before, and because of the intense pleasure caused by my movements, I mistook this pre-ejaculatory fluid for an orgasm. I hurriedly cleaned up, got dressed, and went to bed feeling less than completely satisfied.

It would be less than a week later, after several other similarly produced pseudo-orgasms, that I would experience my first true orgasm. It happened while I was asleep, but I still remember everything about my first and last wet dream. I was fantasizing about being at a swim team practice where none of the swimmers were wearing bathing suits. I remember the image of my being carried on the shoulders of one particular swimmer when I orgasmed.

The first sexual experience that I shared with somebody else occurred my freshman fall at college. It happened the night I described at the beginning when I met Tim for the first time in the library. I will never forget that night for as long as I live. I have to believe had Tim not had the courage to approach me that night that I might not be able to write this paper today. In fact, I might still be denying my homosexuality. I'd hate to know the miserable me if I weren't consciously gay.

As I have already said, Tim and I met at the library. We then went to talk in a classroom in the math building. We chatted for just a few minutes, deciding that it would be better to continue in the secured privacy of Tim's room, where we talked for about two and a half hours about each other and being gay at school. The room was quiet for no longer than five seconds when Tim rose from his desk chair and walked over to his bed where I was sitting. Then it happened. He sat down next to me on the bed and asked, "Would it be all right if I kiss you?"

What was I to say? I thought, "I've been waiting for you to do that for the last two hours." I said instead, "Yes."

It was my first kiss, and it was wonderful. The kiss was tender, yet passionate. It lasted only about two seconds, but it has set the standard for a lifetime. Our lips parted and our eyes met again. Tim asked, "Can I kiss you again?"

This time I didn't answer. Instead I brought my face close to his to be understood as an implicit yes. I was still more than a little bit nervous the second time, but I soon relaxed as that kiss developed into many more. It stirred in me what had been dormant forever before. One thing led to another and soon enough we were undressed and in bed together. That first time was very special for me. It helped dispel the ideas that even I held about homosexuality. Homosexuality was not dirty. Homosexuality was not perverse. Homosexuals do care for each other. Homosexuals can be happy. And I was happy.

That night began my longest and most important romantic relationship. I returned to my room in the wee hours of the morning and was categorically questioned by my roommates the next day. "I was studying very late, and I fell asleep in the study room." This lie was just the first of many. Lying was a fundamental part of my relationship with Tim. I did not lie to him, however. Instead, I felt forced to lie to everybody else with regard to my whereabouts and goings-on. I have never been a very good liar, but I made it through my freshman year without any unwanted exposure. Such exposure was what I feared most. I was very happy with Tim as long as things were very secretive. My extreme paranoia about exposure forced me to hide my true self from my other friends. I do not blame myself for this paranoia. Instead, I blame the overwhelming ignorance of society, particularly that of the college community, with regards to gays and gay issues. This ignorance continues to instill fear in the hearts of most gays, including myself.

The beginning of my relationship with Tim seems like a fantastic blur right now. I can't even differentiate any particular evening from among the many nights we spent together in bed. I remember them all to be loving and passionate, but I also remember that I wanted more. I wanted to have more than a secret relationship which consisted of my sneaking across campus late at night to get into bed with my lover. I wanted us to be able to do things together, openly, without fear of accusation or embarrassment. I, however, was too paranoid to take that first step towards a more "normal" relationship. I was much too worried about what everybody might ask or think about me and Tim. He assured me, though, that my paranoia would disappear and we would do more together than just talk and have sex in his room.

Our first public appearance together, but alone, was playing racquetball at the gym. For a while we were playing quite frequently, at least three times a week. Other than his fraternity's parties, racquetball, and the very routine but passionate sex, Tim and I occasionally shared a meal together. Again, I was always afraid that someone would figure it out if they saw us together a lot. He was not as paranoid, but he, too, was concerned about exposure. Though Tim was then a senior, he did not think, as I did, that sharing a meal or playing racquetball with a freshman (even a cute one) would cause suspicion by others that one was gay. But then we began to get bored with each other, and at least we were honest in acknowledging that it was happening. As I said, the sex was very routine, and Tim wanted more. He wanted to have intercourse, and I didn't.

It really hurt me when Tim went on a trip to a gay bar in Boston with a few friends and admitted to fooling around with one of them. He said all that they did was masturbate each other. "Oh, is that *all?*" I asked, conveying the message that that was more than enough for me to be more than a little bit upset. This was the beginning of the end, I knew, and Tim must have known as well. I was still desperate to make it last though. I didn't want my love to die or to give up someone who had done so much for me. I tried to bring some more excitement to his bed, but it was very obvious that Tim wanted to have intercourse more than he wanted me.

And so our passionate love died before the end of April of my freshman year. We still share a common love for each other though. He is in California, and I am at school, but we still keep in touch. He knows that he will always be very special to me, and I like to think that I am still significant to him.

After Tim and I broke up, and particularly after I returned home for the summer break, I was very lonely. I wasn't about to jump all the way into the back of the closet from which I had recently emerged. I wanted to take some steps forward in the right direction—in the only direction which would guarantee my mental health. I decided to speak to a counselor at school. I saw her several times before I went home for the summer. She listened to everything I had to say, and explained to me why, perhaps, I was feeling the way I was. She helped me a great deal, and for that I will always be grateful. I was feeling great when the spring term ended, and with it my visits for counseling.

During the summer, I told my parents that I was gay.

My visits for counseling promptly resumed upon my return to school. I needed someone to talk to and the counselors at school listened to me. My counselor not only listened to what I had to say, but she also reassured me that I was not alone even at school in my efforts to deal with being gay. She explained to me why I was feeling the way I was, and that these feelings were normal and healthy. She offered guidance, but she never told me what I should do. We talked about my parents and family, my relationship with Tim, and my being gay at school. I never left a counseling session feeling worse than I did when I arrived. In fact, I always felt very secure and confident that my being gay was not something wrong with me, but rather, it was a problem of acceptance on the part of others.

I found the cure for my loneliness in my new family: my friends. When I was "dating" Tim, I neglected my other friends quite a bit and did not foster much development of my relationships with them. Upon my return to campus after the "summer of my discontent," I promptly came out to Dan, who would later come to be my best friend. Dan and I got along great. We played racquetball together and had some classes together. We seemed to hit it off rather well when we first met. Dan is a very open-minded, liberal Californian. I thought that I could trust him with my secret, and I needed to share it with somebody.

I invited Dan to my room and asked him to sit down. He was more than a little bit confused. After about thirty minutes of professing my friendship and other beatings around the bush, I told him I was gay. He barely reacted at all. In fact, he made light of the tense situation by telling me that I was the third person to come out to him in the past two weeks. Apparently, he has a bisexual friend at home, and he used to live with a roommate who was gay. He also told me that there was a point in his life when he was questioning his own sexuality. Dan is not gay, however. I was not used to such a sublime reaction, but I most definitely preferred it to the more recent hysterics of home. Dan was very supportive of me and my struggle, even though he was going through a tough time of his own, as his parents were divorcing. I tried to be equally as supportive.

We grew together that term. We were almost inseparable. When we were with our other friends, we used to love to make comments which only he and I could truly understand. They were usually innocuous as far as the others were concerned, but sometimes Dan would try to put me on edge by seeing how far he could go before someone would ask, "What do you mean by that?" There was never any malicious intent—just good, sadistic fun between friends. I no longer have to hide the truth from my closest friends.

The following term, Dan and I went to Spain together on a study-abroad program. Again, we spent nearly all of our time together there. When we traveled we would usually have to share a bed because we chose to pay less for one bed than to pay more for a comfortable two. Having to share a bed with me never bothered Dan. This was a sign of great trust in me. Granted, I don't think he was worried about my making a pass at him, but his efforts to maintain a relationship where my sexuality was not the central issue was very important to me. I have nothing but fond memories of Dan and myself in Spain. We used to spend a lot of time just talking over a beer and a game of dominos in the town square. I have never been as close to anybody in my entire life as I have been with Dan. I shared my deepest secrets and innermost feelings with him. Likewise, he opened up to me quite a bit.

Dan and I decided to live together during the summer term between our sophomore and junior years at school. For the first seven weeks of the term our relationship continued to develop in the same positive way. After that things started to deteriorate. The reason for this is clear to me: Dan got a girlfriend. Stephanie lived down the hall from us. Dan and I met her at a party so wild he didn't even remember meeting her that night. Stephanie remembered Dan, though. She came by the next day and threw herself all over him. Before I knew what was happening, they were in bed together (a few days later), and I was now well in the backseat of Dan's life.

My analysis of myself with respect to this situation is twofold. First, I feel that I was very jealous of Stephanie. Secondly, I still feel that Stephanie is fundamentally not a good person. Was I jealous because I was being neglected, or was I jealous at a more fundamental sexual level? I have to admit that it would have pleased me greatly had Dan been gay as well. I think he has a lot of traits that I look for in someone with whom I would like to be involved romantically. However, I am being completely honest when I say that I really am not physically attracted to Dan. Therefore, I have concluded that my jealousy of Stephanie is due to Dan's behavior toward me, and not my sexuality.

Since they have been dating (sleeping together), I have seen Dan replace me with Stephanie. He no longer confides in me like he used to. Instead, he goes to Stephanie. He no longer has as much time for me as I am willing to give to him. These things are natural in relationships, but they hurt all the same. Since Dan gained a girlfriend, I feel I have suffered a tremendous loss. Perhaps my investment in Dan was too great, but I believe that it was reciprocal to Dan's own investment in my friendship. He, as far as I'm concerned, has chosen to invest elsewhere, leaving me feeling more than a little slighted.

I left school the next fall on pretty good terms with Dan. However, a new distance was created between us, this time geographical, when I went to work in the city for the winter months. Dan made little effort to keep in contact with me when I was in the city. I did call him occasionally, but I stopped when it started to feel like I was troubling him when I did call. My life in the city was dramatically different than it was at school, and I wanted to share it with Dan, but, apparently, he wasn't interested in hearing about it. Instead, I found others with whom to share my excitement. At the beginning of the fall term when I was at school, I came out to Jack and Paul. Jack is also from California, and even more open-minded than is Dan. He was very happy that I told him about my homosexuality and has shown a genuine interest in me and my coming to terms with it.

I was a little more concerned about telling Paul. I was worried that he might be intimidated by my homosexuality because I had suspected him not of being gay, but of being confused about his sexuality. I am now positive that he is not at all confused about his sexuality. He is perhaps one of the more "hormonal" straight men I know. I told Paul at the end of fall term after we had decided to share an apartment as we were going to be working at the same law firm in the city. I'll never forget what he said after I told him that I was gay. With a smile on his face and a slight laugh in his voice he said, "Hey, I've always thought that it's kind of hip to know someone who's gay." I almost cried. Paul is the funniest man I know. Living with him in the city, even in the close quarters of our studio apartment, was an experience which I would gladly share with him again. He will always be very special to me because he shared with me the very first period of my life in which I felt at liberty to do that which *I* wanted. With friends like these, who needs the support of an unaccepting biological family?

All of this coming out was in the context of my winter work-term in the city. I really miss the city; not only was it the arena for my coming out to three of my closest friends, but it is also where I first really lived. I secured a position at the law firm at which my sister works downtown where I worked hard and interacted well with everybody I met. My sexuality was not an issue, and I enjoyed what I was doing. If I had any concerns about my sexuality and my work at the firm, they revolved around the fear of my sister finding out about my postwork activities. I imagined a situation in which I would run into an openly gay attorney from the firm at a gay nightspot. He would talk about it at work, and through some indirect way my sister would become enlightened and freak out about it. She would call my parents, and they too would freak out. She would call my other two sisters and they, too, would freak out, until everybody in my family, nuclear and extended, all the way to Ireland and Lithuania, would be freaking out. As I am only concerned about keeping my parents ignorantly blissful, I blame them for my paranoia (and, perhaps, overactive imagination).

Of course, this did not happen, but I did meet one attorney at the firm while out for a drink in a gay video bar with two straight friends. Meeting him was special because I now had an ally in the very traditional and conservative law firm at which I worked. We would occasionally get together and have lunch. It was great to see that he was a gay man who was succeeding in the working world, the legal profession which I wanted to enter. However, it was equally as distressing to listen to him tell me how very closeted he was and how very discriminatory the legal profession is against gays, even though it has a very high percentage of homosexuals in its ranks. Apparently, image is of the essence in the legal profession, and openly gay attorneys do not help create an image of stability and competence which ultraconservative law firms demand.

My most important experiences in the city occurred outside of the workplace. Upon my arrival, I wanted to introduce myself to the gay community. I called the gay students' groups at several colleges, as well as the city's gay youth group. I went to one gay youth group meeting and found its membership a bit young for me, but I hit it off rather well with some members of another college group. By my second weekend in the city, my new friends in the student gay group took me out to the popular local nightspots. We first went to a downtown video bar. As we went in, I wasn't particularly impressed by the dark and smoky conditions of the noisy bar. My disappointment disappeared as we passed by the coat check and into the other half of the bar. Everybody in this section appeared to be college-age and very attractive. My whole disposition changed. I was like a kid in a candy store. It had been many months since I had been in a gay establishment, and that was in Spain, which is a completely different world altogether. The people with whom I came were talking to me, but I found it difficult to pay attention to anything except the dark-haired and dark-skinned gentleman standing very close to our circle of conversation. It would be a week later and in a different environment that I would meet Rob.

Rob and I were finally introduced at a gay students' meeting. I was very impressed with what he had to say at that meeting, particularly about the topic of that night's discussion: gay promiscuity. After the meeting he told me that he liked what I had to say also. We talked briefly about a dance that was to be held on Friday, and then we said good-bye. He called the next night about the dance and we decided to go together.

That was the introduction to a very important relationship for me: important because of what I learned about myself upon its dissolution. I really didn't love Rob. I even wonder if I really would find him interesting had we not gone to bed together so soon after meeting. I believe, upon reflection, that I was more interested in a relationship than I was in Rob. I lived a charade with him for over a month, therefore breaking my own rules about sexual activity. I have what some people might call an ultraliberal outlook on the topic of sex. I believe that there is nothing wrong with sleeping with anybody you want to sleep with so long as you meet a particular set of criteria. First, and most importantly, both must be consenting adults. Secondly, and following from my first criterion, one must never force another or be pressured by another to do anything in bed that one does not want to do. Maintaining this level of respect for one's partner is important if my third criterion is to be met. Nobody must be hurt, physically or mentally, by the experience. Lastly, and definitely not least of all, everything done must be done safely. It is obviously too dangerous in today's world plagued by AIDS and other diseases not to exercise the utmost caution as far as sexual contact is concerned. From experience, I would also say that sex where there is an emotional bond is incomparable to that without it, but I do not feel, as some do, that it is immoral to sleep with somebody just for fun, as long as nobody is getting hurt.

I was infatuated with Rob; he made me feel very special. It wasn't really until he came up to school with me for a weekend that I realized what the true story was. At school, I was in my element. He was out of his. I wanted so badly for him to fit in with my closest group of friends. He didn't. He didn't even try. I tried to include him in everything, but he just wouldn't get involved. I realized then that he did not meet the standards that I have for someone with whom I would like to spend, if not all, a good part of my life. When I first met him, I was impressed by what he had to say. That was the last time he ever impressed me. He just isn't an intellectual equal of mine. He isn't even mildly interesting. Again, I found myself with cold feet, and over a very long two-week period, I broke up with Rob. He didn't understand, and for this reason I feel that I have violated the rules surrounding healthy sex; I hurt him. However, I feel that I did the right thing by breaking up with him in order to avoid hurting him more. He told me that he would have liked for me to just have gone back to school and not to have told him how I felt. But I believed that such perpetuated dishonesty would be an even greater infraction of my own rules of sexual conduct.

Upon breaking up with Rob, I started to do some serious thinking about myself and relationships. I had really never had a normal, successful relationship. I have come to the conclusion that there is nothing wrong with this, because it is not written in stone that relationships must work out. In fact, considering my relative inexperience in the relationship game, I would conclude that I have made some very responsible decisions which have helped keep greater harms from occurring. I think, though, that my standards are too high. I am never going to find someone with whom I am completely compatible. I have to learn to accept people's faults as much as I enjoy their good points, just as they must do the same for me. I'm not perfect, and I shouldn't expect anybody else to be.

My friends provide the criteria for a man to whom I would make an emotional commitment. First, but not foremost, he must be attractive. He must also be sincere and willing to share his deepest secrets with me. He must be funny. He must be intelligent and captivating. I see these traits in all of my close friends. Most importantly, he must be able to tolerate me and my quirks. Perhaps I should not be looking for a man with whom I can make an emotional commitment, but for a gay man with whom I can begin a sincere friendship. Only then, when I am his true friend, will I be able to be happy in a more intimate relationship with him. This may or may not be the answer to my romantic blues, but it makes a lot of sense to me. I still uphold my rules of sexual conduct, but I now would add another to the list. One should not become intimate with anybody one feels the potential for becoming very emotionally involved with, without first becoming their true friend.

I do have a couple of gay friends. One has graduated and the other is graduating. They, however, are not as close to me as any of my straight friends are. Why is this? The answer is twofold. First, I do not select my friends based on their sexuality. Second, befriending gays at school can be a difficult thing to do due to the lack of a visible gay community. The people who are openly gay do not seem to be the people whom I would normally befriend. Also, my fear of exposure keeps me from meeting potential gay friends. I would like to have some close gay friends, but I feel that it is more important to have true friends than it is to have gay acquaintances. I am also not willing to put my privacy at risk when I do not have the independence or support that I feel is needed to face opposition.

I have returned to school wiser but definitely more frustrated. There is a gay community, only a minute percentage of which is "out." There is a gay students' group, which holds weekly meetings. I went to one meeting during my sophomore fall, when I was still extremely paranoid about being exposed. I was desperate to find some people like me. I did not find them there. They were talking about marching on the Capitol in Washington. I was thinking about how exposed I was in the strange environment of the student lounge. To make matters worse, a random guy stumbled into the meeting unaware of what kind of meeting he was interrupting. He was picking up something he had left in the lounge earlier. I imagined that the first thing that the intruder did was go tell all of his friends (and mine) that he had seen *me* at a gay students' meeting. Now, more than a year and a half later, my views about this unpleasant experience have changed. I feel that it was one of the first steps I took toward trying to live my life as a gay man. True, it didn't work out, and I have not returned, but I feel that it was a step in the right direction. Indeed, it was a step in the only direction for me. I can't imagine what my life would be like now if I still hadn't confronted my homosexuality and begun to develop positively with it. This positive growth began long ago when I was just a freshman.

Where am I now? I'm very comfortable with being gay, but very uncomfortable with having to be gay at school. Why do I feel this way anywhere? I blame my parents. They will not let me be gay. They want me to be happy, but they don't want me to work for my happiness. I know that if I had the spiritual support (or even the complete assurance of financial support) of my parents, I would be, perhaps, one of the biggest gay activists on campus. Until my parents let me be what I am, I will never begin to realize what I really can do. If I had parental support in gay causes, I might feel very comfortable in the face of campus opposition. I might not fear exposure, knowing that I would always have their love and understanding. Instead, I am a member of my school's huge underground gay community. Here, my activism is limited to my close group of friends who do not need to hear my opinions about gays and gay issues. They are not the ones who need to be reached. The result is a community that refuses to come to terms with itself and its varied sexuality.

I am completing my junior year at school feeling like I am unable to make a difference in my life here or in the lives of other gays. My parents cannot possibly be so powerful! However, their financial grip remains on me. I don't want to hurt them either, but their happiness comes second to mine, as far as I am concerned. The opportunity to put my thoughts down on paper is my greatest step toward public advocacy. I feel that my experiences are similar to those of other gays, and by sharing them with them, and others who are straight, I feel that I am making an impact on others. However, I have not even been able to be honest with my parents about this autobiography project. As far as they are concerned, I am just helping a professor at school with some research.

What have I learned about myself? I have learned that I am a healthy gay man. I am happy with myself, although I could be happier in different circumstances. I feel that I am well on my way to living a productive life. I have learned that there are some things about myself which I must examine more closely if I am to live up to my own expectations. Primarily, I am concerned whether or not my dependence on my family is indeed more than financial. Do I really need their psychological support as well as their financial support? Is my love for them stronger than my resentment of their prejudices? Am I going to be the gay activist that I imagine myself being when I am finally free of my parents' grip? I will only know these answers upon graduating from college and dissolving my dependence on them. I suspect that the answers are complex. I suspect, too, that any other aspects of my dependence upon them will not be strong enough to keep me from living my life as I so choose.

Ben: Eight Years Later

It is almost eight years since I put down on paper my thoughts about being gay in college and the interpersonal difficulties and triumphs connected with it. Recently, I returned to "A Step in the Only Direction" and was struck by how many of the questions that I had asked myself then have been answered during the past several years. I am not surprised that my beliefs and values have not significantly changed, but I am amazed at how the passing of time has allowed me to view many things quite differently.

One statement that I made repeatedly throughout "A Step in the Only Direction" was that I was happy. I would challenge that statement today. Certainly I was *happier,* but to say that I was happy would be a tremendous overstatement. That I still could not be myself with many people who were important to me, including my parents and my twin brother, definitely made me unhappy.

I had told my parents about my being gay, but I was quite disappointed in their lack of interest in what this meant for me, such as my relationships and my development as a gay man. During the three years of my college career that they knew I was gay, they never raised the subject except to inquire if I had changed. Likewise, I never raised the subject because I feared that by doing so I would stir things up and cause conflict. I had had enough of that already.

Strangely, it was not until my *siblings* learned that I am gay that my relationship with my *parents* began to change for the better. When I came out to my parents and they insisted that I not tell my siblings, I agreed because I was doing everything I could to avoid more conflict with them. Shortly after I graduated from college, my parents telephoned to tell me that they had told all five of my siblings that I was gay. They had not told me that they were *going* to tell them; they told me that they *had* told them. When my parents witnessed the support and positive reactions I received from my brothers and sisters, they started to deal with my being gay in a more positive way.

It was not long before my parents seemed quite comfortable with my being gay and with my relationship with another man, Luke, whom I met while in college. It is true that we seldom discussed strictly gay topics, but they manifested interest in different ways. They went to great lengths to make Luke feel welcome and comfortable at family gatherings. This is extraordinary behavior in the context of how my parents generally behave. My parents have not been happy with the spouses of my siblings, and sometimes their dissatisfaction is quite obvious. For them to welcome Luke and interact with him in a genuinely positive manner is shockingly unusual for them.

To this day, more than six years after meeting Luke, my parents continue to treat him with kindness and respect. I will never forget the first time my mother kissed him good-bye as we were leaving a family gathering or the first time she called our home just to speak with him. When Luke and I bought a house together, we needed a rather large loan. When I asked my parents to help, they did not let me finish explaining my request before my father interrupted with, "How much do you need, and where do we send the check?" They accepted only one-fourth of the loan in repayment before gifting the rest of it to us at Christmas one year.

My parents have come a long way since I wrote "A Step in the Only Direction." Then, I was impatient with their inability to deal with me and my sexual orientation in an instantly supportive and informed way. I was oblivious to the fact that their journey to acceptance of my being gay would be difficult and lengthy and that they needed time and education to begin to understand some of the things they were confronting for the first time in their lives. *I* needed many years to begin dealing productively with my being gay. For me not to see that they, too, needed time was immature and self-centered. The journeys, theirs and mine, continue, but we make them with love and support for one another. I am through blaming my parents for any unhappiness I may experience.

When they found out I was gay, each one of my siblings reached out to me almost immediately. They all asked the same question: Why didn't you tell me? There were varying degrees of emotion behind this question, the most intense coming from my twin brother Keith, who was clearly quite angry about not being told. I already had a rocky relationship with Keith, and the uncovering of this deception did not help. The depth of Keith's anger about not being told was revealed about a year ago when he and I were out to dinner while he was in town for a visit. Unconnected with any topic of discussion that evening, he interrupted the flow of conversation and asked me why I had respected my parents' wishes and not told him about my being gay. He was still angry six years after being told by my parents. It was an extraordinarily difficult question to answer.

Although he was angry about that element of our relationship, it is also true that my relationship with Keith dramatically changed once I was outed to him. We used to argue about everything, most notably politics. We seldom asked each other anything personal. We were twins, but we seemed utterly uninterested in each other. I am certain that my lack of interest was founded in the fear of needing to reveal more about myself to Keith. Since he became aware of my sexual orientation, I have felt less constrained about sharing my life with him and others.

Keith and I have become much closer over the past several years, and I have learned that my condemnation of him in "A Step in the Only Direction" was unfair. He is not a fundamentally bad person. On the contrary, I see in him kindness and selflessness, which I see in myself and other family members, including my parents. Keith has gone to great lengths to make me feel comfortable at family gatherings and to inquire about my life as a gay man in a different city. He routinely asks about Luke and has made him feel like a member of the family. These changes in behavior toward me developed over many months and are still developing. I, too, have changed the way I interact with Keith, and I am certain that we both view these changes as positive ones.

In my view, changes in me have facilitated changes in how I view Keith. It is clear to me now that when he did not know about my being gay, I resented him greatly. He could speak freely with our family and others about those things that were exciting to him, including his relationships and love interests. I, on the other hand, had to censor myself to adhere to my parents' wishes. Such self-censorship in the environment where Keith could speak freely and with great excitement and pride fostered in me a remarkable resentment of him and his heterosexual privilege. Since he has known about my being gay and I have been able to speak freely, that resentment has dissipated.

My relationships with my other siblings have generally been strengthened or, at worst, remained unchanged since they learned of my being gay. I was never particularly close to my older siblings, and that did not change dramatically when they learned the truth about my sexual orientation. One noteworthy exception is my sister Betsy. She has gone to great lengths to make Luke feel like one of the family. She has her children refer to him as Uncle Luke. Betsy is a physical education teacher for a public high school. She tells me that she speaks freely to her students about having a gay brother and that she confronts students who make antigay remarks. With the exception of Betsy, I am concerned about how my older siblings will handle my sexual identity and, more generally, sexual orientation issues with their children, my nieces and nephews.

My views about romantic and sexual relationships have also changed since I wrote "A Step in the Only Direction." I still believe, however, in the "rules of sexual relationships" that I enumerated in the autobiography, with one exception. I ended my list with "one should not become [sexually] intimate with anybody one feels the potential for becoming very emotionally involved with, without first becoming their true friend." To that one I now say "poppycock."

My experience with Luke confirms that this rule is simply silly. I slept with Luke the evening we met, and I feel deeply emotionally connected with him. Breaking my silly rule probably facilitated our emotional connection, as the physical intimacy of sex likely eased the way for the more challenging, in my experience, development of emotional intimacy. I wonder how much my "no sex before friendship" rule was actually a manifestation of internalized homophobia or a desire on my part to assign greater value to certain kinds of sexual relationships over others.

This is only one example of internalized homophobia I found in my essay. In another passage, I wrote that I prefer "intimacy with men over sex with women." Describing sexual activity with men as "intimacy" certainly sterilized this public statement, allowing me to avoid confronting others with my being gay and the behaviors that are part of my identity. In one short statement, I took the "sex" out of homosexuality, and I most likely did it to distance myself from what I feared would be judgment from others. What my internalized homophobia brought me instead was judgment from within.

Later in the essay I wrote that "I had really never had a normal, successful relationship." What the hell does that mean? What is a normal relationship? Part of what makes being gay exciting is that being *myself* is enough to break the conventional rules about relationships. To then characterize one kind of relationship as "normal" is to judge those who choose a different type of relationship.

Perhaps the most pronounced example of internalized homophobia is in my statement, "the people who are openly gay do not seem to be the people whom I would normally befriend." Openly gay classmates had the courage and strength to be themselves, for their own good and, indirectly, for mine, but I could not see that. Instead, I saw people who were "making waves," seeking out conflict for their cause, and flaunting their sexuality. I view those peers quite differently now and value them for their remarkable contributions and risks in an often hostile environment.

I, like all lesbian, gay, and bisexual people, must continue to battle internalized homophobia. We cannot eradicate decades of self-hate and doubts about our worth without perpetually confronting those doubts as we develop into self-loving individuals. I make it a point to be out whenever I can, even if sexual orientation does not seem to be pertinent in the setting or situation. I seek not to make others uncomfortable, but rather to make them aware of our differences and to help them to avoid making assumptions about people and their sexual orientations. If my being out does make others uncomfortable sometimes, then I hope they find some value in that discomfort. Certainly that discomfort cannot be comparable to the discomfort experienced by lesbians, gays, and bisexuals who feel that they must perpetually hide who they are from others.

I closed "A Step in the Only Direction" by wondering if my parents' financial grip on me was the only thing keeping me from becoming an activist. I suspected that their influence had a lot to do with my inability to be unapologetically myself—an openly gay man. I also surmised that the answers to these questions were complex. I was right!

My introduction to gay activism was somewhat forced upon me. When I graduated from college, I moved to Providence to be with Luke, who had been accepted to graduate school there. Luke and I were walking down a main thoroughfare in Providence during the daytime when three men attacked us. One of them leapt at me from behind, kicking me in the back; all three surrounded us, threatening to kick our "faggot asses." I have never experienced such fear in my entire life. We ran from them and called the police from a nearby restaurant. When the police responded, I was too afraid to tell them the truth, that we had been gay bashed, assaulted because of our perceived sexual orientation. The next day I contacted the president of the Rhode Island Alliance for Lesbian and Gay Civil Rights.

I became quite an active member of the Alliance. I soon became an outspoken participant at meetings and began working closely with the organization's head lobbyist and political strategist. Speaking directly with lawmakers about the virtues of statutory protections for lesbian, gay, and bisexual (LGB) Rhode Islanders was not an easy thing to do. Although lobbying and organizing others at the grassroots level was challenging, I had very strong convictions to fall back on when the challenges to our cause were particularly intense. No one was going to convince me that we were not pursuing the right thing, because I knew that we were.

I continued to work on political issues for the Alliance; eventually I was elected to its board of directors and then to the position of Vice President for Public Policy. I was privileged to be serving in this role in May 1995 when the Rhode Island legislature passed the bill. The governor signed it into law and Rhode Island became the ninth state to offer protection against discrimination in employment, housing, public accommodations, and credit.

Since the passage of the sexual orientation civil rights bill, I have stepped back from Rhode Island gay politics. Since the summer of 1991, I have been an administrator at a large university. There I have been able to be an activist of sorts as well. I took a leadership role in the university's social group for LGB faculty and staff. In 1994 I was appointed to a subcommittee of a standing committee that examines benefits issues. The subcommittee was charged with exploring and making recommendations about same-sex domestic partnership health benefits. In May 1995 the policy was approved, and I began working on implementation issues with the university's benefits office.

Not long after my involvement with the subcommittee, I was appointed by the provost to serve on the University Committee for Lesbian, Gay, and Bisexual Concerns. The committee is charged with examining and making recommendations about quality of life issues on campus for LGB students, faculty, and staff. The issues the committee explores range from academic, such as curricular issues, to administrative, such as benefits issues. I am currently one of the co-chairs of this committee.

Perhaps the most rewarding activist work I do is actually part of my job. For the past year and a half I have been working very closely but informally with a woman in my office who is responsible for supporting lesbian, gay, bisexual, and transgendered (LGBT) students on campus. She has taught me so much in such a short time about the lives of LGBT undergraduates and their needs on campus. I feel so privileged to have her as a mentor. Recently, working with and supporting LGBT students on campus has become a formal part of my job. This official role change allows me to give the important business of being a resource for lesbian, gay, bisexual, and transgendered students the attention it deserves.

My professional work with LGBT students may be the most rewarding activism I engage in, but it is not the most valuable. By far the most important gay activism I engage in is the daily activism of being myself without apology to anyone. Being out is not always easy. Sometimes it is quite difficult. I believe that if we are to make progress as a society on these sometimes complicated (domestic partnership benefits) but usually quite simple (equal treatment regardless of sexual orientation) issues, society needs to see and know LGBT people. I feel that it is the responsibility of those of us who can be out to be out. Some people cannot be out due to genuine fear of losing their ability to support themselves or out of fear of physical violence against them. I am not one of those people, so I must continue to challenge the assumptions that pervade society and the interactions between gay and straight people as they navigate through a heterosexually biased culture.

So where am I now? As I write this, I am on the eve of celebrating my seventh year with Luke. My parents support me and my relationship, and I feel closer to some of my siblings than I ever have. I am working in a field in which I feel I am making a significant impact on the lives of young LGBT students. My employer is supportive of LGB faculty and staff, and I live in a state where discrimination based on sexual orientation is prohibited. Certainly, many of these positive conditions in my life exist, at least in part, because of influences out of my control, and certainly, there is still much work to be done and progress to be made. It is also true, however, that I have made a difference in all of these areas by working hard for myself and others, and that is extremely rewarding. These successes—both those that are personal and private and those that affect institutional and public policy—are further steps in the only direction as my journey of self continues.

PART TWO

Relationships

Theoretical Overview

This section of the book focuses on relationships, specifically family and peer relationships. Until the 1970s, psychoanalytic and neopsychoanalytic theories yielded the most prominent and influential explanations of the processes by which adolescents' relationships with their parents and peers change from childhood to adulthood. Anna Freud and Peter Blos described the process of adolescents' individuation from their parents (Blos, 1962; A. Freud, 1946, 1958), and Harry Stack Sullivan wrote about the development of intimacy through best-friend relationships (1953). Research has often contradicted these theories, however, and those data led scholars of adolescent relationships to evolve new ways of thinking about adolescent relationships. Some new perspectives, such as attachment theory, draw on earlier psychoanalytic theory; others, such as cognitive-developmental theory, center on aspects of adolescent relationships that were not the focus of the psychoanalytic perspective. This introduction explores some of the most important issues in the study of adolescent relationships that are raised by these theories and related research studies, and mentions some ways in which the cases in this portion of the book may be used to foster discussions of these issues.

Family Relationships

The psychoanalytic understanding of adolescent-family relationships has traditionally viewed adolescence as a time of profound inner turmoil and outward conflict— a time of "storm and stress." Explosive conflict with family, friends, and authorities was thought of as commonplace. This view was based, to a great extent, on the theoretical work of the psychiatric community in the 1950s and early 1960s (Blos, 1962; Erikson, 1959, 1966, 1968; A. Freud, 1946, 1958). Largely on the basis of their experience with adolescent psychiatric patients, these clinicians and theorists described adolescence as a time of extreme psychic and interpersonal stress. Emotional crises and upheaval were viewed as appropriate responses by the adolescent to major psychological and societal tasks required during this phase of life: dramatically reducing psychological dependency on parents, separating from the family, and forming an adult identity. Adolescent turmoil was not only inevitable, but necessary for subsequent normal personality development.

This storm-and-stress perspective of adolescent family relationships is still perpetuated by the media and is often assumed by the public. Scholars of adolescent psychology, however, are in the midst of developing new ways of describing, explaining, and understanding adolescent-family relationships. These new approaches differ from the long-reigning classic psychoanalytic perspective in several ways.

One way these new perspectives differ is in the contention that adolescents and their families are more likely to negotiate changes in power, responsibilities, and modes of intimacy through a continuous series of minor, although significant, daily "hassles," rather than through tumultuous, warlike conflicts. Data from empirical studies with nonclinical populations of adolescents and their families from the past thirty years have led to a radical revision in the psychological community's understanding of how adolescents separate from and remain connected to their families. The majority of research clearly refutes the notion that most adolescents undergo severe emotional stress and family conflict during this period of life. Although experts concur that adolescence is a period of development that requires multiple changes, the current consensus is that adolescence is not ordinarily a time of great turmoil. A variety of studies using such diverse methods as epidemiological surveys (Rutter, Graham, Chadwick, & Yule, 1976), phone interviews (Montemayor, 1983), and time sampling with electronic beepers (Csikszentmihalyi & Larson, 1984) have shown that for most families with adolescent members, serious conflict and disorganization are not characteristic states (Hill, 1987). Evidence drawn from various kinds of self-reports offered by nonpatient adolescents and their parents provides no support for an inevitable dramatic increase in family conflict from childhood to adolescence. In general, the family is not at risk for great turmoil or disorganization during the adolescent years; the search for greater independence from the family is not usually played out in major battle between adolescents and their parents. Instead, current studies look for smaller, although still highly significant and lasting transformations in sharing of power and responsibility and in the nature of family intimacy through daily renegotiations.

This new view does not claim that adolescence is not a time of conflict. It would be a mistake to conclude that conflicts between adolescents and their parents or siblings are insignificant or rare and that their presence indicates family or individual psychopathology. Any valued human relationship undergoes stress at times, particularly when the relationship must adapt to change within an individual. Adolescents usually value their relationships with their parents, and these relationships change and adapt as the adolescent becomes an adult member of the family. Although there may not be striking quantitative rises in the level of family conflict, the *number* of conflicts does rise to some degree in early adolescence and decrease when adolescents leave home. Conflicts are usually of mild to moderate intensity and are rarely about such dramatic issues as drugs or delinquency (Montemayor & Hanson, 1985; Santrock, 1990). In fact, the vast majority of conflicts in adolescence arise over mundane issues such as family chores, curfews, eating practices, dating, and personal appearance. Cases 8, 9, 10, 11, and 13 may be used to clarify your ideas concerning what characterizes an optimal or ideal family for promoting adolescent development. In what ways do these family relationships foster or hinder adolescent independence, achievement, or intimacy goals? What problems might be associated with a pattern of family interaction that exhibits no conflict? How can "normal" developmental tasks of adolescence, like individuation, occur in the context of extremely troubled family relationships, as seen in Cases 9 and 11?

A second important difference in this new approach of the adolescent-family relationship is that it seeks to encompass the description of a *wide variety of patterns* of family relationships, rather than focusing on explaining one primary picture of how "normal" adolescents interact with their families. Instead, a wide range of adolescent family behaviors is considered relevant to understanding adolescent adaptive responses to growth in relationships. This new perspective seeks to include more diversity in the adolescents and families studied. For example, not enough is known about varieties of adaptive family functioning in African American, Latino, Native American, Asian American, and other groups of adolescents in U.S. culture. It may be helpful to contrast the family pictures described by adolescents of European American descent in this section with pictures of family life described by adolescents from different ethnic backgrounds (see the thematic index on pages vii–viii and Case 13) and by other students in your class. Scholars of adolescent psychology also have an extremely limited understanding at present about adolescents' relationships with their single parents, stepparents, and noncustodial parents.

Identifying different pathways to adolescents' new levels of separation and connection with parents is possible by juxtaposing cases in this section. Melanie's (Case 8) family experiences can be contrasted with Chhaya's (Case 9) and Gretchen's (Case 11) family experiences of major conflict and turmoil, exemplars of the classic but less common storm-and-stress model of adolescent individuation from the family. You might ask which adolescent issues trigger aspects of the tumult in these families and which are products of a long-standing family system. These cases provide powerful descriptions of families under severe stress and two adolescents' extreme strategies for coping with that stress. Clearly, some of these strategies strengthen resilience (e.g., Chhaya's perfectionism reinforces her ability to succeed at many demanding tasks, including school), while other strategies (e.g., Chhaya's anorexia and Gretchen's drug use) eventually cause more pain than relief. Chhaya's and Gretchen's cases are reminders of the variety of patterns that lead eventually to successful young adult adaptation and functioning. Case 13, in the Instructor's Guide, and cases in other sections of the book may also serve as examples of a typical family situation leading to severe stress in adolescence (see, for example, Case 2, "Someday My Elders Will Be Proud").

A third distinguishing aspect of psychologists' contemporary approaches to describing adolescent–family relationships emphasizes adolescents' needs for maintaining intimacy and connection with parents and sibling as well as adolescents' wishes for increased autonomy and independence. Earlier psychoanalytic theories focused primarily on the process of separation from the family. Little is currently known about how adolescents establish new ways of being meaningfully attached and intimate with family members while also negotiating greater independence from the family (Gilligan, 1987).

Results from studies that have observed adolescents' interactions with their parents have indicated the importance of family interaction styles that permit conflict between members in a context of support (Baumrind, 1987, 1989; Powers, 1988; Powers, Hausser, Schwartz, Noam, & Jacobson, 1983), acceptance, active understanding from parents (Allen, Hauser, Bell, & O'Connor, 1994; Hauser, et al., 1984, 1987), and parental expressions of individuality and connectedness (Grotevant & Cooper, 1986).

All of the cases in this section, as well as Case 13 in the "peers" section, are strong illustrations of adolescents' heartfelt need to be affectively connected to their families. Chhaya's and Gretchen's cases present particularly significant difficulties in negotiating a sufficient level of closeness and intimacy with parents. Brian's case (Case 10), Melanie's case (Case 8), and Devneesh's case (Case 13) present poignant examples of the struggle to maintain closeness and connections with parents and, at the same time, forge new identities that are not wholly based on being the "perfect child." Brian feels that his new identity is necessary for developing healthy peer relationships and career goals. He is unable, however, to envision a way to coordinate his developing separate self with the self he presents to his parents.

Peer Relationships

Peer relationships may include close friendships, cliques, peer groups and crowds, and romantic relationships. Many cases throughout the book discuss peer relationships, and the reader is encouraged to look in the thematic index following the table of contents for cases that can be found in other sections but include material on peer relationships. For example, "Someday My Elders Will Be Proud" (Case 2) describes the power of peer pressure when an adolescent's ethnic culture is different from those of the dominant culture. The sections on sexual identity are particularly useful for examining romantic relationships.

Close friendships in adolescence may have many facets and functions, such as providing companionship, stimulation, social comparison, and intimacy or affection (Gottman & Parker, 1987; Parker & Gottman, 1989). Rebecca's case (Case 14) presents these varied aspects of adolescent close friendships and their developmental transitions throughout early to late adolescence. Rebecca's description of sexual play with her close grade-school friend in private and at slumber parties, and the confusion that surrounds it, illustrates friendship as an introduction to the sexual aspects of growing up. Rebecca and her friend, Kelly, show us one example of an early adolescent friendship, whereas Rebecca's friendship with Alexandra occurs in college and is an example of the meaning of friendships to these adolescents at different stages of development. Melanie's case (Case 8) provides a window through which to view the importance of close friendships in high school, while Devneesh's case (Case 13) illustrates the crucial nature of close friendships in the transition to college.

Peer cliques and groups may also have a variety of functions in adolescent growth and development. Peers provide a means of social comparison as well as a source of information outside the family, as seen in the cases of Rebecca (Case 14) and Devneesh (Case 13). The role of popularity—fitting in with desired cliques, being rejected or neglected by peers—is acutely felt by all adolescents included within this section on relationships. These cases provide particularly good examples of conformity to peers peaking around eighth and ninth grades and then lessening by twelfth grade (Berndt & Ladd, 1989).

Current theory and research emphasize the connections between the quality of family relationships and the quality of close peer relationships (Gold & Yanof, 1985; Parker & Gottman, 1989). The cases of Melanie, Chhaya, Sarah, Brian, and Rebecca provide excellent material for a discussion of the impact of family relationships on the development of peer relationships. Chhaya's ways of relating to her high school friends mirror the way she relates to her family; she is afraid to show anything other than her "perfect" self. Brian struggles to keep separate the parts of himself that are related to his friends and the parts of himself that are connected to his parents. This division of self is painful and long lasting. Brian's strategies for maintaining these separate selves go through developmental transitions as he faces this struggle from elementary school through college. Rebecca speaks eloquently about the strain between her father's academic goals and her own, and her peers' goals for popularity as well as the influence of her parents on the development of her sexual identity. Theories of intimacy presented by Sullivan (1953) and Erikson (1959, 1966, 1968) are useful for analyzing and understanding these cases. For example, how does Rebecca's (Case 14) friendship with Kelly exemplify Sullivan's notion of same-sex "chumship"? How does friendship or romantic intimacy contribute to the development of identity? Does the research on gender difference in the development of intimacy seem to hold in these cases (Berndt, 1981, 1982; Blyth, Hill, & Thiel, 1982; Buhrmester & Furman, 1987; Burleson, 1982; Coleman, 1987; Diaz & Berndt, 1982; Sharabany, Gershoni, & Hoffman, 1981; Youniss & Smollar, 1985; Zeldin, Small, & Savin-Williams, 1982)? What are the aspects of a romantic relationship that the adolescents in this book value, and how do these values change as these adolescents mature?

8 Courting Danger

A 19-year-old English woman describes her coming of age in the context of a private British girls' school. Melanie enters puberty as a vulnerable and uncertain young woman, torn between compliance with her family's standards of propriety and her own need to crash through what she perceives as the stagnation and regimentation of her life. She finds a haven in an art class where her teacher demands that students break the rules and go beyond conventionality into creativity. This adult validation of her unspoken belief that she is emotionally suffocating gives Melanie the courage to trust her own intellectual, emotional, and physical instincts. She begins to see her needs as having at least as much validity as her parents' expectations of her. The world of intense peer friendships begins to open to her and with it comes a sense that she is attractive and capable in her own right and can make her way in the world on her own terms.

I still have not fully resolved why, at the age of 13, I stood in the corner of a chilly classroom and calmly took off all my clothes in front of twenty or so of my peers. It was a cold, crisp day and I remember watching goose pimples form on my very ordinary legs. There was absolute silence in the room as I carefully undid the buttons and stepped free from our horrible green uniform. The school sweater and skirt lay crumpled round me and my little white panties circled my feet. I felt a strange lack of emotion or horror at what I had done: My eyes stared blankly back at the girls' uncomprehending eyes, and I stood straight and certain. I was very white, very cold, very vulnerable, but very unemotional. Puberty had barely hit me: My breasts were still small and unformed and any waist, as yet, unidentifiable. There was nothing special about my body—I certainly had nothing either to show off or to hide.

I was not aware of doing this for anyone in particular: The girls present in the room were acquaintances rather than friends or enemies, and none knew me that well. The seconds passed slowly; I wanted to ensure that everyone had the opportunity to recognize what I had done. Was it merely the first raw shock of adolescence causing me to act in such an "odd" way? Was this simply a new awareness of the body and an expression of awakening sexuality? What was I trying to say and why did I have to resort to such lengths to make my point? I heard the delayed reactions—"Melanie, *what* are you *doing*?" and "Hey, Emma, come and see this, will you?"—and felt as if I wasn't there at all. I was completely isolated from my body—my pale limbs really had nothing whatsoever to do with me. I have no recollection of dressing again: All I have is that frozen moment when I see myself from an outsider's point of view. I see the goose pimples on my legs as if I were another person looking at this "freak" from a substantial distance. In the weeks to come, my mind would be filled again and again with images of that small figure standing alone in the shadowy corner.

As I started writing this paper, I had no real idea of where it would lead or what, if anything, would be the cohesive factor pulling my adolescence together. Of course the stripping incident had an impact on me—for one, I had never before done anything "unacceptable" in the eyes of society. However, how would all the other ensuing things that mattered to me fit in with that one isolated happening? Many hours of contemplation have led me to believe that stripping was perhaps a first cry to establish who I was—to find some kind of wholeness in my muddled mind. It was a bold statement in order to dare myself, and others, to think about me in a new, and in many aspects, scary way. Although I never did anything quite as "dramatic" again, I see many of the other things that I subsequently describe as further attempts to clarify who I truly was. Things have been painful and often incomprehensible; I have faced an eternal struggle between solidifying my own individuality and maintaining connections with others important to me. As I stood shivering and exposed in that classroom, I still remember realizing that this was the first time that I had been truly "alone"—there was something intangible separating me from "the rest."

A few other crazy things also happened that year. Surrounded by several friends, I stripped down to the waist on the exposed playing fields (faint half-broken voices echoed in the background from the neighboring boys' school) and returned to math without my underwear on. I did cartwheels between the desks in history lessons when the teacher's head was turned, almost longing for her to catch me and punish me. I threw my shoes out of third floor windows in the midst of physics lessons and watched them tumble into the out-of-bounds quad where no girl was allowed to trespass. I leaned over the banisters on the top floor of the school until I was nearly vertical with my head below my feet pointing skyward. That entailed going right to the brink of my physical capabilities and I trembled at the fact that one slight loss of concentration would result in paralysis or death. I was courting danger, but there was something else going on, too—falling from those banisters was the only way I could imagine of doing something truly irreversible, permanent, strangely beautiful, and perfect. No one would be able to brush that off lightly or complain that I could have done it better. It was an absurd thought, but it appealed to the part of me that was wanting some kind of permanence and perfection. There was little, if any, *acceptable* logic behind these acts: I never thought of the reaction my peers would give and never planned my actions in advance. I just knew that I was never caught or upbraided, and that each time I tried a new escapade, I was in part attempting to have my sense of justice restored: Why was I never punished when others so frequently were?

My friendships were, at least superficially, unaltered by my "demonstrations," and there was no noticeable stultification or intensification in my relationships with the rest of my peer group. They certainly regarded me as "weird" and unusual, but, fortunately, I had just enough "normal" endearing qualities to allow me to stay within the realms of their conforming cliques.

Thus began my adolescence in a flurry of self-exposure. I have always been a very shy and vulnerable person, and it has therefore taken me some time to understand why I did things so blatantly *obvious*. I pondered earlier that stripping was maybe the first glimmer of a search for identity. But why did I have such a need to make myself noticed and distinctive when, at the same time, I shied away from drawing any degree of attention toward myself? To begin to answer this question, I shall have to explore my intense feelings of self-doubt and low self-esteem.

Ever since I can remember, I have felt a fraud. I usually surpassed my schools' and my parents' expectations and failed to achieve my own. Often things have been easy academically, but from age 7 onwards teachers have said, "You must be prepared—in your *next* school, things won't be like this. You'll suddenly find yourself a small fish in a very big pond." The problem is that whenever I moved into another academic environment, I was *still* considered a success—still a "big fish." I always fear that the next time will be the one—the next time I move on I'll be exposed for who I really am. Suddenly all these grand perceptions of me will be crushed. When in a new setting, I am often convinced that everyone else is more socially and intellectually capable than I. The more "successful" I become, the more inadequate I feel: *Why* can people not see my limitations when I find it so easy to fault myself and not live up to my own expectations? Although my drive for perfection means I often fail in my own eyes, to others, I have *never, ever* failed. That is absolutely terrifying; I feel I have come so far now that if I do stumble in front of others, it won't merely be a fall, it will be tumbling right over a precipice. Paradoxically, although I don't really value external praise for my success, I still yearn to be reassured and affirmed; I need to be told I am achieving even though I can never fully hear it. And paradoxically also, my perfectionism is complemented by an awful self-sabotaging urge: One part of me seems determined to teach me how to fail in front of others. How can I relate my arrogant perfectionism—which is unable to accept my mediocrity—to my severe lack of self-confidence and feelings of inadequacy?

Sadly, the conscious and logical mind often cannot explain my thoughts. Much of my fear of being a fraud is, I know, irrational, yet I still find it painfully difficult to acknowledge that *really* I am okay. Underneath all this self-doubt, there is something worth valuing. The world of green uniforms was a private girls' school where my scholastic achievements were particularly highlighted (we were valued for what we could *do* rather than who we could *be*). I was the model "do-er," and how I hated it. Thus all my shoe throwing, clothes stripping, cartwheel turning were, in part, attempts at throwing off the role that had been cast in marble for me— that of the good, obedient, successful student. For far from giving me a feeling of pride, achievement, and worth, my role as a "good girl" was making me feel more and more isolated, empty, and disoriented. They were measuring my worth totally on a scale of tangible success. This had two major implications in my eyes: (1) any part of me that couldn't be measured on that scale—that is, who I was as a *person*— was inconsequential and worthless, and (2) since I had no true belief in my own in- tellectual and creative talents, I was certain that I was the largest con artist ever. I became increasingly shocked that I did well in exams; I rationalized it by saying that exams were simply a "knack" that I was fortunate enough to possess.

My ability to analyze myself and spot my fallibilities fits in very well with the general ambience of my family and house where intellect and reasoning are very much admired and where action fades into the background. My family has always been stable and permanent in my life. My relationship with my sister, Sarah, (two years younger) is particularly untroubled. I have always been very fond of, and protective toward, her; she is a very imaginative and almost unworldly girl who seems to exist for much of the day on another planet. Her naïveté and innocence occasionally irritate me, but usually I am amazed and impressed that she has reached midadolescence so pure, old-fashioned, and untainted by the grubbiness of the world. She very much looks up to me and is ever so proud of me. She is in- credibly shy in front of other people; I worry about her low self-esteem (it runs in the family, I think to myself, wryly) and the fact that it is very difficult for her to live up to what she perceives as my enormous successes. Her own very special talents and strengths are unfortunately not as obvious as my damned ability to pass exams with flying colors. It makes me furious to think that my success damages not only me (in a topsy-turvy way) but poor Sarah as well.

Both my parents completed higher education and it was a matter of course that I would do the same. My father is very proud of my academic successes and both my parents nourish and encourage "intelligence." Thus our house is very nurturing to all cerebral functioning. However, because all four of us are shy—we all find listening so much easier than asserting ourselves—I have always believed my affective and social development to be rather stymied at home.

My father especially has a fear of emotions and instability, and he copes by being the most centered and unflappable person I know. Life for him is divided into organized, categorized sections. People, time schedules, objects, relationships, and events all have a defined place in his hierarchical scheme. His constant com- panion is a big scribbling diary incorporating every aspect of his life. Birthdays, for example, are slotted in with an "A" alongside—"A" stands for annual event; "wash sox" has a "3W" (for three times a week); and emptying the vacuum cleaner has an "M" for monthly. Everything is crossed off once it has been recognized (Christmas Day is lined through early on in the morning—thank goodness that doesn't need to be thought of for the rest of the day). He was "green" decades before the concept of "greenness" had even filtrated our society; wrapping paper has always been ironed and the scotch-tape removed by steam so that it can be used again; baths are always two inches deep to conserve water. I see him now, bending over the pine kitchen table and wielding a paper knife and the tissue paper in which wine is wrapped. He folds the paper and carefully cuts it up into six-inch squares that can then be used for toilet paper. My mother always has to rush around the house before our (infrequent) visitors arrive to remove telltale signs of "eccentricity." Our attic is filled with eighty or so identical, numbered boxes that contain all that we don't need on a day-to-day basis. When we need to put up the Christmas decorations, I simply look on his handmade index under "C" for Christmas, notice subsection 1 (decorations as distinct from wrapping paper), and know that all I require is in box 53.

For years it was wonderful for me to be able to believe that life was simply a question of putting numbers on boxes and letters in diaries: It was very reassuring to see a means of control. Although I have never been physically tidy, perhaps some of my mental perfectionism was derived from observing my father's amazing exactitude. He has managed, somehow, to exist throughout his life in this manner, but I gradually became aware of many uncategorizable things. I couldn't just compartmentalize people or feelings—that would be denying their very interconnectedness with other people/feelings—and thus I had to reject my father's philosophy. Nevertheless, I still had to live in a house where emotions were kept very much under control and social interaction was treated as nonessential. I believe my father could exist perfectly well by communicating with no one but the rest of his family. People really are a terrible burden to him, probably because they are unpredictable and tend to resist simplistic categorizing. He gets on very well with strangers when he has to, but can go months without getting in touch with any of the few friends he wishes to keep. He is a very private, mysterious man, and I wish I understood better his way of thinking. He adores my mother and is very fond of both my sister and me but could not recognize that I needed to be meeting new people, talking with my peers about new things, going to parties, and doing all the other "foolish" things that adolescents so desire to do. I think that because I was so successful in the things that were of paramount importance to him (academic work, musical achievement, being a "nice and polite" daughter), he assumed that my social skills were just as advanced.

He regarded nights out with my friends as a waste of time and would usually say no in answer to my supplications. I think his objections to my socializing also implied a real concern with protecting me from the irrational, dangerous world. I found it poignant when he gave as a reason for his negative reaction, "Your mother would be worried out of her mind if you just waltzed off into the night"; of course my mother would be anxious, but the truth was it would be *he* who would be more frantic. As I grew older, I often did not even bother to disturb the family's harmony and ask to go out when I knew they would not approve of the occasion; I thereby forfeited many evenings with my friends to which I felt entitled. I think this issue became somewhat enlarged in my mind: I was convinced both that my father wanted to keep me under lock and key, and that he would never listen to me. In reality, I often didn't even voice my needs to give him a chance to hear me.

In connection with this, I was becoming more and more concerned about my ability to relate and communicate with others—particularly those of the opposite sex. I have always been scared of "maleness." I choose that word carefully; I am not afraid of men as individuals, but I am certainly uneasy about the whole concept of masculinity. I find it difficult to pin down this fear, but I suppose it must be at least tenuously connected to many things: my fear of my father's categorizing, the fact that I never had brothers and their friends round the house, my eleven years in an all-girls' school, my father's lack of social interaction with anyone but his family, and my belief, between the ages of 14 and 17, that I was profoundly repellent and that no man would ever look twice at me as a possible friend, or—God forbid—girlfriend. It was a short step from my shameless undressing in the classroom to a state of shameful embarrassment about my physical presence.

Trapped in a world of schoolgirls where physical beauty was the prime standard by which to judge and compare peers and where the most complimentary adjectives were *fashionable, trendy,* and *slim,* I longed to exist in some dark cupboard where my vulnerability would be invisible. The ultimate aim was to be "trappable"—worth trapping by a member of the boys' school over the wall. (It has always amused me that the school proudly regards itself as very feminist when we as pupils held such conventional and degrading notions of the function of females as simply an object of desire and adjunct to males.) I suffered acutely because I knew that I didn't quite live up to the cliques' standards of fashionable, trendy, and slim. I have vivid recollections of nearly our entire class of thirty-two sitting in lines during lunch breaks comparing the various merits of our shapely and shapeless legs. There were two marks out of ten: one for length and another for "general impression/shape." I, too weak to protest at such behavior, was an unwilling participant. I remember being relieved, and also disappointed, that I was classed as a "double five"; thank goodness I was within the realms of leg normality, but, yet again, I wasn't going to make it into trappable class.

I wasn't really that concerned with my legs: There were, for me, far more worrisome things to think about. I hated my hair, detested my glasses, and was ashamed of the braces on my teeth. For several months, much of my energy was devoted to feelings of physical inadequacy. I defined myself by how others would regard me—and since I was sure that to others I was ugly, awkward, and gawky, I didn't end up with a very strong self-image. Those were days of torment and despair, of hours in front of the mirror trying on every conceivable combination of clothes to make me look the least objectionable. I would curse the inane values against which I was powerless to resist: I knew most of the standards set amongst my peers were insubstantial and trivial, but I was caught up in them all the same—I wanted, and needed, to belong. My early flouting of their rules of normality by undressing in front of them had given way to a desire simply to fit in.

I was desperately trying to define my own identity but was failing so miserably that I turned to others to help me unify my sense of self. My time of conformity was dark indeed, since I had no real core to my being and all was fragmented and amorphous. In addition, I was suffering from bouts of incapacitating depression—day after day of black woodenness and despair. I was sure that if someone were to open me up they would find absolutely nothing there—if such things as souls existed, I wouldn't have one. I would wake in the morning with nothing but a dull headache filling my entire being, and often I would cross off the hours left before I could get into bed again and escape into the oblivion of unconsciousness. I would long with all my feeble heart to sleep for six months so that I wouldn't have to face any of the awful and draining responsibilities that I saw my life entailed. Depressions were deepened by awful feelings of guilt and remorse: What right had I to be feeling this way? I was physically healthy, had a loving family, did very well at school, was treated by all as someone with abundant reasons for having high self-esteem and self-worth. It was plain contrary of me to feel I had a right to suffer. The very fact that I didn't think I had a right to my depressions made them seem all the more immovable and permanent. I remember gazing from a top story window at school (only yards away from those treasured banisters where I had hung so precariously two or three years earlier) and imagining what would happen if I threw myself from it. I saw my body banging heavily through the air and landing on the lawn below. What glorious peace and permanence that would bring—no more mundanities of everyday existence and no more people making me feel so scattered and disjointed.

I would cry monotonously and regularly, both at home and school. My sobs would be silent to the world but huge and deafening to myself. All I could see were the long days stretching effortlessly and emptily to the end of time. How could I possibly fill them, and what good could I do anyway? My family of course sensed that I was not at my happiest, and made a special effort to be understanding, warm, and trusting. However, I was so good at constructing a façade—a semblance—of okayness for the outside world that soon they too began to believe that everything was just fine and treated me accordingly. As I became increasingly competent at maintaining this veneer of togetherness my internal screams shrieked louder and louder, and I felt I must surely be smothered by this dual existence.

But it would be wrong and misleading to pretend that my adolescence was simply month after month of despair, separateness, confusion, and fragmentation. Now I regard all that blackness as a positive force in my development—I *was* thinking, questioning, and acknowledging that everything wasn't all just "fine, fine, fine." I was being torn and stretched, twisted and distorted—but this was a molding into something new and fresh. Indeed I experienced moments of great lucidity and joy between those weeks of deadness. For a few fleeting seconds, existence would seem purposeful and comprehensible. Often it would be merely the tilting of a head, a certain shadow on the sidewalk, a few piano notes caught in the stillness—suddenly I would sense an acute beauty in life that would be almost too expansive to hold inside me. I would struggle to hold onto that sensation for I knew that I was filled with something precious and valuable; my sense of self then was strong and constant.

The depressions began to wane with my first glimmerings of meanings in the world; this coincided both with my achievement of a satisfactory physical identity and with my escape from the acceptance of others' definitions of me. Actually, my transition from—what I considered—a dowdy, gauche 16-year-old to a presentable, even perhaps attractive woman, was the one fairy tale–like thing that has happened in my life. In the space of one short evening I threw off the shackles of physical insecurity that I had been carrying with me for so long.

Everyone had been talking about the school ball weeks in advance, a joint occasion with the boys' school. All of a sudden I was filled with a crazy and wild desire to make an impact at this silly occasion. I was sick to the back teeth of losing at games where others had made the rules; if I couldn't make my own rules, then at least I'd beat them at their own game. If the aim was still to be eminently trappable, then I would do all I could to be as ravishing as possible. I think my intense desire to succeed made things fall into place—how otherwise could it have chanced that I was to have my braces taken off, contact lenses fitted, and my hair cut all the weekend before that damned dance?! I riffled gleefully through all the dresses hanging in the shops the Saturday before and chose the brightest I could find. The "in" color that winter was black, and so I chose crimson. I still remember the sensation when I pulled the red satin over my head and felt its smooth coldness over my flushed skin.

That night my faith in the world and myself was unshakable. I stood before the mirror with my glasses gone, my hair sleek and sophisticated, teeth proud and white, and that wonderful dress hugging me close in all its glory. Somehow, without my acknowledging it, I had become someone reasonably all right to look at after all. I stood there for several minutes: Gradually it dawned upon me that that strange figure in the shadows was a woman, and that woman was me. There was no longer any need to separate my psychological and physical selves: I hugged myself, reveling in that wholeness. That was the real moment of Epiphany: The rest of the evening was perfect but predictable. Everyone was amazed at the "transformation"; by the end of the evening I was satiated with declarations of approval. I danced and danced and smiled and wept. At long last I had no cause or need to feel inferior: Conversely I had no desire to live up to some ideal of perfection. I was *there:* concretely and earthily there. I actually *felt* my feet aching and I laughed in the knowledge that for once I wasn't "floating all over the ceiling" (as I so often tend to do when I feel ungrounded and unsure) and that I had overcome the enormous hurdle of denying my own physicality in a matter of hours.

To this day I have not had a close or intimate relationship—platonic or sexual—with a man. Despite my acceptance of the interdependence of my physical, emotional, and intellectual self and my newly found physical self-confidence, I still feel unprepared and nervous about tackling a close relationship with a male. Remnants of my own fear as a sexual being remain, and as time goes on, I feel relatively less and less experienced in comparison with others. That is not to say that I do not have strong sexual drives or fantasies; even now I occasionally wonder (1) does everyone else think about sex as much as I do? and (2) are other women just as obsessed with the muscles in a man's legs and bum when he walks? Even after one brief introductory meeting I have a distinct and vivid memory of the exact shape of a man's lower body. Faces may fade; legs do not.

Anyway, I have not yet found anyone with whom I feel I can develop a strong feeling of trust. My vulnerability still makes me terribly wary of revealing parts of my psychological or physical self. I kiss and pet as required, but I am never fully at ease—I can never lose myself in the experience alone and never shrug off the question, "Is this right; am I doing okay; is this what's supposed to happen; is this what I'm required to do?" I feel the hands on my back and glimpse my slip rising up my thighs and think "Is this actually me here—are these my hands, my lips, *myself*?" I search for some ideal notion of that overused word "fulfillment" and all that seems to happen is a taste of soggy mouths and sweaty skin.

Occasionally I wish for a constant boyfriend. People cannot understand why I don't "go out" with someone; many of my friends go from one long-term relationship to the next almost without pause. But I still have to find someone with whom I want to make some kind of commitment. I cannot see the point of dating just for the sake of it; I cannot afford to expend a lot of energy on a relationship I don't care about. I have no wish to give a lot of myself to someone I don't truly respect. Thus most of the time I am happy with my decision not to fall into a relationship to be like my peers; I like being free and I am thankful not to be called so-and-so's "bit." I used to believe that vulnerability was the only thing holding me back. "If only I weren't so shy," "If only I didn't worry so much about being wounded." Now, however, I have come to cherish it as one of my inherent strengths. I believe vulnerability has made me all the more sensitive to the vagaries of both myself and others, and I feel that it has helped me to be more self-questioning and willing to take risks. Life for me has never been solid or secure, and so I am all the more aware of what a "risk" is, and how exposed I am to change and new circumstances.

When, at the age of 14, I suddenly found myself immersed in art, its teacher, and the fellow students, I found it incredibly exciting to explore a new part of myself. Art wasn't something I could automatically do and it was wonderfully refreshing to grapple with something that couldn't be classed as "right" or "wrong." In addition, no one had preconceptions of my ability, and I had no one to live up to but myself. However, at the beginning it was not art *per se* that thrilled me; it was the art teacher, Ms. Madeleine Tremayne, in all her strange, beautiful mystery.

To me Madeleine is quite unforgettable. I don't quite know where to start—she is still such an important element of my life that I find it difficult to see her objectively, and I feel a strong obligation to portray her as well as she deserves to be presented. Every moment she is *alive*—questioning us, herself, events, imaginings—and I think it is this constant searching for some kind of ultimate truth of faith that makes her so exciting. It is almost possible to feel the zone of her impact and influence; to my unformed mind this "magnetic field" was fascinating and mesmerizing. She drew people toward her—they would come with love and hate but never with indifference.

I would be painting and slowly my paintbrush would droop and my wrists go limp. I would turn and look—trying to identify what on earth made this woman special. Her uniqueness definitely had something to do with her physical presence and aura—there was a steeliness *and* a softness about her—but I think ultimately her great strength was both her integrity and her sense of risk-taking inherent in her teaching style. Every day she would come in with some new theory about "life's rules"—mingling Buddhist meditation with astrology, reincarnation with existentialism. She did not talk for her own benefit—I am sure she was trying to get us to think about life and art in different and often unconventional ways. Her own life was hardly rosy even now (I remember her saying, "Life's no less shitty to you even when you have got bits of it worked out"). She would ask for our advice and cherish our support when life was being a "real bugger." We would sit enraptured by this woman who actually considered us worthy enough both to share her life experiences and to nurture her in crisis. She would also listen limitlessly to our own tales of conflict and confusion and seemed to possess infinite quantities of compassion, empathy, and suggestions. She forced us to look at what we were creating for ourselves, and pushed us into a new state of awareness and responsibility for our actions.

"It's no good thinking that it's always the other person's fault when things go wrong for you, Melanie," she would say, skewering me onto the wall with the intensity of her gaze (escape or evasion was never possible). "You're always going to be part of the equation when other people are involved, and so you have to work out what you're doing to cause this response." I would look at her feeling peeled and exposed. How did she always know exactly what was happening for us?

"You're still being a victim of your fate instead of an instigator. You *do* have the means to control rather than to be manipulated. In the meantime, instead of faffing around and 'floating around on the ceiling,' put some of this anguish into your picture and give yourself twenty minutes to get emotion into those contorted figures. You see, that's what art is—a means of showing *yourself*, a vessel in which to pour your soul. If you have nothing to show, then all we get is a cluster of meaningless, empty lines. And if I were you, I would go home tonight and meditate for half an hour—you clearly haven't been doing that, have you? Your aura's all over the place." (I would admit that I hadn't been meditating: It was impossible to lie to her.) "And ask yourself why your parents aren't hearing you. The blame's not necessarily entirely theirs. Are you really speaking to them, or are you simply talking in a half-hearted way? By the way, I've just noticed: That tiny bit of blue in the center is really singing; you're beginning to understand the pictorial tension. Maybe something is moving inside you after all."

Madeleine was the one member of staff who acknowledged passion, insecurity, and sexuality—both in herself and in her pupils. She recognized our adolescent turmoils as healthy, joined in with our wildness, rejoiced at our unpredictable inflammability, and treated us as sexual beings. Other teachers denied us the right to be disruptive, sexual, and confused; she loved us for what and who we were and knew that all our "madness" could be harnessed to improve our art. She would stride into the room saying, "Come on. Figure drawing—we're really going to get the hang of internal form today. I want you to see the model as monumental." We looked at the 11-year-old posing in front of us in her green school uniform, her legs skinny and her breasts flat. Monumental was not the word that would have automatically jumped to mind.

"Her legs must be solid—they've got to be big enough to support her. Imagine her as a baronial hall: overwhelming the paper, spilling over. You must be like a little ant crawling around her. If you get this going, you're going to be creating masterpieces—I'm telling you, the experience of drawing magnificently is way, way better than sex. I'm completely serious—so let that be an incentive to you!"

My instinct believed that in the chaotic art room my battered soul could be rebuilt, and that here what I had to give would be valued. For those brief months during my last two years, Ms. Tremayne and the other three members of the art class provided in abundance all the love, frustration, inspiration, and despair that

I needed. For good or bad, everyone else—parents, other friends—faded into the background. Although I had always managed to be fairly popular with my peers (even without reaching the upper echelons of "cliquedom"), I had never before felt a real sense of belonging or connecting. It was with joy that I heard Madeleine talking of:

"Our raft. Our raft's sinking. We've got to support each other. We're all in the middle of this bloody great ocean and the only way we can keep above water is to paddle like mad *together*. It's no good you all standing in your separate corners beavering away at the old still life." All four of us turned, looked at each other guiltily, and dragged the easels closer together.

"The great thing about learning art together is that you pull everyone else along. We create a pool of energy and everyone draws from it. No more of this trying desperately to be better than everyone else. If you're doing awfully, just be grateful that Sophie over here is making up for you."

Art became the focus and the purpose of our passions—a means of catharsis and purging and an outlet for all my emotional and sexual frustration. At home suppers were still pedagogical affairs, but at least now filled with a sense of excitement; my family could recognize that something was happening to me even if they did not fully approve. They realized that I was living in another world, but still struggled to make me hold onto the image of a loving, considerate daughter. After one particularly lengthy argument between my father and me, he said quietly, "Oh, don't be silly, Melanie—just try and be more demure. That's what you should be aiming for—everyone values demureness and femininity." At that moment I was at last able to conceptualize and clarify one of the primary struggles in my development: I was becoming a woman but was fighting tooth and claw against that image of "womanly goodness and obedience." I wasn't only trying to throw off my role as "good student": I was aiming to get to the much bigger issue of what it is to be feminine. I hated the vicelike grip of the word *demure*. Why had I stripped naked, why had I hated those "marks out of ten for leg shape" discussions so much, why was I unhappy with the power wrapped in the words *fashionable* and *trappable*? My fight was *against* the whole belief of girls being quiet, predictable, and dainty. Even when I had joined in that game by going to the ball, it was in a red, angry dress which defied conventional notions of prettiness. I was just learning how to express my darkness and energy through some creative channel, and the last thing I needed to hear was that I should be aiming toward some traditional notion of femininity.

At last I was destroying the semblance of "good girl/good student" and starting to unleash my hidden and suppressed anger. I felt as though I were bringing into the light a half of me which had been hidden and etiolated for years. Occasionally I would stand back, look at my picture, and be amazed that it was the product of my own hand: Did I really have that much blackness and badness in me? It was both liberating and terrifying to be able to see art revealing some of my murky depths. Even so, still I felt choked: If the right point were tapped I would be faced not with a slow welling up of emotion but a full-scale avalanche of desires, bitterness, half-formed needs, unresolved fears. . . . It's a good job that we learned how to do "anger release."

It was a muggy summer's day—the sort of day when one's pores feel saturated with humidity and nothing much seems to be happening. Madeleine was getting fed up with our slowness to get down on paper "what was really happening for us":

"Is this what you really want to say about yourselves through art? All I can see at the moment is a namby-pamby schoolgirl picture—you're painting the wallpaper and thinking about the next tea break at the same time. Do you really want your pictures to look so flabby? I want to see something 'yummy': I want it to look so good that I could eat it. Find the 'wow' effect—do anything but make bloody sure that it's strong enough to knock off anything beside it on the wall. Where's the internal form? The heart? The passion? I want to be *convinced*."

For once, none of us could respond to her exhortations, and so she led us—Jessica, Joanna, Sophie, and me—downstairs to the deserted gym. The school was almost empty since it was after four o'clock, but there was a badminton practice going on in the next-door hall. Madeleine was completely fair: Each one of us was free to leave at any point and we certainly felt no obligation to do what she was suggesting. As I sit here typing, I can still recall the touch of those faded mats as we unpacked them and piled them a foot high; I still see the dust motes hanging in the gym; I still sense that tension of nervousness and expectancy as we stood around those mats waiting to begin. Madeleine began talking in a slow, calm voice:

"Okay, now, I am trained to do this, so you don't need to feel in any way that I am merely experimenting or messing around. I want you all to watch closely and give me energy as I go first. I'm not going to do it fully since none of you would know how to replenish my energy if I let myself go completely."

As usual, my brain understood some of her meanings but not all. What was all this talk of energy and replenishing? What was she actually going to do? I could feel myself beginning to "float on the ceiling"—as I am still wont to do when apprehensive—and I struggled to get both my feet back on the ground. I watched her take off her cardigan and expose her lithe, strong arms and artist's hands. She knelt in front of the heavy pile of mats and locked her arms together by grasping her hands firmly.

"In order to keep me going, I want you all to say insistently something that really pisses me off. I always hate it when people tell me to calm down and so I want you to say just that. 'Calm down!'—again and again. I'm going to shout back 'Shut up.' Okay?"

She gave one of her enormous, reassuring smiles to each one of us in turn. Everything sounded perfectly run-of-the-mill and ordinary. I wondered how she was possibly going to get angry in the middle of a school gym at 4:30 on a Monday afternoon with no real provocation. As I pondered, her face changed: There was absolute focus and concentration, and she started to radiate an almost tangible sense of drive and life force. We felt the tension enveloping us, saw the old, overused mats and heard childish voices from the badminton room. Suddenly there was a whisper of the unknown and the irrational. Madeleine raised her arms high in the air and—Jessica walked out. Her face was filled with an awful fear—perhaps a fear of seeing anger, exposing a weakness, overturning some stable notion of the world? We turned and watched her slam the door, and then drew closer together.

Madeleine didn't break concentration even for Jessica. As if wielding an axe, she raised her arms in a great arc and hurled her full body weight onto the mat. In the same motion she let out a huge and gut-felt cry, "Shut up." The two words lost all meaning as they penetrated the lofty hall. Again and again she drew herself up and thundered back down as we began the slow provocations of "Calm down. Calm down." Her body and voice worked rhythmically; she was both brutal and graceful as the energy surged through her and exploded on the mats. For the first few seconds I was paralyzed by shock and fear. I watched the muscles trembling in her strong arms, the hair in her armpits glistening with sweat, the skin stretching over her temples, and the blood flowing to her lips. Gone were all vestiges of what society so admires and needs: control, etiquette, niceness, and obedience. The figure before me had stripped all our superficial coverings away and taken us back to our brutal and real nakedness. So this is humanity: This is what we all so desperately try to cover with manners and social graces. This untamed beast in all of us. My fear subsided and I looked with admiration at the power curving through my teacher and snarling in her throat. What on earth would a "full" anger release have done to me?

It was hard not to feel overwhelmed and self-conscious as I knelt down and gazed at the mats before me. Why did I have to be the first one after Madeleine? I tried to empty my mind but I could not shut out the sound of girls screaming in the next hall. What if they look through and see us here? How could this be explained to 12-year-olds? I focused on my charcoal-covered jeans and swept the hair out of my eyes. Delaying tactics. I felt an absurd desire to rush out of the room into the sunlight.

"Come on, Melanie," I whispered to myself. "Don't let yourself down; if you get this, think of how much you'll move. Even if you can't do it for any other reason, do it for your picture. Your picture needs it; you need it. Don't think about inhibitions, don't think about what society wants. Come *on*, Melanie." Part of me reeled with the thought of exposing the power within me—acknowledging in public the strength of my dark side. I struggled, finally overcame that fear, lifted my arms, and began. As though from a great distance I heard them shouting—shouting the very phrase my father uses which drives me to distraction. "Don't be silly, don't be silly, don't be silly." I registered Madeleine's voice strong against the rest and shouted back with all the power I could muster, "No!" It wasn't very much of a word, but it was all I could manage. I felt vibrations in my throat and gradually everything—the badminton game, the dusty hall, my friends—became lost, and I was overtaken by wild instinct. I was sucked up into a glorious unity and was expressing that deep and unheard wholeness. As I struck the mats, I had no awareness of my hands growing numb with pain and my voice growing hoarse and incoherent. There was only a sensation of deep and exhilarating release—something was at last pouring from me and I was cleansed and revitalized. I have no idea how long I managed to carry on, slowly the presence of my friends reasserted itself and I collapsed onto the mats, drained and limp. My hands were burning and my throat parched.

I lay there feeling like a newborn babe and recalling the temper tantrums of my childhood years. When had I last been able to express emotions physically?

Had I really been keeping so much inside for so long? Madeleine's olive arms extended toward my white ones and swaddled me in a blanket. I curled over onto my side; Madeleine's breath was hot on my back as she drew me near and held me close, one arm pressed onto my lower spine. My ability to hear seemed to have vanished temporarily and her voice sounded thick as she spoke: "That was good, did you feel good? It was wonderful seeing what no one has seen of you for such a long time. Just lie still—stay still. I'm holding you like this to create a big circle of energy so that my energy can flow back into you. I'm going to refill you. This is, in many ways, the most important part: It's essential that you have someone to give back what you just gave out. I'm trying to make myself as open as possible."

I murmured in reply and felt her body strong and warm beside me as I began to expand and reinflate. I lay quiet and clean amongst the marks made by years of scuffling feet and sweaty toes. The minutes passed and I began to experience a magnificent sense of power and liberation: All the matted junk had been cleared away from my inside and I felt ready to begin again. I saw my big picture—the culmination of our five years of learning with Madeleine—waiting for me. Its primary function was to express, in any way I wished, what really concerned me at that moment in time. Easily six feet long and filled with agonized, contorted horses and humans, it had become nightmarish and abstracted. I was trying to express the enormous conflicts raging inside me, but still couldn't quite get the dynamics working. I had been feeling for the past two weeks as though I was hitting my head over and over against the ceiling.

Ten minutes later (the mats put away and my friends gone home—they were going to do their anger release next week) I swept along the corridor feeling as though I were running on air. I saw exactly what I had to do to make that picture work. It was growing dusky outside and the janitors were beginning to thump around with mops and buckets in the next room. I picked up my pastels and felt entirely alone. The anger release had filled me with such energy that I was sure I could carry on all night if I had to. Taking courage in both hands, I obliterated all the flashy, superfluous marks, rubbed over all the superficial highlighting, erased all parts which were just trying to make me look like an "expert" artist. What would be left? My throat was dry and scratchy and my fingernails filled with the grease of oil pastels. After two hours I stood back, terrified that I had destroyed it all: Had I simply gone overboard with this "anger" and killed everything? My eyes skimmed the image; to an outsider the board looked a mass of messy and unintelligible marks. I exhaled noisily: To me the picture, although now stark and unpolished, had jumped forward more in this one night than it had for the past two weeks. A force was moving within it—oh the joy that that brought. So this is what commitment feels like. I rested on my haunches and thought: This is the first time I have really exposed my anger; this is the first time that I have really experienced commitment to anything. As I sat in that gloomy room, art and that picture were the most important things in my life. Take that away and my life would be meaningless.

By deliberately evading mundanities and trivia by condemning them as the antithesis of art, we had entered a dreamworld where creativity, irrationality, and insubstantiality flourished. It was by no means a stable and realistic existence, but it came at a vital time in my life—all at once no one was forbidding me my rights to feelings of insecurity and inadequacy. I was actually being allowed to ask "What really matters to me?" instead of having to maintain a pretense of okayness. Wow—my art actually improved each time I realized and accepted some previously hidden weakness. The world for me extended not much further than the ends of my fingertips; anything beyond my reach seemed distant and relatively unimportant. I was concerned with how I fitted into life's workings, not how the great impersonal world functioned by itself. I was completely wrapped up in the personal, and set great store on the value and effect of emotion. I began to shun all people—including my father—who appeared to exist without them. Emotion gave my life at that time color and excitement. Experiences were heightened simply because I felt them so keenly; my newly formed relationships were stronger because they were born through feeling. All seemed intense and vital because my spirit was at last being succored while my cerebrality and cold intellect were being starved. At last I was a "do-er" no more.

Unleashed from the restrictions and pressures of cliques, I formed my first real friendship with one member of the art group in particular. Jessica is an extremely powerful, exciting, obsessive, and invigorating woman. She was all that I had been aspiring to be: strong in her convictions, sensitive in her vulnerability, creative in her unpredictability, and powerful in her femininity. She was also incredibly unstable, and there would be days when she was beyond us all—uncontrollable, mad, and irrational. Although she was sensitive and vulnerable, she couldn't really get in touch with her feelings so that she could express this insecure and compassionate side: witness her inability to participate in the anger release. I saw these hidden emotions lurking within her and I longed to tap those resources.

I loved her as I wanted to love myself. My deep compassion for her was intense and exclusive; I didn't have much left to give to other people. Jessie, because of her own need for companionship and security, transferred much of her love onto me. We succored and nourished each other with our crazy devotion. I experienced moments of liberation and commitment that I have never since transcended: Both of us were managing to get over our great fear about exposing and trusting, and we knew that there was much invested in our "other half." But this progress was made painfully; our friendship developed most rapidly at times of suffering.

One rainy afternoon I picked up the phone and I heard her voice devoid of any panic but with a hardness and a tension which meant she was in one of her mad days. Never, till now, had she been able to come to me during one of her deepest crises (she would simply retreat into herself), and I was therefore exhilarated and terrified.

"Mel, Mel . . . um . . . is there any way you can come over?"

"Right now?" (Thoughts fluttered through my mind; two papers to be in the next day, a major piano concert that coming week, my father's refusal to let me out since I was under "such pressure." I had to go; I just had to.)

"Yes. It's that . . . well . . . it's just me. I don't know . . . what's happened."

I placed the phone on the receiver, having assured Jess that I would be over as soon as I could. I faltered on the threshold of the kitchen where my parents were sitting. What do I say—that my friend needs me, that my papers don't matter? I had to find some strength to center my energy so that I could not fail.

"Um, Mom and Dad . . . well, actually, Jessie's just rung. She's desperate and she's come to me for help. I have to be with her. I know you'll understand—and understand how much Jessie means to me." I looked at them, amazed that I was for once being open. As I looked, I suddenly saw their love for me in their eyes. I did know at the moment that they would understand: Why had I always been so afraid of enunciating my needs to them before?

An hour later, I was sitting with Jessica in her room. Of course my parents hadn't thought my papers more important than the bonds of a friendship. On the train I had experienced a new self-confidence: I had come to understand my parents better, and we had opened a new line of communication. Even so, as I stepped into the room my confidence evaporated. Jessica was there but not there: She seemed abstracted from life itself. How the hell could I reach out to her? She was sitting on her bed, her face white and unmade-up and her expression fixed. She looked as though she were made of clay; nothing was going to give. Around her, on the paint-stained rugs, lay half-finished self-portraits, sinister abstracts, angry figure drawings. Her full-length mirror had been propped up against a cupboard. Suddenly there were dead and heavy words amidst this chaotic silence.

"Thanks Mel. Thank you." I looked at her, trying to convey by my eyes what my mouth couldn't express. No, that's inaccurate: I didn't even know exactly *what* I was trying to convey. All I wanted was to make some kind of connection with her.

"I was sitting . . . I was sitting in front of my mirror for ages. I wanted to try and get my self-portrait more intense and mysterious."

Was this some kind of explanation? Terrified, I picked my way across the floor and sat down at the end of the bed. There was something almost inhuman about Jess's lack of emotion and the hardness in her voice. Where had she retreated this time? Do I talk, or sit silently and use my body energy to empathize with her? I had never before been in a position when such responsibility was falling on my shoulders—Jessie had come to *me*.

Again she spoke—continuing the monologue, "And I looked, and after a while, after I had sat there for ages, there was nothing there. I looked in the mirror and—I had disappeared—there was just a crazy head there. Desperate—I couldn't find myself anywhere—I had vanished."

I glanced at her self-portraits—wild eyes, pained cheeks—and back to her own impassive, motionless face. "Maybe we should go for a walk," I suggested pathetically. At least then we could get out of this claustrophobic room and maybe the fresh air would help me clarify what I could do to help her. I led her out into the drizzle and felt as though there were a ghost walking beside me. Impulsively I turned toward her and hugged her stiff and cold body close and hard. I felt the energy in my gut and stomach, and tried with all my force to transfer some of it to her. I could feel myself wanting to cry—wanting to show some emotion myself if she couldn't. My knuckles turned white, and Jess's head drooped onto my shoulder. Suddenly she was limp all over, but still no outburst of feeling came.

We carried on walking, and slowly her voice rose in a whisper, a monotone. It came in fragments: her intense fears about not growing up to be a great artist, the terrifying agony when she feels she "must have vanished." Her days of utter irrationality when she cannot even remember the words with which to have a conversation, the spiderlike fatality of her attraction which draws people toward her only for her to suck them dry, her uncontrollable tantrums. I heard her words and wept inside; my best friend had at last removed her "I'm okay" façade and I loved her all the more for entrusting me with the blackest parts of her character.

What did I say in those next two or three hours before I led her home? I know that I was trying desperately to allow her to let something break inside her. This deathlike passivity seemed so unnatural and unhealthy. I myself felt very strange: I had never—even momentarily, as now—been in a "dominant role" in any relationship, and I struggled to relax. Gradually I managed to forget myself and focus entirely on Jessica. As we tramped homeward through the dismal rain, I began to feel the first flames of energy licking through Jessie's body. She had lost that hardness, but I had to acknowledge that Jessie could not, and would not, recognize her emotions that night.

It was with trepidation that I glimpsed her dark head bent over a book in class the next morning. She looked up, gazed at me, and looked down again; I glimpsed serenity in her eyes. Was this a good sign? Do I stay here or do I leave her to her own intimate thoughts? She lifted her head again and tears were trickling down her face. She did not even attempt to brush them away. I watched the pure clean sorrow in her face and felt real warmth in her pale hands as I grabbed them. I had never seen even a hint of a tear in the past and now she was crying openly and beautifully before me. I could feel in those tears the outpouring of all the tension and deadness of last night, and I rejoiced that Jessica had at last let down her final and most firmly established mask—her mask which stated proudly, "Nothing can get to me: My emotions are totally under control." In the following weeks, our friendship blossomed even further since the remaining few barriers against intimacy had been destroyed. Well, temporarily at least.

You see, this sharing of our lives couldn't last forever. We began to come into school wearing the same clothes without even realizing it, and started using each other's mannerisms and vocabulary. We began to function interdependently—almost as one person. In effect, we were each other's life-support machines. The nature of our union became symbiotic: Our combined power was so strong that it was uplifting to exist as one, rather than to return to our separate loneliness and lack of security. Writing this now, our relationship seems unhealthy in the extreme; the emotions and intensity invested in the relationship were comparable to those in a love affair. But at that time, it was wonderful to know, for the first time, that what I had to give was valuable. The sense of standing alone and being somehow separated was temporarily extinguished.

But the very closeness that was our strength also engendered in me seeds of envy and mistrust. Art, the common ground on which we both stood so firmly, provided the means for comparison. Which of us had more talent? Which of us had greater depths of character to nourish our creativity? The competition inspired our art and put an invisible, paper-thin divide between us. Also, I began to fear that she didn't need me as much as I thought she did. She seemed scared of our closeness, and I sensed that maybe she was starting to reject me. Her periods of withdrawal returned, and in the holidays she would go weeks without contacting me. I would often call her but she was nearly always out with her boyfriend Andrew (was she substituting our interdependence for a new interdependence with Andrew?) and rarely got back to me. Was it possible that she had sucked me dry and was now discarding the empty shell? I hated myself for thinking that, and so whenever she did either write or phone I would forget all my doubts and everything would be wonderful once more. Even so, it was becoming increasingly complicated: Jessie was now deeply attached to Andrew, and therefore there was a third variable to be considered.

I struggled constantly to give the two of them enough room to grow. Whenever the three of us were out with other people, I knew that it was Andrew's, and not my right to be with Jessie. But still Andrew felt in competition with me for her trust and companionship. Jessica is a very striking woman, and I knew he was very proud of her and felt I had no right to claim her. The strange thing is that she defies all standard definitions of femininity—there is something distinctly masculine (if we can call characteristics "masculine" and "feminine") about her "grit" and stubbornness. I would stand there and think: My "best" friend is at the same time the male ideal image of sexual beauty. How does that affect me; *where* does that leave me?

Although one of Madeleine's axioms rang constantly in our ears—"When you feel you can't exist without someone/something, then that is the time to give him/her/it up"—neither Jess nor I had the strength to make a *real* split. Our partial separation had to be forced by the physical dividers of leaving high school and beginning our separate lives. I wonder now: Was it right of me to expect such loyalty from her? Was it right of me to sacrifice so much of myself for her (even now I forgive her every time she "forgets" about me or treats me in an offhand way)? I remember Madeleine's words clearly, "It's no good thinking that it's always the other person's fault when things go wrong for you, Melanie. You have to work out what you're doing to cause this response." Much of my ongoing doubt therefore stems from myself: Is my concept of friendship too intense and distorted? What was I doing to make Jess shy away? Even now I am reluctant to admit the close of that chapter in my life of which I was so desperately fond. In my turbulent and joyful "art phase" it was so clear that I was developing and learning. The storms of midadolescence—with all their agonies and their ecstasies—are over and I now face a period of consolidation rather than complete reformation. It's harder now: I have to look very carefully indeed to identify the few millimeters' progress that I aim to advance each day.

But there have been gains; partially freed from ties with Jessica and the art group, I have been able to reincorporate and reaccept my family. Although I had managed to break down the fear of communicating openly with them during my time of intense friendship with Jessica, I still wasn't treating them as an integral part of my life. My *real* life was my hours spent in the art room; coming home was like having to return to a hotel to sleep and recuperate for the next day. Now, my eyes are free to observe my parents and accept them both as parents and as people in their own right.

The turning point arrived in the form of my first major piano recital. The two weeks preceding this event I had stayed home with my mother and I had felt a real strengthening of bonds between us as we entrusted each other with our intimate selves. On the day of the concert itself, she couldn't eat one thing; it was almost as though she was going to be playing and not me. My father had been like a shadow during this time; he was often there but I never really acknowledged his solidity.

The hundreds of hours of practice for my recital condensed into one short evening. Those rare moments of happiness when I'm playing well—when I feel that I *have* achieved my full potential, and near perfection doesn't seem *quite* so impossible—were quickly over and I was standing bowing. At first I could focus on no one, but then I spotted my father's snowy hair near the back (at the back so as not to distract me). In between bows I strained to see them all clearly. I blinked rapidly and caught my mother's beautiful joyful face and the tears in Sarah's eyes. Thank God I had played my best. I felt on top of the world. Then I saw my father's strong hands clapping and—my father was crying. My father was *crying* because of me. He was being more damned emotional than anyone else in the entire room. I snatched back a sob in my own throat and clutched the bouquet closer to my chest.

I had been so critical of my father's categorizing, and yet I had neatly classified him as "not able to have emotions." I remembered Jessica's tears and now I experienced the same joy as I had then. What tears could do to me! As I lay in bed that night, I knew my eyes were opening to the world; with a sharpness in my chest I realized that my father, and indeed all other people to whom I am closely attached, are infinitely more varied and magical than I had previously been willing to admit. As I lay there in the darkness, I again felt that degree of separateness that I had experienced in that drafty classroom several years ago. But this time I wasn't scared; although there was a thin line separating me from "the rest," there was also a thin line separating each individual from "the rest." (What is "the rest" anyway? Surely it is merely a collection of struggling, lonely souls.) It was incredibly comforting to know that I would never be able to understand fully the workings of someone else—people could never be truly figured out. They would always be able to shock me by their inconsistencies of behavior. One person would cry or one person would strip naked and someone else's notion of the world would be overturned. Yes, it was wonderful to be able to perceive at last each person's own, precious uniqueness and complexity.

Yesterday I was strolling along the sidewalk. It was quite a nice day and my glance fell on my elongated shadow gliding along beside me. I paused: That was *my* shadow. I could never get rid of it, add to it, swap it with someone else, or change its fundamental characteristics. It would always be mine. Just as my "Melanieness" will always be mine. I had never formulated that thought quite so clearly—no matter whom I get involved with, what I do with the rest of my life, there is absolutely no way that I can ever change or add to my shadow. There will always be just one. The only companion it will have is me. I carried on walking and heard a voice inside me: "We must die alone: We *shall* die alone. *We* are our own constant companion. Surely therefore we must learn to live and stand alone." Just as I was about to go inside into the gloom I heard my voice again, "Here I am, whole, eager, vulnerable, and alone. I'm walking alone. I'm existing alone. And I'm *living* . . . not merely surviving."

Melanie: Ten Years Later

For many weeks I have been resisting reacquainting myself with Melanie, finding it difficult to yield to the grip of her tales. It is difficult not because I feel I no longer know Melanie, not because I want to distance myself from "her" or because I no longer am "her." On the contrary, it is because the pain in her—my—words still cuts me to the quick. Reading my case a decade later provokes two simultaneous and contradictory responses: a glorious sense of no longer being constrained by the insecurities I see there, and an equally strong realization that the struggles waged there have a tortuous afterlife. Those struggles—which seem to me to be most caught up with questions of friendship, desire, and autonomy—are not easily left behind. And, of course, commenting on these struggles a decade later before an unknown audience of readers that has its own set of interpretations of and theories about Melanie produces additional, refractory anxieties. I veer between my two responses. I want to tell you that a decade makes all the difference in the world; that shy, depressed Melanie now finds and experiences pleasure that is not marred by debilitating fears about her own self-worth and about not measuring up to femininity. But I want to tell you too that there is no easy escape—and occasionally, it seems, no escape at all—from the grind of anxiety and of painful family configurations that figure prominently in Melanie's life both then and now.

At the start of "Courting Danger," I claimed that I faced "an eternal struggle between solidifying my own individuality and maintaining connections with others important to me." Carol Gilligan, in her commentary, and I, looking back, agree about the centrality of this statement. There is no doubt in my mind that this struggle was indeed the problem that structured my case, both in terms of negotiations with my parents and in relation to the compelling draw of those whom I admired and loved. I want, however, to refine that statement, for the kind of connection I then most desired was, I think, one of peculiar intensity: a bond between another person and me in which, through my abundant love and admiration for that person, I could and would lose myself. That sense of immersion, of being sucked, forcefully, into something in which I was not myself was what framed both that strange scene on the faded gym mats and the devotion with which I tried to model myself on the sinewed insolence of Jessica. It was because of this immersive pull toward those who fascinated me that the struggle between "solidifying my own identity and maintaining connections with others important to me" was so fraught. Maintaining those connections was a question of dissolving the very boundaries of my own identity. I don't mean this in a weak sense—any relationship demands that each person opens in some way to the other—but in the sense that in those relationships my sense of self at times could not be said to exist at all. To lose myself in this movement felt, and still feels, magical.

Part of the pain, the jab of nostalgia that assaults me when I reread my case, comes from experiencing anew the heady passion of those moments. Reading of my friendship with Jessica, a friendship whose intensity I equated to that of a love affair, makes me miss the scorching potency of that tie. And I miss it partly because I know that those days of fervor do seem peculiarly part of, and proper only to, adolescence; those days seem now lost. I do not mean to say that my current friendships are desultory and devoid of passion; far from it. Rather, I wish to point out that the intensity generated by my connections with, say, Jessica and Ms. Tremayne was lined through with boundless idealization on my part. Today my need for people who can become figures of wonder is not nearly so pressing. Part of what pulled me into such dynamics then was the conviction that I myself did not have the confidence or the charisma to be an object of idealization for anyone else. In other words, I was always the one who, in seeking a way out of the straitjacket of a patrolled family life, would fall, awestruck, for others. As I reached adulthood I gradually came to lose the sensation that I was a sham and that I had constantly to escape from others' readings of me as a "good girl." In the process, I also began to be able to take more pleasure in what I could offer my friends and in the possibility that I might have allure for others.

These changes in how I interact with others and how I regard myself have occurred in the context of places of higher education. I have spent the ten years since completing "Courting Danger" studying and teaching in universities on both sides of the Atlantic. I wrote the case while a visiting student in the United States; those six months marked the first extended period of time I had spent out of my home country and away from my family and friends. The writing of my case therefore coincided with a sometimes solitary and wistful period of reflection on those years of high school that I had so recently, and ambivalently, left behind. As I read the case now, memories of that solitariness jump at me: days and countless evenings of reflection when I sat, face to face with the computer, trying to push that just-gone past into line.

I returned to Britain without much enthusiasm, sad to bid farewell to the excitement I had felt at seeing modes of living and of finding pleasure that seemed so different from those practiced by my family. Ten days later, I started my B.A. at that infuriating institution of Oxbridge. There I was taught, mostly mediocrely, by countless men and one woman. There, I became politicized as I began to realize that the structure, pedagogical strategies, and ethos of the university were mulishly impervious to change. I was often bored and unsatisfied by the conservative nature of my social science modules and the unimaginative range of course material, and so I read extensively in feminist, literary, and social theory, took part in many feminist university campaigns, and contributed in various ways to the student governance of my college. My feeling shy stopped, more or less, being a constant predicament. I steered a course through Oxbridge that was both incredibly difficult psychologically (it included several bouts of deep depression) and emblazoned with academic success. In this, there was little change from high school, as few would have believed in either circumstance that behind my frenetically pursued series of accomplishments lay periods of despair. Throughout my time at Oxbridge, no tutor with whom I had close contact had any real pedagogical impact upon me. My intellectual inspiration was drawn instead from my closest friend, who was studying English, and from two professors whose lectures I attended and whom I admired from afar.

Everyday life at Oxbridge was full of various examples of chauvinism. One of my male tutors regularly referred to two of the women in my cohort as bimbos (they, apparently, professed "not to mind"); another male tutor interrogated my closest friend ceaselessly over sherry about her "lapsed" Roman Catholic faith and tried unstintingly to return her "to the fold." I left Oxbridge angry and unsettled. And although I had, by that point, a fulsome understanding of the unchanging institutional structure that so piqued this fury, it still consumed me—hurting me as much as the targets against which it raged. It took me many months to reconcile the contrasts between the joy of the close friendships I made at Oxbridge (and have to this day) and the indignation and frustration I felt toward Oxbridge that took so long to dissipate.

Now I am about to assume the role of teacher and mentor. I am in the midst of finishing my Ph.D. at an élite, hierarchical American university, and find myself perched precariously in a position that demands an intensely maintained subordinate relationship to my advisers and to more established scholars. I feel caught, still infantilized by dint of the lowly position in which graduate students are tacitly held, and thus still longing for the moment at which I will feel fully "grown up." Next year I shall perhaps be starting a job as an assistant professor and feeling the terror and pleasure of having, finally, to take full responsibility vis-à-vis my students. I am anxious about having to inhabit this role, and sense that such anxiety is connected to the difficulty I still have in occupying a position of authority that ideally requires a certain charisma. While I enjoy performing in the sense of giving lectures, seminars, and conference papers, there is something in me that balks at being a possible object of investment, idealization, or resentment for those I am teaching. And so, notwithstanding the many years I have wished to escape what increasingly feels to be an impotent location within the academic hierarchy, part of me still quivers at the thought of taking on a position of great potency. I fear that my default position is still one of tutelage rather than of command.

There is no question that this anxiety accompanies a more general difficulty I still have believing that my concerns, stories, and preoccupations are no less compelling than anyone else's. How much easier it is for me to listen to others—and how much strange pleasure have I learned, over the years, to extract from this role. Although my impulsive tendency to submerge my own identity within those I love has diminished, my fascination with inhabiting others' thoughts and worlds subsists. This vigorous urge to identify with those with whom I interact is, I think, one of my most powerful and double-edged qualities. My desire to empathize with others, to feel their passions and understand their points of view has contrary effects. It often makes it difficult for me to maintain the validity of my own position while responding to emotional and ethical demands of the one who urgently addresses me. My partner tells me, jokingly serious, that in conversations with friends I not only intuit the affective response they might have had to particular events, but also try to make sense of this affect for them, offering an interpretation that they can grasp, leaving them happy without their quite knowing why. I have come to see that the pleasure I gain from such dynamics comes at a cost: the very keenness with which I attune myself to others' sadness muffles my own grief; the fact that I see others' anger, even at me, as understandable often makes my own anger seem unnecessary. And, of course, the very happiness I allow my friends to feel often has the effect of knocking aside their ability to perceive—and sometimes even their desire to perceive—my own emotions and responses. Being a screen on which the thoughts and feelings of others are projected, extravagantly, is a tricky and painful business.

In the context of such comments, I read my repetitive claim of being "alone" that marks the coda of "Courting Danger" as a defensive maneuver. Now I read it as a forced and bizarrely triumphant closure: a proclamation that, through claiming each person's separateness and individuality, promised reassurance that I could "stand alone," not overrun by others' demands and difficulties. My strident hope that others would not overtake my shadow gestures, I think, to a fear that the boundary between me and another person would be no longer ascertainable. To a great extent, I concur with Carol Gilligan's description of how, toward the end of my case, "[m]oral language returns to cover the loss of relationship and to justify giving up a way of living that was 'joyful and turbulent.' " But while I understand why Gilligan reads my lamentations of standing and living alone as a manifestation of my move away from "healthy resistance" and toward "psychological resistance," I cannot fully square that narrative with the path that I remember taking. For although my words then seem to speak of what Gilligan describes as a capitulation to "the ideal of perfection and the conventions of femininity" that I previously resisted, I read them more as pointing to a *fantasy* of both autonomy and familial harmony. Indeed, I read the last few pages of my case as touchingly optimistic: my claim that, once I had partially freed myself from Jessica and the art group I was "able to reincorporate and reaccept my family" was more an intense wish for such an eventuality than proof of its accomplishment.

I think that from my comments here you may be able to see why I have come to disagree with the polarization that Carol Gilligan's analysis seems to suggest. For Gilligan, my describing my time with the art group as "a dreamworld," as "insubstantial" and "unhealthy," is also symptomatic of my move away from healthy resistance and toward psychological resistance. I do not doubt today that my deep friendship with Jessica and my admiration for Ms. Tremayne were crucial and wonderfully liberatory parts of my adolescence. But this opening up of my world was, I believe, located on a precarious knife-edge, one that played suspiciously closely with a kind of hypnotic abandonment of self and stability. I cannot, therefore, make a tidy divide, as Gilligan seems to do, between the good (my "intense and powerful relationships with women," as Gilligan puts it) and the bad (my castigation of such relationships as "unhealthy in the extreme"). For while using the adjectives *unreal-*

istic and *unhealthy* may well have represented too harsh a judgment on my part, I do not think it appropriate to endorse wholeheartedly the dynamics between Ms. Tremayne, Jessica, and me. Those relationships, wonderful as they were, were founded on too risky a ground to be unquestioningly celebrated.

I never managed to show Madeleine Tremayne *Adolescent Portraits*. While I discussed the book with her and said I would give her a copy, a great ambivalence prevented me from completing my promise. My ambivalence derived in part from the adolescent insecurity I felt about revealing the intensity of my response to her; letting her know that my wrists "went limp" as I turned to look at her, mesmerized, was exactly the kind of action that during my school years would have made me feel skewered to the wall with humiliation. But the ambivalence also arises from my confusion, to this day, concerning her actions as a teacher. Madeleine Tremayne enabled me—and I am very sure of this—to break away from many of the limits that I, my school, and my family had imposed on me, but I cannot get straight in my head what I feel about the ethics of her pedagogical practices. Looking back, I see just how tightly and precariously she held us all in her imperious hands. Her tactics, practiced as much unconsciously as consciously, "worked" in the sense that all of us in that cohort ended up with aspirations and fantasies that successfully moved us out of weary ruts. But I do not know whether I can unquestioningly defend the risks she took. I cannot banish the thought that the move out of the rut for some could have ended in psychological catastrophe rather than success.

Another thing I found astonishing in rereading my case is the sensuality of its language, about which I seemed barely aware. I am still startled by the hunger of particular statements—how "I watched the muscles trembling in [Ms. Tremayne's] strong arms, the hair in her armpits glistening with sweat"; how I wondered at Jessica's "'grit' and stubbornness," her "sexual beauty." I have no doubt now that my investment in both Ms. Tremayne and Jessica was deeply eroticized; much of the excitement I felt when being around them was because of my interest in their masculinized unabashedness. Thus, although "Courting Danger" only briefly discusses directly questions of sexuality, I see that much was caught up in trying to pry open and understand the sphere of desire. By desire, I do not mean just sexual longing but a more general urge for and toward pleasure and excitement. This sphere of desire and pleasure was, and still is, incredibly hard to locate in my family. Indeed, I see both my parents and my sister grappling in different ways to find, hold on to, and flee from it. When I was 19, it simply seemed that I inhabited a house full of cerebrality rather than affective engagement. Now I think that it is not so much that my family doesn't have desire, but that the routes desire takes are so circuitous that the final goal of pleasure often seems a washed-out substitute that no longer knows its original aim. The time it takes my family to make decisions and accomplish actions is only one indicator of this. While my father indulges his rituals, my mother and sister endlessly ruminate over possibilities and alternatives. And time moves on, tracking my family's course of repetition and delay.

One way, therefore, in which I have etched a line between the rest of my family and me is through my long-fought-for ability to take pleasure in my own desires and corporeality. It is clear to me that the agonizing adolescent insecurities I felt about my physicality and sexuality are no more. I feel much less burdened by "femininity," and actually take a great delight in taking up, mischievously, stylized forms of feminine performance. The scarlet ball gown of thirteen years ago was the beginning of a series of sexualized celebrations of my femininity. I attended my Oxbridge graduation in a tiny Lycra dress with a criss-crossing of leather laces down its front. (This of course appalled not only my baffled family and irritated tutors, but other doting parents who shiftily tried to edge me out of group photographs in the quad.)

You will want to know about my sexual relationships—who wouldn't want to know what happened to the shy, gauche girl who couldn't get beyond the stage of soggy mouths? A decade does separate that shy girl from me. While at Oxbridge, I had two long-term boyfriends, for whom I still feel great affection, and several flings. In both relationships I offered and received much pleasure and love. The ending of each was painful, of course, but neither was vitriolic or furious. By the time I left Oxbridge, I was relatively sure of my ability to engage in, and maintain, sexual relationships. There is no doubt, however, that my achieving a more animated sexuality is largely due to the relationship I have been in for the last four and a half years.

I met Alex on the first day of my M.A. courses at another university in Britain. She sat beside me in an introductory lecture, oblivious to all those around her; I was immediately captivated. I see still her austere hand on an umbrella and her peak-capped profile that never turned in my direction. I would have to wait nearly three years before a relationship between us would begin—three years in which my desire for her would persist through a series of familiar irritations. First, she was going out with a close friend of mine; I held back from bringing a triangulated crisis upon us all by damping down my desire. Then I was a continent away in the United States: Alex and I strengthened our transatlantic friendship by disavowing our desire. And then, when Alex flew to the United States to woo me, my years of such practiced disavowal threatened to land us in a frustrated stalemate. Our long drive from Boston to New Orleans fixed, decisively, that problem. From the beginning, in Tennessee EconoLodges and Super 8 motels, Alex and I have excitedly recognized how each of us intensifies and brings to light the other's sexuality. Over the last four years this intensification has continued, bringing with it the great excitement and risks attendant upon a relationship that is wedded to thinking itself beyond the immediacies of the everyday. As I luxuriate in a newly found sexual and academic confidence, I am astonished at the shift four years has brought. Many of the insights about the last decade that I have shared here have slowly dawned on me in the context of my interactions, both conversational and unspoken, with Alex. I am as captivated with her now as I was in that lecture hall.

You may want to read my shift from men to women as being foreshadowed in "Courting Danger"—particularly as I have clarified here my long-standing interest in women edged with masculinity—but the line that connects the Melanie of that moment to the Melanie of this moment is not an unbroken or necessary one. I urge you not to ignore my ponderings in "Courting Danger" over whether other women are "just as obsessed" as I "with the muscles in a man's legs and bum when he walks." Those muscles obsess me still. Despite the complex trajectory my desires have traced, I want to stress that my fascination with a particular kind of masculinity and the unlikely ways it may be embodied has been an abiding concern.

I told my mother that I was having a relationship with Erica—the first woman I was involved with, and with whom I fell violently in love—on that fateful day when I was in Lycra, Oxbridge was at its most claustrophobic, and the sun was blazingly un-English. My mother, I'm sure, felt robbed of a moment in which she wanted to be coated in a nourishing fantasy—that all was wonderfully well vis-à-vis the daughter who seemed in so many ways to do no wrong. I felt sick and sweaty all day. My revelation caused immense pain for both my mother and me. But I believed then, and still believe, that my action was the only way in which I could pull a rent in the institutional and familial narrative that was tightly enfolding me. I was driven: driven not to acquiesce to the terms that Oxbridge and its admirers were setting out for me that day, and driven to reveal, not render invisible, a relationship that was for me so full and so immediately on my lips. Two crazy months followed in which I had to bid farewell to Erica (she moved back after her degree to Germany); write most of my M.A. thesis; negotiate with my distraught, uncomprehending, and desperate mother; and come to terms with my own great sense of vulnerability that accompanied the reshaping of my sense of sexual subjectivity. And then, three days after the completion of my M.A., and burning with the loss of people and things I could identify and of those I did not quite yet understand I was losing, I boarded a plane to a strange American city and started my Ph.D.

Without a doubt, much of the psychic work I have been engaged in over the last ten years revolves around the place I occupy within my family. And while the question of my sexuality has added to the difficulties that characterize my family members' relations with one another, it is certainly not the only, or even major, cause of the psychic work I have had to do. What has allowed me to achieve a precarious stability in terms of the place I wish to take within my family is a gradual realization that I have to keep myself to some extent beyond my family's grip. I do not mean I have to disengage; rather, I mean that I see that I can flourish only by stepping outside of the emotional structures my family keeps so firmly in place. The way my family turns in upon itself and fails to confront its problems openly is something that I partly saw and related ten years ago. Those problems, and my family's ostrichlike response to them, have, I fear, only become more ossified over time. For many years, I fought to coax out in my family a vision of "us" I had in my head, which, unsurprisingly, they would never have in theirs. This vision relied on each of us acknowledging, rather than disavowing, the durability of certain dynamics and our role in perpetuating them.

For several years now I have made do without such visions and accepted the intransigence of dynamics about which I can do very little. Nonetheless, the effects of my many years of immersion within these familial structures are long lasting. Isolated relics of the world of my adolescence reemerge in odd ways to disrupt my life now. To this day I shy away from the telephone. As I sit, uncomfortable, with the phone at my ear, it is as if I am unable to brush away the specter of my father. He not only hates being on the telephone, but also rails against the fact that family members take pleasure in using precious time for such a "wasteful" and "baffling" enterprise.

But the frontlines of my psychic work have now moved away from my father. I have come to see my father's obsessiveness as an indicator of his anxiety, as his ferocious attempt to keep at bay those increasingly large segments of the world that threaten his equanimity and desire for control. (In "Courting Danger," in contrast, I read his obsessiveness as a function of his being "centered" and "unflappable": at that point in my life, I think it was too hard to acknowledge that my father was scared of many things, since this would have entailed a questioning of the authority I saw and vested in him.) Sadly, my father's anxious rituals and eccentricities have become more unyielding over the last decade. Once I, and then my sister, departed for university, my father came to have fewer and fewer encounters and experiences that, in relation to his static and controlled life, inevitably seemed unruly. Thus he has been able to consolidate and expand his curious world of obsessive routine. His one connection with, and buffer from, the world outside is, of course, my mother. Frequently, his anxiety in the face of a mess of chattering people will be accompanied by a pitiful lament, "Where's my wife? I want my wife." My mother in turn has become accustomed to subsuming her own wishes and expectations to others' demands, especially his. Hence, she has ended up helping him maintain his circumscribed world while at the same time feeling an ever greater disjuncture between it and the remains of her life outside of it. When I allow myself to think about this, I am convulsed with rage and sorrow, as much with my mother's capitulation as with my father's cruelly all-encompassing pathologies.

I think my account here makes it clear why the father–daughter battles are over. The very fact that those battles were openly fought meant that my anger and anguish could dissipate. In addition, the clarity with which I now see my father's fragility means that I no longer need to fight for a change in him that I see can never come. And while this of course will never stop being upsetting, I am no longer possessed by this unfilled and unfillable gap. Instead, I am more attentive to how my mother's and my sister's inability to move away from the bind of familial dynamics has detrimental effects not only for those, like me, who are subject to the gravitational pull of their insistent discontent. I watch with acute sadness as my sister replicates my mother's confidence-less trajectory; I cannot help but feel that the anxiety of both my parents is distilled with fierce concentration in Sarah.

I should make clear that much of my academic work over the last six years has centered on psychoanalysis and late nineteenth-century psychiatry. Reading countless psychiatric cases has made me much more wary of the genre of the case study. I wrote "Courting Danger" in a frantic and agonized manner, perhaps seeing its form as halfway between a diary and a confession. Although I rewrote those thirty or so pages endlessly—I was oh so invested in how "properly" to do justice to each high-school scene, to each reconstructed conversation—I remember that my overriding sensation was one of startled relief. For after the scenes had been collated, after my tears had been spent while excavating forgotten actions and sorrows, a new sensation of clarity appeared. I had a very real sense of having properly recounted, and therefore digested, my history. I have undertaken writing this update very differently. I was reluctant, as I have already mentioned, to robe myself in adolescent anguish—anguish ten years old and still so keenly felt—at a time in which I am struggling to complete that most grueling of writing projects, the doctoral thesis. I also feel a guardedness that I had not fully anticipated about telling anything more at all. For many weeks, I was unsure whether I would be able to write anything about my family, sensing somehow that my words would not capture the intricacies of their stories and would offer too bleak a narrative. And I shied away too from describing the newly won pleasures in my life—most obviously those experienced in my relationship with Alex. Wanting to protect those pleasures has not sat easily with the demand that I share them.

I have blushed behind the anonymity that "Melanie" affords me as I have felt forced to pass judgment on the changes that a decade has brought. I see, frustrated, how those ten years have brought me far greater psychological freedom and exhilaration, and apparently brought my family so much less. I cannot shake the thought, guilty and stubborn, that my "escape" has somehow entailed the continuing imprisonment of the rest of them. Today, I see more clearly how I am the linchpin that keeps the family dynamics in motion. I mean this in two ways: I am both that which prevents a falling apart (my family turns, unhesitatingly, to me whenever there is a crisis) and the motor that helps keep the familial structures in place (my decisiveness exacerbates, I fear, their indecisiveness). It is to the arduous task of unpinning myself that I am devoting myself now.

9

Falling from My Pedestal

Living in a family characterized by disharmony and constant threat of divorce, this author traces her serious eating disorder to her attempts to compensate for her parents' unhappiness by being a perfect child. But no matter how hard she works or how perfect her grades, Chhaya's parents remain unhappy and even criticize her efforts. The emergence of adolescent sexuality creates a crisis in her sense of perfect self-control that is followed by the devastating news that despite her obsessive hard work, she will not be valedictorian. Drastically restricting her intake of food becomes a compensating obsession and means of asserting self-control and achieving perfection. Her health deteriorates and she is hospitalized. She learns that she must discover her own realistic goals and give up her "insane drive for perfection." Her recovery proves to be arduous and long, but by the end of her story she feels she has turned the corner.

So many people have asked me "How did you become anorexic?" that I'm about ready to tape-record my life story and play it back the next time the question comes up. I try to explain using the analogy of a rainbow. The entire spectrum of colors comprises the rainbow, but no single color can be extracted—they all blend together to form a continuum. The same can be said of the illness. Anorexia wasn't something that just "happened" to me—I didn't one day suddenly decide to stop eating. My problems ran much deeper than simply "not eating." The disorder was my desperate attempt to maintain some semblance of control in my life. It was a cry to establish who I was, to pick up the pieces of my shattered identity. To make sense of this insidious disease, and ultimately of myself, I must confront and examine the issues that led to my using the eating disorder as a coping mechanism to deal with the turmoil that surrounded and threatened to suffocate me.

I am convinced that my childhood represents the beginning of much of what led to the anorexia. My identity problem goes back as far as the elementary school years, and starts with my ethnic heritage. I come from what you might call a mixed background. My parents could not be more opposite in their histories if they tried—my father is East Indian and my mother is a typical WASP. As for me, I've gone through my entire life not knowing exactly what I was. I've always despised filling out standardized forms that ask for personal information, because I never know what box to check under "ethnic origin." The categories are neatly defined, literally black and white, and people who are "melting pots" like me present problems for this efficient form of classification. Technically, I'm more Indian than anything else, but I always feel deceptive saying I'm Indian when I'm really only a half-breed. Thus, I end up the perpetual "Other," an unclassifiable anomaly.

No one would guess merely by looking at me that I'm part Indian—my hair and eyes may be dark, but I'm quite fair-skinned. The one thing that gives me away is my name—my horrible, terrible Sanskrit name which I'm convinced no one on this planet can pronounce correctly without help. I have lambasted my parents endlessly for sentencing me to a lifetime with this albatross around my neck. I can't even count how many times people have completely massacred my name, either in pronunciation, spelling, or both—the number is utterly unfathomable. I'm forever giving what I call my "name spiel," explaining the origin and meaning of my name. Since such an understanding requires knowledge of my background, the subject inevitably leads into a discussion of my family, one of my least favorite conversational topics.

Even though my parents' relationship was tenuous (to say the least), they never fought in public. No one would have guessed they were anything other than normal as far as married couples go. At home, though, the masks came off, the farce ended, and the boxing gloves were donned. The match would usually begin at the dinner table. Supper was the only time we all came together as a "family," if you can call it that. It typically started with something insignificant like, "Why didn't you fix mashed potatoes with the steak," and escalated inevitably into the divorce fight. You could always tell when one was coming on. First, they'd bicker for a few minutes, then the voices would rise. The remark, "Why don't you just leave?" by either of them was the cue for my exit, for I could recite practically verbatim the arguments that would follow. Mom would snap, "You should go back to India. You haven't been happy since you left." Dad's bark ran along the lines of, "Why don't you move in with your parents?" In spite of all the fighting and all the threats of divorce that were made, though, it was always just words. Neither of the two ever acted upon their vow to end the marriage.

I think the instability and uncertainty of their relationship bothered me the most. The dark, intense fear always loomed in my mind—would this be the fight that leads to divorce? Is this fight going to be the straw that's going to break the camel's back? What if they're really serious this time? I'd be fraught with anxiety after every one of their quarrels. Within a few days, things usually returned to normal, meaning the usual strained relations in the absence of verbal brawls. Once I knew things were "safe," that divorce was not imminent and that we would remain a foursome, I could breathe a small sigh of relief, at least until the next argument.

When you're young, you think the world revolves around you. Given my egocentrism, I blamed myself as the cause of my parents' marital strife. I felt it was up to me to salvage their marriage, which I tried desperately to do. After each fight, I would ask myself what I had done wrong and how I could rectify the situation.

Harboring intense feelings of guilt, I lambasted myself for not pleasing them and not living up to their expectations. Maybe if I'd cleaned my room like they'd asked . . . I wondered. If I could just be good enough, I thought, they'd love each other and, in turn, love me. I erroneously believed I could bring my parents together by the sheer force of my will. Frustration over my inability to positively influence their relationship caused me to feel completely ineffective and inadequate. My solution was to be more perfect than anyone could expect a child to be, to hide all signs of anger and rebellion, in order to deserve and gain their love.

Being achievement-oriented in school was my answer to many of the problems I faced. By making the grades, I was sure (or so I thought) to gain the love and attention I so desperately craved, not only from my parents, but from my teachers as well. Because my family life was like an emotional roller-coaster ride over which I had no influence, I turned to school for comfort and security. I knew that by working hard, I could do well—in the classroom, I could exert complete control. As the perfect student, people would respect and admire me. Only if others saw worth in me could I be truly assured of my substance and value.

Unfortunately, my plan backfired on me. The more As I received, the more my parents and classmates began to expect I would continue to do well. I strove endlessly (and fruitlessly) to impress my parents with my good grades. At the end of the marking period, I would rush home, report card clutched in hand, hoping to have glowing praise lavished upon me. Words can't begin to describe the crushing disappointment I felt when they merely remarked pointedly, "We knew that's what you'd get." Part of me was angry at having my hard work and accomplishment minimized. Whenever I mentioned my grades, all they did was preach about how "Grades aren't everything in life." Another common point they made was that "Common sense [which they felt I lacked] will get you farther in this world than will good grades." I felt I could never win with them. It seemed as though no matter what I did, no matter how hard I tried, there was always something lacking, something else I could and should have done better. I yearned for reassurance and affirmation of my worth, but because I felt that I could never be perfect in their eyes, I could never be truly convinced of gaining their love.

These traits I have described were present throughout my childhood, but no one ever recognized them as potential problems. On the contrary, my drive to be good, to achieve, to live by the rules, and to avoid disappointing or arousing the criticism of others was what made me a model child, even though I never felt like one. The severe misconceptions I held became dramatically apparent, however, with the onset of adolescence, for I was pitifully unprepared to meet the issues of this period.

As I entered high school, I became even more rigid in my interpretations. My self-doubt intensified and my self-esteem plunged even lower. I was convinced everyone else was more capable, both socially and intellectually, than I. Never comfortable with myself, I constantly devalued my abilities, thinking I wasn't good enough for anything. Striving for perfection, for being the best (and then some), became my all-consuming goal, my purpose in life, to the point where I sacrificed all else. I studied all the time, believing that if I let up in the slightest bit, I would inevitably slip up and fail. All of my flaws would then be revealed, and I would be exposed for the imperfect person and the fraud that I was. To me, failure represented the loss of control, and once that happened, I feared I would never be able to regain it.

I became petrified of showing any signs that could possibly be interpreted as imperfection. I felt compelled to live up to and surpass the expectations of my parents, teachers, and peers in order to avoid arousing criticism, which I took as a personal attack. While others may have expected 100 percent from me, I pushed for 110 percent. So driven was I to succeed—or rather, to be seen as a success—that I imposed the strictest of standards on myself. Rather than creating a sense of pride, worth, and accomplishment, however, my role as the good, obedient, successful student—the girl who had it all together (at least on the outside)—caused me to feel increasingly empty inside. Paradoxically, the more "successful" I became, the more inadequate I felt. I began to lose control of my identity more and more as I fell victim to the Perfect Girl image in all areas of my life. I had no idea of who I *was*, only who I was *supposed* to be.

I denied myself pleasure throughout high school, never allowing myself to simply have fun. To do something for the sake of enjoyment brought forth incredible feelings of guilt and self-indulgence. I think part of this conflict arose from my parents' disagreement over issues regarding my (non)social life. My mother always had a tendency to be overprotective. She tells me that when I was an infant, she used to peek in on me, sleeping soundly in my crib, and pinch me ever so slightly, just to make sure I was still breathing. I think her reluctance to let me out of the house had to do with her overriding concern with shielding my brother and me from the dangerous outside world. At the time, though, I felt she was trying to suffocate me. I would vehemently protest against her fears; what reason had I ever given her not to trust me? "It's not you or your friends I don't trust," she would respond, "it's the rest of the world." My father, on the other hand, pushed to get me more involved with my peers. "Why don't you invite your friends over here?" he'd prod. I always found that suggestion rather amusing, given the nature of our household. If I asked to do something with friends, I was always bounced from one parent to the other to obtain permission, and usually they ended up arguing over the incident. As a result, I ended up feeling guilty for being the cause of their marital strife, a position that tore me up inside. Rather than jeopardize the family harmony (or rather, lack of discord) I often didn't even bother to ask to go out. I tried to avoid the conflict by removing myself from the situation.

I had friends throughout high school, but I always kept them at a distance, scared that if I let them get too close, they would see that I wasn't perfect and reject me. Relating to my peers was extremely difficult for me as a result, because rarely could I talk about my inner feelings. I equated the expression of emotion with weakness and vulnerability, so I always remained deadly serious and kept things on a strictly superficial level. To others, I must have seemed frigid, removed, and detached. I myself felt lonely and isolated. I desperately wanted to reveal the true me, but my intense fear of exposure silenced me.

Two specific events, both of which occurred during the spring of my junior year in high school, catalyzed the emergence of the eating disorder. One of these two major happenings involved my very first romantic encounter with a member of the opposite sex. Prior to meeting Kevin, I had had no experience whatsoever with guys. My self-confidence being what it was (practically nil), I thought no one could ever possibly be interested in me. An extensive "screening" process, with stringent standards that few guys could measure up to, was a way of protecting myself from unnecessary pain and hurt. If in every guy I met I found some fault that immediately made him undesirable as a mate, then I'd never have to worry about him rejecting me. I could remain in control and would therefore be safe.

My encounter with Kevin changed things dramatically. I met him in March at a two-day science symposium held at our state university. I had mixed emotions about Kevin—on the one hand, I found myself incredibly attracted to him and excited at the prospect of what might lie ahead, but at the same time, I didn't want to open myself up for fear of getting hurt. I wanted badly to be "swept away," to experience all the wonderful emotions described in romance novels, but reminded myself I should remain calm and levelheaded. After all, I was treading on completely foreign territory. My intelligence was of absolutely no use here, and since I couldn't rely on previous experience, I had to make sure I protected myself. Despite all of my hesitance, I was able to let my guard down long enough to experience my first kiss. Kevin and I, along with another couple, parked in his car in a secluded area of the campus. As the two in the back seat started going at it immediately, I sat uncomfortably in the front, eyes focused straight ahead. I was afraid to even look at Kevin, sure I'd flush with embarrassment. He would see right through me and realize how inexperienced with guys I really was. He was definitely the one in control here, as I had absolutely no idea how to behave.

We talked for a while (with his friends in the back continuing their dalliance), and then it happened. By "it," I am referring to one of the most monumental moments in a person's life—the first kiss. I had wanted mine to be as passionate and romantic as they come. After practicing on pillows for so long, I thought for sure I'd be ready when the time came. All of my rehearsing turned out to be in vain, though, for in no way did it prepare me for the intense emotions I felt. I remember more the mixture of thrill and nervousness that jumped around in my stomach more than I do the actual physical interaction of our lips (which I simply recall as being warm and wet). Thinking back on the event, I have to laugh at how it came about. I had undone my seat belt while we were parked, and when we were getting ready to leave, I couldn't rebuckle it. As I fumbled with the strap, Kevin leaned over to lend a helping hand, but instead ended up giving me much more than just a hand.

I was exhilarated by the thought that this tall, intelligent, incredibly gorgeous guy actually saw something good in me, something more than just my grades. He validated my sense of worth, and I began to think that perhaps I wasn't such a horrible person after all. Maybe there was something inside me other than the empty space that all the As in the world couldn't fill. Whereas my academic accomplishments gave me only a transient sense of self-satisfaction, the knowledge that Kevin liked me provided a warm feeling inside me that didn't fade away. For the first time in my life, I felt truly happy just to be alive.

In addition to the positive aspects of the relationship, there was, of course, a down side. I feared losing control of myself, a worry that was intensified by the fact that I was in completely new and unfamiliar territory. The incredible power of my feelings scared me immensely. In my family, I had learned the importance of always being rational and logical, of keeping my emotions in check and exhibiting self-discipline. Now here I was being "swept away," throwing all caution to the wind and acting purely on impulse and desire. The guilt I felt was extreme.

When I related the incident to my mother (the fear of telling my father loomed so large that I never talked about the relationship with him), I was thrown totally off guard by her reaction. I had pictured her throwing a fit and saying I shouldn't be getting involved with members of the opposite sex at my age. But just the opposite happened—she was glad I had met a "nice boy." Perhaps if he had lived in our town she might have reacted differently. Given how far apart we lived, dating was never feasible, so she didn't have to worry about my going out late at night doing God knows what.

Kevin and I had been writing and calling each other on a fairly regular basis, and I began to entertain the thought of asking him to the junior prom. Though absolutely terrified at the prospect of rejection, the encouragement of my friends and mother (who actually offered to have him spend the night at our house!) finally convinced me to take the risk via the mail. At the post office, my hands shook and my stomach quivered as I took a deep breath, opened the mailbox, and dropped the letter down the chute. As soon as the deed was done, though, I thought, God, what the hell have I done?! I'm setting myself up for the biggest fall of my life! How stupid could I be to think Kevin would want to go with ME?!

I awaited his reply with nervous anticipation, checking the mail every day as soon as I got home to see if it was there. When the letter finally arrived, I was so nervous I could barely open it. My stomach was literally doing flip-flops as I began scanning the note for signs of his reply. When I read about how he would love to be my date, how he thought we'd have a great time together, and how he looked forward to seeing me again, I was euphoric. I was practically bouncing off the walls, so full of exuberance and utter joy that I thought I'd burst with energy.

Within a week's time, I found an outfit (gown, shoes, clutch purse—the whole works), made dinner reservations and a hair appointment, and bought the tickets. Everything was in place when the big night finally arrived. After I finished getting ready, I decided to risk taking a look in the mirror. I was worried that I would find a brainy nerd who was trying hard to fit in where she didn't belong. The image that reflected back at me, though, caught me by surprise. With my hair pulled up and with flowers in it, my mother's pearl choker around my neck, the teal-colored gown flaring out around my waist, and the rosy glow of my cheeks (due more to my excitement, I think, than to the makeup I had applied), I was actually not half bad to look at. I felt as though I was looking at a stranger, for I knew the elegant young woman in the mirror couldn't possibly be me, the same person who always felt awkward and ugly. I truly felt like Cinderella, transformed if only for one night.

I was anxiety-ridden about seeing Kevin again—it would be the first time we had seen each other in some months. Everyone, both family and friends, loved him as soon as they met him. They all thought he was attractive, intelligent, and an all-around great guy. I floored everyone as I made my entry with him—not only had I myself been transformed, but here I was with a gorgeous date at my side. Finally my feelings of inferiority melted away. I had always been recognized as smart, but now on top of that, people saw me as attractive. The culminating event that evening was my election to the junior prom court. Normally a popularity contest, I never dreamed of standing among the four couples who flocked the king and queen. When my name was announced, I arose from my seat, mouth agape, as everyone around me applauded. Again I had stunned everyone, especially myself—smart people simply did not make the court. Proving them all wrong gave me a sense of uniqueness that I cherished. I reveled in my now complete blossoming from a former ugly duckling into a beautiful swan.

In spite of all its magic, the prom experience stirred up the same mixed bag of emotions I had felt when I first met Kevin, only to a much greater degree than before. At the dance, Kevin's open display of affection bothered me tremendously. I felt uncomfortable expressing my emotions in public, especially since I wasn't even sure exactly what I was feeling. I had no idea how to behave, and so I distanced myself from Kevin. If he moved his chair closer to where I was sitting, I moved in the opposite direction. If he tried to hold my hand, I would fold my arms across my chest. I wouldn't even let him kiss me in front of everyone. He was probably totally baffled by my behavior—I know I myself was, but I couldn't help it. Since I felt out of control and didn't know what to do, I turned to the only defense mechanism that I knew from previous experience had worked—isolation.

After the weekend of the prom, Kevin and I stopped writing and calling each other. To add to my confusion, my mother and friends expressed their disdain for my handling of the situation. They reminded me that I had had the chance at a relationship with a wonderful person and had blown it, big time. My mother, who had thought Kevin was one of the nicest, most polite, handsome young men she'd ever met, laid the worst guilt trip of all on me. She made it seem as though he had done me this enormous favor, for which I should feel some sense of undying gratitude and obligation. "Here this nice boy drove all the way over here just to escort you to your dance, and how do you treat him? Like dirt." As a result of others' reactions to my behavior, I became even more miserable and disgusted with myself. This relationship represented the first time in my life that I had tested the wings of independence and trusted my own feelings, and I had failed. The incident reinforced my belief that I was worthless and incapable of making decisions on my own.

I mentioned before that the prom was one of two important events that helped catalyze the emergence of my eating disorder. The second event, which occurred within a month after the prom, was my guidance counselor informing me that I was not ranked as first in my class. My very first reaction was that some terrible mistake had been made. There was absolutely no way I could be anything but number one. I was the only person I knew who had maintained a 4.0 GPA, with nothing less than As on all of my report cards. Becoming valedictorian had become my life; every aspect of my identity was in some way wrapped up in it.

When I expressed my disbelief to my guidance counselor, he assured me that no mistake had been made—I simply was not first. That's when the shock set in. I sat in his office thinking, "I have to get out of here NOW." The walls were closing in on me and I felt as though I was suffocating. I quickly mumbled something about having to get back to class and practically ran out of his office and into the nearest bathroom, where I let the intense pain that had been welling inside me burst forth. My heavy sobs shook my entire body, and I was hyperventilating so badly I could barely breathe. I leaned up against the wall and slid slowly to the ground, clutching my knees to my chest and pressing my hot face against the cool wall tiles. "How could this be happening to me?" I screamed in my head. Why? What had I done wrong? Hadn't I sacrificed everything for the sake of the almighty grade? Wasn't I the perfect student? How could I pretend everything was normal when inside I was falling completely apart? Afterward I fought desperately to keep up my false image of control and stability, stuffing my pain down further and further inside me in the hopes it would somehow magically disappear. Everyone expected me to be number one—what would they think when they found out I wasn't? If only they knew. . . . I felt duplicitous and deceitful, as though I was projecting a false image that was just waiting to be debunked. I was falling from my pedestal, and I knew the fall would be a long and hard one from which I might never recover.

The fall was even more profound than I could have ever anticipated. It devastated my life to such an extent that now, five years later, I am still trying to put back the pieces and recover. An eating disorder, however, was the last thing I expected. In my mind, I had imagined people losing respect for me, devaluing my abilities, and seeing me for the incapable fool I felt I was. That didn't happen. The only person to turn her back on me was me. I was truly my own worst enemy, endlessly berating and cursing myself for being so stupid. Gone was the radiant, smiling teenager from prom night, so full of life and exuberance. In her place was an ugly, sullen person who could barely drag herself out of bed in the morning because she saw no purpose to her life. The change was dramatic, but no one ever commented on it, perhaps because I was so good at putting on a happy face, and perhaps because they felt (or maybe hoped) I was just going through one of the low points that characterize the average adolescent's life. What others didn't realize was that this was not simply a phase that would pass in time—it was to become a deadly disease that would grab me by the throat and nearly choke the life out of me.

I don't really know when the anorexia actually hit me. Thinking back, it seems to have been more a progression than an event whose full impact hits all at once. Why I turned to food as a means of establishing control in my life, I honestly have no idea. I had never been concerned with my weight prior to this time. I was always thin, but ate whatever I wanted—in fact, I was the ultimate junk food addict. Chocolate, candy, cookies, chips—if it was bad for you, I loved it. These items were, of course, the first to go when I started my downward spiral, and as time went on, the list of "forbidden" foods grew while my food intake gradually but steadily diminished.

The earliest recollection I have of anorectic behavior involves its isolation more than the self-starvation. During the spring of my junior year, I began skipping lunch. My friends and I usually sat together during the lunch period, eating and chatting. Instead of going to the cafeteria with them, I started holing myself up in the library, where I could be alone with my pain, as I felt I deserved to be. My friends immediately noticed my absence and commented on it. I told them I was simply doing my own research into the different colleges that interested me. I wasn't completely starving myself at this time, but what I now know were the early signs of my eating disorder went unnoticed at the time.

It wasn't until that summer that the disease began to intensify. With the school year over, I no longer had to deal with my teachers and peers on a daily basis. Thus, it became easier to isolate and confine myself to my own internal world, a jail cell out of which there was no escape. I felt I was divided into two separate personalities—one jailer and one prisoner, simultaneously beating myself up while begging for mercy. I would lie on my bed, behind the safety of my locked bedroom door, crying endlessly. One part of me was saying, "I hate you—you're stupid and worthless," while another part was pleading, "Please don't hate me— I'll work harder to make you like me." It was a no-win situation, though. There was no pleasing the jailer, no matter how hard the prisoner inside me tried.

As the prison walls began closing in on me, I fought desperately to hang on. I got a job waitressing at a nearby restaurant, and tried to keep busy by working as much as I could. My work schedule made it easy to hide my eating patterns from others. Since Mom and Dad worked full-time, I was safe for most of the day. "I ate something before going to work and then had dinner on my break," I'd lie. If anyone at work asked about my eating habits, I'd say my mother was saving dinner for me when I got home. I was really clever about deceiving others, as most anorectics are, and delighted in the thought that I was able to pull the wool over everyone's eyes. No one would be able to figure me out, I vowed. By keeping to myself, I'd be safe and protected and could get back some of the security that I felt had been brutally snatched from me.

I started cutting back on my intake with the initial goal of becoming "healthier." I'll look and feel better if I get toned up and shed a few pounds, I told myself. After a period of restriction combined with exercise, I lost between five and ten pounds, and did in fact feel better about myself. The source of my improved self-image wasn't so much being thinner as being able to accomplish something with tangible results as reinforcement. I could step on the scale and watch the number drop from day to day, just as I could feel my clothes getting baggier around my waist. Here was something I could do successfully! Maybe I wasn't good enough to be first in school, but I certainly seemed able to lose weight, a task that presents enormous difficulty for many American women.

I read every article on health, nutrition, and weight loss I could find. I sought the diets that offered the quickest route to losing weight, pulling together bits and pieces from each to develop an elaborately detailed plan of my own. I learned what foods were "good" and what foods were "bad," and became a careful label reader, comparing caloric and fat content for a wide variety of foods. Going to the grocery store was a big production—I would spend ages in each aisle, trying to hunt out the products that would give me the most food for the fewest calories. Almost paradoxically, food became my obsession, the center of my world. Pouring myself into losing weight became a substitute for pouring myself into my schoolwork.

As with all other areas of my life, I gave 110 percent to the illness (when I commit to something, I do a thorough job). My insane drive for perfection, however, once again turned on me, in the same way it had done with my schoolwork. Losing that first bit of weight left me feeling good about myself for a little while, but then I began to question the greatness of my accomplishment. After all, I told myself, five pounds really wasn't that much—anyone could lose that amount of weight in no time with minimal effort. Now, if I could lose ten pounds, *that* would be something—shedding that much weight requires more commitment and dedication. If I could do that, I'd really feel capable of doing something important. Thus, longing desperately for that feeling of self-worth, I readjusted my target and continued in pursuit of my new goal.

Of course, once I reached this new weight, the same thing happened, and a vicious cycle developed. No sooner would I finish patting myself on the back than a little voice in the back of my head would squelch my pride, saying okay, maybe you achieved that goal, but I bet you can't meet this one. . . . I found myself getting caught in a cycle of self-destruction. Even though I craved success, I would go out of my way to ensure it eluded my grasp. As soon as I reached one goal, I'd set a new, higher standard. I was doing to myself the very thing I hated my parents for doing to me. Whereas I could detach myself from my parents, however, I couldn't escape myself. I internalized the frustration of not knowing how to please them, to the point that I was unable to recognize and meet my own needs and desires. Because I didn't even know how to satisfy myself, I was forced as a consequence to look to outside indicators of my value. My life became dominated by the numbers of the scale, which governed all of my feelings and emotions. If the number fell, I was secure and happy (for at least a little while). If it moved in the opposite direction or not at all, I panicked and tried frantically to think of a way to regain control of my body. I based my every mood on my weight, not realizing that in doing so I was setting myself up for failure—though I didn't realize it at the time, self-worth comes from within, and can't be found outside oneself.

As I continued my quest for a "wholeness," an identity I thought thinness would provide, I failed to recognize the self-destructive path I was following. My body became more emaciated, but all I saw in the mirror was excess flab that I had to be rid of. I rejoiced when the skirt of my waitressing uniform became so big I had to use safety pins to keep it up. One day while going through my clothes (which were becoming baggier with each passing day), my eye caught a glimpse of my prom gown, sheathed in plastic and hanging at the very back of the closet. I decided to try the dress on, just to see how it fit. As I removed it from the plastic, I thought about how far away the dance seemed—almost like another era, even though in actuality only a few months had passed. I pulled the dress on and zipped it up, only to have it fall past my bare and bony hips to the ground. Gone was the elegant gown that had transformed me into Cinderella. All that remained now was a mass of teal-colored satin lying in a pile around my feet. Though somewhat wistful over my inability to recapture the magical quality of prom night, I comforted myself with the thought that at least I wasn't fat like I had been then. Thinness was the one measure I could grasp hold of to convince myself I was better now than I had ever been.

I deluded myself into believing I really was doing fine. Though I experienced all the telltale symptoms of the eating disorder—constantly feeling cold (especially my hands and feet), hair falling out, problematic bowel movements, insomnia, amenorrhea, dizzy spells, skin discoloration, and the gnawing hunger that penetrated to the bottom of my stomach—I brushed them off in denial. I can recall only one instance that summer when I was forced to face the gravity of my illness. I remember getting out of bed and heading for the bathroom to take a shower. As I reached my bedroom door, I got a swift, overpowering head rush that nearly bowled me over. The room started spinning and I had to clutch the door frame just to keep from collapsing. My heart started palpitating and I felt as though my chest was going to explode. For the first time in my life, I truly thought I was facing death. I leaned against the door frame and let my body go limp as I slid to the ground. Stabbing pains pierced my heart so sharply that they blinded me. Oh my God, I thought, what have I done to myself? I prayed to God to please let me live. I'll eat, I promise I'll eat. . . . I won't try to lose any more weight. . . . I'll go back to eating normally. . . . Just please make the pain stop and don't let me die!

Being faced with the all-too-real prospect of death shook me up enough that I did fix myself something to eat. The frightening impact of the incident faded rapidly, however, and within a few days I was once again back to restricting. I passed off this danger signal, reassuring myself that since I survived the episode, I must be fine. When I tightened my grip over the food, I was in control—I was invincible, and no one could touch me. The eating disorder gave me an incredible feeling of power and superiority, a sense of independence. I could prove that I had control, that I could accomplish something on my own.

You may wonder where my family was in all of this mess. Didn't they see me slowly wasting away into nothing? I vaguely recall them nagging me from time to time to eat. I don't feel any resentment toward them for "letting" me become anorexic, for not catching me before I got as bad as I did. They were, I'm sure, in as much denial as I was. Acknowledging my disease would (and eventually did) open a Pandora's box full of problems, ones that went far beyond my not eating to include the entire family. My mother did get worried enough toward the end of the summer to call my pediatrician. When she explained my situation, his advice was to get me to take vitamins (just the solution to an anorectic's problems!). His failure to recognize the severity of my illness made it easier, I think, for my parents to gloss over the situation. Having a doctor's reassurance probably put their minds at ease. The family problems could stay safely locked away, at least for the time being.

I somehow managed to make it through that summer, and the beginning of my senior year in high school soon arrived. My mother tried to warn me of the reactions people at school would have to my emaciated appearance, but I could see no difference in how I looked now as opposed to how I looked at the end of junior year, when I was at least twenty pounds heavier. She was right on target in her assessment of the situation. I'll never forget the looks I received from my classmates and teachers that first day of school. Their eyes bulged and their mouths dropped in horror as they stared at the withered, drawn figure before them. Three months earlier, I had been a healthy teenager and now all that remained was a skeleton covered with skin. I was incredibly self-conscious walking through the halls, certain all eyes were on me and that the topic on everyone's mind was my dramatic weight loss. Feeling like a queer anomaly, I tried desperately to cover my twiglike arms and hide my body under baggy clothes. My answer to the stunned looks was that I had been sick and was run-down as a result. Though I found it perfectly plausible, my explanation was met with skepticism. No one pushed the issue, though, probably due to my unwillingness to discuss the subject, evident by my curt responses to their questions.

Within the next few days, the nurse called me down to her office. Apparently, nearly all of my teachers had voiced their concerns regarding my health. I offered the same excuse to her as I had to everyone else—yes, I had lost some weight, but would be fine once I had a chance to recoup from being sick. She was skeptical at my insistence that everything was okay, but I promised to work hard to get back my health. I was, of course, lying through my teeth. I had absolutely no intention whatsoever of returning to what I considered my grossly fat previous weight. Did people think I was going to abandon my quest for thinness just like that, simply because that's what they wanted me to do? No way was I going to let all the hard work I had poured into this project over the past three months go to pot! I was annoyed with others meddling in my life. Rather than seeing their concern for its genuineness, I was convinced they were trying to undermine me. They just wanted to see me fail at something else so they could laugh in my face. Well, I wouldn't let that happen! I'd show them that I could achieve! They would marvel at how well I could shed those pounds and admire me at least for that, if nothing else. I thought that perhaps by being successful at losing weight, I could somehow make up for my intellectual flaw of not being valedictorian. I was knocking myself out to impress others for no reason, though. The only one who cared that I wasn't first was me, but ironically, that was the one person I was unable to satisfy no matter how hard I tried.

I remember one key experience that clued me in to the severity of my problem. While going through candid photographs for the yearbook, I discovered two of myself. I picked them up to examine more closely and gasped in horror as I looked at the ghastly image captured on film. Her face was as white as a sheet, her eyes sunken, and her cheeks severely drawn. The blue veins bulged out of her sticklike arms, and her clothes hung limply on her fragile frame. She looked morbidly depressed, a pathetic creature who seemed ready to snap at any moment. Surely that person couldn't be me! Tears started welling in my eyes as I looked at that picture. What had happened to the smiling, vivacious teenager of the previous spring? She was like a rose that had bloomed and then withered away. I bawled uncontrollably as I realized I was falling apart. The life was being slowly sucked from me, and I was growing increasingly weak and helpless. Please God, help me get my life back together, I prayed. I don't want to die!

You may think that, having recognized myself as having this disorder, I would be well on my way to recovery. I know that's how I felt—now that I really *wanted* to get better, to get back to a normal life, I would. I tried to convince myself and every-one else that I could tackle and overcome this problem on my own. The solution was simple, I thought—all I have to do is eat and gain back the weight I had lost, and I would be fine. Unfortunately, it wasn't quite that easy. Anorexia nervosa had come to symbolize seventeen years of emotional instability, psychological turmoil, shattered dreams, and bits and pieces of my fragmented identity. There was a lot more that needed fixing than simply my diet—all of the issues that permeated my entire life needed to be confronted and dealt with before recovery would be possi-ble. It took everyone—my family, friends, teachers, and even myself—a long time to realize this and to recognize the full, devastating extent of the disease.

Though I really did want to get better, I was unable to regain the weight my body required. Having gone beyond the point of no return, so to speak, I continued to lose poundage. The nurse finally suggested my mother take me to a specialist, someone who might offer the assistance I needed to get better. I became absolutely irate at the very mention of the subject. "I am NOT crazy, and have no intention whatsoever of seeing a shrink!" I hollered at my mother. But she was adamant. The psychologist I went to see was unable to help me, though. My disease had pro-gressed much too far by the time she intervened. About a month later, she told my parents there was nothing more she could do for me, and recommended I be eval-uated for admission into the Eating Disorders Service at a nearby children's hospi-tal. Though I strenuously resisted the idea of hospitalization, my mother calmly but forcefully put her foot down: "We can commit you without your having any say in the matter." My parents were finally taking charge.

In terms of my treatment in the hospital, Mom and Dad focused more on the outer me—my body and its weight—than the evolution of my inner self. When-ever I spoke with them on the phone or whenever they visited, the very first ques-tion was always, "How's the weight doing?" My recovery became framed in terms of numbers, the very thing I was trying so hard to get away from. I had based my entire identity on tangible indicators of my worth—grades, class rank, weight—at the expense of my true inner being. As a result, I never established a self-directed identity. My work in therapy to evoke an awareness and understanding of the im-pulses, needs, and feelings that arose within myself was incredibly difficult and emotionally draining.

Before my admission, I had been closer to my mother. She was always the more reliable one. If I had a problem or needed something, I always went to her first. My father, on the other hand, was a lazy bum. I couldn't count on him for any-thing except for material objects. When I was in the hospital, this changed dramat-ically. Mom was like an ice woman. All the other parents felt guilty, thinking they were in some way responsible for their child's eating disorder. Not my mother. She staunchly and promptly informed me that she was not going to take the blame for my problem. At the time, I saw her as cold and heartless. I *wanted* her to feel sorry for everything she had ever said or done that caused me to be the way I was. She *deserved* to feel guilty for creating the sham of a family life I had to endure. My fa-ther, on the other hand, was easier to deal with when I was heavily dependent on him, as I was when in the hospital. I think he needed to feel needed by me, to feel in control of my life. He called me every night, just to find out how my day had gone. On his frequent visits, he would always bring fresh flowers, and we would sit and talk, watch TV, or take a walk. I remember on one occasion, we even made the bed together. It was times like these when I felt closest to him. I wanted to be taken care of, and he seemed willing to do the job. The combination of my not wanting to grow up and his wanting me to stay daddy's little girl helped to sustain this dependence. Though at the time I saw his behavior as a form of care and affection, I now recognize it for the power game it was.

Paradoxically, our weekly family therapy sessions failed to reflect these newly developed interactions. During that one hour, the family roles reverted to their usual prehospital form. At first, I actually looked forward to family therapy, thinking it would expose some of the important and volatile issues that had always been buried underground. Finally, we would be able to resolve our problems and, I hoped, become a loving, cohesive unit, the perfect family I longed to be a part of. Unfortunately, this miracle transformation didn't occur. Our problems ran much too deep for even a therapist to tackle. The sessions became as much of a sham as our family itself was. Every week it was the same thing. Everyone, with the exception of myself, shied away from the real issues, the potent problems we faced as a group of four individuals collectively termed a "family." My parents always wanted to discuss specific aspects of the Eating Disorders program, details that were "safe" for them—for example, "Why isn't she eating any red meat?" or "When is she going to get back to eating normal foods?" Getting them to recognize that food was not the main issue, that the eating disorder cut far deeper, to the very core of my identity (or lack thereof), was the most difficult task I faced. I would try to bring up a particular aspect of our home life—for example, my parents' marriage or my brother's attempt to shut himself off from the rest of the world. Before I could even finish my account, though, my father interjected, shaking his head and protesting, "She's making too much of this and blowing things way out of proportion."

The dismissal of my emotions as trivial wasn't nearly as bad as what came next. "Our family life may not have been wonderful," Dad admitted, "but it was relatively normal until she began this whole mess and disrupted all of our lives. She's the one with the problem, not us." I sat dumbfounded, not believing my ears. How could he possibly lay the entire blame on me? Did he honestly believe I had planned on becoming anorectic, that I set out on some mission to destroy our family? I refused to just sit back and let him heap any more blame on me. I had meekly taken all the denouncing for so long that I had internalized and turned it back on myself, resulting in incredible feelings of guilt and self-doubt. I couldn't stand the torture any longer. "You're wrong if you think I'm the cause of everyone's problems," I told my father point-blank. "We had problems long before I got sick." To my surprise, my mother then spoke on my behalf, saying to him, "You can't blame her for everything. We're part of the problem, too." Finally, someone was taking my side! I looked over to my mother with gratitude in my eyes, silently thanking her for saving me from drowning in a sea of guilt and self-worthlessness. At least she was beginning to recognize my problem encompassed much more than a simple decision to stop eating. Throughout this entire scene, my brother remained isolated and detached from the rest of us. When confronted, he would usually just shrug his shoulders. He had a grand total of two standard responses to the therapist's questions—"I don't know" or "I try not to think about it."

After six weeks in the Eating Disorders Service, I returned to the real world—back to my home and family and to my teachers and friends at school. Everything was pretty much the same, though. My parents still fought and my brother still shut himself off in his room. I was still obsessed with food. Though I had gained weight and was now eating more, I still kept a meticulous log of every (measured) bit of food that entered my mouth. I refused to touch red meat, junk food, or any kind of fat whatsoever.

Eventually, I had to resign myself to the fact that I alone cannot repair the immense damage that exists within our family. Without the cooperation of others, my endeavor is doomed to failure. I have relinquished my role as the family savior, realizing I am unable to control the behavior of my parents and my brother. I can, however, change my own actions and reactions within the family structure. An important, and difficult, part of the recovery process has been extricating myself from the dynamics of the family in order to develop and accept my own independent sense of self.

I can't believe I'm almost through with my college career. So many things have changed since I was a clueless, teary-eyed freshman. Now I'm half through my senior year. Within the past year alone I have undergone a complete metamorphosis, beginning with my revealing my anorexia to the world. I had wondered for so long whether I would ever be able to overcome this wretched disorder, and finally, I have reached the point where I can eat when I'm hungry and stop when I'm full. My recovery has been due in large part to the drug Prozac, which has also made me less obsessive and less high-strung. My recovery, however, has had its ups and downs. This past summer I fell into a deep depression. I felt like my life was spiraling out of my control, that everything I had worked so hard for was falling apart. I spent most of my days crying and mulling over things. I didn't even want to go back to school in September to finish my senior year, but everyone convinced me to do so. I got treated for the depression, and finally decided to take medication for it. I had adamantly refused to do so in the past, though an antidepressant was recommended by two of my previous psychiatrists. When I think back to how bad I was this past summer, I'm so thankful that I got help in time and was able to turn things around before they got completely out of control. I'm finally starting to feel good about myself, comfortable with who I am, and actually happy!

A big part of the change in me is due to LOVE. Yes, I finally met someone who was as attracted to me as I was to him. He has stood by me through some of the worst times of my life, through fighting the eating disorder as well as depression. I started seeing him nearly a year ago. Things were rough at first, mainly because of my inexperience and the issues I was having to deal with about myself. I was freaked out about sex and mostly about opening myself up to someone. I had been so egocentric for so long that it's been hard to give some of that self-centeredness up. I also had my first sexual encounter with him. That was another issue I had a hard time dealing with at first, but now, after having lived with him for the summer, it seems pretty silly.

I thought for sure that we would spend the rest of our lives together, deliriously happy and in love. But this past summer really put our relationship through the wringer. We've been fighting a lot, but more than that, I think we've been starting to pull back from each other. We pretty much both know that June will bring with it not only graduation but the end of our relationship. It's been really hard for me to accept that what I thought was an infallible, perfect romance is actually not immune to problems. I really wish things had worked out the way we planned them, but I guess I should have learned by now that life doesn't always follow the plans you make for it.

So, you might ask, what happens next? Well, I have moved ahead, and after four long years, I have finally beaten this disease. I feel as though an enormous weight has been lifted off my shoulders (no pun intended), and that I am finally ready to move ahead with the rest of my life—to "live, laugh, and love," as they say. I'm optimistic about the future, for if there's one thing I've learned, it's that I'm a fighter. . . . And, more importantly, I'm a survivor.

10 At Least We Got One Right

In this case, Brian describes his close, intense relationship with his parents. The third of three children, he is the "perfect son," the one who will fulfill his parents' dreams of academic, social, and economic success. Even as Brian appreciates and responds to his family's love and support, he finds that he must hide a great deal from his parents in order to explore friendships and relationships in school and later at college. Catholic school contributes to his sense of the conflict between the ideals and illusions people maintain and the realities of his own life and the lives of others. Brian struggles to live up to his parents' and siblings' expectations, to maintain the stable family environment, and to figure out who he is and who he will become.

It is Christmas. I am 19. My brother, 33 years old, is crying alone in the next room, his old bedroom. My father is not speaking, has been stoking the fire for the last hour, his face burning from the heat. My sister, a bruise on her left arm, is trying to explain things, screaming so loudly at my mother that her voice starts to scratch and fade. My mother's face is wrinkled with tears. Choked from crying, she barely has enough breath to tell my sister to get out of her sight—she says if she hears any more about it she will throw up.

My brother has just told us he is gay. For me, it is not really a surprise, more of an explanation, a confirmation of something I had already known for some time. A reason, almost, for why he has always seemed so closed-off and passive. I feel many things—scared and sorry for him, confused and happy for him, repulsed and empathetic—all at the same time. I would like to express these feelings, but I hold back. I don't let anyone see. Because I have always been the responsible one in the family, the flawless one, it suddenly becomes up to me to fix the crying and desperate silences that are now invading all the rooms in the house. I will have to start to calm people down, to change people's minds, to pull the family back together. It's simply the way it's always been.

For a while, even I thought our family was lucky, that somehow we had been blessed. Looking back now, after all that's happened, it is easy to see how we thought this, how comparing our own little family to our extended family and to the families we watched on the news or saw on the talk shows made us feel virtually untouched by life's tragedies. Sure, there were minor arguments (my sister spending too much money, my brother spending too much time away from home), but these were usually smoothed over before they got out of hand. Never were there any of the chronic troubles, any of the violence or drugs or pregnancies that rooted themselves into so many families we knew, problems that lingered and eventually tore them apart. We prided ourselves on the fact that these kinds of things had not happened to us and felt almost consciously that we deserved the peace we'd been granted. For this reason, my mother and father and older sister and brother and I considered ours the luckiest family in the world. We thanked God every day and threw that word—lucky—around without a second thought, always saying things like, "I'm so lucky to have a mother like you," or "You're the greatest sister anybody could ever want." We were always hugging each other, and we never left each other or hung up the phone with each other without saying I love you. In these very sincere words and gestures we professed how much we cared; there is no doubt in any of our minds that we all love each other deeply and with all we have. But beneath these words and gestures and love lay all the things we were all either too scared, too embarrassed, or too proud to say. Beneath it all lay the addictions that we kept to ourselves, the private pain that we hid for so many years and for so many different reasons. Today, provoked by a single night and a single announcement that forced us all to confront what we meant to each other, my family is just beginning to realize the cost of keeping too much inside. But in spite of all this and in spite of the soul searching and sharing my family has been forced to do, there are still secrets that I find myself clinging to. There are still some illusions of myself I can't afford to shatter.

Here was the American success story, the stuff of miniseries and Fourth of July specials: A man and his young bride fled war-torn Europe for America, settled down in the poorest area of the city, and began to make their lives. The husband, my father, worked seventeen-hour days on an assembly line. The wife, my mother, got a job at a dry cleaners that she had to walk an hour to and from each day. Once, walking home, she was thrown against a wall and beaten up for the change she kept in her stockings. To get out of this area, they saved up money and began a succession of moves into increasingly nicer areas until they reached one secure enough to start a family. This theme characterizes their whole lives: the quest to move up and out. They sacrificed everything and anything to make sure that their children would have a more stable and comfortable life than they did. It became an obsession, not just a goal or a hope, to keep climbing this imaginary ladder. And if they couldn't climb it themselves, they would climb it vicariously, through their children.

They had a girl first, my sister, then my brother the year after. My sister married at 19 (not because she was pregnant, of course, but because she was in love with a man with a good job who came from a wealthy family). She got a good job and gave birth to two athletic and bright boys who are now breaking records in their respective grade schools. Together they live in an area at least five rungs up from the area my parents settled for, in a house we used to gaze at from the road and only dreamed of living in. For a while, we were able to blame her husband's temper on his Italian blood. We called it part of his "color," and my sister laughed right along with us.

My brother never married or went to college or had very much money but did live the life of the swinging single, having the looks and the charm to do so. For a while, watching his age increase, his energy sink, and the women decrease in number, we feared his true love would never come. In his company, though, we called him the family Casanova and pretended we weren't worried. My parents saw education and marriage as the ways to climb the ladder and so my brother grew up constantly pressured to concentrate in school and date girls seriously even though it was obvious that he simply didn't have the knack for school or the commitment to a steady relationship.

I was born fifteen years after my brother, when my mother was 41. I am what my parents have come to refer to as "the best accident they've ever had." It is said that from the minute I was born I was something astoundingly special, that I lifted my head up instantly when my mother first held me, looking around at the world with a fierce curiosity and excitement. It is said that I was reading the *TV Guide* at 2, that by the age of 3 I was already writing my name and entertaining visitors with little shows and stories that I would create in my head. In grade school I won countless academic and service awards and never got a grade less than an A. In high school I won national writing awards and even spoke on national television. I'm not only the first in our extended family, one as far-reaching as Sicily and as numerous as seventy members, to go to college, but the college I attend has an internationally known and respected name.

In direct contrast to my brother, I did everything right. If my parents were always harping on my brother for screwing up even the smallest things, they were always praising me for even the smallest things I would do right. An example of this is how they took my sister and brother to Europe when they were in grade school. My brother cried the whole time he was there, clung ferociously to my mother's side, refused to do anything, and basically ruined the trip for everyone involved. When they took me when I was roughly the same age, I was "an angel." It's a wonder my sister and brother don't hate me for being the perfect one. I always felt guilt for the constant praise I got and shied away from acknowledging it when I was in their presence. It used to embarrass and anger me terribly when, in their company, my parents would lavish praise on me and simply smile at my brother and sister as if to say, "at least we got one right."

I can't remember one single time when our family sat down together and talked about anything important, any problems any of us were having. No Brady Bunch family meetings were ever called in our house. It was simply assumed that no one was having problems and there was nothing to talk about. Whenever one of us did something good, got a raise, a good grade, a new stove, we all talked about that for hours, praising each other and saying how happy and lucky we were. But never the problems. It has been easy for my family to think that because I am "a genius" in school, popular socially, and stable within the family, I am able to handle anything. It's not true, never has been true, and much of the control I may have been assumed to have has been an illusion. It is an illusion, however, that I have created myself and that I still persevere. I have let them see only my brightest pieces and have successfully covered up the others.

I was always a very lonely and morbid child, in spite of (or should I say because of) the academic success I had in grade school. Everyone knows the class brain is no fun, and boy was I no fun. I swear I used to wear three-piece suits to the second grade (there are pictures!), and my hair was always combed and parted so severely you'd think I was from Transylvania. And I was too mature for my own good, excited not by the things little boys should be excited by (mud, frogs, cars) but by fun things like what the last chapter in our math book was about and could the teacher promise we would get to it? Once, a month after our first grade teacher had randomly mentioned that no word in the English language was spelled with two consecutive *i*'s, I found a 45 by a singer named Amii Stewart in our stack of albums. I was excited to the point of shaking that I had proved my teacher wrong and actually brought the 45 in for Show and Tell. I got booed. I think even the teacher booed me. From then on, I was labeled as the geek.

Because of my geek status, I had no friends until the sixth grade, when I befriended the other weirdest kid in the class, Richard. We spent our recesses walking around the playground singing songs, and everyone called us fags. When I wasn't with him, I was at home making up math problems to solve or watching television. On Friday nights, instead of sleeping over at friends' houses or playing moonlight football in the neighborhood, I would sit up with my mother and watch soap operas. Many of my conversations with my mother centered around these soap operas, what would happen to J. R. or to the Ewing ranch, and we used to laugh and joke and pretend we lived in a huge house with servants and fancy cars. During the sex scenes, though, all conversation would cease and we would look stone-faced at the screen, not breathing, hiding every emotion, pretending it wasn't happening. When they were over, she'd laugh guiltily and say, "if your father knew I let you watch this . . . " and that was the extent of any discussion of sex that ever went on in my house. Any hint of sexuality outside of "doesn't your sister look pretty?" or "look how handsome my sons are!" was never expressed. As a result, I learned everything about sex from *Dallas* and *Dynasty.* I learned that it was dirty and unspeakable.

On those Friday nights my mother and I would sit in the family room with the windows open and I remember that I could hear all the neighborhood kids yelping outside, riding their bikes and making mischief. I remember feeling two conflicting ways: very sad and sorry for myself, sure that I had some kind of disease that made me an outcast and a weirdo or that, maybe, I was *so* special that I was too good for those boys. I know I was most convinced that there was something wrong with me, that there was some reason why no one talked to me in school and I spent my recesses helping the teacher clean the classroom, but what was it? I concluded that, fundamentally, I was an awful person. Or was it just that I couldn't swing a bat or catch a ball to save my life? Or were they just jealous of my academic prowess (my parents' explanation)? Or did I just need to be more friendly, more receptive? I was plagued with self-doubt and self-loathing, the fear that I was a freak. But I had also bought into my parents' notions that all of my hard work, all of my concentration on school, would pay off later and that I just had to wait. I was a mass of contradictions, sure I was headed for greatness but convinced deep down that I didn't deserve it, that I wasn't good enough, that I would be found to be a fraud.

I know that my parents noticed how unpopular I was, that no one ever came to the door for me, but they considered this a necessary sacrifice. I realized later that they were happy that I was unpopular, glad I wasn't associating with anyone who would expose me to interests outside of school. I think that they were lonely, too, my brother and sister having moved out, and that they were counting on me to keep them young. They wanted to keep me all to themselves, and in grade school I grew fiercely attached to them. I considered them my best friends in the whole world, and I loved being with them. I have fond memories of driving in the car with my father, playing games with street signs, him teaching me jokes and me trying to say them back. We would test-drive expensive cars we could never afford just for the fun of it and watch cartoons in the afternoons that he had off from work. He taught me card tricks and jokes and prayers and laughed when I could never get them right. I remember trying to teach my mother how to read English, using the old blackboard we had downstairs, giving her tests and quizzes and hamming it up as the teacher. I would put old 45s on the record player in the basement and practice little shows for her, then call her down and dance and sing my little heart out for her. I would bow at the end and she would clap and clap and say that one day I would get an Oscar, and I believed her.

My mom and dad would always say, "Friends will always let you down, but your parents will never leave you. We are the only ones you can ever count on in this world." Though I know that they meant no harm in telling me this all the time, that they were just trying to express to me that they loved me with all their heart, it is an example of the distrust they instilled in me, one that stays with me yet. They both always had a fundamental distrust of anyone who wasn't a member of the family or at least a member of the same ethnicity. I understand this distrust and paranoia and know that it is attributable to their own upbringing and the hardships they had in escaping the war and fighting prejudices in America, but I still resent the fact that even today it is very difficult for me to trust people. Even today it takes a lot for me to be convinced that my friends are really my friends.

My attachment to my parents, I think, is the cause of virtually all of the problems I am having today. As much as my parents came to depend on me (to keep them young, to fulfill their dreams, to fix all the minor problems), I came to depend on them to an unhealthy and ridiculous degree. After all, they were all I had, and they needed me. I have never felt so needed by anyone as I have felt needed by my parents. Because they are from a different country, they are very naive. To this day, my mother cannot read or write and my father can just barely get by. By the fifth grade, I was balancing their checkbook, filling out insurance forms, addressing letters, and writing birthday cards to their friends. A very interesting dynamic began to form: I treated them as children, and, as far as certain things went, they treated me as an adult. No wonder I acted so mature in school! I worried about my parents all the time, terrified I would lose them. Once, in Bible school, we learned that when someone contracted leprosy they were taken instantly from their home and never heard from again. For a while I lived in a paralyzing fear that my parents would contract leprosy. In school I would find myself short of breath, heart racing, worrying about returning home at the end of the day and finding them gone, my only friends in the world gone. Those, I think, were the first instances of the panic attacks that would recur later in high school. I was always conscious of the fact that my mom and dad were older than most parents and convinced myself that they would die before I got a chance to grow up. Still today, every time my parents are five minutes late I am convinced that they are dead in a car accident. I am always snooping in my parents' room for their medical records, making sure that they aren't hiding the fact that they have cancer. These fears are more rational than they sound. My parents are the type of people who won't tell their kids they are sick until they are on their deathbed. When my mother was going into labor with me, she told my brother and sister she was going shopping. When, two years ago, my father went in the hospital for a minor but pretty risky operation, my mom said he was working late. I can't even count how many different nightmares I used to have about going to their funerals.

I have always been a TV junkie. I think that I watched so much TV growing up that I sometimes find it difficult to separate what really happened to me during my childhood from what happened to characters I saw on television. Growing up, my greatest longing was to have the boyhoods I saw on TV. I wanted to track mud in the kitchen, to catch frogs with my bare hands, to race Matchbox cars up and down the walls. I wanted to step up to the plate and, for my teammates and the crowd around us, hit the winning run. I wanted to be carried home on their shoulders. I wanted to get in trouble with the neighborhood boys, to come in late, to skip school; to be one of the guys, to break the rules and risk the consequences, and then have my parents find out, get angry, but then laugh it off and chalk it all up to "boys will be boys." This, I knew, would never happen. Any rebellious action, any action that didn't involve bettering myself or bettering my academic career, would mean disappointing my parents and taking away their dreams. I refused to let myself do that, and so I never let myself get caught doing anything remotely wrong or making any sort of a mistake. Instead, the times when I did get caught were devastating to me. Once, in the fifth grade, I got a 58 percent on a social studies test, which meant that I had to have it signed by my parents. I was white as a ghost the whole day, barely able to eat or speak. I remember handing the test to my mother and crying uncontrollably. She called my father into the room and, after their initial anger and confusion (how could this have happened?), they began to *console* me because I was completely out of control. When I finally stopped crying, they told me that it was okay, that I could always make the test up, and that they weren't mad. But I was inconsolable. They asked me why, and I had no reason for why I was so upset. Now I know it is because that small failure, that fifth-grade fluke, was a chink in the armor that I had so painstakingly fashioned for myself. It was a mistake I couldn't cover up, and it meant that I wasn't perfect. How upset I was symbolized that I would never be brave enough to rebel, never brave enough to let them know that I was not perfect, that I was just like the rest, just like my brother; that not only did I have no friends, but that I wasn't even as smart as everyone thought. I always knew that I wasn't as perfect as I'd always been told I was, but that didn't matter as long as my parents didn't find out. I know that it is all still true today, that because I never let them see me make a mistake from the beginning, it's impossible to start now.

As a kid, I felt I had to protect my parents from the bad things going on in the world, the things like bad language, breaking rules, and sexuality that I was beginning to notice in grade school. These things were brought to me courtesy of a group of friends that I remarkably gained late in my grade school career. It came slowly, and it started with one person: Mark. He was the class clown, the most popular person in the class, and he lived down the street from me. He was one of the kids I used to hear from my window, and I would have given anything to be his friend. We had walked home from school together in the same "Walkers" group since first grade, but it wasn't until the seventh grade that he struck up a conversation with me and, to my amazement, invited me over to his house. I was beside myself with joy. I couldn't believe it! We hung out, watched TV, lit off firecrackers in his back yard. Soon we were walking home together every day, spending hours sitting on the curb in front of his house talking. It was a dream! I helped him with his homework and he taught me how to be "cool," how to dress, how to play sports. He introduced me to his friends, the cool crowd of my class, and assured them that I was all right. Acceptance from them came more slowly, but eventually it came. Suddenly I had a group of friends who called and came over, and I began to look at myself differently. There were people who admired me for how smart I was, and thought it was funny that I was too scared to be as rebellious as they, to go pool hopping or steal condoms from the Rite-Aid. Of course they didn't know that I was scared of disappointing my parents, but that was okay for then. The times I spent with Mark and my new friends were times I cherished and replayed over and over in my head. But the joy I got from these times, from the water fights and stickball games and popularity, was not enough to commit me to giving up my role as the class brain and family treasure. My parents disapproved of Mark because he was the dumbest kid in the class and because he had introduced me to sports. They didn't like me hanging around with him, but felt I was mature enough to pick my own friends and they didn't forbid me to hang out with Mark. My times with him, though, began to be plagued with guilt because I was always told by my parents that "You are only as good as the company you keep," and that Mark was not good enough for me. The crazy thing was that I believed them! I actually thought that I was somehow above Mark when I actually had so much to learn from him: how to get along with friends, especially boys, how to let loose, and, ultimately, how to enjoy just being a kid. I was trying so hard to uphold my perfect image to my parents that I learned to lie about everything I did with Mark. Instead of playing or riding our bikes across the highway, we were doing homework. I got to be a very good liar, and, since my parents were so naive and trusted me so much, they believed me. I felt incredible and irrational guilt. Here I was trying desperately to be the perfect kid, and all the time I was lying! Here my parents were supposed to be my best friends, and I had abandoned them for the dumbest kids in the class! I wanted so desperately for my parents to think that everything was great, that I was great, that my friends were great but that they didn't compare to them, and that they didn't have to worry. I lied because I didn't want them to worry, because I feared not their punishment but their disappointment. I wanted punishment! I wanted to be sent to my room without supper! The funny thing is that the things I was doing—climbing trees, sneaking down to the creek—weren't even that bad! They were "normal" boy things to do, according to TV at least. I didn't understand why my parents would be so freaked out by them if they knew I was doing them! The truth was that I never knew what their reactions would be because they never found out about them. I told them only the good things and they never found out about any of the bad things I did, with the exception of that 58 percent.

I went to St. Joe's for high school, a notoriously strict and athletics-oriented Catholic boys' institution that also had a great academic reputation. I was terrified of this place from day one. The Catholicism didn't scare me, since my grade school had also been Catholic. It was all those guys: 1,500 of them roaming the halls next to me, guys three times my size who traveled in packs and spoke with the deep voices I still hadn't acquired. Where was the tiny grade school where I was a star? Where was the softness of all those girls in their plaid skirts? All of my grade school friends were gone, the beloved group it took me eight years to win, and I had no vocabulary for these Cro-Magnons I now found myself with.

Mark was my only friend from grade school who went to St. Joe's and I clung to him as much as I could. But because he was tracked much lower than I was, I never got to see him during school time. I banked on the fact that because he still lived down the street from me, we would still hang out and he would ease me through all the parties and dances and football games that we went to together. It took me a while to realize that high school friendships are defined by the quantity of time that you spend with someone and not by the quality of that time. Because we spent the bulk of our time in school in classes with different kinds of people, the amount of time we spent together was cut short and we began to grow apart. We still got together and chatted every once in a while, and we still told each other things we would never have told anyone else, but outside of these times, I simply didn't feel comfortable with his jocular friends guzzling beers in the backs of jeeps, and he felt uneasy with the "smart people" whom I slowly began to befriend. We still considered each other "best friends," though, and somehow at the time just that label was enough. But our relationship was often tense: At the random party when we would run into each other, we were both conscious that the "geek" was talking to the "jock." Groups of friends on our respective sides would stare us down as we spoke, or at least that's how it always felt.

Those first two years were very lonely ones, surpassed only by my first year of college. I spent most weekend nights writing in my journal, writing angst-ridden poems about the fleetingness of happiness and the burdens of being young and alone. I wrote fake suicide notes to myself and dreamed of how horrible everyone would feel when they found out how disturbed I was. I would call in to those radio shows where people dedicated songs to their significant others and give fake names, pretending I had someone, feeling overwhelming bouts of self-pity. I wasn't doing as well as had been expected in school, either, getting my first grade ever lower than an A on my report card: a C in algebra. I was a wreck showing this to my parents, who promptly scheduled a meeting with this teacher and myself. It quickly became apparent that math and science (I was getting a B in Biology as well) weren't my things and that English was where I really shone. My parents were very relieved by this, assured that an interest in English would turn into an interest in law (I don't know who they got that idea from) and that I would make lots of money as a lawyer someday. I had a fabulous English teacher who encouraged me and inspired me to love literature and writing. At parent-teacher meetings, he would tell my parents I was one of the most talented students he had ever had, and my parents would glow for days. They convinced themselves that if I really wanted to, I could do well in math and science and that, if I had to, I could always go to medical school and become a doctor. It was simply a matter of putting my mind to it. I just shook my head, letting them believe what they wanted. What was the point in disappointing them?

It wasn't until my junior year in high school that I found a group of friends that really affected me, a handful of guys who seemed both winnable and exciting. These were the "alternative" guys, the ones who wore black and painted peace signs on their bookbags, who smoked pot and memorized Allen Ginsberg poems. They fascinated me and I felt a real kinship with them. Like me, they didn't really fit in with the rest of the people in school. Like me, they also seemed to think they were too good to hang out with the "cool guys." I made a conscious decision to become a part of their group. Since they were all smart, they were all tracked in the higher classes with me, and one or two different members of their group would be in all of my classes. I campaigned unabashedly—desperately—for their friendship, sitting next to them, striking up conversations with them, dressing like them, and saying things in class that they would agree with. I remember kissing up to their hippie contingent in my history class by asking, "Could you tell us more about the peace movement in the sixties?" It was very blatant, but it worked, and soon Gabe, the ringleader of the group, began talking to me. He invited me to sit at their lunch table (an absolutely crucial and risky first step), loaned me some of his tapes, and invited me to hang out with them on the weekends. Again slowly, and again with the help of one guardian angel, I had a group. I knew I was one of the gang when I roomed with them at a weekend retreat we were all required to go on our junior year. We smoked pot and did whip-its in the bathroom and I was in heaven. Here was real rebellion! Never mind the unbelievable guilt I felt doing drugs on a religious retreat, I had finally found a group of my own in high school. Now I was ready for Happy Days.

I began to drink and smoke pot regularly with Gabe and his crew, lying to my parents all over the place. Though they waited up for me every night no matter how late I came in, they were too naive to notice that I was drunk or stoned. My grades didn't suffer—they actually improved, I think—and things were relatively easy and fun. I was frightfully insecure about my group, though, no matter how much I was accepted. It came back to the learned mistrust I had gotten from my parents. I was constantly afraid my new group would discover I was a geek in hippie clothing and send me back to the abyss of nerddom. Even though they respected me for my talent in school and my eagerness to "try anything once" (as long as I could do it before curfew), I still held on to these fears. I would panic every weekend that they wouldn't call. When they did, the high from that renewed acceptance lasted for days. My insecurities came from the first six years in grade school and the first two years in high school when I had no one except my parents and a couple of Friday night DJ friends. I would do anything to keep from returning to that.

My senior year of high school was the best in my life as far as friends were concerned. There were parties every week, and I gained popularity with all different types of people. Though I still maintained the same group, which I by then was co-leading with my new best friend Gabe, I made other friends who were "cool" and, through them, even started to hang out a little more with Mark. I entered short stories and essays in contests and won national recognition, trips, and money for them. I read in a nationally televised ceremony in front of an audience that included ex-presidents, Nobel Prize winners, and published writers. I was accepted on scholarship to a top-rated school and my parents and family radiated pride for a whole year. "It was really happening!" they thought. I had the whole world open for me, and my family was convinced I was going to be a millionaire. By the time I graduated, I had gained a new security within my group of friends, which by then included girls from our sister high school, St. Anne's, and during the summer before college we spent every moment we could together. We were all going to different colleges, and we knew things were going to end, so we clung to each other as tightly as we could.

So much for friends. What about those other complex entities called girlfriends? The fact is that girlfriends, at least the gaining of them, has always come easily to me compared to the gaining of guy friends. It might have been because I was always told by my parents and family that I was very handsome and attractive to girls, which helped me to maintain some self-confidence when it came to talking to them or going to dances. More likely, though, it had to do with the fact that I have always been a little confused about my own sexuality. Though I have always been attracted to women, and still am, I have always felt an attraction to men that was stronger than merely wanting to be their friend or a part of their group. I didn't want to admit it then, mainly because I didn't really understand it, but I did know there was something different about me, a reason why when the other boys called me and Richard fags in the fifth grade it affected me more deeply than it should have. I had crushes on the most popular girls and the most popular boys in grade school, wanting to kiss them and touch them and be as close to them as I knew how to be at the time. Though I knew this about myself in grade school, and knew it clearly, I refused to believe it and waited for it to pass.

I never had a crush on Mark or Gabe, but there were plenty of opportunities in an all-boys school for these kinds of crushes. I mostly had crushes on the cool and popular guys, on the rich, clean-cut ones with the nice cars and beautiful girlfriends.

I think I had a crush on heterosexuality, on the strong man who knew how to handle a woman, on the guys who seemed more slated for the life that was expected from me by my parents than I ever seemed. More than wanting to be close to these guys, though, I wanted to *be* them. I longed for their strength and confidence, their coarseness, the sure movements of their hands. I was too sensitive with the girls I dated in high school, too cautious, and always scared I was offending them or pressuring them. Though I was incredibly and frustratingly attracted to them sexually, I was too "nice" to try anything more than kissing. I wanted to have my way with them and not care about their feelings, to treat them badly and have them love me anyway. I wanted to tell the guys in the locker room what I got off them. Just like in grade school, though, I wanted to want to do these things more than I could actually bring myself to do them. I was too uncomfortable with my attraction for the guys in the locker room to ever discuss girls with them and too uncomfortable and confused about my sexuality to ever be very aggressive with a girl, afraid that she would somehow figure it out if we got too close. Again, I didn't understand why the "normal" youth experience was denied me, why my life wasn't a sitcom, why I wasn't one of those skirt-chasing guys with a great smile and a whole lotta heart. Everyone around me, including the members of my group who everyone considered the hippie fags, seemed to be having fabulous heterosexual sex and wild experiences while I was stuck on first base.

I had a stream of steady girlfriends from the beginning of junior year when I first became accepted by Gabe's group. I went on dates with girls and had month-or-two-long relationships with them that included drunken explorations of each other's bodies and passings of notes that expressed the love we said we felt for each other. I dated Kim my whole senior year and we proclaimed our eternal love for each other. We even came close to sleeping together, but she decided she wanted to wait. We broke up before she could decide, and I left high school a virgin, the only one, I thought, to come out of there since St. Joe himself walked the halls. Though I did tell Kim I loved her, I never felt the kind of love I had come to expect from all the movies and TV I'd seen. There were none of the Bobby Brady fireworks, none of the puppy love I'd expected. Romantic love, to me, meant not being able to eat, sleep, or breathe without thinking of the person you were in love with. It meant that your mind was always consumed with thoughts of her only, that you'd rather be with her than anyone else in the world at every given moment. By those rules, I had never been in love with any girl, even, as it turns out, the ones I dated in college, and again I didn't really understand why I was being denied. I began to get scared that I would fall in love with another man. I hid my frustration and confusion over this from absolutely everyone and didn't even write about it in my journal in case anyone found it. I was waiting for it all to pass. I was waiting to wake up as the Fonz.

Now that I have had more time to put things in perspective, I realize that going to Catholic schools all my life has had a lot more to do with my adolescent difficulties than I originally thought. I think both schools I went to were fundamentally unhealthy environments because of the hypocrisy inherent both in the Catholic doctrine they taught and in the codes of discipline that were built from this doctrine. Both schools seem to have had a deliberate agenda: to establish a community of unquestioning believers through strict discipline, guilt trips, and discrimination against those who didn't fit in. Grade school, I think, is survivable because all the crucial questions about one's self haven't yet come to the forefront, and it is a time when you are still completely trusting authority. High school is the time when all these questions come to the surface and demand attention, and so it is the Catholic high school that has a responsibility to address these questions and help its students become strong individuals.

St. Joe's and Catholicism in general say they build themselves on one fundamental maxim: Love your neighbor as yourself. My earliest memories are of hearing this phrase over and over and believing that it was possible. At St. Joe's, we heard it every day and learned to feel guilty when we couldn't live up to it. The problem was that the school itself couldn't live up to it and yet would never admit it. Catholicism, a religion that stresses love and acceptance in its teachings, couldn't be more intolerant when it is put in practice. St. Joe's was a very sexist, racist, and homophobic place, a school that encouraged regarding women as objects (all the whistling and grabbing of the St. Anne's girls in the halls that was laughed at by the administration) and that favored its white majority by discriminating against its black students. (If you compared the percentage of detentions and expulsions given to the handful of black students at St. Joe's with the percentage of those given to white students, you'd find a frightening imbalance.) Heterosexuality was taught as the only way of life besides celibacy; homosexuality was evil and sinful. The school's goal was to combat the turbulence of adolescence by providing a regimented and strict set of rules, to provide a stable and reliable backdrop to the instability of the teenage years. It worked for the students who couldn't see the discrepancies in the church teachings and who didn't recognize the appearance-orientedness of the discipline code: the fact that it was OK if you harbored hate for a certain group as long as your hair wasn't too long or you were wearing a tie. I still clung to the beautiful parts of Catholicism—Christmas, Easter, all the pretty rituals—but was forced to reconcile what I liked about it with what I found disgusting: its hypocrisy and intolerance. Catholic school taught me the importance of keeping things hidden, the stakes of being different: losing your god, your family, your well-being, your peace of mind. This only fueled my crises of personal and sexual identity. The school that was supposed to love me condemned me and my brother, and swept us under the rug.

The Catholic religion, in spite of all I did to combat its hypocrisies, did manage to ingrain some very conservative views in me. I hate feeling this way, but a part of me still believes we were better off when mothers stayed home and gender and societal roles were held firmly in place. This comes, I think, from my years of TV (all those fifties shows) and from my longing for a stable environment that mirrored those families where everything was always resolved, where no one was divorced or gay or on drugs. Of course I know these families were fantasies, that everything that goes on today went on then as well, but that doesn't seem to make a whole lot of difference. In spite of the fact that I believe in equality for all people and tolerance of virtually every difference, in spite of the fact that I vote that way and do what I can to combat ignorance and intolerance on a personal level, these conservative feelings and wishes and expectations still creep up. I fear that I am just as racist, sexist, classist, and homophobic as I have accused my church and family of being.

My first year of college was a nightmare. I cried every day for the first two weeks I was there, going home every opportunity I got (my house was only an hour away and my parents were more than happy to pick me up) and feeling lonelier than ever. I missed my parents terribly, scared that without me they would grow old, grow sick, and die. All my kid fears resurfaced. I missed the everyday routines of home and neighborhood, the kids playing stickball in the street outside my window, the lulling landscape of suburbia I had taken for granted. I was paralyzed by nostalgia. I couldn't believe anything in the future could compare to my high school experiences and the friends I had there. I was forcibly detached from my parents, and I couldn't deal with the fact that my childhood was over, that I was no longer their little boy. I didn't think I could survive without their protection and stability, and I missed the babying and unconditional love that I had grown accustomed to. Who would love me like they? Who would be as committed to me, as believing? No one, I thought. I was a wreck.

Everyone seemed to be so well-adjusted, comfortable with all these new, incredibly intelligent people. The same way I was scared of all those guys in high school, I was terrified of the leagues of geniuses who weren't just in my classes but living right next door to me. I was scared of all the issues and all the melodrama that surrounded them, all the anger and hostility of activism. There was not one stupid person on campus, no dumb jocks or flitty girls to feel superior to. It was now time to prove myself, to really rise to the occasion, and I was sure I couldn't do it. I had always believed my smarts were a fraud because they came very easily. I hardly ever studied and I always managed to do extremely well. I relied on my talent in writing to get me through and distinguish me from those who could use both sides of their brain equally brilliantly. Mostly, though, I felt like the dumbest person at school and convinced myself I would never fit in. I was silent in all of my classes, scared to open my mouth, thinking my insight was juvenile. I rationalized that these geniuses around me were nerds who needed to get a life, who weren't as cool as I found I could be. I told this to someone on my hall—someone who would drink with me when I asked her—told her how I thought college would be, all keggers and one-night stands and hangovers. She flatly stated: "You're at the wrong school." I wanted to do all the college things I saw in the movies, all the constant partying and practical jokes. Instead, everyone seemed so serious, so into their academics that they had no time for fun. They acted like I did in the third grade. I started drinking more than ever to escape from it all, and, as is common to too many college experiences, that's when I started making friends.

By the end of my first year, I had established a set of friends that I loved, and I was very happy in that regard. I managed to find people with similar backgrounds to me and strike a balance between hard work and hard partying. I dated several women, but the kind of love I had always expected never happened with Jane or Hannah or Maria. Though Jane, the woman to whom I eventually lost my virginity, told me she loved me and I told her I loved her back, it never felt to me like true love. It always felt pretend. Though I had a very good sexual and emotional relationship with Hannah for a while, I never felt the all-encompassing love for her that I so desperately wanted to feel. We broke up amicably after three months, knowing we were meant for different people. I started dating Maria soon after Hannah and I broke up, and we had a sexual relationship instantly, but nothing outside of that. We enjoyed each other's company, but our relationship was mostly physical and we didn't pretend to try and stay together after she graduated. Through all these relationships, my feelings for men increased, especially after I found out about my brother and heard all those statistics about genetics and environment. I am terrified these feelings will eventually take over, in spite of the fact that I have never had a semblance of a romantic relationship with another man. Every recent relationship I've had with a woman has been a comfortable one, one I have settled for but not initiated, one I've sort of fallen into and gone along with until it was obvious it couldn't go on any further. There was always something missing from these relationships, something that prevented me from feeling truly happy about them and about the women attached to them. So many times after being intimate with Jane or Hannah or Julie, I would be overwhelmed with a tremendous sadness and guilt; sadness for my inability to give myself totally to them the way I had always wanted to give myself up, and guilt for my unwillingness to be completely truthful with them.

I grew to love college life, the freedom of it, but I still needed to go home every Sunday. I needed a break from all the intensity and I needed to see my parents, to make sure they were okay. My mother cried every time I pulled into the driveway and every time I left to go back to school. My not coming home, though, would have killed my parents, who centered their weeks on these Sundays, preparing feasts made for kings on my arrivals and pampering me shamelessly. It made me feel guilty; guilty, I think, for growing up, for moving away from being their baby into becoming my own man. I regressed in their presence. I didn't want them to think I was having any growth experiences, and so I, of course, lied about what I was doing in school. According to my parents, I did nothing but study and go to the occasional movie. They knew none of the real stories, none of the drinking or drugs or the men I was fantasizing about or what I was doing with the women I was seeing. Again, this was my fault. How were they to know if I didn't tell them? And how was I to start? How was I going to sit them down and say that this had been going on for years, that who they had known as their son for twenty years was someone completely different, someone with desires and faults and addictions?

What does a family do when its tradition of lies and covering up starts to break? What does a family that has never let the word *sex* come over its lips do when one of its members says he is gay (i.e., a disgusting pervert, a demon, doomed to hell?). Mine reacted with tears and anger, and it was up to me, the one who supposedly had no secrets, to patch things up.

My brother apologized to me, said he couldn't help the way he was. He said he hoped I wasn't embarrassed by him. My sister hugged me, said she knew I would understand, because I was the only one with his head on straight. My father shook his head, then said, "Thank God I still have one real son." My mother clutched me so tight that my ribs ached, while crying into my shirt. She managed to say, "You are the only one who has ever made me happy."

But they were talking to a stranger, someone they didn't know. I wanted them to know me, and I wanted to say to my brother: "You don't have to apologize. More and more I am being convinced that I am just like you. Despite all the pretty girlfriends I've had, there has been an inkling of something different about me, something I refuse to acknowledge. You are not alone, and my head is not on as straight as they think." I wanted to say this, to assure him that he was not alone in this, but I was too scared. Instead of saying what I wanted, I hugged him and said, "Everything will be all right. Mom and Dad will understand because they love you, and I understand because I love you." He hugged me back tightly, tears of relief streaming down his face. He hugged me as if I was the last person on Earth, and I envied him because he had the courage to begin to free himself.

I wanted to tell my sister that it was time to follow my brother's lead and come clean with the problems she was having in her marriage, to leave Bill and get out of that situation. I wanted to tell her that I understood how badly she wanted us all to think she had the perfect family, how it was the only thing she had ever been appreciated for and that she didn't want to screw it up and seem like a failure. Instead, I took her arm and said: "Stop yelling at Mom; you're not making things any better. She'll be okay; I'll talk to her later. But now you should just go home." She said she trusted me to calm things down.

To my father, I wanted to say: "Don't count on me to make things right because I'm terrified of life and of my future. You have two sons, and you should remember that more often, because I won't be able to cover my tracks for much longer and you'll see that I'm just like the rest—not smart, not talented—that I'm just as bad as the rest." But instead, I told him in the deepest voice I could muster: "He's going through a rough time right now, and he needs us. Sure, you don't have to worry about *me* (I can't believe I'm saying this, digging my hole even deeper), but *he's* your son, too, and he needs you. Don't abandon him this way." He considered this, because my words carried weight, and kept stoking the fire.

To my mother, I wanted to say: "Don't you know how many times I've made mistakes, how many times I've come home stumbling, driven the car drunk; don't you know I've stolen things from stores, had sex with girls, fantasized about men, lied about grades; don't you know how sad I've been, petrified of my future, how I've wanted to get out of this house and this area of the world for so long, to break free of you and Dad, and yet have been too scared to leave you by yourselves? Don't you know how I have been paralyzed with fear that I would lose you and yet, sometimes, I have wished for that very thing? Don't you know I'm not as innocent as you think?" But instead I said, stroking her hair, "Shh, it'll be okay, I'm here, Shh, things will work out, I love you, Shh, stop crying now, there's no reason to cry, I'm here, Shh."

I played the part like the actor I have grown up to be.

Today, it is disturbing to me that I am still wearing the same masks I have worn since the first grade. The stakes have risen, though, now that I am about to graduate from college and begin to make my way in the world. There is a lot that's expected of me, and the overwhelming feeling that I have as I think about the future is guilt: guilt for the lies I've told and the people I've betrayed into a false hope. I know that what I want to do with my life—write—won't be enough for my parents. I know they are expecting more than I will ever be able to deliver, from the amount of my paycheck to the structure of my lifestyle. Scarier than how well I know that I can't keep all the pretending up for long is how much keeping my perfect image intact matters to me. I won't let myself disappoint them—I can't—because with every chink in my armor a little love will be lost, a little respect taken away. I won't settle for anything less than the hyperbolic love I've received from them throughout my life. I knew it as a child and I know it now: There is no one else out there who will love me the way my family has loved me. Unlike my family, others are not blinded by any happiness or hope or expectations that they have invested in me over these many years; therefore, others see my mistakes and faults and realize that I am nothing special.

I do consider myself lucky for the love I have received from my family. There are some people out there reading this who have never felt or will never feel the strength of such a love. But it has been a mixed blessing: It has given me support and protection and many happy memories, but has also stifled me from being all that I could be. To fit it into a popular cliché, the love of my family has given me roots, but no wings. For now I am desperately holding on to my roots, scared to shake things up any further, playing the role of the perfect son with however much pain and deceit it takes.

Brian: Three Years Later

It is Memorial Day. I am 24. My brother has invited me to a barbecue at his partner's house; he never misses a chance to spend time with me, hopeful that this will be the summer we finally connect. My sister is organizing a party of her own to celebrate the sprawling stone mansion she and Bill have just bought. Bill is calmer now since being promoted, but my sister has spread herself thin with the worry of a forty-something working mother; her physical bruises have been replaced (as far as I know) with intense anxiety and the panic attacks we've both inherited. My parents, still in the dark about any of their children's anxieties, have never been happier. I've chosen to spend a month with them before returning to grad school; they've fixed up my old room, cooked my favorite meals, and treated me like a movie star forced to lay low a while. Sometimes I catch them staring at me, starstruck, amazed at their luck at having me home. But when they stretch their arms to hold me, bury their heads in my chest (I'm taller now and can rest my head on my father's when he hugs me), I feel mostly grief, a profound longing for the life we've never had. We are still strangers.

My relationship with my family has always been defined by longing. I have lived six hours from them for the past three years, but I still speak with my parents every day on the phone, mainly for us both to make sure that we're still alive. We never discuss anything beyond the weather, what we've made for dinner, or how we're doing at work and in school. I experienced a minor victory when I convinced them that I didn't need to talk to them on Thursdays or Fridays, that I was just too busy to call, until Thursdays and Fridays would come around, and I'd feel that same fear I felt when I was younger—that while I was off living my carefree, selfish life, they were somewhere in danger, dying, in pain. I braced myself every Saturday morning when I called them, and when I heard both of their voices, I'd relax and settle into the pleasantries of conversation, feeling guilty but thankful to have them in my life. During our conversations, the longing would always mount: I'd want to tell them about my life, have them share in my worry and confusion, but instead I'd keep silent, focusing on my honors and intermittent happinesses; after I hung up, the anxiety would rebuild until Sunday morning, when the cycle would begin again.

My friend Gail told me recently that I was unhealthily obsessed with my parents. At first I took her comment the way I took it when my ex-girlfriend Hannah years ago accused me of not being close to my parents—I refused to believe either comment was true and vigorously defended my family's unique understanding and abiding, if blind, love. Now I know both women were right. I am not close to my parents because they don't know me, and though I'm obsessed with the fact that they don't know me, I'm completely unable to make myself known to them. Though my therapist maintains that my parents never allowed me to express myself openly to them, that they carry the bulk of the blame for our shared inability to be honest about our mistakes and fears, I take on most of the burden. I feel that my parents raised me the best way they knew and that, if I were stronger, I would be able to be honest with them, and we could enjoy each other for the rich, complex, beautiful, flawed people we are.

Though I feel I have come a long way since writing "At Least We Got One Right," in the presence of my family I am still the same high-achieving, peacemaking, jolly savior I described then. If anything, because of my graduate school and work experience as both a high school and college teacher and my ability to live independently in a distant city and yet keep close ties with friends and maintain an active social life, they view me even more as a hero. I have since learned that no one in my extended family has ever lived more than two hours from their original home (not counting emigrations, of course); one of my cousins, for example, attempted to attend college across the country but dropped out only three months later. She returned home emaciated and depressed, apparently malnourished on a life away from her overprotective family. Within, I am like this girl—seething, scared, lonely, anxious, dreamy, vaguely hopeful, and constantly waiting for my life to begin, yet I have somehow been able to hide all of these conflicting emotions under an elaborately detailed mask of control, reason, and satisfaction.

I am amazed at how much I both knew and didn't know about myself when I was 19. As you can already tell, the same issues are still as salient now as they were five years ago—a fact that is even more startlingly disheartening when I remember they are the same issues that plagued me as a child—and I am impressed that I was able to isolate these issues as clearly as I did in that piece. That I was able to recognize my constant fear of being found a "fraud" (still a major fear today), my inverted relationship with my parents, and that "my attachment to my parents . . . is the cause of virtually all of the problems I am having today" convinces me that adolescents are all too aware of the nature of their needs and fears, and that they may even know how to address them. Though isolating these issues (then and now) has not prompted me to actively improve my family dynamic, I believe it has allowed me, over time and by much risk taking, to be more honest with myself. Most important, it has given me the courage to make myself known to others (to friends, co-workers, etc.—anyone not related to me).

Three major issues have marked my past five years: the remembrance of sexual abuse I endured as a child, a continued conflict with my own sexual orientation, and the treatment of my panic disorder through therapy and antianxiety medication. Though I have taken decisive steps to deal with these immense issues, I still have a long way to go to achieve some sense of peace with them and to integrate them healthily into my family and social life. Attempting to separate these three issues from each other, to order them or arrange their cause and effect, is as difficult as distilling the subtleties of my identity development down to ten thousand words or less. Yet, mercifully cathartic, writing this essay helps me to see that certain issues remain broader and less unique than I once suspected. I know now more than ever that I'm not alone, and it helps somehow that you the reader are sharing a part of my life with me.

I spent an anxious and lonely year living at home after college, teaching at a local high school and attempting to salvage a social life out of the few friends left in the area. That Christmas my parents and I vacationed in Europe in the country from which my parents emigrated, and though I felt connected to my heritage there, identifying strongly with the passionate esthetes in my mother's family, I was distanced by language and oppressed by my parents' constant presence and attention. They were literally the only people I could talk to; we ate every meal together, slept in the same rooms, and packed ourselves tightly into tiny cars on endless sightseeing tours. Midway through the trip, I began having inexplicably gruesome nightmares of being chased, trapped, or smothered. One day toward the end of the trip, as I was peacefully writing in my journal about watching my grandmother with my mother and enjoying a rare moment to myself in the early morning, I began to think about those Friday nights I wrote about so nostalgically in "At Least We Got One Right," when my mother and I would watch soap operas, and I would listen longingly at the window for the neighborhood boys playing outside. It's true that I learned that sex was "dirty and unspeakable" on those nights but not only from the soaps we watched and my mother's dubious censorship. I came to remember, simply by writing it down during that day amidst the beauty of my ancestral home, how, after the soaps were over and before my father got home, my mother and I would crawl into her bed together, and she would sexually mistreat me. There was never any physical penetration, anything that could have been construed as rape, but mostly a lot of inappropriate touching that seems now a lot like wrestling or horseplay. At first the details were very vague but real; unfortunately, since remembering them, they have become more and more real, and they are clear, damaging, and frightening. I was so young, so trusting, and so entranced by my mother (she looked like Audrey Hepburn and acted with as much style and sophistication; she was my best audience for all my silly stories; and she was my best friend) that I never thought twice about expressing affection to her then, about touching her and letting her touch me. Our family was always very physically affectionate, so this did not seem extraordinary at the time.

In the last few years, dealing with these memories in therapy and on my own, I have felt a range of emotions both all at once and in stages: intense confusion, disbelief, anger, guilt, sadness, embarrassment. I have felt like damaged goods; I have felt betrayed. Writing this feels like another betrayal. I still love my mother, but I will never forgive the physical, emotional, and metaphoric ramifications of her actions— my inability to trust anyone (especially the women) I've dated or see them in any way other than as suffocaters (there is always the image—and sensation—of my mother's body on top of me, crushing me; it's as real as if it were happening to me now); my fear and intermittent repugnance of women's bodies; the feeling of fear at the end of every night with a woman or a man that I will be forced to please them. In the four years since I have remembered those nights, I have not been able to maintain an intimate (sexual and emotional) relationship with a woman or a man. Every time

I am with someone romantically, I am 8 years old again, and he or she is my mother, and I am being seduced against my will, forced to do what I feel duty bound to do, not what I actually want to do. I don't really know what I want to do or whether I even want to do anything except feel safe. I am left lying next to my boyfriend or girl-friend, ashamed and heartbroken, scared and embarrassed, pouring my heart out to him, trying to explain, telling her the whole story (I don't lie to anyone except my family). Everyone I have dated has always been patient, kind, and understanding—with few exceptions anything but suffocating, demanding, or sexually aggressive—and offered to see me through my problems, but I don't let them. I've rejected and broken up with all of them, hoping that with the next person I'll be okay, I'll be over it. I'm still waiting, longing for that next person. I am most afraid that my mother's abuse has ultimately denied me the capacity to love anyone fully, that her systematic betrayal has forever prevented me from achieving what I've always regarded as my highest goal: a family of my own to love and care for, to whom I would be devoted. I spend hours alone in restaurants and coffee shops now writing in my journal, look-ing around, glancing shyly at attractive strangers, hoping for some glorious revela-tion in his or her eyes, hoping to be rescued by them.

Of course no one in my family knows about the abuse; I have only told my therapist, two close friends, and the three people I have dated since my trip to Eu-rope. I can't bear my own shame in reliving it again, but I especially can't bear the look of pity in their eyes that says, "how awful for you; you must really be fucked up." The only way I've found to coexist peacefully with my mother is to mytholo-gize her, to find reasons for what she did. I know she was lonely; I know she thought she was doing nothing wrong, that we were just "playing"; I know she has always been a very seductive woman, taking pride in—and using—her beauty and personality to get what she wanted; I know those nights were her way of letting me know she thought I was just as beautiful as she and that she loved me. I also know I was desperate for attention and that I must have enjoyed feeling "special," yet I can't determine whether my lifelong need to be the best in everything began before those nights or after. These days, I can barely hug my mother without shuddering, though I do it anyway. It's difficult for me to tell her I love her, though I do it almost every day and though I'm constantly—without reserve or hesitation, with only boundless affection—telling my father that I love him.

Before and after my trip to Europe, I believed that being with a man would be the answer to my fear of intimacy and my inability to truly enjoy sex or feel com-fortable in a relationship. I had convinced myself that my biggest problem was my inability to accept my homosexuality and that once I came out, I would (like my brother) finally achieve peace. I had a short, secretive, and purely sexual fling with a man during my last year of college, and though at first it felt exciting, instinctual, and good, I eventually began to fear him and distrust him, afraid not so much that he would tell people (I had already begun that process, coming out as bisexual to my friends) but that he expected more from the relationship than I could give him. He was talking love, but I wanted only to feel physical closeness with a man; I didn't see that the two could go together. Eventually, I turned him into my mother and avoided him. I had a similar experience with a female housemate a year or so later: We drank, we had sex, we talked, she wanted more, I turned her into my mother, she betrayed me, I fled.

My most significant relationship has been with an older man named Mark who I met in grad school. At first the relationship was all very romantic, like something out of a movie. We met at a party (my first all-gay party) and talked the entire night on the couch, unable to get enough of each other's company. He was a doctor (a real catch!) and handsome, if not exactly the boyish type I always desired. We went on a few dates, taking it slow, revealing ourselves to each other soberly, jumping into bed with clear, informed heads, one eye on safety in this age of AIDS, the other eye on pure excitement about sleeping with someone you knew and were beginning to fall for. This experience in itself was new: None of my relationships had begun so maturely. Most were stereotypically "college romances," where the sex and alcohol came first and the questions later. For that reason, I think, I was happy the first few weeks I dated Mark; I felt grown-up, honest, balanced, and protected. I was in control of my own emotions in a relationship that was a true partnership. I hated my inability to tell my parents about us, but since lying to them has always been second nature, covering up our relationship proved easy; if all worked out, I told myself, I would stop lying and present Mark to them saying, "love me, love us," or some equally dramatic gesture.

But soon, not really surprisingly, the pattern reemerged. Mark talked of the future, of love and destiny, and I grew repulsed by his sentimentality and uncomplicated approach to such immense possibilities; I was afraid of his clinging, of his expectations that I could never fulfill. I grew to feel trapped and put upon; every moment with him felt like a chore I had to perform before gaining permission to seek fun somewhere else, with anyone but him. I told him all of this, along with what I believed to be the origin of these feelings, and he was patient and understanding—so patient that I began to lose respect for him, thinking him needy, desperate, and of questionable taste (I am, of course, one of those who would never belong to a club that would have me as a member). We are friends now, despite the last few weeks of our relationship when he painfully attempted to reconnect with me, and when I—guilt-ridden but with equal force—pulled away, shutting him out of my heart, mind, and social life. I look to his friends, as I look to strangers in coffee shops, as potential lovers now. The answer lies always in whomever I haven't yet chosen; then when I choose him or her, the answer lies in someone else. My most enduring fear is that no one will ever prove good enough—that there is no real answer. I fear that that awful, repeated, physical and metaphoric violation of will and desire I experienced those Friday nights will blind me to any "answer" in a man or woman that I might one day love and feel safe with.

I have called these fears my "ugly" side and noted that the reason my immediate family never talks to each other about anything substantial is because we are all afraid of making our true selves known; we are afraid to show our "ugly" sides to each other, choosing instead to believe that we are all perfectly happy, in perfect control, and on the straightest paths through life. Showing our ugly sides means disappointing, scaring, and upsetting each other; it is much safer to appear happy and to suffer in private or with our friends. I have learned that I am not the only one who is hiding; this house is filled with expert pretenders. Like bluffers in a poker game, we hold our cards to our chests pretending we've got royal flushes, but no one will call anyone else's hand. We just sit around the table staring at each other, edgy but professional. When we lose a hand—that is, say "I'm gay," lose our temper, admit we are sad, cry in frustration—we rush to each other's aid immediately, feeling guilty that we had such a better hand and never knew it, guilty that we didn't realize how lucky we were. But soon enough another round begins, and the stakes are raised. . . .

Constant hiding implies constant fear of exposure. No time is ever your own. Something always threatens to expose you, to force you to show your hand, to hold you under the lights. Always on edge, you never feel safe from discovery. As I described before, I grew up with a constant, irrational fear that something would disrupt my life, take me or my family away. The fear started to surface in late high school in the form of panic disorder: short (but overwhelmingly powerful) attacks of sheer terror striking without any apparent warning, cause, or signal. I'd be driving in my car, and suddenly my heart would race, my stomach sink, my skin tingle, and my hands shake, while a burning sensation ran up and down my legs and spine. Or I'd be in bed reading or talking to my friends or waterskiing—I was never safe. The aftershocks of these daily attacks lasted nearly the rest of the day, so that just as I was getting over an attack, a new one would begin.

I lived this way for seven years. Then one weekend several years after college and after writing the original case, after taking allergy medication that (unbeknownst to me) aggravates panic disorder, I had a panic attack that didn't go away after a few seconds. It lasted all day and into the night until, sitting in a restaurant the next night surrounded (safely, I thought) by all my friends, I jumped up and said I had to go to a hospital because I was going crazy—finally, I believed, my lifelong fear of going insane was coming true. A friend calmly walked me to his apartment and called the campus police, who put a therapist on the line. Hearing her reassuring voice explaining the disorder to me clinically but empathetically, rationally but warmly, I settled down, and the fear subsided. We talked for hours, me spinning countless family stories. She convinced me to seek professional help, informing me that panic disorder is common, treatable, and beatable.

The psychiatrist I met the next day, who prescribed me a very low dosage of pills that I still take, told me the story of my life, as if the details of my complex and seemingly unique childhood were merely bullets in a textbook: He asked, having never met me, questions such as "Did you feel when you were younger as if you were the parent and your parents were your children? Were either of your parents sexually inappropriate with you or your siblings? Are you struggling with your sexuality? Do you have strong separation anxiety? Is your mother or father overly anxious?"—questions that, though commonly asked by the stereotypical psychiatrist, defined the core of my identity. (I remembered once looking through my mother's medical records and finding the one-line diagnosis scrawled in the corner: anxiety. I didn't understand it then.) I took immeasurable comfort in knowing that I was not alone in my distinct brand of anxiety disorder, finally understanding that my problems were part chemical and part environmental. My psychiatrist and I agreed that to mitigate the disorder, I somehow needed to merge the many lives I was leading and piece together a cohesive identity for myself—with the help of the medication (that, much to my relief, eliminated the panic but did not diminish my everyday neuroses) but, most importantly, with the help of talk therapy. I arranged to meet with the woman I talked with on the phone, and I have been seeing her for the past two years. Slowly, we are devising methods to deal with my life's stubborn patterns and to work through my conflicted feelings about every member of my family (not just my mother). And though it is difficult to keep up the energy and summon up the courage, and though I fail constantly, I work every day to be honest with myself. There seems to be simply no other path to sustainable happiness for me and no path more difficult in my family.

I can see the pieces of my life before me, how easily the pattern fits together: the precedent of lying (and anxiety) set long before I was born, the disruption of safety early in my childhood giving way to a longing for "normalcy" during those crucial early years of adolescence, the panic that ensued from that early violation coupled with growing awareness of ("abnormal") sexuality. Threading through it all is my vigilance to maintain order and peace, to transcend my history, to beat it and come out the victor—a vigilance that places immeasurable weight on my conscience and spirit and that leaves me always guilty, put upon, unsafe, and scared. I am, of course, still 8 years old, putting my parents' needs (to see their children happy) before my own (to be honest, to be happy). I am still constructing finely detailed masks at so quick a rate, one of top of the other, that I've lost the original face beneath them. When I look in the mirror, a cast of strangers stares back. I long to meet somewhere among them the boy I never got to be. I imagine him more beautiful than the many boys who have taken his place since, masquerading, performing, protecting, passing for him. They have done a great job covering for him, but their work is done—the boy needs his own chance.

11 Bad

In this essay,* Gretchen, a 21-year-old white woman, tells the story of her eventual recovery from the psychological injury done to her by others' misunderstandings of her attention deficit hyperactive disorder (ADHD). Within her family, Gretchen was labeled a problem child: poorly organized, prone to school failure, and apt to become distracted. Perhaps as a result of her parents' marital difficulties—which destabilized the family generally—Gretchen was afforded little room for error, and as her problems persisted, she was subjected to escalating emotional and physical abuse by her mother. Finally, during her senior year of high school, Gretchen dropped out and ran away to live in the city with her boyfriend. After months in a drug rehabilitation center and a stint in an outdoor therapy program, she chose to return to high school.

Writing as a college sophomore, Gretchen challenges the conventional belief that ADHD is nothing but a problem, a syndrome to be cured, a disease to be eradicated. Instead, based on her own experience, Gretchen believes that ADHD can be a source of joy and life energy, a part of a person's cherished uniqueness. Accordingly, Gretchen advises her readers to adopt a more curious and open stance toward ADHD, warning that failure to do so can result in the misjudgment and abuse of persons like herself.

I woke to the sound of my mother's footsteps hammering down the stairs to the kitchen. Through sleepy eyes, I looked out at the glorious fall foliage, the bright sunshine warming my face as I sat up and stretched my small body, thinking, "It's finally Saturday!" I loved Saturdays in the fall; it was soccer season, and Saturday was the one day of the week I spent with my dad. As part of our Saturday ritual, Dad would always bring doughnuts for me and my sister, one chocolate and one honey-dipped. The smells of coffee, doughnuts, and the newspaper surrounded him when he came to pick us up for my soccer game. I loved the way Dad looked on weekends, his hair messy, his face unshaven and salty from his early morning jog. Handing me the doughnut bag, Dad asked if I had my gear ready, and I realized I didn't know where my uniform, cleats, or shin guards were, though I did know where to look.

*From Rodis, Garrod, & Boscardin, Learning Disabilities and Life Stories, published by Allyn and Bacon, Boston, MA. Copyright © 2000 by Pearson Education. Reprinted by permission of the publisher.

I darted upstairs to examine the heap of things on my bedroom floor. I first looked under the bed, where I found one shin guard and one cleat behind my Scrabble box. Beginning to feel frustrated, I scurried around my room, finding only two dirty soccer socks in my doll clothes drawer and a pair of soccer shorts from last year's uniform. Wanting to appear organized, I threw on the mismatched pieces of my uniform, just in time to hear my father's call up the stairs, "Ready, Gretchen?" As I ran down the stairs, I was something to behold wearing my wrinkled shirt, still dirty from my last game, a pair of shorts that were too small, and my dirty soccer socks, carrying one cleat, and one shin guard that had a doll hat stuck to the Velcro strap. I squirmed as my father examined me, his thick, dark eyebrows raised, his eyes squinting skeptically. I spotted my sister's gear stacked neatly in the corner; dropping mine, I scooped hers up and followed Dad out the front door, feeling somewhat relieved by the cool morning air. My very organized father followed with a shopping bag full of cookies and punch for the team; it was his turn to bring the postgame refreshments, and I thanked God for letting me remind him of that yesterday, and not on the way to the field.

We sat in silence as we drove to the field, but I was happy just to be with Dad. I loved watching his strong hands shift the car, which smelled just like his office: a mix of leather, paper, coffee, and new carpet. I liked to feel part of my father's world, and this for me, this time alone, was a bonding experience. I would often pretend I was one of his clients and that we were on our way to a meeting. I'd also pretend that the air of seriousness that surrounded my father was comfortable.

Before the game, I huddled with my team, shivering because I had forgotten my sweatshirt. When my coach shouted, "Get out there girls, let's hustle," I stared blankly, wondering why she hadn't put me in the lineup. Then I heard my dad yelling from the sidelines, "Weren't you listening? GO! Get out there, you're playing defense, pay attention! GO!" I ran onto the field, with my too-small shorts riding up my behind. My mind drifted as I watched my teammates dominate the game at the other end of the field, and I started mentally going over the moves I had learned in gymnastics that week. I started to do a cartwheel, and as my legs kicked over, I saw the ball heading straight toward me. My coach screamed from the sideline, "Gretchen, for Christ's sake, this isn't GYMNASTICS, it's SOCCER! Why are you doing flips in the middle of the game? PAY ATTENTION!" I glanced at the laughing parents standing on the sidelines, saw my father's embarrassed look of disgust. My coach took me out at halftime, and I sat with my back to my father for the rest of the game, hating myself for being so stupid, wondering why I could never be as organized as everyone else. The car ride home was silent. I was filled with shame and devastated that my day with Dad had been ruined. I was not, after all, his client, but merely his unreliable child whom he couldn't understand.

"I would hear my name being screamed from the front of the class."

When I think back on my years as a young student, I can laugh at some of my behaviors in class. I was constantly told to sit down, to stop talking; if the teacher gave instructions, I was always one step behind everyone; if we were supposed to hang up our coats, I would be easily distracted by something else. I was constantly yelled at for being disruptive, and I remember feeling very guilty, but, also confused: I did not mean to disrupt my class, and I often didn't even realize I was doing anything wrong. I realize now that I was not a child with a discipline problem, but a child with ADHD.

But, at that time, nobody knew what my real problem was, and at school embarrassing things would happen to me daily. I was constantly in trouble for taking too long when I went to the bathroom or to sharpen my pencil. I would look out the window and totally forget I was in class. Then I would hear my name being screamed from the front of the room. The thing was, I could not control my behavior. I felt I was not in control of my own mind and body. My frustrated teachers and my parents always wanted to know why I was not paying attention or why I was acting up in class, but I would only tell them, "I don't know, I just did." Often I couldn't even remember what I was in trouble for! But no one ever believed me, and soon I was pegged as a liar—a label that followed me for a long time. Every teacher at my school knew me because I was always in trouble. I was regularly kicked out of class, which bruised me emotionally because I could not explain my behavior. I felt like a really bad kid.

"There are days when I can actually feel my ADHD taking over my mind and body."

ADHD is not merely a part of me or an influence in my life. It is me. It is the main force that controls me mentally, physically, and socially; I cannot separate it from myself or keep it under control. It is hard for me to explain what it feels like to be driven by an inner force that is so powerful and primordial. There are days when I can actually feel ADHD taking over my mind and body. It's kind of like being on a ride at the fair that goes 'round and 'round in circles as it jolts up and down and side to side, and everything is a huge blur of lights, smells, and noises, and you try really hard to single out your friends down on the ground watching you, but you can't focus because it's spinning so fast. That is how hard ADHD can hit. Imagine that happening when you are in class trying to listen, or when you are trying to do your homework. In class, I often have the feeling that I am sitting in the middle of a drain, and I sit there at my desk, spinning furiously, trying to stop the motion. When the force erupts, my anxiety starts to take over, and I have to fight the urge to scream with frustration. My body reacts to this rush, and I have to move. There is nothing that can bring me back to the moment, and the only thing that helps me to relax is space and open air. An escape! This is an extremely complicated psychological state to have to describe when someone asks, "What's the matter?" or "Why can't you just sit still?" I feel that someone would think I was psychotic if I tried to describe the feeling.

The strangest thing about this state is that, though I know what I am supposed to be doing, I have absolutely no control. I can have a huge list of things I know I have to do, or else pay severe consequences, but I still will not do them. There is a force stronger than my own will controlling me. For example, if I have an important assignment to complete for school the next day, I'll go for a run or clean my room, all the time thinking, "I'm not doing my assignments." Then I might read the paper or go out with my friends, still conscious that I have this assignment, but still not doing it. I want to, but I really can't stop not doing it, can't stop doing something else. This also happens in class: I get the urge to do something else, like go for a hike, and I go. It does not matter what else I should be doing—I have to go. I'm driven.

"How come no one ever saw the fear in me?"

As a child, the hardest part of the day was the bus ride home. I always had a bag full of notes from my teachers, and I knew the school had already called my mother to tell her I had them. I would get off the bus scared to death and very sad. I would contemplate running away, or wonder whether things would be better if I were dead. I would close the front door very quietly, knowing what I would get when my mom knew I was home. I always felt like I had worms in my stomach, and would sometimes vomit from the anxiety. I'd develop a migraine, which my mother would say I was faking because I knew I was in trouble. I often felt like I was spinning out of control, and my parents would make me spin even harder, until finally I would just shut down and cry myself to sleep, feeling worthless and scared. I always felt very misunderstood.

My mother had a mean and violent temper when I was a kid. I know now that she was unhappily married and felt neglected by my father, and she would take out her anger on me and my sister. But as a child I just thought that this was how my mother was. I always got it worse than my sister—I added more stress because of school. When my mother got mad, she screamed so violently that I did not recognize her. She also hit. Instead of sitting and discussing why I was having trouble in school, she would usually beat me. This made me fearful; I started to lie to my teachers and hide my bad reports from my mother because it was my only defense from the abuse.

The first time I was caught forging my parents' names to a progress report was in the third grade, when I was 8 years old. The consequences of lying were always worse than the bad report, but I could not stop. I had to protect myself somehow; nobody else understood what it was like for me. I felt that the only way for me to avoid punishment was to lie, and though I was often caught and punished, for some reason it didn't stop me. It became a habit, and I found myself lying even in situations where I did not have to. I never got in trouble at school for problems like fighting, but I was very dishonest, which gave me a bad reputation. My parents and my teachers overlooked my learning problems and focused on my behavior.

How come nobody ever saw the fear in me? Why did I have to be so deceitful so young? This overwhelming fear started very young, and stayed with me until recently, like a terrible weight I carried inside. I was a nervous child, and the stress caused migraine headaches and a nervous stomach. Stress can do many things to people, especially children, which I feel is one of the largest factors behind my failure in school.

As I got older, things only got worse. I was evaluated several times at my school, which showed only that I had deficiencies in copying from the board, work completion, math, and spelling. I was always off the charts on my vocabulary and comprehension abilities. They always told me that my testing scores were way above average and that I was capable of the work, but that I was careless and lazy.

I was often told that I didn't have my priorities in order, which was why I was doing so poorly in school. When I was in seventh grade, my parents decided to put me in private school, hoping that it would solve my problems. This may have been a good idea, but, in fact, it only brought on a new wave of problems. The private school had parent advisory slips—commonly known as PA slips—that would be sent home if you were disruptive in class, did not do homework, or if you were basically not doing well in a class. I probably hold the record at Cabot Academy for the most PA slips! As I explained, bringing home PA slips was not an option for me because I was so scared of my mother. So, once again I forged and lied daily. I would hand the forged slips to my teachers, but they usually found out my mother had not seen them and would then tell me I was caught. For the rest of the day, I would conjure up possible escapes, imagining myself living on the streets or in the woods, lonely and afraid. But I always went home. I would get home, where I would be verbally tormented by my mother. I would try to explain that I didn't know why these things were happening and that I was as confused as she was, but all she could say was, "You're lying," or "You're a lazy, stupid, selfish child." I was called an "insensitive brat," a "lazy, fat ass," and I often heard my mother say, "I could fucking kill you!" As she screamed at me, she would twist my arm or smack me or push me, then send me to my room, saying, "I don't want to see your face for the rest of the night." I would wish that she could understand that acting that way was only hurting me and killing my self-esteem. I wanted her to realize that I was not doing these things because I was a bad person. I wanted her to realize that my problems in school were caused by something that I didn't understand. Instead, my mother only added to my problems.

Several incidents will never be erased from my memory. I hope that sharing one will help explain why I stayed in this pattern of lying, why I was just too scared to stop. I was in bed one night when I heard the phone ring. I thought it could be one of my teachers telling my parents that I had failed a math test. I heard my mother say, "Thank you very much for calling and letting me know." I knew I was right. I heard my mother scream from her bedroom and come flying down the hallway to my bedroom. The door burst open, and standing in the light of the hallway was my mother. She stormed into the room with a belt in her hand and started to whip me where I was lying in my bed. She was screaming cruel things at me and whacking whacking whacking me with the belt. Finally, my sister ran into my room and pulled my mother off me. It was total chaos. My sister and I were screaming and crying, and my mother was totally flipping out. I was confused and embarrassed that my sister had seen this. I know she felt bad for me, but I also know that she was angry at me for causing this. I put a chair in front of my door and huddled under my blanket, crying and getting sick to my stomach until, finally, I fell asleep. All this because I failed a math test. By the time my father got home from work, the house was silent and we were sleeping.

"I don't ever remember my parents getting along well."

It is amazing to me how much my family influenced how I see myself and shaped who I am. I will start with my parents. I believe that my parents' marriage was doomed to fail from the beginning. They were married at 25, and within two years they had my sister Meredith and me. My father started a job at an accounting firm in Boston, where he has worked for the last twenty-one years. My mother stayed at home for the first few years to take care of me and my sister. The main reason my parents are no longer together is that my father is married to his job; it's the reason they started fighting. My father worked twelve to fourteen hours every day of the week. My mother thought it was unfair that she was left home all day with two babies to take care of and that she was totally alone all the time. When my father did come home, my sister and I were usually asleep; we never spent time with him. I believe that my mother felt neglected, and that she felt bad that my sister and I never saw my dad either. My mother could not handle my father's work schedule, and she became very depressed and angry, and my parents fought regularly over the fact that my father was never home. I think my mother was so angry that she couldn't tell my father that the problem was that she really missed him and wanted to have a better marriage, so she would yell and scream and push him away even further. Eventually, their arguments became violent, and my mother would hit my father. The first time I witnessed this was horrific. It is hard to see your parents acting so irrationally. I was scared my parents would end up killing each other.

Looking back, I understand my mother's frustrations. I know she needed much more affection and communication than she was getting from my father. I know she tried to make their marriage work in many ways. She became an excellent cook and homemaker. She kept herself looking great, always beautifully dressed, and in great physical shape. She was envied by her friends for being so domestic and desirable. Only my father never recognized her efforts, never complimented her or gave her more time. That is why my mother became a very angry person.

My mother's temper became the thing that scared me the most. She would hit me and my sister when she became angry, often enraged over little things like spills or messes around the house. My mother treated every situation with violence. My father never really knew what was happening, and there was no one to help us. My mother's erratic behavior was confusing: After she hit me, she would give me a big hug and a kiss and tell me she loved me, but it never made me feel better. I wanted her to feel bad for what she had done, not kiss and make up. I often felt I was living in the middle of total chaos, but was too small and powerless to stop it.

"The doctor told them I had ADHD."

When I was in eighth grade, my parents decided to take me to see a specialist. I had been evaluated many times throughout the years, but I was still not improving. My parents were desperate to get some help for my problems. I remember the ride to the hospital: It was no big deal for me, since I had become accustomed to being taken to psychologists and doctors. As I went through yet another series of testing—the ink blots, the puzzles, the building blocks—I wondered how these simple games would tell these people anything about me. At the end of the testing, my parents and I met with a doctor, who told them that I had ADHD. He said the drug Ritalin was the latest treatment and told my parents how it was used. I had never heard of ADHD, and at the time it did not mean much to me. I just figured, "Well, that's one more thing we can add to the list, so can we go home now?" That was the extent of my diagnosis; we never got any information about ADHD and we never talked about it again. My parents never thought to seek any advice about my condition, and, for me, it was just another name of another syndrome that was not going to change who I was. It didn't really bother me that we never talked about it because the doctor didn't seem to think it was a big deal. By the end of that school year, I was kicked out of private school and back in public school still without any mention of my ADHD.

I now regret so much the way my parents and I let my diagnosis be pushed under the carpet. If I had had some help, I could have accomplished so much more and been spared the humiliation I felt when I was expelled from school. The guilt was even worse; I was so tired of disappointing my parents. I knew I was doing poorly in school, but I never expected to be kicked out. I think this was a turning point for me in many ways. I think this is when my parents finally gave up on me and when I gave up on myself. I was tired of not being understood and of being hurt so much that eventually I stopped caring about myself. I became so afraid of failure and admonishment that I was unable to take a risk or try really hard for things. I became scared of conflict or even the possibility of conflict. I couldn't trust anything I believed, and I became a sponge for other people's opinions. I never told anyone my feelings because I was so embarrassed about myself all the time.

Yet all of this did lead to something positive: I became a listener! The one area of my life that gained something from my bad experiences was my ability to be a good friend. I have had the same friends for many years, some since the first grade. I always put a lot into my friendships. All my friends would come to me with their problems because I was a good listener. I wanted to make sure these people felt that their problems were significant and that they were being understood. I never wanted anyone to have their feelings misunderstood as I did. I would change plans for my friends, even if it meant missing the biggest events; I would never desert a friend. I never let myself be in a clique and made it a point to try never to hurt anyone's feelings. I stuck up for kids who were being picked on and felt good about helping people. I was so well liked that I never had to worry about being picked on like I was at home or by my teachers. I was never a victim. Many teenagers have a hard time socially because kids can be really mean, but I never experienced that. This was great for me, but it also became a problem. I became so involved with everyone else's lives that I totally ignored how I was really feeling. Helping other people did make me feel better, but it was not enough.

During my sophomore year in high school, I became involved with Rob, a boy I had known throughout my school years. Rob gravitated to me because he had a lot of emotional difficulties. In elementary school, he had cancer for seven years, but cancer was the least of his problems. When Rob was diagnosed with bladder cancer, his father took off, and Rob never heard from him again. After later bouts with lung cancer and a tumor on his spine, Rob went into full remission when he was 12. A week later, his mother announced that she had cervical cancer and that it was too far gone to help. She had never told anyone because she wanted Rob to be taken care of first. She died when Rob was a freshman in high school, and he blamed himself. This kid had major problems, and he became my new project.

I went out with Rob for five years, devoting myself mainly to his problems. I believe he'd be dead by now if not for me, but it sure didn't get me anywhere. He was a drug user, and I got into heavy drugs with him—acid, pills, coke. For two years straight, that was all we did. It was great: I was "helping" Rob, and I was too fucked up to feel my own pain. Rob hated school as much as I did, so we stopped going after a while, and if I did go, I was high. My parents separated the year I met Rob, so they were dealing with their own problems. My mother was such a wreck throughout her divorce that it was easy for me to get away with things.

But midway through my senior year when my mother had an emotional breakdown, I totally lost it. She wanted me to affirm her and comfort her, but I was so angry at her for what she had put me through that she made me sick. I could not even feel bad for her, and I let her suffer. My dad and sister were gone, so I was left alone with my irrational mother. And I just lost it. I quit school and ran away from home. I got an apartment with Rob and two of his friends in a part of the city surrounded by crack houses. This was the worst possible environment, but I did not care. I felt like I was losing my mind and just had to get out of my house. I have never been so depressed in my life; I totally hit rock bottom. I was still seeing my therapist through all this, and one day I showed up for a therapy appointment to find my dad waiting there with two guys in white coats. My father forced me to take a drug test, after which I was locked up in rehab for a few months.

"Those three months in Minnesota were a period of rebirth."

When I got out of rehab, I had a hard time motivating myself to do anything. The whole world felt dead to me. My relationship with my parents was not great, and my self-esteem was at the lowest place it had ever been. I couldn't pretend I was happy; I couldn't even smile. I was able to put a lot of effort into figuring out what I needed to do to be happy again, and the one thing I was sure of was that I needed to get away from my family, my friends, and my hometown. I needed to see myself in another setting, to cut myself off from the rest of my world and totally concentrate on myself. My father suggested that I try an Outward Bound course for the summer, and I instantly agreed with him. I knew a little about the philosophy behind Outward Bound, but I didn't know what to expect from my trip. I think the main reason I agreed to do the trip was because the distance and seclusion sounded so right.

I spent three months in the woods of northern Minnesota backpacking, kayaking, and canoeing. There is something so amazing about living without a clock or a schedule hanging over your head. Getting away from the noise, hustle, and stress of life, I was able to reflect and think. I found a calming silence in nature that soothed my mind and gave it the time to expand without unnecessary chatter and noise.

My Outward Bound course was the most significant experience I have had, the best choice I have made in my life. The changes I experienced during my trip were so strong and unbinding that I could feel them as they were occurring. I had moments of great clarity that allowed me to separate myself from the cloud I had been living in for years and to free myself from insignificant worries and fears that I had been holding on to my whole life. I think this was the first time I recognized myself as an individual person, rather than as a mere part in the lives of all the people I knew and all that I experienced. Before, I had absolutely no sense of who I was; I viewed myself according to what other people told me I was. Outward Bound gave me the personal freedom to explore inwardly and form an identity for myself. This freedom was the crucial aspect of my experience. I was in a group of seven strangers who did not have a clue about my past, and this was the first time that I could be the person I knew I was. I did not fear that these people would ana-lyze my behaviors like my family did. I had lost the faith of all the people who were close to me and was used to getting few words of encouragement.

Those three months in Minnesota were a period of rebirth. I shed about nine-teen years of unwanted skin that was trapping my spirit. With every step I took, I sweated out the toxins in my body and mind. Every day, I struggled and cried, and I released and released all the pain inside me. For the first time my nerves settled, and the sick feeling I had in my body left. My stomach felt empty and happy with-out the butterflies that had lived in there for years. I smiled and I laughed out loud, and I was happy!

Equally important to my rebirth was that I gained a lot of insight into my family. I had had so much anger at them for so long that I could not distinguish the good in them. I know that I had an inner demon eating away at my spirit, and my family was that demon. In time, I was able to conquer the burdens they had placed on me and recognize my own faults and the ways I had contributed to the deterio-ration of my family. I had put so much emphasis on defending myself that I hadn't seen my role in the problem. I went home from my trip feeling settled and open to them. The trip also gave me time to decide what I wanted in the future, and I de-cided to go back to high school to get my diploma.

There is a part of me that would never want to change the fact that I have ADHD. I believe that this condition can be positive in many ways for the person who has it. The main setback for most people with ADHD, especially children, is that they are misunderstood. If I had been taught to believe that ADHD was a learn-ing difference rather than a learning disability, I feel I would have had a more posi-tive view of myself while growing up. ADHD has caused me problems as far as learning goes, but not because I cannot learn. I just do not learn the same way other people do. But then, everyone learns differently, not only people with ADHD. ADHD becomes a learning disability when teachers try to put many different kids together in one room and expect them all to learn the same way. I feel that a lot of the problem for children with ADHD lies within the education system. Most schools have a set curriculum and routine method of teaching, but it is ridiculous to believe that all children will be stimulated by the same things. The problem is that not all classroom settings incorporate a multimodal form of teaching. There are simple strategies that can be incorporated into the classroom that can greatly help all students learn more effectively according to methods that work best for them.

Many specialists believe that medication is the most effective treatment for students with ADHD. This is something that I am very afraid of. I have experimented with a few of the drugs that are prescribed, like Ritalin and Dexedrine. When under the influence of these medications, I am a completely different person. I lose all my energy and emotions. It is like the driving force behind who I am is sucked out of my body leaving me feeling like a hollow shell. My ADHD is the source of my energy, and it is vital for me to have that. I feel that my personality would not be what it is if I did not have ADHD. There are so many positive aspects of ADHD. For example, I can do many things at one time successfully. My mind is always in motion and always looking for something to do. My main goal is to be able to control my ADHD in certain settings, and to use my ADHD as an advantage, rather than taking drugs to suppress all my creative energy.

Although most people look at ADHD as a negative condition, I disagree. I believe that if you were to ask anyone that has a friend with ADHD, they would say that all of these crazy symptoms are what they love about that person. ADHD makes a person an individual unlike anyone else. I know that at times my erratic behavior and spontaneity aggravates my friends and family, but those are the qualities that make them laugh and appreciate me. The problem is that most of the literature about ADHD is written by people who do not have ADHD. They generalize ADHD and say that the symptoms are concrete. This is extremely offensive to me. I understand my symptoms, and I know how my ADHD affects me, but it's all personal. My situation can be totally different from another person with ADHD.

I am happy that I have the opportunity to write about my experiences. They are me, and they are real. I hope this essay will help some people see the importance of dealing with learning disabilities so that they or their child will get the help they need. I also hope people can learn from my story so that they will deal with this issue differently from the way my family did. I want people to understand that ADHD should not be labeled a disability, that it only becomes a disability when it is not understood and when people fail to see the benefits and the positive aspects of it. I believe that my ADHD caused people to look down on me and tell me that there was something wrong with me. I had hundreds of tests for that reason alone; everyone wanted to know what was wrong with me rather than just seeing the energy and passion that I had for so many things. My teachers and parents overlooked all the areas in my life where I was succeeding and instead concentrated on my faults. If I had learned earlier how to turn my ADHD into an advantage, I would have had a better outlook on life and I would have had more respect for myself as a person. It has taken me a long time to be able to see the good in me. Because of all the people telling me there was something wrong with me, I was unable to recognize any part of myself as positive and "normal." All I wanted was for people to listen to me and to really see me, not what the doctors were seeing.

12 Beyond the Euphoric Buzz

This author, a college junior, describes her double life as a high school student—respected student leader and secret weekend drinker. Growing up in a permissive family in Florida, Sarah slips into a pattern of binge drinking, drunkenness, and promiscuity. With utmost skill, she manages to keep her high school responsibilities and her drinking compartmentalized and for a while sees no need to change her habits. However, finding "common ground" and romance with a Chinese American man at college compels her to reassess her life and to master her addiction. Now a wife and mother, she commits herself to "a whole new appreciation for the sober life" and to caring for her husband and infant child.

Someone go find Luke! His girlfriend is puking."

I'm lying on the bathroom floor of the hotel room. Luke and I had been going together for only a month, when he had asked me to be his date for his junior prom. We drank together plenty in those four weeks, but this was the first time I had gotten sick. In my excitement at the after-party, I had veered from my "Beer then liquor, never sicker" rule, and that's how I came to be in my present situation.

I wake up to see Luke walking through the hotel room's bathroom door. "Oh, hi." I try to smile, but the room is spinning wildly. I can't make it stop. I close my eyes. Oh, worse. I grab the toilet bowl to puke some more. I hate vomiting. It feels like my guts are being yanked out through my mouth for everyone to have a look at. But there's nothing I can do to stop it. I keep waking up, feeling the room spin, puking, then falling back asleep.

At some point Luke decides I need to get in the shower. I argue with him because I can't move without the entire room turning into a carousel gone mad, spinning and spinning. Eventually, he ignores my whimpers. As he stands me up, dizziness overwhelms me. I begin to fall in slow motion. The world is tipping, like a bottle of tequila, and I'm inside, sloshing back and forth sickeningly. . . .

I am lying in the bathtub. Every movement creates another current in the water around me and the bottle sways back and forth. I slosh from side to side, bumping my head on the glass side. Luke is trying to hold the small plastic trash bin for me to puke into. I stop throwing up as the waves die down. I move my arm to get comfortable. More waves. More vomiting. I knock the trash bin on its side and vomit spills into the bath water. For just a moment I'm watching the room from above. I see myself lying there pitifully; sopping clothes, stringy hair, unable to control my bodily functions, bits of vomit floating around me. Then I'm back inside me, inside the bottle that almost finds equilibrium to stand up straight, but then something sets it rocking again. After what seems like hours I drift back to sleep, with Luke holding my head above the water. I'm too exhausted to keep up the fight.

Luke says I need to change into some dry, clean clothes. I look at him. He's never seen me without clothes on. But there's no way I can argue. I obviously can't go to bed like this, and I can't even stand up by myself. My body is not my own. He pushes my pants down to my ankles and sits me on the toilet to pull them off and to put on dry ones. I relax into his arms as he carries me to the bed.

Looking back at that night, I marvel that I never apologized to Luke. I remember feeling awkward because I had never become so ill from drinking, and I wasn't sure how to act. But apologizing was not my instinctive response. Instead, as soon as I had the realization that I had ruined Luke's big night, I began making excuses for myself. "It was only his *junior* prom," I told myself. My philosophy had always been that when I make a mistake, I should resist guilt and invest my energy in learning from the experience instead. But learning from my mistakes assumes some logical cause—something solvable. When drinking became the source of my mistakes, my already formed habit of avoiding guilt became a perpetuating force for my mental addiction. If I didn't feel guilty about the negative consequences of my drinking, what would motivate me to quit?

Today I can answer that question easily. I am finishing my last year in college, I am a wife and mother, and I comfortably identify myself as a nondrinker. But I cannot pretend that the person I am today is unconnected to my past. Just two and a half years ago I was driving home drunk, with a six-pack on the seat next to me, and I cruised into a tree in my front yard, putting a sizeable dent in my mom's car hood. So I must ask, how did things get so bad? Are there aspects of my personality that allowed me to sink so low or was this a simple case of alcohol addiction? And what keeps me from having a drink tomorrow, starting the whole cycle over again? What I've found is that the more I uncover in the complex networks of my mind, the more I see how this will be a lifetime process of realization and readjustment.

I am the youngest of four girls in my family. So, I learned everything about growing up from watching my sisters go through it. School, boyfriends, adolescence, alcohol, high school, drugs . . . I saw it all—first through the eyes of a little girl, and then later as I experienced it myself.

Lilliana, my oldest sister by six years, was my idol growing up. She was a cheerleader. She was on Homecoming Court. She was popular. She drank, she partied. After a while she even did drugs. Pot. Acid. Probably more. But I knew her only as my beautiful, glamorous sister whom I wanted to be just like when I grew up.

Her teenage years were extremely hard on the family. Lilliana was anything but subtle in her disobedience. She would yell and scream at my mother at the slightest cause. It was not unusual to find my mother chasing her around the kitchen table, out the front door, and around the rickety old station wagon parked in the driveway. She wielded a wooden paddle and a fierce look—intent, not on hurting her, but on disciplining her rebellious spirit by punishing her defiant acts.

My parents learned a lesson in dealing with Lilliana—you can't force a teenager to do what you want. So they never took an authoritarian approach with the rest of us. Whereas my parents would try to tell Lilliana to come home at one and she would purposely stay out all night, I never had a curfew. Their strategy with the rest of us was to persuade us to do what they thought was best by reasoning with us, discussing the issues, telling us about their experiences. But ultimately, the decision was ours. They understood that sometimes hearing about their mistakes wasn't enough. We needed to experience and learn for ourselves too.

And that was our relationship, for as long as I lived in that household. I respected my parents, obeyed their few rules, considered their abundant counsel, and made my own choices. I could say that not having a curfew was conducive to excessive partying. I could say that being allowed to drink at home was convenient for heavy drinking. But I don't. I never blame my parents for any position I found myself in. I made my own decisions and I dealt with the repercussions myself.

As the offspring of genuine hippies, drugs were never a taboo topic. Growing up, I knew that my parents had lived on a commune with a diet consisting mostly of tofu and pot for the majority of their young adult lives. I was raised on all the "psychedelic" music of the 1960s and by the time I was 12 knew all about the allusions to drugs in the Beatles' songs and many others. But drug use was not a subject that I took lightly.

A memory is imprinted on my mind not because it had great meaning or emotional impact, but from sheer repetition. My mother would be doing something around the house and talking to me at the same time. Suddenly she would stop—always midsentence, sometimes midword. It appeared that she was just pausing in order to concentrate better on what she was doing. I would wait for her to finish the task, expecting her to then complete the sentence, but she never would.

"Mom. What were you going to say?"

"What?"

"What were you going to say? You were just telling me to do something."

"Oh," she would say with surprise. "I was? I'm sorry, honey, I don't remember."

"But *Mom!*" I would reply, drawing out the "o" in exasperation. "You were *just* saying it."

"I'm sorry, sweetie." And the conversation was over. Now for that to happen once is understandable, twice is forgivable, three times a little trying. But over and over and over . . . it's something you can't forget. Later when I found out that this is a typical symptom of being "burnt out," this memory served as the greatest incentive I could ever ask for never to try pot.

By the time I was 13, both Lilliana and Rachel, eighteen months my elder, were heavily into drugs. Everyone knew it, but there wasn't much we could do about it. I resented the huge role that pot played in Rachel's and Lilliana's lives. They totally dropped out of family life. Not just by neglecting chores, but also by retracting all emotional investment. They couldn't stand to be around the family without the buffer of being high. They only valued smoking and people who smoked with them. They were always off in their fairy-tale land where everything was cool and chill and nothing really mattered.

High school was a wonderful time, filled with new experiences, new faces, new challenges. Our freshman class was composed of six hundred students. Wandering through the halls I saw many familiar faces from middle school, and many new ones. I smiled brightly and said hello to everyone, without hesitation. During the second week of school I was in the attendance office and I saw sign-up sheets for anyone who wanted to run for Freshmen Board. Instantly, my mind was flooded with memories of helping Lilliana run for student office. Late nights spent making stickers that read, "Vote for Lilliana Fox!" with little legs and a bushy tail drawn around the "Fox." It sounded like fun! I put my name down for treasurer, a notable title without a lot of work, I thought. The following week I made posters and stickers that looked like a sun and wrote "Vote for Sarah Sunshine!" To my surprise, I won.

The following week a freshmen student assembly was called to introduce the Freshmen Board. The four elected ones sat in four lonely chairs on the vast gymnasium floor. The kids who filled the seats in the towering bleachers were full of that first-week-of-school, fidgeting, bottled-up kind of energy. The assistant principal spoke (for too long) and then began introducing the board. Finally, it was my turn! "And here is your newly elected treasurer, Sarah Fox." Applause, stomping, yelling. Wow! Was that louder than they had cheered for the President? It sure sounded like it to me. But as I approached the microphone, the mob before me was still daunting.

"Thanks for electing us to Freshmen Board," I said with a smile. "Our goal is to make school a more enjoyable place. And I think we've done good so far. We got you out of class today, didn't we?" Hooting, hollering! I was beginning to blush. They hadn't cheered during anyone else's speeches. As it was getting quiet again, Ted Williams, hunk of the class, yelled out, "We love you, Sarah Sunshine!" That started another round of rowdiness. Realizing that I could control this great throng, I willed my bashfulness to disappear. "Okay, okay," I said, as if I was used to this, unimpressed. I continued with my speech, and glancing up, I saw it. People were actually listening to me! With this reassurance, I flashed smiles at faces I recognized. When I came to the end of my note cards, I headed to my seat. The compulsory applause followed. But I couldn't stand such a mediocre ending. Just before I reached my seat I dashed back to the podium. "Freshmen class rules!" I cried into the microphone. They exploded! They stood on their seats, they went wild! But I wasn't a participant in the excitement—I was the leader of it. Yes, that's right, follow my lead, I chuckled to myself, as I sat down.

Looking back I see that this experience had quite an impact on me. That feeling of power over the multitude was intoxicating. Until then I had lived like a little girl, without a care about the consequences of my words and actions. But in the course of that speech I lived my first calculated moments. I did not smile or speak as I always had, out of an impulsive, friendly instinct. I acted in order to produce a desired effect. I was rewarded for my calculation with instant popularity. As my high school career progressed, I treated every action as a political statement.

Being on class board was not just about popularity, for me. I quickly involved myself in every aspect of the school's inner workings. The principal of the school once introduced me saying, "This girl runs the school. She holds everything together around here with her sunshine smile." I once let a curse word slip out in class and was sent to the office. "Look," I said to the assistant principal. "I've heard you use that word how many times? How are you gonna punish me for it?" Not only did I have administrative immunity, but I was making honor roll without trying terribly hard and all my teachers loved me.

I seemed to spread the fairy-tale glitter of my life over everything and everyone that I came in contact with. And the better I became at playing to the crowd, the better my life seemed to get. I couldn't have asked for more. This was every girl's dream of high school. So why shouldn't I become totally immersed in it? Yes, it required some acting, putting up of façades, surrendering of my hopes to live life with childlike innocence. But it was worth it. Hell, it was more than worth it. What I had was better than innocence. It was perfection.

Throughout junior high and freshman year of high school I never drank. I had always been firm in my refusal to drink, to the point that I never had to mention it; it was known. I was confident in my role and I felt I was being wise. So when I decided to get drunk for the first time I could honestly say it was a choice that I made for myself when I felt I was ready. I wasn't just following the crowd. *I* wanted to try it. I set the date in my head and then I told everyone else. "Next Saturday I'm going to get drunk," I said.

"All right! We'll have to get some good stuff, then!" That was Frank. He was two years older than me and had this incredibly charismatic personality. He had an air of relaxed confidence about him, as if he were so cool he could just relax about it. We were part of a group that hung out on the beach every night. He lived near me so he often drove me home in his jeep.

All that week I looked forward to it. On Friday, Frank asked, "Why don't you just do it tonight?"

"Nope. Tomorrow. Don't worry, Frankie, it'll be just as fun!" And was it ever! I drank a beer and felt giddy. I was talking and laughing, which is not uncommon for me. Everything just seemed to have an extra sparkle. Then I drank another and I was off and running. Weighing one hundred pounds, I knew it wouldn't take much alcohol to affect me. "Let's go down to the water!" I said excitedly. I met with groans and sighs.

"It's too far."

"Aw come on, Sarah, just sit down and relax."

"Come on, come on! It'll be fun!" I urged. "Come *on!*" I said pulling on Frank's arm. Finally Diana, who had not yet tried drinking, decided to go down with me. And then I convinced Frank to come too. "I'll race ya," I said to Diana and set off running. I arrived at the water's edge out of breath. Diana was trailing behind me, laughing.

"Sarah, you're such a nut!" she cried happily.

"Oooh!" I said, as I had another thought, "Let's go swimming!" And before she could respond I was running toward the water. As soon as it was deep enough I collapsed into the water. I felt it close in around me, hugging my body, making me warm. I moved and turned, feeling the water swirl around me. And after a while I popped my head out of the water, took a gulp of air, then let the water envelop me again. I just lay there this time. Letting the lull of the waves move my body for me, relaxed completely. And then I felt arms around me. Real, human arms. Someone was dragging me out of the water.

"Oh, hi Frankie!"

"Diana thought you were drowning," he said flatly. He didn't sound amused.

"Oh. Well, I wasn't," I explained. I began thinking how unfortunate it was that he had pulled me out. It was so much warmer in the water! He set me on the ground. And then I caught sight of the sky. "Ooooh! Diana look at the stars!" I said. "Let's spin!" I stretched my arms out, let my head fall back, and spun around and around and around, looking at the stars in the heavens. I was a little girl again. Grinning so widely that my cheeks bulged out to twice their normal size. No cares outside of the here and now. Ah life! What joy! I sat down and pondered with amazement, while the world slowly stopped spinning around me.

This is the story of the first time I got drunk. But it is also the story of how I fell in love with the drunken state of mind, and still love it today. Being drunk is like being a kid again. When I was drunk I could experience careless bliss. Once I tasted the forbidden fruit, I couldn't give it up. When I discovered that being drunk was like artificial childlike innocence, I couldn't resist. And why should I? I could have my cake and eat it too.

Sophomore year I was elected class president. I was passionate about the work I was doing to improve the school. The people around me seemed to sense my dedication. It was the same with all the people I worked with: facilities managers, administrators, students, teachers. They worked extraordinarily well with me and for me because they respected me professionally, liked me personally, and thought that the final results of my work repaid their efforts. My products were inherently more valuable because I put so much of my self into my work. I wasn't just the president anymore, I became a public figure. As much depended on my personal integrity as on my capability.

Sophomore year I was partying with all the most popular kids on campus. Yes, I stood out from the crowd, but only because when I wanted to have fun, I *really* had fun. No inhibitions, no quiet reservations. Everyone had a "One time Sarah was so drunk . . . " story to tell at school the following Monday and I thought it was great.

I always drank to get drunk. And I usually passed out sometime during the night. I knew people thought it was a big deal to black out but it didn't make much sense to me. Passing out to me was just like falling asleep. And when can anyone remember the exact circumstances of falling asleep? I remembered my nights in the form of a flash: action, feeling. And the emotion washes over me, in that flash, with an intensity that can hardly be paralleled when sober. Why dilute that memory with specifics and particulars? In my eyes, I was sucking the marrow out of life.

From the second or third time I got drunk I began to think about alcoholism. I still wonder, was my instinct warning me, from the very beginning? Could I have known somewhere deep within my subconscious that I was *too* in love with being drunk—that it could become a problem for me? I wanted to find out more about alcoholism, but I was scared my political career would be over if my secret concerns became known. In eleventh grade the opportunity I had been waiting for finally came. I had to do a documentary on a topic of my choice. I immediately knew I wanted to interview recovering alcoholics and counselors for substance abuse; then take what I learned from them and apply it to students who were known as fun partiers. I wanted to show that what most people thought of as harmless fun was truly dangerous. Looking back I realize that I wanted to increase social awareness so that people like me would be taken seriously. The best definition of alcoholism I heard from those interviews was, "When your alcohol use begins having a negative effect on more than one area of your life and you continue to drink." The only problem is that the more addicted one becomes, the more subjective one's judgment becomes. The definition of what's "bad enough" keeps sliding.

Going into the summer before senior year I had it all made. I was managing to keep my school responsibilities and my drinking compartmentalized, balanced. At that time I was involved in my most serious relationship yet, over one-and-a-half years long. His name was Luke. His family was moving to Orlando at the start of the summer, about six hours upstate, and he was leaving for the state university in the fall. Lately, I'd noticed myself looking at other guys. I was just hoping to stay faithful until he left, and then I'd be free. I had already convinced him it would be better not to attempt a long-distance relationship.

Two days before Luke's departure, we went to a party. When I had become sufficiently intoxicated, I pulled aside Steve, a friend of his that I had always thought was cute. "So, listen," I said. "Luke is leaving on Tuesday. Why don't you give me a call and we can go party or something?"

He looked at me quizzically, peering into my face to confirm the implications he thought he had just heard. His face broke into a broad smile. "Sure."

Tuesday came and Luke left. Thursday came and Steve called. We went to a kicking party. The end of the night found us skinny-dipping in the jacuzzi. We made out passionately in the steamy water. He pressed himself against me, and for the first time in my life I seriously considered not saving myself for marriage. Luckily, I was too nervous about the whole situation (nude in a strange place with my recent ex-boyfriend's good friend) to do anything.

A few nights later I went to another party at the same girl's house. There was an attractive guy there who I had my eye on. He had graduated from my high school two years earlier. When I introduced myself, he said, "I know. I used to watch you during lunch when you sat outside." I was flattered. He used to watch me from afar! I always wanted an admirer! As the party cleared out, Christopher and I were left on the fold-out couch. We started making out and it got pretty intense pretty quickly. At some point he asked me whether I wanted to "do it." I said I never had and he dropped it. A while later he brought it up again and after a few minutes of pondering I said sure. Just like that. That night seemed like it never ended. I don't know what girls are talking about when they say the first time hurts.

I thought it was terrific. Over and over. At times I would forget his name, then the next time I woke up I'd remember it.

I awoke the next morning and knew right away that everything had changed. Why had I decided to go for it? I asked myself. I had no answer. Saving myself for marriage was such an integral part of my self-identity as a moral, good person. Without my virginity, I was left devoid of any positive self-image.

It took less than one moment to decide my response. I would not regret losing my virginity to Christopher. No regrets! I would make it a meaningful experience by developing a real relationship with him. And if that worked, wouldn't it be fantastic if I actually ended up marrying my first?

For the next month, there was little time that we spent together when we weren't drunk or having sex. But we were getting to know each other a little more. For instance, I learned he was much more uptight than I was, he had been a complete loser at school, he had been kicked out of two state universities in the past year, and none of his friends or family thought highly of him. In fact, anyone who knew about us tried to convince me that I shouldn't be with him. Not many people knew, though. If any of my friends from school heard I was with him, they might also hear that I was sleeping with him. And that, I knew, would be the end of my perfect reputation at school.

Our relationship was a constant roller coaster. Every time something came up that put us on less than good terms, I panicked. I could sense that Guilt was just out of eyesight, impending, threatening, and if we didn't stay together it would come barreling down on me. It got to the point that the simplest interaction, like calling him up, required having at least a few drinks to calm my nerves and rally up my courage.

After about five weeks I stopped caring. I found what I needed in my drinking. I finally ended it by kissing another guy. While we had been together, I told myself that Christopher would be the only exception to my sexual abstinence. But once we broke up, Guilt again threatened to overcome me. I still did not want to surrender to it. The only alternative was to keep going without looking back. That's just what I did.

All summer I partied every night. Drinking was starting to lose its excitement. My new thrill was hooking up with whomever I wanted. There was a certain satisfaction in knowing that I could seduce anyone. My conquests were always one-night stands and I never became emotionally involved. Looking back it was as if I became a completely different person when I went out drinking. Never would I have done those things sober. I knew they were wrong, and I would have felt too ashamed. But as the summer went on I could plan who I was going to get that night, before I ever started drinking. By the end of the summer drinking was not a necessity. Although it was a large part of my lifestyle, I didn't have to be drunk to carry out my conquests.

I was drinking more and more during the day. Partying all night left me depleted of energy during the day. Drinking made the daylight hours bearable, made me feel physically better, more energetic and happier. Not only was my physical health failing, but my emotional health was also deteriorating. My sexual conquests required cutting off all emotions. Once I learned how to cut myself off, I found myself doing it all the time. Not only was it easier to live life without a conscience, but there was a convenient aftereffect: since I didn't care about anything, even when alcohol was having a negative effect on all areas of my life, in my mind things never became "bad enough" to quit.

When school started in the fall I hardly paused. I was president of student council, captain of the debate team, and treasurer of the National Honor Society. I was enrolled in two AP courses and three honors courses. I stayed two hours after school every day, and sometimes arrived an hour early, to take care of the official business of my various positions. I was dedicated to my academics, but somehow I still found the time to drink. On Wednesdays I arrived home from school at four o'clock. My church orchestra practice started at six. On my way home from church, I stopped by 7-Eleven and bought some brew with my fake ID. A few of my nonschool friends would be waiting for me when I got home.

I was able to keep my reputation and positions at school because no one there knew about my drinking. I never partied with people from school. At the time it was because I thought they were superficial and their mere presence annoyed me, inhibited me. In retrospect I see that I was successful in the various spheres of my life, and in order to maintain that success while continuing to drink, I had to preserve barriers that would never be crossed.

About halfway through the fall of my senior year I started getting a bit bored by my drinking routine. It had lost its excitement. I felt so old and tired. I could feel myself getting numb. I decided to clean up my act. I wanted to start a real relationship. My plan was to build up a relationship slowly, and at the same time cut down on my drinking and partying. Eventually we would spend all of our time together and I'd have no need to drink at all. It was a good plan.

I picked out a sweet, innocent underclassman, Ted. By the next week we were passing notes between classes. Already I felt like a normal teenager again, excited at the mere hope of being someone's girlfriend. I could almost feel the spiritual calluses softening up.

And then came the big football game that Friday. I hadn't gone to a game sober in ages. At first I tried to make plans with some of my old nondrinking friends. But I hadn't even called them in ages. They couldn't just drop their new friends and welcome me back with open arms. Friday came and I couldn't resist. My drinking buddies bought a bottle of tequila and we drank a good portion of it before walking over to the field.

Before I could get very far I ran into Ted. What terrific luck! I was actually hoping I'd see him here. We saw each other from a few yards away and we both burst into smiles. I ran into his open arms. He picked me up and he swung me around. This is the way it should be, I thought to myself. I stood with him for a bit, until I spotted my friends, looking impatient as ever. I gave Ted one last hug.

The night was still young, the halftime show had just ended. I was beginning to tire of putting on fake smiles for my superficial school friends. Then I ran into an old acquaintance. Not just anyone, mind you. Rick Marciano. Wow! What a hotty! He had graduated two years ago, and he was still known as a legend amongst the lady folk. I greeted him with an extra close hug and barely stepped away after the embrace. We talked for a few minutes about nothing and then he told me about a party after the game. I already had plans, so he gave me his number to meet up later. "You'd better not forget my number!" he said as we parted.

Don't forget his number? Who was he joking? Did he really think he was the pursuant here? Or that any girl in her right mind would give up such a golden opportunity? I walked away feeling even happier than the eight drinks had made me feel.

And what about Ted? Well, I did think about him for a moment, as I walked away from Rick. But this was such a once-in-a-lifetime opportunity that I couldn't give it up. By this time I was so good at making excuses for myself that I hardly had to think twice to defend my actions. Ted and I hardly have anything going, I told myself. I mean, it's not like we're going out or anything. Plus, maybe it was a bad idea to try to have a normal relationship. Maybe I'm not ready for it yet. And that was that.

That night one of my only true friends from school was throwing his first big party. When I arrived, all the popular kids from his grade were there. After a few drinks, I called Rick to invite him over.

The next thing I remember Rick and I were making out in the bushes in front of the house. Of course, everyone saw. Wilson persuaded me to at least find somewhere more discreet to do whatever I wanted to do. So Rick and I hopped in his car and drove away. That was all that people needed to start the rumors.

It wasn't long until Ted heard the stories. He called me on Sunday night. It was horrible. He told me I was the first person who ever made him feel like a real man. Why did I do this to *him*? Was he not fast enough for me? He was crying. There was nothing I could do to make amends for what I had done. Not just to Ted, but to myself, my family, my church, God. I could feel the weight of the world bearing down on me, about to collapse. In that moment the gates opened up. Feelings of worthlessness, guilt, shame, sadness—all the emotions that I had been refusing to feel, that I had intentionally dammed up inside me by drinking alcohol, alcohol, and more alcohol—it all came rushing out in a torrent. I felt like Jesus Christ, all the sins of the world cast upon me in a matter of moments. Except these weren't the sins of the world, these were *my* sins.

Do you know what a shock it is to the system to feel so many emotions all at once, after not feeling anything—nothing—for months on end? It's paralyzing, to say the least. He was sobbing. What could I do? I was bawling inside. But I had forgotten how to express those kinds of emotions. Or maybe I should say I had unlearned it.

I slept for only two hours that night. I dreaded Monday. I considered staying home from school, but that would be a cowardly public statement. At school I could feel the stares, hear the whispers as I walked by. By the end of the school day I felt extreme blackness cover my insides like a blanket. It was too much to bear. I had to shut myself off again or else I would have a nervous breakdown. I was sure of it.

The worst part was the Student Council meeting. Ted was a representative. He sat quietly in the back row, like the martyr that he was. The meeting was complete disorder. Everyone thought they had the right and the duty to condemn me. This was their way of showing their disrespect.

Eventually things at school died down. I didn't get back my ability to feel, but I didn't really expect to either. I had undergone a trauma. I would never be the same again. Sometimes I pitied myself. I'm still a kid, I would say to myself. I'm not supposed to have to grow up this fast. But I knew I had only myself to blame for it all.

It took this harrowing experience for me to realize I had become obsessed with the powerful feeling I obtained from controlling men. Through it all, I never thought to quit my drinking. I knew that my lack of self-control was worst when I was drunk. But quitting drinking would disrupt my whole life. And I just wasn't ready for that. I needed all the comfort I could get at that point.

In many ways college was just like high school. I quickly got a reputation that I was fun to party with, and everyone had a funny, "One time Sarah was so drunk that she . . . " story to tell. The most important difference was Dan. I met him my second day on campus. The moment I saw him my heart started racing. He wasn't just good-looking, he was strikingly so. This guy was *gorgeous*. And as we began to talk I saw that his beauty was not just skin deep. Our friendship was like love at first sight. From that first night and every day after, my amazement, admiration, and enjoyment of Dan just grew and grew.

We spent all our free time together. We could be found lying side-by-side on the lawn doing homework, meandering through town, and eating breakfast, lunch, and dinner together. Not only did we have a terrific time, but I was constantly in wonder of how alike we seemed, despite our apparent differences. He from the Northeast, me from the South; he from the big city of Boston, me from the midsized tourist town of Sarasota; he Chinese American, me white, Cuban American; he the oldest of his siblings, me the youngest. But we seemed to find common ground in everything. We were like two puzzle pieces made of different materials, by the hands of different craftsmen, who had spent their lives adjusting to the fact that we would never quite fit in with the rest. Then all of a sudden, by some twist of fate, we discovered that we fit—together, perfectly.

It was three months into our friendship before we confessed our romantic love for each other. The ensuing months were heavenly. We were so in love and happy about it that the most frequent comment we received from friends was, "You guys make me sick."

The only thing we didn't have in common was drinking. Dan wasn't a big drinker. His social scene in high school had never included drinking as a regular activity. Our freshman year he went to the frats, because that was the main social activity, but he didn't derive his pleasure from drinking, like I did. About four months into freshman year—we had been together as a couple for only a short time—my partying became a problem for us. Dan was getting tired of staying at frats until midmorning, when he wasn't even having a good time. But this was my way of having fun and I wasn't ready to give that up for any reason. I don't think it was a matter of being addicted to alcohol at that point. I just enjoyed that scene—the people, the noise, the drunk intellectual conversations, and, yes, the drinking. But maybe that lifestyle is part of the mental addiction.

Dan and I never discussed these issues. About three months into our romantic relationship I kissed another guy at a frat after Dan had left. It wasn't a long, passionate kiss. A quick peck. But the guilt was overwhelming. I confessed to Dan the next morning. We talked about why it had happened, how I needed to control myself when I drank, but we hardly scraped the surface. The real conversation started when I confessed to a much greater sin. Two weeks after we started dating we had a one-month vacation. On my trip back home I slept with my recent ex-boyfriend, Keith. Dan almost couldn't handle it. We practically broke up. But my begging and pleading finally convinced him that *he* was the one I wanted to be with, that I would never let it happen again.

Other than those incidents, our relationship was wonderful. It was the happiest, healthiest relationship I had ever been in. We never came out of the "in love" stage. We were affectionate and snuggly and passionate, but we also had stimulating intellectual discussions and challenged each others' perspectives.

At the end of our freshman year, we were faced with a summer apart. I had an internship in Miami, about five hours from my hometown, and he had an internship in Boston. I knew I'd be spending several weekends at home, and a part of me wanted the freedom to be able to hook up with people at parties, if the opportunity arose. I explained that I wanted to be with him. In fact, I wanted to marry him, eventually. But I needed this last chance to be free and irresponsible, before I grew up and settled down. He couldn't understand how we could be anything but monogamous and still stay together. Finally he put his foot down. Either we stayed exclusive or we broke up. I agreed. We would stay exclusive.

All summer we talked every day. We talked on the phone at night, we e-mailed each other from work during the day. All was going well. I had visited home a few times and I was confident in my ability to stay true to my promise.

Fourth of July is always a big celebration in my town, and it's a huge drinking affair. By the time the fireworks ended, I was very happily drunk. I had invited a few of my old drinking buddies over, for old times sake. While we were all hanging out on the front porch drinking, I began to notice how attracted I was to one of my old friends. When everyone else had left, we began to kiss. One thing led to another and we ended up in bed. I didn't really want to have sex with him. That wasn't at all what I had in mind. But that's what happened. I was so drunk that I didn't really care. All I could muster was a questioning, "Um, Rob?" As if to say, what are you doing? But I didn't feel strongly enough about it, at the time, to put up much of an argument. Needless to say, it was terribly unenjoyable.

The next morning came and I felt like shit. I knew I had to tell Dan. That had been his one request. "Sarah, if you care about me in the slightest, you'll give me the respect of telling me if anything happens over the summer." I boarded the bus back to Miami and thought about how I was going to tell him. How I was going to explain that it wasn't passionate, it wasn't meaningful, it had just happened. Most of all, how was I going to keep him from dumping me?

I called that night. I cried. He was silent. He had expected it, he explained. He had felt something, a certain foreboding, about me going home for the holiday. He called me late on the night of the fourth, hoping that if the thought of him was fresh on my mind, it would stop me from doing anything. But it hadn't. He broke up with me. I said everything I could to win him back. Finally I told him I would quit drinking.

"Good! You need to. But that's not going to make what you did any better. And it won't solve the problem, either. I want you to want *me*. No one else. Whether you're drunk or sober, I need to be the object of your love *and* your lust. You need me, but you don't want me." Maybe he was right. But I had to do something. I called AA that night and found out where the meetings were held.

For twenty-four hours Dan and I were in Hell, separately. I called him the next night. We were miserable. I don't think he even liked me, at that point. I could hear the distaste in his voice. I didn't deserve him. We both knew it. I had caused him so much awful pain. But we were even more miserable apart. So he took me back. It was going to take a long time to mend his broken heart and regain his trust. All I could do was hope—hope that our happiness together wasn't over for good.

Quitting was the only thing I could actively work on to improve things with Dan. I stopped drinking cold turkey. It was easy while I was in Miami. I barely had a social life there, so I rarely had the opportunity to drink. My visits home were the true test. My family had become so accustomed to my drinking habits, that they questioned my sudden abstinence. Over the next few months, my sisters and parents each took their turn explaining that I need not be so extreme. A little alcohol surely couldn't hurt, they implied. But I knew myself. I knew I couldn't drink without getting drunk. I never had experienced that mentality. My mind only worked a certain way. Once I have the first sip, my only goal is getting wasted. I knew that my craving wouldn't be quenched by one drink. It wasn't the taste that I desired, it was the feeling. That euphoric buzz that leads to a numb semiconsciousness. No, I couldn't even have a sip.

When I first quit drinking, I felt like I was missing out on the best of life. Who can go back to a normal lifestyle once they've experienced the passion and extreme highs of living for the moment, completely rid of the inhibitions of societal norms and personal conscience? The memory of my fast-paced, extravagant lifestyle was not enough. I wanted to experience more. Being at a college where drinking makes up the bulk of social interaction did not help. When I saw crowds of drunk people meandering through frat row I felt so much hostility. I wanted to be there, I wanted to join them. I didn't want to grow up yet. And, damn it, I shouldn't have to. I'm 18 and I deserve to be still having fun, I told myself. What I knew had been fun and exciting. How could something else be anything but dull and mediocre?

To Dan, my decision to quit drinking on July 5, 1998 was a statement that I had recognized, at last, all the pain and injury that my alcohol use had inflicted on myself and those around me. But that's not what it was to me. To me, it was admitting that keeping Dan was more important to me than continuing to drink. Realizing the myriad of ways that alcohol had affected my life would be a long process.

Before I could see that my alcohol use was the cause of many problems, I had to admit that I had problems. I needed to admit that *by my own standards* my life had gone to hell. I had to admit that I had slipped so far from where I wanted to be. I thought of myself as a failure. The first step is admitting to myself that I feel this way and then recognizing that the source of these feelings is me, my perspective, the way I think life ought to be.

I feel like I have done a lot of harm in my day, to myself and to others. I've broken the hearts of guys who were foolish enough to invest feelings in me, during my alcohol and sex binges. And I never to this day even thought about what I had done to them. I've seen sides of myself that I never wanted to believe I was capable of. God gave me the ability to influence people, to captivate them, and I desecrated these gifts by using them for sexual conquests and to further myself politically. This is not religious guilt, put on me by someone else. It's the way I feel inside.

It took me two years just to gain enough distance to be able to talk about drinking without wanting to be engaged in it, deep inside. I'm finally secure enough in my identity as a nondrinker to be able to look objectively at my experiences. I have just started this process. It seems like I'm rather late—two years and I haven't made much progress in all that time. But the way I look at it, at least the process has started. With the birth of my daughter six months ago I became responsible for a brand new life. Today, my desire to take care of my family gives me a whole new appreciation for the sober life.

13 In Search of My Voice

Born in Bombay and living in Malaysia for part of his childhood schooling before returning to India, this college student tells of the path that brought him from the East to a small liberal arts college in the American Northeast. Eager to be accepted by American society and his college peers, Devneesh is devastated by the racist and misogynistic attitudes his first-year roommate harbors. He is compelled in this hostile environment into a period of profound self-questioning and self-contempt, viewing himself as a tan dog paraded around by the college trustees to make his predominately white college seem more diverse. Only when he has forged close bonds with a young Jewish man and an East Asian woman, does he begin to discover his own voice and reconcile his ethnicity with his environment. He emerges from his college experience with a new acceptance of his identity as a "wanderer" and with a strong desire to contribute to American society and make part of this country his own.

I was a complex ball of pride and insecurity as I passed through the immigration post at Boston's Logan Airport. I remember standing, bags and passport in hand, in a patch of sunlight streaming through a window, surrendering to the moment and feeling like the emperor of my life. I felt exhilarated. Liberated. Accepted. Welcomed. Now I could finally try to realize my dreams, I thought. But the truth is, I was running away, away from the shadowy patches in my memory. Ashamed of the person I knew myself to be, I was far from being the person I wanted to become.

I was alone for the first time in a strange land of beautiful, graceful white people. I was taken by how structured and controlled the faces around me at the terminal were. They all looked so smart and mature. So civilized and polished. I felt suddenly immersed in opulence. The abundance and obvious prosperity, however, struck me as being somehow cold. There was also a curious strain on these faces. What burden could these Children of Fortune possibly bear that would explain their placid, dispirited demeanor? They smiled out of habit and laughed occasionally, but it seemed their hearts were not in it. I figured people must just get bored when they have everything they could possibly want.

I was picked up at the airport by Sunil. My father and his had known each other for decades, and though we had met only briefly before in the security of my home in Bombay, I was delighted to see a familiar face and kept close to his heels. The cab we rode in was huge. I worried about how many precious dollars would be spent on this lavish form of transportation. I was beginning to feel the strain of my journey. My mind had been in a state of alert for quite a while, absorbing, observing, learning, unlearning, listening, tuning, and mostly worrying. Sunil was talking rapidly, about the rich history of Boston, his two years as a graduate student, and the developments in his research since we had last met. I could see him talking to me, but his voice began to fade away. My mind was fatigued, and I was getting weary of the adventure. I wanted to be in the comfort of my mother's presence, and I longed for the soothing smell of her saree.

Nevertheless, I was excited and anxious to meet my roommate-to-be. Jon arrived at Sunil's humble apartment the next day in a BMW and we shook hands, expectantly. His palm enveloped mine, his grip was firmer than I was comfortable with. Although I had nibbled on some breakfast, Jon and I set out to grab a bite. I couldn't help but gaze in wonder at his brown eyelashes. His fingers were so fat. His manner so stiff and controlled. His voice so monotonic. And his expression so condescending. I soon found myself fighting the thought that to Jon we were clearly not equals.

We zipped around Boston and came to a cafe he was obviously familiar with. I was taken by the name, Au Bon Pain, which I dared not try to pronounce. I followed him closely, picking up a tray and looking at the menus, just as he did. I was in for a shock: "What? Two dollars for orange juice! Even more for a muffin. What the hell is a muffin anyway? You have got to be kidding. I don't want to spend that much especially when I'm not in dire need of it." Resolved not to drain my wallet, I picked up a carton of milk, and sheepishly told him that I wasn't hungry. He was visibly irritated, and offered to treat me. When I declined, he was provoked further, telling me I had no reason not to be hungry, and that I shouldn't have eaten before, since we had arranged to have brunch together. His derisive tone left a strong impression. I would have liked him to be more understanding about my obvious embarrassment at not wanting to spend the money. No doubt it was an awkward situation for him as well, but there was clearly a significant difference between Jon and me.

I had thought about all the things we could do as roommates exploring a new college setting for the first time together, making friends, playing games, and talking about women, but now I began to feel a little worried. He was asking me if my mustache was a "normal" thing for people in Asia. He was curious to know if I was a hero back home among my villagers, since I was coming to an institution that was obviously superior to anything within their reach. Surely, he surmised, I must come from one of the richest families in India to be able to afford an education here.

On the ride back to Sunil's we were briefly interrupted by Jon's mother calling him on his car phone. Later in the year, casting his caution away, Jon would joke to me about how his mother had asked him during that phone conversation if I smelled like curry. I did not suspect it at the time, and noticed only that he was uneasy and eager to denigrate his mother to give me the impression that he was less dependent on her than he really was. I wondered if Jon and I would ever grow to see each other as individuals, past the obvious differences that distracted us. In all my excitement about college and the wonders of partaking in the American melting pot, it had thoroughly escaped me that I might be an unwanted intruder, an alien entity from a backward planet, whom some Americans, out of generosity and magnanimity of spirit, had allowed to study and work here, and to marvel at their superior, evolved nature of being.

I was greeted in Hanover the next day by a brief respite of beauty, where these concerns receded again. The Environmental Orientation Trip was perfectly suited for a wide-eyed novice to nature who did not know what Gore-Tex shoes and sleeping bags were. Eternally thankful for every moment of the experience, I was taken by the untouched purity of nature around me—the clear river water, the age-cracked pines, and the cleansing mist in the mornings. The hope that the natives of such a heavenly abode might also be pure in their spirit of humanity seeped back into me. I especially liked my trip leader, and two others—a gentle Vietnamese girl and a quiet Puerto Rican guy. I was happy to have them as friends, with whom I ate my meals, trekked the woods, canoed the placid river, and even did some good old-fashioned bird watching. Rationalizing that they were both naturalized Americans, and therefore not too far from the people I would soon live among, my optimism that Dartmouth might indeed accept me grew stronger, and therefore more dangerous.

I met many people the next few weeks, attended many orientation sessions, and took many tests. Throughout the whole first week, Jon and I never managed to say more to each other than a polite greeting. We agreed he could take the bigger of the two adjacent rooms that made up 102 Sage. He brought in decorators, including his mother, to carpet his room, wheel in the television, VCR, and music system, and help him put up posters of cars, women, and all the different types of condoms one could ever want to use.

A lot happened that fall term; Jon positioned himself as J.J., and Devneesh shied away into Dev. Calling myself "Dev" eased the burden of enduring introductions, but I soon started feeling like a cheap imported car. I felt stared at and patronized in social gatherings, and learned to make clever excuses to avoid them. J.J. found a few like-minded males to bolster his image, and soon used alcohol and his critique of those things called women to pretend he was at ease. Ironically, he was seen as the mature, sensible guy who carried his wealth in style, and was magnanimous enough to bear the burden of living with "one of them alien types."

J.J. was a key figure in my process of adaptation. I would occasionally wake up to his morning mantra, "Dev's a fag." He introduced me to his buddies, who would poke and test my cultural beliefs. "Dev the Man, tell them why you don't eat meat." "Devdom, tell them about why you don't drink." "Dev, is it 'cuz it's bad Karma or something?" And they would chant "Karma Man" for painful lengths of time. I once retorted that I didn't need alcohol to bring down my defenses. "But don't you just wanna let go for a while?" they asked. Let go from what? I thought then that these defensive pink angels were all playing a game none really wanted to be part of, but that societal and parental expectations forced them to play roles from which weekend binges provided brief relief.

As J.J.'s pictures of his family disappeared from his room to save him the embarrassment of showing attachment, mine surfaced from the folder I had kept them hidden in, to keep me from giving up. I finally felt I could bear to see them without breaking down. Oh, I missed them so! But I couldn't let myself admit it, lest I shatter to pieces. I was working in the College Cafe, learning to flip omelets, make sandwiches, mop the floor, and run the dishwasher. When I would return from my shift on Friday nights at midnight, looking to sleep off the strain of the week, there would inevitably be a party in our suite. I would sob into my pillow while I held it over my head to muffle Axel Rose's disturbing "mother-fucker" and "bitch" and Nirvana's anguishing screams that made me shudder with fear. I would try to quiet my mind with a little prayer, and then lie awake wondering if at any moment J.J.'s friends were going to barge into my room and beat me up as a way to release some of the aggression their music seemed to breed. I would curl into my ten-dollar polyester blanket and peer through the holes I had made in it.

I did not exist to J.J. and his friends. In the room that always had its door closed, there was no human being, no feelings that hurt, no intellect that mattered, and certainly no one who was being kept awake. Nothing. They could blare their music, flaunt their phobias about immigrants and "faggots," and all would be well. J.J. would tell me how he felt international students at Dartmouth—heck, in the whole USA—should all just go back home. They were leeches that took away valuable slots that local students were denied. They drained the financial aid that his parents were indirectly paying for. I, as an "import," was just getting in his and other people's way.

While peering through my blanket one night, the door swung open, and in walked a few of J.J.'s friends. They seated themselves on my bed, used my phone, ate my chips, and tottered around for a while completely oblivious of the curled-up bump under the blanket. They appeared to me to be shouting in argument about something, but that could just have been my fear exaggerating their intimidating presence. They left eventually, and I tried impotently to find relief in sleep.

When I expressed timidly to J.J. that I hadn't slept much the previous night, he said, "Dude, it's a party. Dude. Everything is cool." I desperately hoped I had appealed to his sense of pity, and scrambled away thanking him. Soon after, however, it happened again. I came back from the cafe, my bones feeling brittle and my nerves throbbing, to a smoky, noisy room of judgmental eyes. My confusion and fatigue gave me an extraordinary temper. I lay in my bed, fuming and humiliated, for a couple of hours. Then I picked up my courage, opened the door, and requested that they turn the music down. "Oh, sure thing, Dude," replied a sniggering voice, and after I closed the door, the music got louder.

"I have had it with you, J.J.," I raged to myself. I put on my jeans and rushed out of my room, heading across the green toward the campus police office. But as I got closer, my courage seemed to abandon me. By the time I crossed the green, I was contemplating giving them a few more hours to enjoy themselves before I went back. After all, I reasoned, I was only an import. They had a right to their fun, and there was no sense in my getting in the way.

So I curled up on a bench and tried to snooze away the growing lump in my throat. A black dog with a red collar sauntered around the green and soon settled itself comfortably near me on the ground. Though I have been afraid of dogs from a very young age, this dog felt like my soul mate. He understood me. He was me; I was he. My position at Dartmouth College was like that of a tanned dog that walked on two legs. When my owners, the college trustees, pleased, I would walk around, parading myself, contributing to their vision of diversity. In return they paid for my college expenses. The humiliation and worthlessness that I felt that moment on the bench still make me very angry. I had reduced myself to a state in which I was glad just to be patted on the head, fed now and then, and allowed to wander freely, as long as I didn't bother anyone. The indignity numbed me. I curled up, defensive and weak, too empty for tears.

But I asked myself a fundamental question. Why did I let them do this to me? They are not to blame, really—I am. I let them taunt me. I didn't have the courage to face them, to ask for what I deserved: basic respect, not for special accomplishment, but for the simple reason that I was a human being. And something changed in me that night. I saw myself for the proud, arrogant, overachieving geek that I was. I deserved every bit of the abuse I had gotten. What a coward I had been. In my desperation to make America my home, a place where I would be accepted, I was giving in too much. But I was going to take it no more. The lesson was learned, and it was time for me to raise myself up, for my own life, my own happiness, and my own free will.

I returned to my room feeling empowered. It was deserted, and I slept. The next morning, I firmly told J.J. there would be no more parties in our room. And to my amazement there were not. I slowly began to change my accent, listening intently to those around me and practicing my American voice in whispers. I put on a mask of the stoic male that I felt would keep the curious at bay. My classes became the focus of my attention. It was time to start bridging the gap between who I really was and who I wanted to be. I had reached the nadir of my existence, and now felt cleansed and ready to undertake a process of building. For the remainder of freshman year I erected my scaffolding for this ambitious construction project that I intended to last a lifetime.

While I struggled to handle my roommate's bigotry, I fought another battle— a crush on a woman I imagined would be the answer to all my problems. One of the first acquaintances I made at Dartmouth was with Farha. On the first day of fall term, I was eating alone in the dining hall, contemplating a bland salad and wondering if I would be able to sustain myself as a vegetarian much longer. When I got up to surrender the dirty plates, my eye caught someone else sitting alone at another table. She looked Indian, and I was struck by the radiance of her face and her shiny black hair.

I excitedly went over to her table, trying to appear casual and comfortable, and introduced myself. She said she was Farha from Pakistan. To me she was Sunshine from Good Land. She spoke with almost childlike mannerisms that betrayed her full, bright red lips and big shining teeth. I shook her soft Vaseline hands and

helped myself to a chair across from her. We talked about simple things, like adjustment difficulties, and she responded with the most sympathetic eyes I had ever
seen. After I left, Farha grew on me, like a fungus.

I thought of her constantly, using the memory of her soft manner to bolster
me during the first few difficult weeks of that fall. In my imagination, I told her my
deepest fears and secrets, and confessed that things weren't really as good as I pretended they were. When we finally did get together, though, I would tell her she
was naive and unrealistic and portray myself as experienced and practical. I looked
upon her with disdain as a mere romantic who wouldn't survive in the real world.
But when we played pool, I would stand at a distance looking at her wondering if
she would ever see through the masks that I skillfully put up to distract her. Would
she ever see the aching, sentimental, romantic part of me? I fired a spear at her now
and then that punctured any desire she might have had to try and get closer to me,
and sure enough she stopped trying to understand me altogether. I thought less of
her for having let me win in the battle to defeat myself. I gave up the hope that
Farha and I would ever be close friends. J.J., in sympathy with my failed hopes, explained that I needed to find myself an American woman who wasn't going to has-
sle me with "all this Islamic shit."

J.J.'s bigotry, Farha's rejection, and a growing feeling of academic incompetence made me miserable that year. I vividly remember one afternoon in that first
winter, when I went down to the river, lay on a hammock, and contemplated walking onto the frozen river, not caring if I would fall through and freeze. As I lay
there, I asked myself a key question: "Why should I go on—what is there for me at
Dartmouth or anywhere else?"

I don't think I was serious about doing anything drastic to endanger myself,
but it was the possibility of suicide that spurred me to think of reasons to live another day. I was working hard, plodding away at physics and math classes that I
did not care much for, and also working grudgingly at the cafe. What was it all for?
To graduate from Dartmouth and work myself up the ladder so that J.J. and I could
one day sit at the same table, drive the same cars, and live in similar houses? I knew
that, beneath my insecure shell, material respect was not what I craved. The over-
achievers and super-competitive people at Dartmouth that I lived and worked
with were not role models for me. And if their lifestyle was all that my time spent
in Hanover was leading up to, then I didn't really care if it ended or not.

As I lay there, my mind wandered into the depths of my latent childhood
memories. Although it felt like I had come such a long way from places I had once
called home, in another sense I was still facing the same conflicts. I remembered
that there were actually a few times when I had pondered taking my own life.
These times came invariably when I did not meet the standards that I or others had
set for me. My right to live in this world, I thought, was earned every day by my
achievements, failing which, it only seemed natural and fair that I should forfeit
that right.

I think I must have made the connection between parental affection and high
achievement during my first few years of schooling in Bombay. Report Card Day
was easily the most important time of the year. It surpassed birthdays, festival

days, and certainly vacation days. There was a ritual that I practiced every Report Card Day. I would be playing in the street outside my house, growing excited in anticipation, waiting for sight of my father returning home. Just as his car turned the corner, I would abandon my game and my friends to race home, wildly, and hide under my bed, clutching my brown report card. As he entered the house, exhausted and hungry, he would hand over his briefcase to my mother, Amma, and with a twinkle in his eye would play along with my game, asking Amma where I was. She would call out for me, and I would emerge from my hiding place, pretending to be afraid to face my father, hoping to mislead him into thinking I had done poorly. I would look down at my feet, report card hidden behind my back, trying to act grief-stricken. Amma would tell him it was Report Card Day, at which point I would unveil my hidden treasure, flashing the gold star pasted on it that indicated I was first in my class, the passport to my father's affection. He would chuckle in satisfaction, beckon me to him, plant a noisy kiss on my cheek, and shower me with a string of nicknames. They made little sense, but they made my year worth living.

This annual ritual was altered one day when I stayed indoors on Report Card Day, shaking genuinely with fear. I had gotten a silver star instead of gold, and was at a loss as to how I could possibly face my father. Would I be beaten? Or perhaps just bitterly scolded, which was usually worse. Maybe he would cast me away, disowning me, and renouncing his ties to a failure like me. Instead, he simply washed up, sat down for dinner, and conferred the title of "The Second One" on me. I was taunted and teased for being "The Second One," and the newcomer who was first that year became my prime target of hatred and competition. I held him responsible for taking away my father's loud kisses and nicknames, and made sure that I never relinquished my gold star again. After that year I never heard "The Second One" again.

The thought of losing my father's attention and affection gave me the motivation to achieve and earn my parents' pride. I also saw my achieving as fulfilling my *dharma,* or duty, as the way to assure them that their generous investment in me was not in vain.

When I was younger, my father ruled the house with firm discipline. The hierarchy was very clear: The decisions were made by the head of the household, my father. My mother had the right to voice her views, and my sister and I had the right to voice a suggestion, but it was my father's firm nod of the head that made legislation. I loved my father dearly and longed to be strong and wise like him someday. He had no qualms in showing affection and would often make me laugh by playfully wrestling with me, dancing around most awkwardly, and making faces impossible for me to replicate. I relished his barrage of affectionate nicknames and squirmed with delighted embarrassment when he got into those affectionate moods. And I felt that on each Report Card Day, I extended my lease on the right to be his son for yet another year.

Soon, though, my father's scrutiny extended into everything else in my life. He felt he needed to correct my habits, my etiquette, my speech, my English, my posture, my behavior, my temper, my style of handling situations, my need for tact, the volume of my voice. He helped me develop an introspective view of myself, to know how to identify my weaknesses and improve upon them. That trait helped me a lot when I found it necessary to stop, take stock of a situation, evaluate where I was headed, and then make the changes I felt necessary, all without inflicting too much pain on my bloated ego.

However, my father's constant vigilance also made me very self-conscious. I had to put up the front of being the ideal son in his presence. When we moved to Malaysia after my seventh birthday, I came to associate this "ideal" identity with my academic performance. Indigestion before exams was my measure of sure success. My other Indian friends chose to keep a distance from me, as I became unpleasantly competitive in every field. On Report Card Day, I beat all my enemies, as well as all my fears and insecurities. I earned the bronze medal for my class every year, and prided myself in being the top Indian student.

The Chinese believed they were naturally a superior race, and established themselves as the hardworking, deservedly prosperous ruling majority in Malaysia. The darker races, Malay and Indian, were lulled into a submissive role as lesser peoples and accepted what little came their way. But I was never an easy person to suppress. I had a mouth too big and a voice too loud, which made many people uncomfortable. I was spurred by parental pressure as well as by the need to champion my race. I built my life around competition and achievement.

In sixth grade I was faced with a mammoth challenge to these aspirations. My parents had set their sights on St. Joseph's Institution (SJI) as the best place for my secondary education. Now it was up to me to work toward getting into it; I hated that whole year. I had nightmares for months before the nationwide exams that determined who got into which school. I spent the majority of my time at my desk, mostly worrying. That year, my indigestion gave me little comfort that I would be able to succeed. I needed something alternative to fall back on in case I failed to get into SJI. For years I had walked across a bridge over a canal on my way to school. I decided that if I was not accepted at SJI, I could easily climb over the green sides of the bridge and put myself at the mercy of the cars and the canal below. The thought of thus escaping facing my father comforted me at night, and I waited for the day of the results. As I went to school that fateful day, I marked the spot on the bridge that would be ideal to jump from. But I had indeed gotten into SJI—the premier secondary school for boys in Malaysia.

Until then I had largely been ignorant of my life as a pawn in the success story that my parents had designed for me. But now, as I approached age 13, I was beginning to understand more of the world around me, and came to realize that for the most part, that world did not include me. I saw that I was entrapped in this game of parental expectations, but did not have the courage to try and change the rules.

My first week in St. Joseph's was spent in admiration of its traditions and its hundred and sixty-odd years of high achievement. In my first year, I was initiated into the various conflicts that plagued the remainder of my years in Malaysia: fighting for my space, defending my race against the Chinese, struggling to relate to the other Indians who were of a different worldview, trying to sustain myself on a vegetarian diet, and struggling to live up to my father's expectations.

My Indianness centered mostly around classical Carnatic music, vegetarianism, and my newfound interest in meditation. The other Indian boys, because of their different interests, stuck together, spoke in their slang, idled on the stairs, and did badly academically. Although I found myself defending them to the Chinese, I didn't really identify with them either. I found myself rationing my time and efforts among all the groups, not wholly respecting or belonging to any one, but trying to fit in with all of them.

One aspect of my lifestyle that set me apart was my *mridangam,* a drum that is played in classical Carnatic music. The tradition is strong in my family, and many relatives hoped that I would follow suit and become a famous Carnatic percussion player. In Malaysia I began taking lessons. I enjoyed the first few years, and basked in all the attention I got. I performed on stage and on TV and radio a few times in Malaysia. However, once I entered SJI, academic excellence became my foremost concern and *mridangam* was relegated to a mere hobby. In my second year at SJI, I got tired of making excuses to avoid the required two hours of daily practice. Complaining that schoolwork was just too hectic, I turned away from *mridangam.* My father soon came to accept my change of heart, although he predicted that after I grew up I would look back and regret having quit.

My father was right. I do regret it. I could have grown to relish cooking up rhythmic patterns in my head, to revel in expressing my creative energy. But there was one glitch that made me stop. I had tried hard to get the exercises right, but it wasn't easy. I would practice till my hands bled on the rim of the drum, but I just couldn't seem to get it right. The thought that I could try so hard and fail at something was devastating to me. I had built the illusion of being a super-achiever. Everything else came easily to me, and *mridangam* had to as well. When it didn't, I decided to pack it up. My father bestowed on me another title—"The Quitter."

My father came home soon after with news that when I finished the school year we would have to relocate to India. We had lived in Malaysia for nine years, and it had affected my view of my homeland. India, with its lackluster economic performance, was a frequent butt of jokes in Malaysia, where material success was the all-important element of survival. Even to the local Indians, I would try to defend India, talking about its history, its benign nature, the endearing humanity of the people, and so on. But now, faced with the idea of going back and living in Bombay, I found myself quite opposed to the thought of ruining my career prospects, stuck in a rut in an unknown corner of the world.

Knowing that I was going to be gone soon, my ties to friends became stronger and more sentimental. I cried through my entire farewell ceremony at SJI. When our departure day came, I was touched to find twenty-three of my friends at the airport to see me off. As I walked to the plane, I turned to take a last look and saw a line of dark faces lining the windows of Gate 34, making me feel like the most loved person in the world. They gave me the confidence that I was indeed ready for India, and I tried to look forward to my first breaths of winter air in as long as I could remember. It would be a stark difference, I told myself, and I must try to make the best of it. In retrospect, I am glad that we moved to Bombay. The tough streets of Bombay were an ideal classroom to have my identity and core beliefs bolstered in preparation for my giant leap across continents to an American college. In the two years there, my own voice grew louder and more confident both within my family and in school; indeed, Bombay ultimately helped show me who I was.

We landed in Bombay on January 9, 1989, almost ten years after we had left. My initial reaction was one of simple shock. We landed at night and were guided through the airport and the streets to the hotel. I still see the images: a mass of dark oily faces pressing themselves on the glass windows of the airport; the taxi cab, an arcane remnant of the 1960s; the empty, narrow, dimly lit streets of Bombay; and the hotel room that served as our home for a month as our apartment was renovated far behind schedule. It was a tough experience for all of us, and tensions grew.

One evening my father returned from the office and noticed that I had left my sweater unfolded on his bed. The smoldering volcano finally began to spew lava. He began shouting at me about how I was completely irresponsible, uncooperative, and an utter pain in his rear. Finally I emerged from the bathroom, fed up with the abuse. I don't know what came over me, but I just didn't feel like hearing my father's inconsiderate noises any more. "It's not fair, Appa. I'm only 16. There's a limit to what I can take, too," I answered back.

For the first time I had found my voice and stood my ground, though fleetingly. We argued about the sweater for a while, and then I let him have the last word. He then asked us if we were ready for dinner. We normally alternated lunch and dinner between a Chinese restaurant in the hotel and a South Indian place farther down the street. The latter was my father's favorite, as it was the closest place he could get to home-cooked food. But being quite tired of the same Indian fare, I asked if we could eat Chinese for dinner instead. Old Faithful vented his steam yet again. "Don't you talk back at me. You either come with us, or don't eat at all."

I retorted, my voice quivering in fear, "It's just not fair. Not fair. We have our problems, too, you know. It's tough for all of us. You're the one who got the transfer to Bombay, and you go to the office and that's it. I have no idea what's going to happen from here on. I'm scared too. You're not the only one with problems."

My father gave me the look of a predator, too angry for words. He was beginning his strongest attack on me yet when the phone rang. While he talked my sister said that it was all over for me, and that the only sensible thing for me to do now was to apologize to father after he got off the phone. "Apologize for what?" I asked. And she said, "Just tell him you weren't thinking." He got off the phone and there was a cold and uncanny silence. I walked over meekly and told him I wasn't thinking. He looked up, and with his next words raised himself from being a mere policing benefactor to an adored role model. "That's not true. You were thinking. And you're right. It is tough on all of us. We'll go eat Chinese."

My sister couldn't believe it. My mom, glad to see the storm pass, bravely went up to my father and placed a supportive hand on his shoulder. At that moment, I loved my family. I believed that we were now ready to take whatever lay ahead for us in Bombay, for we were finally beginning to act as a unit that shared its fears and respected one another's needs. I understood, and even felt, my father's pain: He was scared, too, of what was going to happen to all of us. That incident represented a remarkable victory for me. I had taken a big risk in speaking out for something I felt strongly about, and the reward was quite sweet. I had been scared out of my wits, yet had taken a leap of faith, trusting my instincts that the just outcome would prevail. This incident, though minor, stuck with me thereafter. It flashed before my mind before I finally confronted J.J. at college, and again before I mustered up the strength to express my feelings toward Farha.

In the next couple of years my father and I became good friends. My sister attended university in Australia, and that left just three of us at home. My father had his frustrations and his lessons in adaptation at the office, and I had my daily trials at school. We brought them to the dinner table, where we shared our thoughts and grew to respect each other more. Knowing that I was trying my best to adapt and survive in school, my father didn't pressure me as much. I was discovering a confidant and a role model in my father.

Father also made no attempt to hide his pride in his son. He was happy with the way I was flourishing and maturing, growing in stride with the incremental measures of freedom given to me. I know that my growing older must have had something to do with it all, but I'm convinced that it was the softening of my father's nature that made Bombay bearable. Gaining his approval and making him proud of me, for who I was, for my ideas about people, for the way I dealt with situations, gave me tremendous encouragement and confidence.

Bombay went beyond just being a catalyst in the changing relationship with my father; it shaped my understanding of myself and of the people around me. It's a tough thing, becoming disillusioned with people. And I was disillusioned, over and over again, by the people who I came into contact with in Bombay. It was especially hard, since I had looked to India to fill a void that I felt in my identity. I went back to India thinking I was finally among my own people. We would understand each other, and we would be better accepted for the values and common faults we shared.

In short, I had been convinced that I would meet more like-minded people in Bombay, that I would develop strong connections that complemented my connections in Malaysia. I just had to! It was my culture—I was Indian, wasn't I? I had read the Mahabharata and Ramayana, hadn't I? I was initiated and reasonably religious, right? Put together, in my head, that meant that India and I shared a common "culture." I was to learn, much to my dismay, that culture goes beyond books, food, songs, and religion. It strikes at the core identity of a person, and Bombay and I were clearly not cut from the same cloth. The educated middle class in Bombay seemed to be caught up in living for societal approval, mainly by accumulating piles of money. I saw a society that was immensely cynical in its fatalistic surrender to suffering, and surprisingly aggressive, given its nonviolent modern history.

I soon found myself at Bombay Public School (BPS), the most expensive private school in Bombay. What I saw at BPS was nothing short of appalling, and it did not reassure me that I would soon fit in Bombay. The students would sit quietly and attentively when "Sir" or "Ma'am" was around, but the moment the authority figures left the classroom, mayhem broke loose. Chairs toppled, bodies clashed, as the boys, all younger than I, got together to play a game that they had invented, hitting a tennis ball against the back wall. There was absolute pandemonium at the back of the class where I sat.

A large part of my time was spent worrying about the state of affairs in Bombay. The education system, with its blind emphasis on pure percentage points and admissions tests, coupled with parental pressure, was wreaking havoc on the character of the students. All anyone cared about was grades. Character mattered not; as long as a student had the grades, every misdemeanor in the world could be justified. This bothered me a lot, for many reasons. What were these boys going to be like when they grew up? What kind of a society were we going to have? It was such a shock that I was going to be living with people like this; I was terrified that in a couple of years I would grow to assimilate and take on characteristics that I did not respect. Even if I didn't want to, the pressure to perform, given the yardsticks that others measured me by, would demand that I cheat on exams, and take every opportunity to push someone else down in order to climb a little higher myself. The survival game, played by trees and insects in the Amazon, was being enacted "live" in Bombay Public School, and I was probably the only person there detached enough to see it.

I had to do something. Anything. I stood for elections in my class and became a representative of the Students' Council. I decided to start with the smallest unit—my own classroom. I convinced my classmates to be more organized in maintaining and caring for our classroom. Soon they got the desks put in orderly rows, the floor swept, chalk for the teachers, and we started to actually feel proud being Class 11-F. Spurred by my success, I ventured into other classes. Soon thereafter I was walking up the stairs from recess when a group of boys "escorted" me into the bathroom; there they beat me up. "Just who the hell do you think you are? Just go back to Malaysia or Hong Kong or wherever it is that you came from. This is India, okay, and we like the way things are just fine." I was able to stare down their leader, again finding a determination that I did not know I had. This boy then actually apologized for the "misunderstanding," pulling something straight out of a Hindi movie. "Hey, man, we could use someone like you in our group. Why don't you join us? Here, take my hand in friendship." Although I turned down his invitation to join their gang, he went on to buy me a mango drink, apparently convinced that I was worthy of more respect than he originally thought.

After that, though, my attempts at organization slowly fell apart. I had hoped that the momentum of my early success would inspire others to join in and start contributing positively. Instead, as my energy waned, so did the condition of the classrooms. I was attracting more cynical derision than I was inspiring, and I soon learned to bear down and start working toward my escape from what seemed to me like Alcatraz.

The first year of Bombay, with its encounters with prejudice and closed-mindedness, took its toll on me. I grew cynical and aggressive—emotions that I felt I needed to get by from day to day. I also picked up the important Hindi expletives and managed to keep a few friends happy once in a while buying them drinks during recess. I met up with some of the more sophisticated girls, and was invited to dance parties; repressed and socially unknown as I was for much of my time in Malaysia, I thoroughly enjoyed the popularity I received in Bombay. But that was the public image of Devneesh in school. On the way home, I would release my tension and anger at the hopelessness around me by punching and kicking the back of the seat in front of me. By the end of the two years, that bus endured a lot of abuse from me—the metal seat was dented and mangled by the time I graduated from BPS.

I should say, however, that I was a markedly different person at home. I thought about each day, satisfied that I had pulled it off. Whew! I saw myself as playing a role in school to survive. It wasn't really me. Oh, no. The real me had to be securely hidden away. I nurtured myself at home, in the evenings, by meditating, in private, with the lights off, floating away to a distant place buried deep within me. I was amazed at the extent to which I learned to perfect the art, and soon grew to look forward to the two or three hours in the evenings when I sat by myself and worked diligently, toying with my thoughts, emotions, and beliefs. Meditation helped show me my strength and nurtured my idealistic beliefs, just as BPS helped to show me how low I could stoop.

I didn't really live in Bombay or go to BPS after that. I was distant from almost everybody I met and soon retreated into an inner shell where nobody was allowed. I rarely spoke in class and liked to spend recess on my own. There were not many strong connections of my liking to be made in Bombay. Taking the SATs and running away to an American college or university seemed like my only real option. Dartmouth was the only college for which the early decision deadline hadn't passed when I received the forms, so I put all my effort and prayer into that application and waited for the decision. When I was notified that I had been accepted, I shouted and jumped in my house for twenty minutes nonstop, for this represented an escape from Bombay and what the city had come to represent for me.

It is difficult to put into perspective the influence that Bombay had on me. It gave me a lot of strength and confidence in myself, as a person with mental ability and social skills. However, it also took away from me a certain mirth I had. Life became an endless struggle against suffering and disappointment. Defending myself against the challenges that faced me every day, I also learned to broaden my views about other human beings. I had never before been exposed to such magnanimity of spirit, or such depravity of morals. In Bombay, my ideas about what humanity and suffering meant gained broader, deeper definitions. But it had become clear to me that Bombay would not nurture the person whom I thought I wanted to become.

As I flew over western Asia and the Atlantic on my way to Dartmouth, my excitement and anticipation grew. Dartmouth was my final chance, my final hope for finding a place where I belonged. Turning away from Malaysia and now India, I looked to America to fill a void of identity and acceptance. Would I find a home? Would I find friends? Would I both give and receive love and respect? I admit it was a lot to expect from a new land, but Dartmouth was to be my very own unhindered opportunity to realize my ultimate goal—to know myself.

Which brings me to that afternoon in the winter of my first year, when I went down to the river, lay on the hammock, and contemplated walking onto the frozen river. In the calm of the frozen riverside, where the trees were laden with snow, I vaguely remembered a song from what seemed a long-forgotten distant past. During my second year at St. Joseph's the senior assistant used to lead us singing:

> If I can help somebody, as I pass along.
> If I can do my duty, to a world upwrought.
> If I can spread Love's message, that the Master taught . . .
> Then my living shall not be in vain.

That song had always made me feel happy, and it did this time, too. It made me think about what use I could be to a society and about what really gave me happiness. If I could make a difference to somebody or someplace, sometime, I thought that would make me happy. It would satisfy my need to do something lasting and productive. I could go on at Dartmouth, doing all the things I was supposed to, obeying the ingrained habits of my upbringing and my present company, but secretly hoping to make a difference, in my own private way, in my own private time. In doing so, I could perhaps know myself and be happy with what I knew.

The Devneesh that had been bred to succeed and achieve, for security and recognition, finally allowed another Devneesh some space to breathe and grow. The second Devneesh wanted to do what made him most happy—to try to live unconditionally. That day a small battle started between my two halves—one side accountable to my parents, seeking their approval, and the other stressing my independence, accountable only to itself and the few selected people that it respects. Foremost among the selected was Michael, who was my closest American male friend. I looked to him for a gateway into American life, and he always explained as patiently and sincerely as his listened. He did it without being condescending, as though he recognized that it was an effort for me to adjust. I wondered how Michael came to be so different from the other males that I had met. He was the reverse image of J.J., and I was eager and hopeful that our budding friendship would grow with time, and that we would continue to respect each other as we came to know each other's strengths as well as weaknesses.

I longed to be seen as an equal by Michael, for I saw that he was a good person and I wanted to have him accept me as such as well. I couldn't identify it then, but we shared a common thread: Both of us had been through times that were painful and that made us look beyond the immediate, requiring us to grow and shape ourselves to deal with the pain. Perhaps both saw ourselves as outsiders at this college: he, a Jew from Texas, and I, a Hindu from Bombay. As a result, we both had a certain measure of confidence and respect for ourselves, which not only enhanced the quality of our conversations, but also made us look to each other for understanding and empathy.

Friendship with Michael was played by strict rules. And I often worried that words spoken during a disagreement or in a bad mood would permanently come between us. There were many times when Michael saw me in one of my more insecure of defensive moods. He would see me put on airs to impress someone, or be rude to a mutual acquaintance. He saw me be socially rough around the edges, and saw me make my blunders. Sometimes he would say something about it: "What was that all about, Dev? I didn't really understand why you did that." Caught in the act, I would find myself scrambling to hide my nakedness. Realizing that defensive explanations, regardless of how creative, were probably not going to fool him, I'd find myself discussing my faults with him. As a result, he got to see me more completely, and the fear that he would reject me for my faults was slowly assuaged.

The other person who has commanded my enduring respect is Farha, who has since evolved from being a "fungus" in my imagination to becoming a part of my every day and night, my daily thoughts and feelings, my anger and my tears, such that I feel incomplete when she's not around me. I love her dearly, and she has given me what nobody else has before—honesty, trust, and respect. And she had brought out the same qualities in me, which I never really gave anyone else before either. She has become the active part of my conscience, which keeps me in check. She gave me the warmth of a mother, the support of a friend, the attention of an equal. We learn every day from each other, as we grow to understand each other more.

Yet as I explained earlier, it wasn't always like that. Our present relationship, cordial and occasionally intimate, began in the fall of my junior year, after I returned from a summer internship in San Francisco. After our dismal interaction during freshman year, we hardly met or spoke to each other during the fall of our sophomore year. That winter though, I decided to take the initiative to break the ice. It worked, and we cautiously experimented with getting to know each other as friends. Because of my friendship with Farha, I threw away an application for transfer that I had requested to MIT. There was too much I could potentially lose, I felt, if I left Dartmouth now.

After reuniting with Farha I got a summer internship, and the next few months turned out to be the most important three months of my first two years at college. It gave me relief from Dartmouth—from its fraternities that I felt excluded from, and from the constant competition and politics that plagues me there. It also gave me a chance to be alone, working hard, earning money, resting well on weekends, and cooking my own food. For the first time I started to feel I had a niche where I was cozy and comfortable. I also learned a most important lesson that summer.

It was a Saturday that summer, when two friends and I made a trip to Mount St. Helens. As we hiked up the volcano, we soon came to a point in the trail where a patch of snow lay dead in our path. If we were to go on to get a glimpse of the open top of St. Helens, we'd have to cross that patch and walk on for about an hour more. I looked down and saw that if I slipped while trying to cross it, I would slide for about a hundred meters and then fall right off the face of the mountain. I could feel my legs preparing to mutiny. I wanted so badly to get across, but was entrenched in the belief that I couldn't do it. I would fall. I would slip. I would die. I would look like a fool. I couldn't do it. It was a dumb idea. What would father say? He'd say it was a dumb idea. He's right, he's always right. Turn back now—and there won't be any trouble. No risk. No danger.

I wasn't going to look like the coward to my friends, though. Halfheartedly, I started to try to cross the iceberg. One step, left foot forward. That was okay. Next, move the right foot. Good. Now, move the left foot over. . . . Oops! . . . My foot slipped, and I panicked. I still had my right foot in place, and so I dug my fingers into the icy slope to keep from falling. Then my fingers started to freeze and I realized I had to do something fast. This was it. I was going to die. I began to run through a list of the things that I thought I would regret if I were to fall from that cliff. I wouldn't realize my dream of helping India out of its poverty, and I wouldn't live to give Farha the silver ring that I had made for her birthday. I remembered my parents, and thought to myself that they were going to be heartbroken at my death. One of my friends steadied me, and we inched our way backward off the snow. I was only too glad to be on firm ground again and thought that it was best to give up and head back.

We reluctantly turned around and started walking back, and I faced head-on the realization that I had given up on myself. It was my fear that had enlarged a simple patch of snow, not much different from those abundant in Hanover, into an imposing iceberg. I realized I was running away from an opportunity to do something that was within my reach because I was inhibited by my fear. And that patch symbolized many fears: my fear of never being completely independent of my family, my fear of failure, my fear of letting down those important to me, and, yes, my fear of not being able to face Farha without worrying about rejection.

I decided to try again, trying not to think of my fear of falling. I instead recited the Gayatri Mantra to calm myself, to remind myself of who I really was. I pushed away other thoughts, inhibitions, warnings, and fear signals, and just thought about getting across. Much to my amazement, in my newfound courage, the patch appeared no greater than a harmless speck on the ground. Before I knew it, I was across, and so were my friends. We went on to get a wonderful view of the side of the mountain that had been blown open, and I was amazed at how easy the whole thing had been. On our way back, we came across it again. There were a couple of middle-aged women trekking across it. Ashamed as I was that such a simple thing had almost gotten the better of me, I vowed that once I got back to campus, I would give Farha the ring, and I would tell her all there was to tell, tossing my defenses to the wind.

And that is exactly what happened. I told Farha quite plainly that much of the person I had shown her in the past two years was a hoax. I revealed that I had been scared of letting her see me in my natural state, lest she reject me. Vulnerable though I now was, I felt my affection for her flow through me. Farha, who had never been intimately involved with a male before, took some time to get used to the idea that she was interested in a guy. Given her family's strict objections to her being in a relationship, especially with a non-Muslim, it took inordinate courage on her part to take the steps that she did to get to know me better. She ventured out of her cocoon, and we spent days and nights finding out about each other, and finding ourselves in the process.

My upbringing was not geared toward taking risks. I am from a traditional conservative background that would have been only too happy if I had turned out no different from the generations before me—mild, passive, salaried, educated, and none too ambitious. But the events in my life, coupled with the impulses of my soul, ended up taking me out of that cozy cocoon, so much so that to go back would be akin to incarceration.

All through my adolescence, I have been struggling to find a community outside my home, struggling to find my own voice, to define my own dreams, to carve my own path. My parents will always be a part of me, even after they are not physically around to comfort and guide me. However, I still am looking, in earnest, to build a community of close friends who understand and stimulate me.

I struggled in Malaysia through my first ten years of schooling. Just as I was beginning to adapt adeptly, just as I was venturing out of my shell, learning the rules of the society vastly different from that in my home, I moved to Bombay. I thought I'd finally be home, but that too soon turned out to be a mirage. Unwilling to give up looking for a nest, I came to the United States, attempting to find that elusive community that would nurture me. Have I found it here in the four years that I've been looking? The answer perhaps lies in the fact that I know I can't go back to either Malaysia or Bombay now. I couldn't give up my links with Michael and Farha. I couldn't give up feeling hopeful again that my goal is still reachable. Here, in America, I am free to chase my goal of growing endlessly. I am free to give my voice freer reign than it ever had before. And as a result, I am the least cynical and unhappy that I remember ever being.

Still there are times that I feel America will never really be home either. I can be happy that I am around friends I love, but to most people I meet, I will always be a "legal alien." Alas, the age of the immigrant is over in America. A community of English-speaking Europeans have lived here long enough for their indelible cultural stamp to dominate. I fear I will be a member of a minority group wherever I go. Such is the life of a wanderer. Some enjoy wandering and may look upon my state with envy. I, however, am tired of wandering and want to feel a link to the land I am in, to the people I am with, and even to the air I breathe. I want the words I voice to be familiar to people around me, to have a deep relevance to their core being.

I want to feel like I helped build this American community. Helped it grow. Helped shape it so that it is better off in the future. I want this for me. I was born too late to fight in the American Civil War, too late to struggle in a sweatshop in New York during the Great Depression, too late to work alongside Gandhi while he built modern India. But my generation will also have its struggles, and I am perfectly poised to contribute a lion's share in the drama of the twenty-first century. So I continue in pursuit of this mirage, except I am, for the first time, enjoying the chase, relishing the risks, and loving scoping out the next opportunity that will give me a strong sense of connection with the people around me.

Trying experiences help one see oneself and know oneself better. My experiences have helped me get to know and love myself, and I'm more capable of respecting and loving others because of it. I know I have my own battles, my own challenges, my own red devils in the night, my own snow patches on cliffs, my own childhood fears and inhibitions, but I'm trying to grow out of them, one at a time, painstakingly moving toward a more fulfilling time, as I know and respect myself more. I am trying. I am doing it with a certain honesty and courage. And I can't give myself a better compliment than that.

14 Loving Women

This author describes the evolution of her sexuality from childhood sexual play through heterosexual relationships to her present identity as a lesbian. Rebecca was close to her father, who encouraged her intellectual interests, until she finds that in junior high school she needs to discount her intelligence and shun academic success in order to be popular. The resulting breach with her father is never repaired and seems to be a turning point; if the price of a man's love is conformity to being what he wants you to be, she can live without it. Toward the end of high school, her troubled boyfriend overwhelms her with his emotional needs and reinforces the sense of emptiness and not being fully understood in heterosexual relationships. In college Rebecca develops close platonic relationships with women in which she feels for the first time appreciated for her intellectual and emotional strengths. She finds that being comfortable with herself is most possible in intimate relationships with women.

When I think of my preadolescent years and who I was, I seem to remember myself being much the same as I am now. I remember the same moments of standing still, listing adjectives that located me in my world. I'm sure that my list changes, as my context has surely changed and shaped me with its changes. Yet I have remained remarkably similar in my method of taking stock. I start by sitting alone either in my bed with my fan or my clock, or outside on some type of rhythmically moving object—a swing or something. I like a regular beat. I first describe in detail, to myself, the physical surroundings and the time frame that I'm in. I guess it gets me into an observant framework.

After I establish the framework, I recount each of the relationships that are crucial to me at the time, usually concentrating on their expectations or perceptions of me and following with expectations or desires of my own. If I'm feeling strong joy, resentment, anticipation, or confusion, I try to list or chronicle the events or tensions that led to these feelings. If I think that I want to cry or scream, I definitely do it now—I find that I can't *really* cry spontaneously or in front of anyone else, unless it's my mom or my brother and I'm frustrated or angry—loneliness or heartbreak crying happens when I decide I'm ready for it. Finally, I think about myself as a part of a bigger structure—sometimes I ask myself if I'm believing in God at the time, and that varies. If I am, I first do the Catholic prayers that I learned growing up, very quickly, followed by a very slow analysis of them. For instance, I say, "Our Father, who art in heaven, hallowed be thy name. Thy kingdom come, thy will be done. . . . Is God a father, is he like my father? Can He be in Heaven, is Heaven a different place from this one, how is it different? And is God's will what is done? Who is to know what He wills and how to do it, especially when it seems so improbable that everything priests say that God wills should actually be done?" It goes on like that, which is the only way that I can eke meaning out of it.

In the last few years, I've articulated to myself a direct challenge to my idea of God—that is, when I'm believing in God. I do not believe that God is actually a He. Now, my mother thinks that I'm crazy to be so concerned with the male-oriented language of prayers. She tells me that I can, of course, imagine a gender-less God. But this isn't really true, or at least it's not that simple. It's not just a product of intellectual acceptance of feminism and the fact that I've learned to criticize anything produced out of a patriarchal system. It's that I honestly can't pay attention to praying in any religious language that I've learned. I fall dead asleep at night when I try to pray in any form that I associate with Catholicism. And I'm sure that it's because I've incorporated the image of God as man—not a physical man like that trite grandfather image, but just someone who doesn't understand women, or at least me. Someone distant and very analytical and fair, but in a strident, formal way. I guess God just doesn't appeal much to me as "He" is constructed by the church.

My next step in the debriefing process is to bring it back into myself. I list the things that have always been true of me—most of them having to do with how I interact with others, but not all of them. I'm smart, I'm motivated, I'm eccentric, I'm honest (blunt), I'm caring. I'm high strung, I'm independent to the point (sometimes) of being selfish or claustrophobic or cold when pressured. I take stock of myself physically, describing myself as if I see me walking down the street. I end up with my mom and my dad—how I'm so like both of them and how I am also so different that they could not have anticipated how different I would be.

The first real memories that I have of myself outside of my familial role are based in what I remember of the descriptions and actions of my first best friend, Kelly. Apart from my family, who obviously contributed most to my sense of myself, she really shaped a lot of my view of me. She told me a lot about what she thought of me, but she also modeled attitudes for me, which I either absorbed or rejected. She introduced me to the idea of sex, of romantic relationships, and of physical maturation, all of which dramatically affected my own feelings toward approaching adolescence.

I met Kelly when I was in second grade, and the school that I moved into was a very small private school for girls. We had only thirty girls in our grade, and the academic and social roles were already well established when I came into the middle of second grade. These roles barely shifted in the six years that I attended the school, with the notable exception of Kelly's leading role in both areas. I don't remember how we established the best-friend-ship, but I do remember it happening almost immediately. I am pretty sure that it had to do with academic success. Kelly was the "smartest" when I got there. Within one or two weeks, I was her rival. She made the overtures, and we started an intense and very competitive relationship. We were always together, and we were always competing. We wrote plays, and we did extra math in our playtimes, racing with each other to finish the exercises.

Kelly told me once that I was smarter than she was, and it completely floored me. My immediate reaction was to protest vehemently that it was she who was the smarter, because I had always sensed a territorial tone and aggressiveness that had been the precipitating factor of our entire competitive dynamic. It seemed to me that our friendship worked on the premise that she was the dominant mind and I was her most worthy challenger. I was comfortable in the role. It was worthwhile to me to be second if it secured our friendship. A mutual friend told me that Kelly had said that she had always envied my intelligence—that she had always had to work harder than I did to end up at the same level. It made me feel displaced from the friendship all over again.

Kelly was the first person who made me aware that I was intelligent. She was the first person who showed me how dangerous intelligence, especially intellectual comparison and competition, can be to a friendship. She was also a positive precedent, however, for future friendships based on intellectual compatibility.

Kelly told me that I would get my period, which meant that I could have babies. She told me that I'd bleed a lot, uncontrollably, and that it would happen every six months and it would keep on for weeks. She told me that it would happen any day now (we were 8 years old), and that when it did happen everyone would know because my breasts would get big and I'd have to wear a bra. I was incredibly distressed about all of this. I cried and cried and spent hours pressing my chest in to keep it from growing. I dreaded the blood and somehow I connected it to growing old and separating from my mom. I was too ashamed to tell her what Kelly had told me. Finally I had a nightmare and she figured out what had happened and then set it straight for me, trying to convince me that menstruation would be a wonderful event and that it probably wouldn't happen to me for a few years. I felt a little better, but never entirely confident that I would adjust to it all.

Kelly told me a lot about sex. In fact, she told me everything that I knew about it until late in fourth grade. Kelly's parents had given her some information about the actual act of intercourse early in second grade. I guess that they told her about male and female genitalia, which I already knew, but also about how intercourse actually works. They also told her that intercourse takes place in heterosexual romantic situations, and that they did actually have and enjoy sex themselves. This blew my mind.

Kelly explained to me all about the penis and the mature vagina and told me that I would definitely want a penis in my vagina, that I would have a boyfriend or a husband, and that this would be something I would do. She also explained something about being sexy, which was certainly nothing I had thought about before. She had all these old *Playboy* magazines from her dad's closet which gave us very explicit ideas about both the act of intercourse and the sexy woman. I remember being very excited about all these pictures, but very sure that all of this was a big sin. Still, my admiration for Kelly and her vast knowledge won out over religious restraint and it became our secret fund of coveted information.

Kelly first suggested that we play games based on sex in third grade. She would always act the man's part—she'd be my boyfriend. I was supposed to be sexy and receptive, and she'd seduce me. We tried to switch it around, but that never seemed to work. In retrospect, I guess it was because Kelly was always dominant in our friendship. She made up the rules for these games, and she had to be the one to control their progress. We would lock the door to our rooms, take off our clothes, and try to figure out how to pretend to have sex. We were really scared of getting caught, especially me.

Kelly publicized our expertise and her magazine store. We were already leaders among the girls, so we kind of started a trend. Third and fourth grades were the slumber party years, so Kelly set forth a slumber party game which became sort of routine. We would all get dressed and made up, designate judges, put on music, and have strip shows. These became more and more elaborate, despite the risk of parents figuring it out. That was the extent of it—we never got as physically close as Kelly and I did. There were some girls who were really into it, and some who weren't, but we all did it. I never let on that it was really exciting to me; I always acted nonchalant and waited for Kelly to suggest it.

In fifth grade there was a huge turn of events. The whole attitude of the class toward academic achievement changed dramatically. All of a sudden, with the increased attention to boys at other schools, a new *type* became popular. It was not at all cool to be smart, nor was it cool to be at all involved with teachers. It was cool to be making bad grades, to be disrespectful to teachers, to smoke, and to drink. The best thing to do if one was smart was to deny it. To be "modest"—in other words—I deprecated myself constantly, in hopes of remaining popular. It was a constant struggle to continue to please myself and my teachers, which I wanted to do, and to please my peers. The main connection here is that Kelly refused to deny her intelligence and she remained openly assertive about what was important to her—pleasing her parents and teachers and making good grades. Everyone turned against her, and the weapon of choice was the accusation of lesbianism, which fit conveniently with everyone's newfound interest in boys. I was incredibly relieved when Kelly switched schools in sixth grade, because I had been afraid that she would tell them what we had done. She was a constant reminder of something I wanted to forget.

My self-image, although influenced in key ways by my peers in my early adolescence, was always colored by my perceptions of what my father thought about me. Throughout my childhood, my father was my role model. I remember spending a lot of time with him until I was about 8 or 9. He was funny, interested, and challenging for me during those years. He was always intent on hearing what I had to say and encouraging me to express my ideas. It isn't surprising that I imagined growing up and practicing medicine as he did, and he certainly did encourage me to believe that I could accomplish whatever I wanted. He told me that I was very intelligent when I was about 7 or 8 years old, and I understood him to mean that I was like him, that we shared a special and elite bond. I asked him how he knew, and he told me that he could tell by my ability to converse.

For as long as I could remember, we had had intellectual play—we worked together constructing plastic models of the human body, and he would take me to the lab on Saturdays so that I could work with the lab equipment to run experiments. I remember researching and writing a twenty-page report on the cell just for fun, to give him as a present. It was understood that I was to excel in school; he certainly ascribed to a competitive model of assessing academic success. He always knew which other girls in my class were my rivals, and he was very interested in my comparative analysis of all of our performances. My mother had a problem with this, and Dad and I kind of went underground with the commentary sessions, sort of forming an alliance against Mom, who clearly didn't understand the importance of all of these measurements. I was impressed by my father's obvious intelligence, and I trusted that he was absolutely right to push me as hard as he did. I felt no resentment at that time, only admiration. I think my father picked me out to succeed, to fulfill his hopes, and this is why he never harped on the negative impact that being female would have on my chances. I'm glad of that, even if I resented the extreme pressure, since I feel it gave me strength as a female that many of my female friends never developed.

My interests started to diverge from those of my father in fifth or sixth grade, when academic success or ambition became taboo for the girls in my peer group. In our setting, a small private girls' school, peer opinion was crucial, and deviants from the accepted trend were treated very cruelly. There were no alternative social groups in our class of twenty-five, so it was adapt or be absolutely miserable. The girls devised ingenious tortures, which really scared me into line. Name-calling, mostly, but sometimes they would steal lunches, or write on lockers, or call up the boys who would be, I supposed, appalled at these academic statistics.

The only acceptable reaction was public, intense self-deprecation and real deference to the loudest ringleaders (inevitably not those making good grades) in every extracurricular group event. Sometimes, we were even required to cheat for them in tests and homework. Above all, tattling or visible signs of distress were reactions that were punishable by being ostracized from the group. I managed to stay in with the "popular" girls and, perhaps more amazing, to convince myself that I was happy at the school and in their group. I missed test questions on purpose, though never enough to seriously jeopardize my grade. I just wanted to avoid the announced list of A+ tests. I was really torn. I had always looked up to my teachers, and they liked me. And my father, of course, was fit to be tied. He sensed, as did my teachers, that I was purposefully decreasing my academic standards.

Over the course of these three years, my feelings about the kind of interaction I had always had with my father changed dramatically. Instead of enjoying the intellectual exchange, I shied away from it. I don't think my dad could understand why this happened. He's very "logical," very driven, and very emotionally distant. I never felt comfortable discussing anything personal with him; I felt he thought my friends were really silly and unworthy of his or my time. It wasn't until I switched schools in that first year of high school that we were able to reestablish any connection at all.

I had strong friendships in high school, but none of them had as much impact on my current view of myself as my first real "love" relationship. At the very end of my senior year of high school I became involved with Jason. It lasted throughout my first year of college, and it has conditioned my responses to love relationships since. I suppose, in retrospect, that it was very serious or intense, although it really crept up on me. I had always intended to avoid the dependence that eventually developed on his part, yet I seemed to miss obvious clues, or at least to avoid confronting them straight out.

Jason was two years older than me, and although I had been vaguely aware of him in high school, I never planned or even anticipated getting any more involved with him after he graduated. He initiated the dating, and when he came home for the summer, he avidly pursued both my time and my emotional involvement. Because I had just recovered from a breakup with a guy who didn't have the inclination to be committed at all, Jason's attention came as a welcomed change of pace. He was very charming, very attentive, very interested in my family, and very interested in finding out about things I enjoyed—books, plays, whatever it was that I wanted to do. Within a month we were together constantly, and he was saying that he loved me. I thought that I loved him, too, although I knew that I was attracted to him because of the way that he felt about me. He came across as very glib, witty, and carefree—people were drawn to him. I felt privileged to penetrate that act—as if that was what intimacy was all about. In a bizarre way, I was really attracted to the disturbed, depressed side of his personality, which often came out when we were alone; I loved feeling as though I could help him.

I felt like I was a crucial source of positive energy for him. He would confide in me—he was angry with his father, he was worried about the alcohol and drugs on which he depended, he couldn't see any positive future for himself post-graduation, he was convinced that he couldn't be happy on his own, he would rather die than be alone. I would listen to him cry, and I would tell him that there were things worth doing—emotional and intellectual. I would tell him that we would do them together, and that then he would be okay on his own. I guess that I started feeling stifled after this scene replayed over two months, but by the time I noticed a desire to spend time alone and the need to rethink the benefits of all these pursuits, I was already inextricably involved with Jason. I worried that he needed me to help him find some self-esteem. He had mentioned suicide enough for me to feel a heavy responsibility. Probably worse, nobody could believe the seriousness of his depression, since his carefree social demeanor was so well constructed. My mother and my friends thought that I exaggerated, and I knew that his friends would never believe it. It seemed completely impossible, since he was manic in public. This increased my sense of being isolated in a relationship which was only real to the two of us. I considered it selfish of me to want to be alone or away from him, so much so that I rarely consciously articulated the desire to do so. Instead, I just felt frustrated.

I made the decision to have sexual intercourse with Jason in the middle of that summer. I decided then that the intense attachment and need I perceived and felt must be love, or the strongest feeling that I was capable of at that point in my life. I discussed this in depth with Jason and also with one of my best girlfriends. It was an extraordinarily difficult decision to make, especially because I knew that I would not be able to discuss it with my mother. Both of my parents are serious Catholics and had always taken a firm stand against premarital sex. I remember thinking that I might never be involved in something so serious again, although I don't remember thinking that I'd be involved with Jason forever. He did not directly pressure me to have sex with him, but he made it clear that he thought that sexual intimacy was a natural step in our already intensely developed emotional relationship. We went through God, sin, lying to my parents, birth control, and my fears about the actual act countless times. I went to Planned Parenthood with my best friend and cried the whole way home after the physical and the Pill lecture.

I definitely decided to have sexual intercourse because it seemed important to him. I had never been very involved in the sexual aspect of our relationship. I was completely alienated emotionally from the physical interaction, so I never really had any physical response worth mentioning. I certainly never had an orgasm, and he didn't ever ask if I had or, if not, why I hadn't. It never crossed my mind to care—I just assumed that the sexual dimension of the relationship wasn't important to me in itself. The actual act, which I had never really planned for, didn't impress me as very different from the foreplay stuff that we had been doing all along. I don't remember disappointment; I hadn't been expecting anything amazing. Intercourse seemed inconsequential compared to my reaction.

My response seemed completely bizarre to Jason, but to me it made complete sense. I kicked him out of my bed (my parents were out of town) and I started reading all of my old letters and journals from camp and high school. I played my favorite tapes and informed him that I wanted to cry alone. After he was gone, I cried about leaving my mom and my room and my high school routine. I cried about growing up, which I had never wanted to do. I didn't feel guilty then, although I knew that I had been rationalizing my way into a sexual relationship that I had learned was sinful. At the time, I just felt old. It wasn't horrible. It was just the event that I needed to release all of the separation anxiety that I was feeling before leaving home for college. It definitely didn't have much to do with Jason.

As soon as I left for college, Jason broke down. He called daily and cried on the phone; he was usually so drunk that I had to call his friends at home to tell them to go pick him up at the fraternity. So, feeling guilty about my responsibilities to Jason and the resistance it evoked in me, and simultaneously attempting to rationalize some sort of separation from him, I started in on myself with a guilt trip about my sexual relationship with him. I had nightmares about Hell and I told him that I wanted to break off the sexual aspect of our relationship, or at least the intercourse. He reluctantly agreed. The guilt culminated at Christmastime, when I decided that I should confess the whole thing before Christmas Day.

I hadn't been in a confessional since eighth grade, but I managed to drag myself in and tell the very old priest that I had had sex with my boyfriend. He said, "Fornication!?! How many times? Less than fifty? You are very lucky that you have come for forgiveness, for you were going straight to Hell. Do you steal, too?"

Needless to say, I barely made it through the prayers, and when I emerged shaking, my mom asked me why. I couldn't tell her, and that made me cry. The religious guilt served both to reinforce my sense of desperation to get out of the relationship and my anger at myself for arriving at that point. It gave me an impetus or even an excuse to leave Jason, even if it left me more confused about the place of sex within intimate relationships.

It took the rest of the year to get out of it. Jason wasn't willing to let me loosen it up at all; he definitely fought it. I told him that I would not see him until summer, when we would discuss it again. I started seeing someone else, which ended with him calling at all hours of the night to make sure that I was in my room alone. His friends called me to yell at me. I told him in May that I wasn't even willing to try to work it out over the summer. He pulled out every insecurity that he knew that I had and tried to throw them in my face. He took my confidences about my family—my fear that I was really selfish with them, even unable to move out of myself in dire situations when Mom (especially) really needed my support—and used them to retaliate. I remember him telling me that he was the best that I would ever have, that he knew that deep down I was too selfish to ever care for or love anyone, and that no matter who tried to tell me otherwise, he knew me better, and he knew the truth. I was afraid for a long time that he was right.

This relationship precipitated a screening process which is just starting to break down in my final year of college. I find myself unbelievably conscious of my own emotional independence, almost to the point of being incapable of sustaining any "love/romantic"–type relationships once they require a commitment. As soon as I detect any signs of a lover's "neediness," I start to back out of the involvement. I am reluctant to become involved with anyone who seems emotionally inconsistent; I'm very wary of tears or "melodrama." And I'm definitely reluctant to become involved with any men sexually. I like to have my physical space to myself—I have since refused any sort of cohabitation with my male lovers. I'm not sure how much of a correlation there is between my lack of interest in intercourse and the associations I have from its role in my relationship with Jason, but I'm sure that it is connected. Often that guilt which seems to be religion-based emerges in these situations. I think, though, that this guilt marks a reaction to being pressured by the men with whom I am involved, and from whom I would like to break away. I think that this guilt serves as an easier route away from oppressive relationships than confronting the claustrophobia I feel directly.

In the winter of my first year I took my first women's studies class. It was challenging, and it provided the first real professor–student contact that I had had at the college. I had been surprised at the distance I had felt from my professors first term. In high school, I knew all of my teachers well. I spoke often in some classes, depending on how the boys treated me. For my first term at my college, I hadn't spoken in class nor had I spoken to any of my professors outside of the classroom. The women's studies class was very small, discussion-oriented, and my professor insisted on seeing each of us in her office for conferences. She encouraged me to continue taking Women's Studies, and she gave me a sense of confidence about my academic work.

I also came into contact with some of the more active feminists on campus through the class. I began to be aware that there were women and some men on campus who were interested in the issues that interested me; I became somewhat involved in the countermainstream politics on campus, especially with (mostly white) women's issues groups. I also began to develop and articulate the unstated concerns, especially about stereotyping, that I had had during high school, and even before then. I learned more about feminist theory, and I developed a framework for the arguments I had always had with the way that I had been treated. I began to feel stronger, more concrete about my ability to be actively in discord with an institution or group or society that made me feel marginal. Looking back, I know that I depended a lot on rhetoric to develop this stronger stance; I don't think that issues of differences among women had made an impact on me then. But I know that it was a time of expansion for me, intellectually and socially. I knew that I had a lot to learn, but I was so excited that academics could offer me something that seemed to have to do with me and my experiences.

I still hadn't found a real group of peers with whom I felt comfortable enough to expand and act on these feminist issues. I was going to meetings, but I was still tentative and concerned about how to make personal connections with these very impressive but intimidating women. My best friend and roommate, Jane, was involved along with me, but we were both in a similar spot—reserved, shy, but very interested. The pivotal connection occurred my sophomore spring, when I took a history class on national liberation movements in Third World countries. I was grappling with issues of racism and cultural imperialism for the first time, which really complicated but expanded what I had been learning in women's studies classes that I had been taking. I remember being overwhelmed by the information; I was almost immobilized by the impact of information so radically different from anything in my world. I met Alexandra in this context. She was in the class, and she was very vocal and very intelligent. She was also beautiful, a physically engaging presence. The amazing thing about her was her ability to express all of the anger that I felt while also including all of the facts, and to make clear, pointed analyses of the situations. She clearly believed that she could channel all of her conviction into some effective action. As we were preparing to write our first paper, she asked me about how I was going to approach the question. We had an involved discussion, and we made plans to write the paper together at the computer center. I surprised myself at my own ability to debate with her; I think that I gained confidence because she obviously considered my thoughts intelligent and worth hearing.

That was the start of a very involved intellectual friendship. We spent the remainder of that class conferring over paper questions, our own questions, and questions raised by active members of the political left whom she knew. She was involved in feminist issues, but also very involved with the radical left of the international students association on campus. She constantly challenged me, and she constantly involved me in protest actions on campus. I made the transition that I had held back on for my first one and a half years—I became a visible member of the college's political left. I was nervous because it meant being recognized and often ignored or treated with hostility. Alexandra took me on as her protégé. She had such a sense of mission, and I was so impressed and awed by her, that I jumped into anything that I could be involved with.

At the end of that term, visible feminists were being harassed by "anonymous" hate mail from hostile conservative campus groups. Also, many women students had been sexually harassed in dorms, and while members of the women's issues group had heard about it through the grapevine, none of the incidents were being reported because there was no clear protocol or support system for these women. A group of us took these incidents to the college president and received little active response. So the group decided to sit in pairs, wearing gags, passing out statements about how women were silenced on campus when they tried to speak out about harassment. I was afraid to "sit in" in front of the fraternities, in the dean's office, and the ultraconservative newspaper's offices, but because Alexandra encouraged me, I did it. I remember that she told me that I was brave, and I remember thinking that it was worth being petrified and being verbally abused to be in the middle of a direct, antiauthority action with her. I felt stronger and more effective than I had ever felt.

As my friendship with Alexandra progressed, we moved out of the intellectual somewhat. I realized that I was dying to be included in her personal life. If she called me to come over and hang out, I was thrilled. I loved listening to her talk about her women friends—they were entertaining, smart, politically impressive, and always involved in some scandal or other. I liked it when she confided in me about strains or stresses in her group; she thought I was perceptive and that I offered a good perspective on what she would tell me. But I hated it when she told me about her lovers. I didn't really formulate why I hated it then; I just felt frustrated.

Sometime over the course of my junior year in England I realized that I was infatuated with her. I got used to the idea of being attracted to, even infatuated with, a woman through trying to figure out why I felt so strongly about Alexandra. I knew that I wanted to be her confidante—her intimate friend. But as I tried to imagine what it would be like to be one of her most preferred friends, I also admitted to myself that that wouldn't be enough. I knew that I would still feel disappointed. I was both emotionally and sexually attracted to her; I couldn't separate those two impulses at all in my feelings for her. It was the sexual attraction that I uncovered slowly. It had not been a conscious element throughout the process of getting closer to her. Also, I had never related personally to lesbianism. I was interested in my homosexual friends, and I had been politically involved in gay and lesbian issues at my college. But I had never felt as if the word or concept *lesbianism* had anything to do with me. Part of this was, I'm sure, that I had never had any models. I never encountered a single person who was openly homosexual until I came to college. The only contact I had had was with Kelly, who was labeled *lesbian*, derogatorily, by our peers.

I came back from London into my senior year having decided, after thinking about Alexandra, that I would be open to a lesbian relationship if someone who interested me came along. This decision was monumental, for once I admitted it to myself, I developed a resolve that I knew would back me if I did get into a situation that seemed to require it. I was scared, but I was proud of myself for making this mental step. Since Jason, I had been involved with two other men, and both of my relationships with them ended similarly to my relationship with Jason. We would start dating, and in what seemed an inappropriately short amount of time, the men would be emotionally involved to a degree which seemed unwarranted, frightening, and claustrophobic to me. Also, the sexual aspects of these involvements, although not oppressive, were not crucial or even consistently satisfying for me. I liked these men a lot before I got involved with them—both were good friends with whom I had similar political and intellectual interests. Both were sensitive about my emotional and sexual needs, but I had the same feeling of distance and constraint that I had felt with Jason, only to a lesser degree that was not frightening, only frustrating.

After Alexandra, I decided that part of the reason that these relationships were occurring was that it was always a man with whom I was involved. I thought that the emotional nurturance that I was providing and rarely receiving had to do with a communication gap or a difference in emotional expectations somewhat rooted in gender. I hadn't had trouble in the numerous close relationships that I had had with women friends. I had two wonderful women friends with whom I could consistently communicate and reciprocate emotional needs. Then, Alexandra tilted the balance by introducing in me both a sexual desire for a woman and a real drive to be totally immersed in her life. I had the resolve; the mental preparation had occurred. However, I didn't think that I would get involved in a lesbian relationship at my college. The lesbian community here was so small, so catty, and so prominent that I couldn't imagine wanting to get in the middle of it.

I met Marie fall term. I had known that she was gay, although she had graduated and was somewhat removed from the lesbian undergraduate community. She was intelligent, experienced, and wise—she had been through so much more than I had encountered in my sheltered life. I was impressed with her strength and her self-possession. She was interested in me; I suppose she sensed that I was open to the idea of a gay relationship. We talked about it extensively, and she was amazed that I had mentally prepared myself before ever making any actual steps. We got involved in a romantic relationship, although I wasn't in love or in awe as I had been with Alexandra. We developed a close bond, and I concentrated on the differences that I perceived between this relationship and my previous ones with men. I felt that I had a sense of proximity, or sexual familiarity, that I had never had before. I attributed this to the fact that we were both women. We had a much more similar approach to sex than I had had with the men I had dated. I felt that sex was much less goal-oriented, much less alienating, and much less demanding. I was more comfortable with it than I had been, and I didn't experience the guilt repercussions that I had in the past. I never felt like I should feel ashamed for enjoying it. We had an easier time relating to each others' views about feminism and, more importantly, we had a better understanding about how to talk about things on which we didn't agree than I had had in past relationships with men. Instead of defensive or aggressive counteracting of my feelings, she was able to honestly set out how she felt, and I could usually find a correlating or analogous feeling in my experience. I was looking for something which could integrate a sexually satisfying relationship with the comfortable, open communication I had had with my women friends. I got closer to this with her than I had in the past.

However, after some time I felt constricted. I tried to confront this feeling with Marie because we had established an open channel of communication. Although we tried to work with giving me space while allowing for her desire to be with me often, we couldn't seem to find a resolution. It was really hard for me to face the feeling of claustrophobia again, when I had hoped that it would not recur if I were involved with a woman. But it did, and I think (in retrospect) that I have some understanding of why it did. First, it was very hard for me to integrate this relationship with the relationships I had established with my other women friends. My friends were initially very supportive, and in theory they were all prepared to accept that I had a woman lover. But Marie's obvious attention and possessiveness interrupted the well-established dynamic. My friends, especially my two closest friends, felt sad, jealous, and somewhat displaced. Instead of asking for support as I probably should have done, or even taking more time just to talk about Marie with them, I tried to play it down for them. I was constantly trying to compensate for my relationship with Marie. Of course I ended up denying any of my own need for support and also hurting these friends as they sensed that there was so much that I wasn't sharing with them. This took its toll on my enthusiasm for the relationship with Marie.

Second, and perhaps more disturbing, I felt some of that demand for intense emotional sustenance similar to what I had felt in previous claustrophobic relationships. I didn't think that I could handle what I perceived to be serious demands on my time, space, and emotional availability. I had to acknowledge that this pattern in my relationships was entirely due to me. However, it did teach me something about my own space and time limits and the importance of my friends as they affect my love relationships. I knew that I would have to be clear from the start about what kind of interaction made me feel threatened or constrained. Anyone with whom I would get involved would have to be able to deal with my wariness, which would probably require a lot of patience. And I would have to be very careful not to compromise my relationships because of my women friends, and also not to alienate my women friends from my relationships with women as lovers. I did feel that to become involved with women as lovers was a positive move. Challenging, but worthwhile. The feeling of proximity in both communication and sex convinced me that it was an important step in ascertaining what I want in a love relationship. I know that it doesn't bypass every relationship hitch. But it makes a positive difference for me.

The only really disturbing aspect of identifying myself as a lesbian is that I worry about my family. I have not told my parents or my sister, and although I did tell my brother, he has not given me any support or feedback. This decision has been a major turning point in my life—even though I worry about my family and sometimes about my future, I feel better about myself now than I ever have. I have learned a lot about my own needs, likes, and dislikes in both love relationships and friendships. I have a new relationship now, and I feel for the first time the ability to get over this pattern that has felt inevitable at times in the past. She is the first person with whom I have been able to relax and share space comfortably, and I feel that even though there is a strong physical attraction and emotional involvement, I am not threatened or claustrophobic. I think that this ease derives in part from an understanding of my limitations and also my abilities, mostly newfound, to be comfortable in an intimate, emotional, communicative, love relationship. She is very independent, very motivated, and very concerned with listening to me and expressing herself clearly. She is able to cultivate an emotional side to a very comfortable relationship without setting up what I perceive as a need too great for me to handle. Also, I have learned how important it is to be straightforward and thorough with my women friends, especially Jane, my best friend through all of my college career. I really love her, and it has been hard to let her know that I will always be with her despite the fact that I will have women lovers. We have learned, however, that it is best to talk to each other about exactly how we both feel about our relationship and about our relationships with lovers, no matter how painful it may be. I think that the intimacy is worth the painful moments.

PART THREE

Challenges

Theoretical Overview

Within the field of adolescent research there exists a debate over whether adolescence is typically a period of storm and stress, of alienation and separation, or a more harmonious evolution in which positive feelings about self and family are extended into the larger realms of peers and society. Each of these perspectives has merit and accounts for the different individual circumstances and coping styles of a complex period of human development. One point of agreement in this debate is that adolescence is a period of radical transformation of the physical and psychological self. Even under the best of circumstances, adolescents travel an exquisitely poignant journey through difficult developmental terrain. Finding one's way would be challenge enough. But when the ground is continually shifting with the ongoing physical, emotional, and cognitive growth of this period, the journey becomes full-time work for most adolescents. When the ordinary stresses of adolescence are overlaid with extraordinary additional stresses, there emerge important risk factors for healthy development. The cases in this section explore both the dangers and strategies for coping with such challenges.

Our notion of "challenges" implies obstacles or special difficulties that must be negotiated in addition to all the more "typical" preoccupations and developmental tasks of adolescence. Challenges are important both because of what they tell us about adolescent coping strategies in general, and because many adolescents face such circumstances at some point. If we add up all the adolescents who must deal with challenges such as physical disabilities; serious illness; divorce; the death of a parent, sibling, or close friend; physical or sexual abuse; mental illness, and so on, we can see that significant challenges, whether acute or chronic, represent, if not the norm, at least a sizable subsample of all adolescents. An autobiographical exploration of challenges also provides the reader a window into resilience. It allows us to learn which coping strategies and character traits appear to be most protective and even promotive of adolescent mental health.

Each of the five cases included in this section represents a distinct challenge to healthy psychological growth at multiple developmental periods: (1) a severe

stutter and serious sexual abuse in early childhood, (2) the emotional crisis surrounding an abortion in adolescence, (3) a journey from war refugee to immigrant
to the United States and gradual acculturation, (4) a family breaking apart under
the stresses of emigration to the United States and the mental illness of a parent,
and (5) the special obstacles faced along the adolescent journey posed by a significant physically disability. Taken as a whole, these cases highlight both what is
unique and universal, at least for Western culture; unique, in terms of specialized
issues these problems raise for adolescent development; universal, in that the cases
highlight the way in which the tasks of adolescence remain relatively constant
even in the face of powerfully destabilizing events. The emergence of adolescence
represents both a difficult context in which to bring preexisting problems, and a
new opportunity for overcoming some of the more debilitating psychological effects of these issues.

Self-understanding is one of the more important aspects of emerging adolescent abilities for overcoming serious challenges. Prior to adolescence, childhood is
characterized by the embeddedness of the child in his or her family and the profound tendency, whether for better or worse, to identify with important persons
and norms within the family. The increasing importance of the peer world and the
simultaneously evolving capacity to see parents as less powerful and more fallible
are conducive to a loosening and diversification of earlier identifications. This
evolving capacity for perspective can facilitate healing through important substitute relationships such as teachers, mentors, peers, families of friends, and others
(Noam, Powers, Kilkenny, & Beedy, 1990). Such healing may be necessary when
families have not been sufficiently nurturing, protective, or enhancing of self-
esteem. While these relationships may also be important at earlier periods, the
adolescent can increasingly see her *self* through the eyes of these important others.
This fresh perspective allows the adolescent to take a more autonomous approach
to creating a self of her own choosing. There has long been recognition that this
emergent ability to gain self-knowledge and perspective through interaction with
others—this "looking glass self" (Cooley, 1902; G. H. Mead, 1934)—helps explain
why positive relationships can have such a restorative effect on the damage of earlier events. This "mirroring" becomes especially salient in peer and romantic relationships during this time (Sullivan, 1953; Erikson, 1968) as the adolescent learns to
take a perspective on herself by means of gradually modifying the self she sees reflected in the eyes of peers.

Self-understanding has been shown to be an important "protective factor"
(Beardslee, 1989) in ameliorating the risk to healthy psychological development
from serious life stressors. Ideally, self-understanding should lead to action that
transforms one's adaptation to circumstances or changes the circumstances themselves. It is only when insight leads to new and better means of coping with life's
challenges that we can say the individual is rising to the challenge. Indeed, insight
without action can reflect a profound sense of hopelessness. The cases presented
here all reveal the adolescent biographers to be reacting to significant stress by first
developing insight and then taking steps to make things better.

An important emerging field within developmental psychology is devoted to studying individuals who are resilient or seemingly invulnerable to serious risks and stresses that have been shown to affect negatively the mental health and long-term adjustment of many children. This relatively new field represents a significant historic shift from studying almost exclusively those individuals who succumb to developmental risks to studying those who are equally exposed but who overcome the risk and remain healthy. Among the factors shown to place children at risk are serious mental illness of a parent, physical or sexual abuse, serious marital discord, poverty, emotionally unsupportive relationships with parents, foster home placement, and parental alcoholism (Rutter, 1975, 1979; Werner, 1989). While different studies find differing degrees of relative risk for each of these and other factors, it is found that, when only a single risk factor was present, the probability that a child would suffer from a psychiatric disorder was no greater than for a child in a family without any of these risk factors. However, two risk factors produced a four-fold increase in the chances of a psychiatric disorder in the child; four risk factors produced a tenfold increase in risk. It would seem that most children can cope with a certain amount of stress stemming from these risks, but when overloaded with multiple stressors, they become exponentially more likely to succumb. Many children and adolescents, however, do not succumb even under such stress. Therein lies a hopeful avenue for understanding how some children are protected, or protect themselves, against the vicissitudes of serious stress. We might speculate that, whatever these protective coping mechanisms are, they appear to promote good mental health in general and could therefore be helpful even in low-risk individuals.

Three of the most important protective factors to emerge from research are: (1) personality features, such as self-esteem, (2) family cohesion and lack of discord, and (3) external support systems that encourage and reinforce the child's efforts to cope (Garmezy, 1985; Masten & Garmezy, 1985). Protective factors are not fixed attributes; they are subject to development or reduction over time within the same individual, and those that may aid in coping at one time may not work at another. Thus these factors should be seen as dynamic; the resilient individual is one who can adapt his or her coping strategies to changing situations. In this sense, protective factors should not be seen as fixed traits of the individual or circumstance, but rather as interpersonal and interactive. This is what Rutter (1987) refers to as protective *mechanisms* or *processes* that the individual may apply or modify as needed.

The cases in Part Three reveal a variety of risks and developmental vulnerabilities, as well as a number of protective coping mechanisms. These mechanisms are employed to secure important emotional needs, and with the dramatic emotional development during adolescence these needs themselves undergo transformation.

In the case of our sexually abused adolescent, "The Simple Beauty of a Conversation," a severe stutter during childhood and adolescence (that may or may not have been related to his abuse) devastated his self-esteem and his relationship with his parents. This devastation had a profoundly negative impact on his social relations. But the functional needs and possibilities of adolescence propelled him into new relationships—warm mentors at work and an accepting and affirming girlfriend—which gave him belated self-confidence to overcome the more debilitating effects of his stutter and abuse. In this sense, the functional tasks of adolescence became for this young man more than merely something to be achieved on the road to adulthood; they became a crucial opportunity for redressing the developmental damage incurred in his childhood. Each phase of life, therefore, not only provides extra obstacles for adolescents with special challenges, but also represents a fresh chance to redirect the inexorable movement that phase will require. His ability to seek and utilize the support and encouragement of adult mentors, as well as his self-understanding, are the protective mechanisms that may account for his resilience against the vulnerabilities from his abuse and speech problem. These mechanisms and the developmental task of romantic intimacy that emerges in adolescence combine in a powerful protective partnership.

Case 15 represents a long-term challenge, whereas Case 18, concerning adolescent abortion, "Proud of the Strength I Had," involves an acute crisis that results in an extended period of depression, anxiety, and guilt feelings. The resulting effects on this autobiographer's self-esteem, attitude toward sexuality, and capacity for intimacy represent risks to her healthy transition to adulthood. A variety of studies find that many women who undergo abortions experience periods of depression, regret, and guilt (Cvejic, Lipper, Kinch, & Benjamin, 1977; Ford, Castelnuovo-Tedesco, & Long, 1971; Smith, 1973) but that these feelings are typically mild and abate in the short term without negatively affecting general functioning. Other studies have found that the primary response to abortion is relief (Adler, 1975; Ewing & Rouse, 1973; Monosour & Stewart, 1973), and that in the case of adolescent abortion in particular it "is neither psychologically harmful nor in other ways damaging to the patient" (Olson, 1980, p. 440).

In comparison with adult women, adolescent females are found to have somewhat more negative emotional responses to abortion, though not severely worse (Adler, 1975; Bracken, Hachamovitch, & Grossman, 1974; Margolis, Davidson, Hanson, Loos, & Mikelson, 1971; Payne, Kravitz, Notman, & Anderson, 1976). This seems to reflect the experience of our autobiographer, who describes somewhat more lasting negative feelings, perhaps because as a middle-adolescent at the time, she was unable to fully anticipate her sense of loss and to prepare for it psychologically as older adolescents appear better able to do (Hatcher, 1976). The sense of betrayal and isolation was intense—her former boyfriend offered no support other than to pay for the abortion, and she felt unable to tell her parents or even her twin sister. She describes how this crisis led to her participation in a college support group for other students who had terminated pregnancies. Emotional catharsis and gradual understanding of her feelings led to active participation in reproductive-rights events and close friendships with other women who shared the same experience. The integration of self-understanding and action is central to her eventual success in managing this stress and recovering from her depressed feelings. This emerging insight also brought into focus her family's inability to communicate emotionally and her determination to redress this constriction of her own emotional openness. When her younger sister thought she might be pregnant, our author took this opportunity to soothe her own feelings of isolation and abandonment by providing the type of support to her sister that she wishes she had. Thus the opportunity to reflect on the linkage between how she became pregnant—"not being able to talk about sex and contraception" with her boyfriend—and her family's emotional silence—"I grew up in a family that stuffed their feelings and never talked about anything, including sex"—led to an important self-understanding about the ways she wanted to change. This crisis illuminated an underlying and ongoing challenge to her happiness: her family's dysfunctional emotional communication.

The developmental vulnerability of an unwanted pregnancy is itself reflective of the adolescent tasks of balancing intimacy, identity, and sexuality. In this case, we can witness the painful beginnings of learning how to develop and employ protective mechanisms—sharing intimate feelings with trusted friends, providing the type of support to others she now knows she needs, searching for an ideology that gives meaning and purpose to her experience, and actively identifying with other women who assert their feelings. Her moves in this direction are tentative, but she seems to have a solid understanding of the cause of much of her unhappiness and the means of redressing it. Similar to the lessons of the other cases, the challenge to her emotional development is met by interaction of protective mechanisms and developmental tasks.

In Case 19, "Seeking the Best of Both Worlds," the adolescent tasks related to separation and individuation become especially poignant in the context of an immigrant family having fled a war-ravaged Vietnam. The traumatic experience of emigrating under such circumstance can understandably have profound effects on both the individual and the nature of family relationships. The author describes feeling both great loyalty and respect for his mother's heroic role in rescuing the family from an impossible situation, and feeling shame and contempt for her unwillingness to allow him to adapt to the U.S. culture to which she had exposed him. He wants acceptance and permission from his mother to live in both worlds—the western world to which she brought him and the traditional world of his family. Even though he is willing to accept the dichotomy of worlds and to live according to the rules of family when at home and of society when outside, his mother seems unwilling to make any such accommodation for herself and thinks he should not either. The result is that he chooses to segment his self into "dutiful but resentful" son at home, and "Americanized" adolescent in school and the larger world. He must resort to constant lying and other subterfuge to keep his mother from knowing his other self. This stress of a double life and the alienation from his mother leaves him emotionally isolated and increasingly depressed.

In addition to all the normal preoccupations of adolescence, and beyond the typical parent–child conflicts of the period, this author demonstrates how hard it can be for immigrant adolescents to integrate the best of both cultures if their family demands exclusive loyalty to the native culture. His strategy of alternating his behavior to whatever culture he finds himself in is often effective for immigrant adolescents (LaFromboise, Coleman, & Gerton, 1993) and is even associated with positive mental health (Rogler, Cortes, & Malgady, 1991). In this case, however, we can also see the tremendous emotional stress and developmental risk this form of adaptation can cause. At the same time, the case also illustrates how his increasing competence and validation in the larger culture gradually creates a new and respected role in his family as the intercultural go-between. By the time he writes his autobiography in college, he describes ways in which he has been able to influence his mother in rearing his two younger siblings so as to lessen some of the pain and conflict he experienced.

In Case 17, "Pa Jam Decourajer," the story is also one of immigration to the United States. The writer describes her recollection of her family's life in Haiti as stable and economically comfortable—at least in relation to the larger Haitian society at the time. Her description of life in the United States is one of poor housing, dangerous neighborhoods, and severe marital discord between her parents. The subsequent separation of her parents eventually leads to her and her sisters being placed in a series of foster homes where she is, at the least, emotionally neglected. Upon reunification with her mother, she and her sisters are chronically abused physically and live with their mother's worsening mental illness, itself an important risk factor (Garmezy, 1987). Despite this chronic neglect, abuse, and high levels of stress, this writer was able to graduate as her high school valedictorian and gain acceptance to a prestigious college where she did exceptionally well. Her self-understanding is demonstrated by her ability to reflect on the continuing emotional damage she suffers as manifested in her inability to experience intimacy and let herself trust others. Her awareness of this as a problem, and understanding of it as a protective mechanism to avoid the hurt and betrayal she felt as a child, is itself a hopeful sign that she will work on overcoming this residual damage as she has so much else. Research on resilience underscores what a remarkable outcome this case represents in light of the enormous risk factors.

Studies show that African American adolescents who show self-motivation and autonomy are more likely to have parents who exercise warmth, careful monitoring, and firm control (Hauser & Bowlds, 1990). In a similar vein, Garmezy (1985) found that resilient black inner-city youth who come from troubled communities are more likely to live in homes that are orderly and have parents who are actively engaged in promoting their children's emotional and social development. Such parents are also likely to engage other supportive adults who provide guidance and encouragement to their children. The parents in Case 17 were not able to provide any of what Rutter (1987) describes as protective processes or mechanisms. Instead, we see a young woman who must essentially raise herself in trying circumstances, where her parents represent more of a risk factor to her healthy development than an active support in overcoming the family's circumstances. What this writer does have as a protective mechanism is high self-esteem (as a student), self-understanding, hope for her future, and the ability to distance herself emotionally from some of the turmoil surrounding her. Rutter (1987) studied individuals who manage to adapt successfully despite chronically stressful and adverse circumstances. This research points to a cluster of personality traits that buffer such stressors: high self-esteem, hope, optimism, a strong personality, and a well-founded belief that there are steps one can take to control and overcome one's circumstances.

Physical disabilities can also pose additional challenges along the adolescent pathway, as in Case 16, "Forever an Awkward Adolescent." The physically challenged autobiographer describes how he used to experience closeness with his father by allowing him to do virtually everything for him, including helping him dress each morning up until high school. He states that as adolescence and his desire for independence emerged, better late than never, he began to insist that his father restrain "his legendary penchant for interfering." His need for independence, however, didn't obliterate his desire for closeness with his father; it caused him to redirect it along more age-appropriate lines, like shared ideas and interests. We can see how the developmental tasks of adolescence, here for greater autonomy, have similar transformative effects on parent-child relations for a severely disabled adolescent as they do for others. The difference is that it is adapted to those particular circumstances, and in the case of a physically disabled adolescent, the importance of the struggle for autonomy has special salience regarding how much independence they will be able to achieve as an adult. For another adolescent, the same autonomy task might lead to a demand for greater privacy or a right to choose his or her own clothes but with less long-lasting implications.

In addition to the press of developmental tasks, the autobiographer's coping is enhanced by the remarkable self-understanding he demonstrates in his attempts at adaptation. He repeatedly stresses his own responsibility for his adjustment and happiness, and the need to find some means of "fitting in" with his able-bodied peers lest they give up trying to relate to him and leave him to his "'default' pigeonhole . . . of a short, oddly-postured disabled kid." And he writes repeatedly of having to create "a persona I could live with" by mirroring himself in the eyes of his peers. This search for identity by means of acceptance and validation by his peers is another important task of adolescence. Thus he demonstrates the interaction of developmental tasks and protective factors, identity formation and self-understanding respectively, which together serve to compensate for the risks of isolation and dependence his physical disabilities represent.

"Forever an Awkward Adolescent" was originally published in the first two editions of this book. We have brought it back in the fifth edition because the author has now written a retrospective update, "Thirteen Years Later." Now in his mid-thirties and a successful executive in a disabilities advocacy organization, he reflects on his original perspective as a college student on what his future might hold. He writes about what has held true and consistent in his life, and what new challenges and opportunities for growth he has faced and anticipates in his future.

These five cases reveal much about the opportunities of adolescence for growing stronger through challenge. Unfortunately, not all such challenges are met so successfully. These autobiographers do, however, represent the fortunate fact that most adolescents who face such circumstances do somehow find a path to productive lives. The following cases tell stories of how such challenges can be met, and though the life stories could not be more different, their pathways to overcoming have much in common.

15 The Simple Beauty of a Conversation

This author's shocking discovery of his speech impediment in first grade leads him to feel insecure and self-conscious regardless of academic and social accomplishments. Ray's "identity as a stutterer" makes him give up in school, because it is "easier not to attempt something than to fail at it." He plagiarizes and cheats his way through high school without being caught, as much a rebellion against his parents as a way of getting by. His religious faith, a close friendship, and his work in the library help him through some of the most difficult years, providing support and contributing to a growing sense of himself as a valued person. Ray experiences a setback when, early in college, his girlfriend is raped, an experience that causes memories of his own early sexual abuse to surface for the first time. He feels like a stronger person now, "standing on his own two feet." His stutter reappears only occasionally, reminding him of the difficulties each of us has in our lives.

As I started high school many teachers and friends held high hopes for me, but by the end of my senior year there was a question as to whether I was going to graduate or repeat the year. My academic problems did not all stem directly from my learning problems. The most accurate description would be to say that I was burned out. I desperately wanted someone to recognize that I was having problems and to offer help. That never happened and I continually failed at all attempts to get myself on track. It became easier not to attempt something than to fail at it. I could see no future for myself. I never even tried to think about what I wanted to do after graduation. I couldn't handle the present, so trying to plan my future was an impossibility.

I got by the best that I could. High school was very painful and difficult for me, and as a way of protecting myself I pretended that I didn't care about the school or my classes. If I had let myself feel that high school could be a very positive experience for me if I was successful, then the pain would have just been worse. I did very little homework, cheated on almost every test, plagiarized all my critical papers, and skipped school as often as I could get away with it.

I need to go back to my early childhood to explain all the problems I had with school. At the age of 5, I went through kindergarten. I enjoyed it and as far as I knew I was just like all the other kids. However, I found out that while all my other friends were going on to first grade, I was going to go to another kindergarten class. No one ever explained to me why I was repeating kindergarten. When I got to the new class I was with a bunch of other kids who were pretty normal. For one hour a day, however, I was taken aside with a special teacher who came to the class just to work with me. I didn't mind because I remember thinking she was pretty. She would show pictures and ask me to tell her what I saw. For example she would show me a picture of a dog and I would say, "dog."

"No, that's not right. Try it again," she would often say.

I had no idea what I was doing wrong. The picture was very obviously a picture of a dog and as far as I knew I was saying the word "dog." This would happen with pictures of trees, cats, farm animals, and many other simple items. I would tell her what it was and she would say, "No, try again." She never told me what I was doing wrong.

The other kids in class must have picked up on what was going on because pretty soon they all started calling me names like "retard" and "moron." I didn't understand this either. I went home crying to my mother one day and asked her why I was being called these names. I can remember the most pained expression I have ever seen come to her face and she said simply, "Because they're not very nice children."

I made it through that year in pretty good shape, all things considered. In first grade the same teacher came to see me every day again. We would go to a small office in the basement and do the same things we did in kindergarten. I know it was unintentional, but one day she did one of the most cruel things I have ever experienced. I went to see her that day and we went through the same routine. This time, however, she had a tape recorder. She recorded the answers I gave to the pictures. Then she rewound and played the tape back to me. I'm not even sure how to describe my reaction to the tape. I was about $6\frac{1}{2}$ years old and like every other little kid I wasn't all that self-conscious or worried about the differences between myself and other kids. But that tape crushed me. The voice I heard was absolutely unintelligible. The voice was stuttering terribly and all the pronunciation was completely off. I couldn't even recognize what it was saying. The voice didn't even sound human. I was sure that I had said "dog" but when the tape got to the point where the word should have come, something completely foreign, not even resembling "dog," came out. I started crying and screaming, "That isn't me! You put another tape in there! That isn't me!" She couldn't calm me down.

I guess everybody assumed I was aware of my speech problems because they were so severe. At the very least I must have been aware of my stutter. But I wasn't aware of it at all. As I've said, no one, my parents included, had ever talked to me about it before.

That tape had an immediate effect on me. I became very withdrawn and would hardly talk to anybody. I particularly avoided talking to my parents, both because I didn't want them to hear me speak the way I did and also because I felt betrayed; I wanted to hurt them with my silence. That might sound like a lot for a 6-year-old but it is very true. Everything that had happened—staying back in kindergarten, the special teacher, all the kids making fun of me—became clear to me and I became very bitter toward my parents for having never talked with me about it. I really hated them. Over the next ten or eleven years I spent much of my time finding little ways that I could hurt them and get back at them for the way they had failed me.

My relationship with school didn't fare much better. Soon after the tape was played to me, the special teacher told me that she was transferring and that we wouldn't be working together anymore. I have no idea if the tape incident had anything to do with her decision, but I am sure now that it did play a part in my parents' decision not to get any more help for me. They couldn't deal with the pain, and I think they felt that the best thing to do was to ignore my problems and hope they would disappear with age. So I no longer went to any special classes. In the regular classes I did everything I could to keep from having to speak in front of the class. I didn't want the other kids to hear how I talked. Through the rest of grade school every teacher I had just about killed himself or herself trying to get me to apply myself more. They all felt I had great potential if I would be more outgoing. I resisted all these efforts. While my pronunciation improved somewhat, my stutter had not improved at all by the time I entered junior high.

It is very difficult to discern how much my stutter affected my image of myself and how much it affected others' image of me. Trying to look back objectively, I would say that for the most part it had its greatest influence on my own self-image. When I was growing up it sometimes seemed that everybody was laughing at me and pointing me out, when in reality probably only a few did so. There are some events that make me realize now that my friends and classmates must have held me in fairly high regard. In the fourth grade I was elected class president. In sixth I was given awards for sportsmanship, leadership, and math ability. In the seventh grade I was chosen as the "Most Intelligent" out of a class of about 150. Still, these did very little to raise my self-esteem, so sensitive was I about my stutter. The effect of these positive reinforcements was minimized to the extreme by my self-consciousness. The only identity I had for myself was as a stutterer. None of my other accomplishments came close to having the effect on me that the fear of stuttering and speaking incorrectly in front of others did. I felt that no one else knew who I really was because I had become so proficient at hiding my speech problems. I saw myself as hiding who I really was from others. To some extent this was true.

In junior high my self-esteem reached its lowest point. My outlook on everything was dictated by my view of myself. I built a reputation at school for being able to get away with cheating, skipping classes, forgery, and other things like that. During lunch at school a lot of kids would come to me looking for help. I'd make a cheat sheet, sell an essay, or do whatever the occasion called for. This was my first niche in junior high and freshman year. It was fun at first because it was novel and it got me a lot of attention. Sometimes it was more innocent and sometimes it was of a much more serious nature. For example, I went through the honors English sequence in high school and plagiarized almost every critical essay I was assigned to write. Some other students were caught doing this but I never was. I learned how to choose obscure, yet valid, sources and how to change things around just enough so that there was very little chance of getting caught. I cheated on almost every test I took and spent a minimal amount of time on homework.

I was shy with girls and doing things like this created opportunities to talk with them. This was very important. I've been attracted to girls as long as I can remember. My first kiss was in kindergarten—the second year that is. I was embarrassed afterward and I was afraid the girl would start telling the other kids that I had kissed her, so a couple of days later I went back to her house and beat her up, which sounds worse than it was. I had my first opportunity to have sex when I was in the sixth grade. The girl was in the eighth grade and I'm pretty sure she was drunk. We were behind some bushes in the church playground across from my house. She came over to me and took off all her clothes. She kept saying, "Come on over and lay me." I had never done more than kiss a girl at that point and I didn't know what "lay me" meant. I went over to her and she stuck her hand down my pants. I ejaculated as soon as she touched me. She laughed at me and said she wanted me to do that again but this time while I was "porking" her. I didn't know what that meant either. To be honest, I had no idea what to do at all. We fooled around for a while but we didn't actually have sex because I didn't know what to do. She kept laughing at me the whole time. I put my clothes back on and left her lying in the bushes. Immediately after this experience and for the next few days, I felt awful. I was cold and shivering all the time and I couldn't stand to have anyone closer than a few feet away from me. I didn't understand why I felt this way but then I didn't understand anything to do with sex at that time.

I went through puberty at an early age. By the end of the sixth grade I had had a couple of wet dreams and I was masturbating often. The incident with the first girl made me curious about and interested in girls. A friend and I used to climb trees in our backyards together. It started a few years earlier as an innocent childhood pastime and we just kept on doing it. One late afternoon during the summer after sixth grade, we were sitting up in the tree talking quietly when we saw a light go on in my neighbor's house. It was the bedroom of a girl who was about a year older than we were and who was my sister's friend. My friend said to me half jokingly, "Wouldn't it be awesome if she changed and didn't pull her shade down?" I agreed, of course, but we really didn't expect anything. But then she did change into her bathrobe without pulling down the shade. We sat for a while without saying anything. I think we were both embarrassed to talk or to move because we both had erections and didn't want the other to know.

One day later in the summer the girl we spied on, Jean, stopped by to see if my sister was around. I was home alone that day and told her so. She came in for a while anyway and we started talking. I got an erection and since I was wearing my bathing suit it wasn't long before she noticed, although I tried to hide it as best I could. At first I was embarrassed, but pretty soon we started talking dirty. We kept daring each other to say dirtier and dirtier things and to shift our clothes around to reveal more. Eventually we went into the shower and I lost my virginity. I think it was her first time also, but I'm not sure.

The time in the shower felt pretty good to me but I don't think Jean enjoyed it very much. She looked like she felt very guilty. Nevertheless she started coming over often when I was alone. We fooled around and tried a lot of things. She must have known more than I did because I really didn't understand how girls got pregnant, but after the first time in the shower she never let me penetrate again. Instead we did other things. At the time we did it I liked it, but I always felt dirty after she had left. Every time we fooled around she would ask for a few of my father's beers to take back home (he never kept track of them). One day she came over with a *Penthouse* and read some of the letters to me. She said she would try those things if I could get her a full bottle of wine. My father had one and I gave it to her. I had heard about prostitutes in church and what it meant if you got into that stuff. I started thinking that what we were doing was almost the same thing. I had a terribly guilty conscience, but every time she came over the same thing would happen.

There was something more than just a guilty conscience though. I couldn't bear having people being physically close to me. If I ever was in a crowd, such as in a mall, I would get lightheaded and have dizzy spells. I also hated to have anyone stand behind me. If I was in any line I would stand a little off to one side to prevent people from being directly behind me. I thought that maybe these feelings had something to do with what Jean and I were doing but I didn't understand them.

When school started again, Jean stopped coming over. We never talked about what we had done again and I think both of us really wanted to forget it. I have never bragged about these experiences to anyone. There are just too many painful feelings and too much confusion connected with it for me to be able to talk about it lightly. As a Catholic I felt what I did was morally wrong, and then there were all those other feelings which I couldn't figure out. In college I told the first girl I slept with that I was a virgin. She said she was, too (and she was probably telling the truth), and that it made it more special because it was the first time for both of us. I've only slept with one other girl since, and I told her that my only experience was with the other college girl. Right now I just don't feel comfortable letting anyone know about what happened.

After the summer with Jean I entered junior high school. That's when most kids start dating, but I became very shy with girls. I knew what sex was like but I had a lot of trouble talking to girls. Each day I was becoming more and more self-conscious about my stutter; I felt that no girl would ever go on a date with a guy who talked like I did. As a result I didn't have any dates in junior high or high school, although I did begin to talk to girls more. I had other problems then as well. I've mentioned what my academics were like. My grades were respectable but they were not earned honestly. My parents and I were moving further apart. About the only time we ever talked was when we were fighting.

As a result of my problems with my family and in school, I needed to find a place I could find some solace and security. Actually, I found three areas: religion, friends, and work. I was raised in a fairly strict Catholic manner. My mother took me to church every Sunday and we fasted before and after mass. I went to classes preparing me for all the sacraments and attended service on every holy day. Sometimes the tedium and monotony of these rites would get to me but overall I have always been a religious person. Often prayer and hope for the future has been the only outlet I have had when times have been really bad. I have never had a serious question about my belief in God and the scriptures, and for most of my life I have prayed every day. While my religion is and always has been an important part of my life, I have often questioned the attitudes of the Catholic Church itself. Nevertheless, I do have strong faith and I try to follow as best I can the teachings of forgiveness, forbearance, and humility. I take pride in my faith.

When I was a sophomore in high school, a priest in my parish, a person whom I really admired, came to me and tried to convince me to enter the priesthood. I actually considered this for a time. In the end I decided against it. But that is not the significance of that incident. This was the first time that someone I really admired let me know he saw some value in me. He was seeing good in me that I couldn't see myself. It had a profound effect on me. I didn't turn myself around in a day because of it, but I did have my first thoughts of where I was going and the person I was as opposed to the person I was capable of being. These were brief, very scattered thoughts, but the seed had been planted. It was the encouragement of other people like him that helped me learn that many people saw me in a better light than I saw myself. I had very little self-respect so I had to get it from others, most of whom have been very religious. At least they are religious in my estimation of how the religious should be; they practice their faith and they show their belief in how they treat other people rather than by preaching to them. And they are secure enough in their faith that they can accept faiths that differ from their own. I have a lot of respect and admiration for these people. I learned from them that a strong belief in the self often goes hand in hand with a strong belief in a set of principles and precepts.

The Catholic Church requires public worship and professing of faith, but I was always very private about it. In that sense I made a poor Catholic. In fact, along with most of my friends, I denied holding any beliefs. I made jokes about the church and about older adults who were very religious. It's also true that I outwardly denied my faith because my mother was Catholic and worship was an integral part of her life. I didn't want to be anything like my parents, and it was a form of rebellion. But, still, inside I found it a source of comfort and hope. As I grew older I started understanding the readings at mass more and saw that they could be applied to my life. I often looked at myself as a modern-day Job. I suffered through trials and hardships as a test of my faith. Not only my faith in God but also my faith in myself and my ability to keep hope alive in my breast and work for something better. I had occasional thoughts of suicide, and three times I made concrete plans to go through with it, but there was always something inside that wouldn't let me give up on myself. Religion helped add to my sense of identity, but that still wasn't enough. There was only so much I could get through my private contemplations and beliefs; I needed experience on a more social level.

This leads to the other two areas—friends and work. I had enough friends that I didn't feel like an outcast, but I had only one really close friend, the one who was my peeping-Tom partner. The two of us had met when we were 5 and have been best friends ever since. The strength of our friendship cannot be overstated. We never pressured each other into doing anything (like trying drugs) and we could share our secrets and problems. My friend, Bill, had a much better relationship with his family than I did, so I adopted his family as my own in a way. I didn't look up to or respect my parents, but I did his. Their opinions had more weight with me than my own parents' opinions. I don't mean to imply that my mother and father were failures as parents, but I held hard feelings against them and looked to Bill's parents for guidance.

Bill and I did everything together. We liked the same shows and music and hung out together all the time. In fact, it wasn't uncommon for teachers and other kids to get the two of us mixed up. There was a great amount of security in that relationship for me. I felt that Bill accepted me for who I was; he was the only person who I wasn't afraid to stutter in front of. Bill and I were (and still are) blood brothers. When we were very young, probably 7 or 8, we slit our thumbs with a knife and rubbed our bleeding fingers together. I assume that isn't done much today. We took everything from swimming lessons to guitar lessons together.

Our parents all worked and much of the time we were left to ourselves. During the summer we spent most of every day unsupervised. Some of our activities were questionable. For example, there was the summer that a moose was spotted in our town. A moose had not been seen in our town for over a hundred years so the news stirred up some fear along with the curiosity and fascination. Only a handful of people had seen the animal, and it was assumed that it had just moved on out of town. One afternoon Bill and I came up with a brainstorm. Our local paper had carried a picture of the tracks left by the moose so we cut that out. Next we got some wood and cut out models that resembled the prints. We tied the models to the bottom of our sneakers and walked in the backyard. Sure enough, we left tracks in dirt that were very similar to those in the picture. The next few nights we snuck out of our houses and went to the swampier areas of town. We put the moose feet on the bottom of our sneakers and walked in the mud of several backyards. A couple of days later we read in the paper that the moose was back and, the paper said, it was possible now that there was more than one. The police had been placed on alert. Aside from our terror of being found out by the police, we loved the whole episode. We had fooled the adults again.

The two of us did everything together and continually made future plans. In the long run this may have come close to hurting me; I relied too much on Bill's friendship and didn't try to be more outgoing and build my confidence. On the other hand, if I hadn't had Bill and the security of our friendship, I never would have learned how to function well socially.

The summer before high school I got a job at the town library, and I was excited about starting work. I had spent a lot of time at the library (it was very close to my house) and I knew several of the librarians. My immediate boss, Mrs. Johnson, turned out to be one of the most special people I have ever met. She was kind, friendly, intelligent, always quick to praise but also ready to point out mistakes in a constructive way, and an all-around lovely person. She could discern everybody's personality. She must have known that I needed a place where I could feel I belonged because she soon gave me many important responsibilities that were within my capabilities. This helped my confidence tremendously. I felt everyone there wanted to see me succeed, and when I made mistakes they treated them as very minor in comparison to all the other things I had done right. It wasn't long before I was working very hard at my job. I would do everything they wanted done—and more if I could find other little jobs. If they needed someone at an awkward time on short notice, I always volunteered. At first it was simply that I wanted Mrs. Johnson and the others to keep giving me praise and that their good opinion was very important to me. Eventually, though, I began to realize that to do a task with integrity and diligence was important and was its own reward. Before working at the library I had never felt what it was like to accomplish something that I had spent much time and effort doing. There was great satisfaction in it. It was a long time before I applied this to schoolwork, but that would come.

I worked at the library for about six years. It's hard to summarize all I learned and all the feelings connected with the library and the staff, but there are a few key points. First is the dedication of the staff. Many of the full-time employees held a master's degree in Library Arts and yet were making under $22,000 a year. They unfailingly did their best to work for the community in what was often a shamefully thankless capacity. I admired their dedication. I felt I wanted to emulate that, and often now when I feel I'm unfairly overloaded with work and responsibilities I think of those people and remember that I should appreciate what I have going for me. The other staff—the part-timers, custodians, and such—were the same. They all did their jobs well and created an enjoyable atmosphere for everyone. Sometimes I wondered how so many good people could be concentrated in one small place. Maybe I'm a naïve optimist but I came to the conclusion that it was the atmosphere, the congenial and supportive feelings around us all, that was responsible for it. Most people have it in them to be their best but the circumstances surrounding them are not as favorable. And where did this atmosphere come from? I think it came from Mrs. Johnson and a couple of others there who were much like her. They were very supportive, generous, and kind to everyone, and so everyone else began to emulate and encourage this attitude. I don't know how well I have succeeded, but I have tried to hold this attitude and to project it to those I come into contact with. I've learned that how you treat people can really make a difference. Sometimes a kind word from the right person at a certain time can make all the difference in the world.

Another aspect of the library that was very important to me were the patrons, whose questions and requests for help had a great influence on me. I felt I held a certain power. If I knew the answer to a question, then I could solve a person's problem. Perhaps if a person was particularly nasty I could purposely misdirect that person (I never did that but I was aware that I held the power). It really built my confidence. I was given certain responsibilities and I was living up to them. This was something I couldn't find in school.

After a couple of years of working at the library, I noticed that many people recognized me outside of the library. For a very shy person this really fed my ego. One of my favorite memories happened right in the library. A mother brought her little girl to check out some children's books. The girl was no more than $3\frac{1}{2}$ years old. She could walk and talk only a little bit. Her mother sat her on the counter as I checked out her books. I was talking to the girl like I usually did with little children; I asked if she enjoyed reading or if her mother read her stories at night. When I was done checking out the books and the mother was taking her off the counter she smiled and said, "He's a nice man, isn't he, Mommy?" Her mother agreed. I felt about ten feet tall the rest of the day. I knew from my experience at the library that I wanted to work in some capacity with people.

The problem was always that I couldn't seem to apply myself to anything outside of working at the library. I matured a great deal while working there, but I needed to extend that to other areas. I continued cheating on tests and papers throughout all of high school, but after freshman year I stopped advertising it. I quit helping my friends cheat and bragging about my crooked accomplishments. I wanted to become a more serious student, but I wasn't secure enough in my abilities to give up cheating. I felt I needed to cheat to get good grades. It was also partly force of habit; I was accustomed to cheating—not studying—and that was hard to break. I was still very withdrawn in class and did not participate. I avoided all high school social events. Overall, high school did not have a great effect on me because I put so little into it. What I did outside of class was of greater consequence.

When I wasn't working and my friend Bill wasn't around, I spent most of my time by myself feeling very lonely. Only those who have experienced extended periods of loneliness know what it can do to you. Fortunately, I had enough interests to occupy some of my time. For example, I was very interested in astronomy, and early in July there is a meteor shower that appears every year. One summer I decided to get up in the middle of the night to watch it. I had never seen a meteor shower before and I was not expecting it to be anything too spectacular. I got up around one in the morning and went outside the house. It took a while before I could discover the section of the sky in which it was taking place, but when I first saw it, I was frozen in place. Every few seconds a bright streak would shoot across the sky and disappear. Each one couldn't have lasted more than a second, but the power they seemed to display left me awestruck. They sped over the sky so quickly that they were hard to follow and I got dizzy from turning my head so quickly.

Then I decided I wanted to enjoy this more. I went inside and made a couple of sandwiches and got a drink. On leaving the house I caught a glimpse of my father's old pipe. It was a big, awkward thing but it seemed to match the moment perfectly. I had never smoked before—I had never even considered it—but I grabbed some tobacco and some matches and went outside with my little package. When I got outside I wasn't satisfied with my view. My house is on a hill but the house next to mine was taller and was blocking my line of sight. Nothing was going to get in my way of enjoying this show so I decided to climb up my neighbor's roof. I had scaled the side of their house several times before a few years earlier (to peek in their windows) but I had never been on the roof. The house had a fairly sturdy drain pipe so I tied my things in a bundle around my waist and climbed up to the roof. It was an old house with a lot of nooks and crannies in it so I found a good comfortable spot which couldn't be seen from the ground and sat down to rest. Lighting up the pipe took a few tries, and when I did light it at first I felt sick from the smoke. After a while I got used to it and started on the sandwiches. There was no moon that night and the sky was very dark. I looked upward and watched the lights streak from one side to the other.

I was all alone. I could see no one and no one could see me. The darkness of the sky was very soft and deep and the warm yellow streaks painting a path across the backdrop every few seconds were both magnificent and calming. My troubles were all below me and the show I was watching seemed to put everything into its right place. This was so much larger than anything else I had ever seen. How many trillions of miles and billions of years had these meteors travelled only so I could watch them burn out in flame? Everything else seemed insignificant. There were no happy families, no unhappy families. No good students and no bad students. There were no words locked inside my head refusing to come out right. All of us were little and of no importance to what I was witnessing. A quote from Dickens floated over me and didn't seem as harsh as when I first read it: "The universe makes a rather indifferent parent." I stayed on the roof for a couple of hours and for that time all was right in the world. Unfortunately, that was only a passing moment—no matter how good it made me feel, it didn't help me deal with everyday life.

After barely graduating from high school, Bill and I went together to a community college. It was something of a joke academically; my high school classes were more difficult. In spite of skipping a lot of classes we ended up with As and Bs and decided to transfer to a technical college. A couple of weeks into the semester I realized engineering was not for me and decided to transfer again in order to become an English major and live at school. It meant separating from Bill the next fall, but I felt it was time for me to try going out on my own.

That summer I met a girl named Ellen and soon started dating. Everything seemed perfect—almost too good to be true. We understood each other's feelings and problems and were able to give support to each other. For example, one day we were talking and I stuttered a little bit. She asked me directly about my stutter. No one had ever done that before. People had avoided mentioning it because they thought it would embarrass me. That attitude carries the implication that there is something wrong with having a stutter. Ellen asked me about it very straightforwardly. I realized that she accepted it as simply a part of me—just like my hair is brown and my eyes are blue. It had a great influence on me and I felt myself falling for Ellen. I took her to her prom and we saw a lot of each other during the summer.

So much happened that summer that it's hard, even in my own mind, to organize it all. Most was due to Ellen's influence and the nature of our relationship together. She was the first girl I ever developed an intimate and supportive relationship with. We shared our secret hopes and dreams and could rely on each other if we wanted to talk over problems we were experiencing in our lives. We each knew that we could depend on the other. We took things very slowly as far as a physical relationship went. When I think back to the time we shared, I think my favorite memories were when we went to the park and had a picnic. We would lie on the grass, sometimes I would lay my head on her lap, and talk or just sit quietly. There was something very special about being able to spend quiet time with someone as close to my heart as she was. All the days we spent together seemed to be sunny, happy, and fulfilling. I'm probably romanticizing our time together, but that is the quality of my memories of Ellen. Being able to build a relationship like that, particularly since Ellen and I were so well matched, resulted in my maturing a great deal.

I can't give a surefire explanation for it, but my stutter was decreasing markedly. By the end of the summer, stuttering had become a rare incident whereas before it had been the norm. Perhaps it was because I was at the age when men finally stop growing. My metabolism may have changed slightly. Maybe it was because I was maturing mentally and emotionally. By the end of the summer I was almost speaking normally. I am determined never to forget, however, what it was like having a problem such as that and what it was like to have people judge me and put me down for something over which I had no control. I'm very fortunate to have experienced that and to have had it corrected for whatever reason. I work with the mentally handicapped now, and it's always surprising to see how far they can go beyond what is expected of them. I've learned never to place restrictions on the abilities of other people, and more important, on my own abilities.

Ellen was going to a school about 1,500 miles away. We could have made a commitment at the end of the summer, but we both thought that we should go off to school with full freedom and then see how we felt. It was difficult because we were both very much in love by that point. It was a good decision though, and we promised to keep in touch. Without Ellen's support, I don't think I would have had the confidence to leave my home and all my established friends and go off to an unfamiliar environment. She was never even aware of that. It was one of the ways she helped me without knowing it.

We left for school and, as promised, we kept in touch. I wrote her every day, and she called me often. After three weeks we found it very hard to be apart. We kept on saying how much we missed each other. Toward the end of September, Ellen said that she was coming home in a couple of weekends. She wanted to get together and spend a day with me. I'm pretty sure we were both ready to make a commitment—we were going to become engaged, so to speak. Ellen hinted that she felt ready to begin a sexual relationship. We started talking on the phone more often, and Ellen began thinking about transferring to a school in my area so we could see more of each other. I was on top of the world.

Friday night around 11:00, about a week before Ellen was to come home, I was in my room studying when I heard the phone ring. It was Ellen and she sounded upset. She said she had been assaulted that afternoon and described what happened. When she had finished, I said, "Ellen, you keep saying that you were assaulted but I think it's important that you admit outright that you've been raped."

It was a painful phone call for both of us. We talked for an hour or so; I said I knew a place I could call to get some information and I would call right back. I called a rape crisis hotline and found out all the medical, legal, and physical aspects I could. I called Ellen back and we decided to fly her up here, take her to a hospital, and see what she wanted to do as far as pressing charges. She felt she couldn't tell her parents what happened, so I had to help her on my own. I did what I could for her, but I don't know how much help I was. I was very upset. It was an extremely difficult weekend. She went back to her school in a couple of days, which was probably the hardest thing of all. I wanted to keep her with me and protect her. But she had more courage than I did and went back to finish the semester.

I was in a bad state after she left. I didn't eat for a total of six days and when I did start eating, it was only in little bits. I couldn't sleep, and when I did I was having terrible nightmares. I would dream of people chasing me and then setting me on fire; people surrounded me and hacked at me with knives. The nightmares were bad, but I wondered why they were always about me. Ellen was never in any of these dreams. I felt very selfish, like I didn't really care about her. This brought on a tremendous feeling of guilt.

Soon the dreams started to change and seemed to reflect something that had actually happened. I couldn't put my finger on it, but each time I woke up I seemed to be close to recalling something I hadn't thought of in years. Bits and pieces started coming together, and it just got worse and worse. I began calling back memories in my waking hours. For over thirteen years my mind had withheld these incidents and blocked them from coming forward. However, now with Ellen's experience, it all came back. I remembered being a small child and a man I knew brought me into a bedroom. I remembered him laying me on my stomach and his hot breath on the back of my neck and the pain as he pushed down on me. It happened more than once; he did things that I didn't understand then but I understand now. I can't say how many times he did this because they are all blurred together. The experiences had been locked in my memory for years—I had never recalled or spoken about them to anyone before. I must have been afraid at the time to tell anybody, including my parents, what was going on.

By the end of the semester, I was a mess. I was in a crisis situation and my grades were horrible. I did pull through it, but the next semester I decided to get counseling. I started understanding a lot of things. I understood now why I hated crowds and having people stand behind me. I understood why the experience with sex brought up so many confusing emotions. What I have never learned to understand is why some people will use other people weaker than themselves to satisfy their own selfish wants. I still know the man who did the things to me and it really seems he doesn't remember it at all. Maybe he does and is suffering with a terrible conscience, but I don't think so. I have been watching him since to find out if he has been doing it to any other child. I don't think he has. If I find out that he is, I'm not exactly sure what I would do. Most likely I will kill him if I think I can get away with it. I don't have violent feelings toward most people, but if someone like him keeps hurting innocent people in that way, I don't think he should live. I want people who do things like that to know that they are in a lot of danger.

The relationship between Ellen and me was never the same. We stopped dating. She wasn't able to continue a physical relationship with me, or start one with anyone else at that time. It wasn't a complete loss because we developed a very strong and supportive friendship. I eventually told her what had happened to me as a child, and we helped each other in many ways. Our friendship became something very important to each of us, and we have both benefited from it. I learned from her what love and generosity in the face of pain really is. Since then we have both gone on to date successfully and are both happy and contented people. We both had something horrible done to us, but neither of us is guilty of ever hurting another person.

I have found a role for myself. It was very painful growing up, but through the pain and all my mistakes I have learned a lot. I do very well in school, and I'm working my way toward studying counseling psychology in graduate school. I earn As and a few Bs now, and I'm finally the student that I've always wanted to be. In fact, I'm more successful in college than anyone else in my family. I'm not spiteful and bitter and don't rub it in my family's face, but I do like the feeling (and the place in the family) it gives me. I find that even now I tend not to participate in class discussions as much as I could, but that is more from old habits than from shyness. I date girls, but I haven't dated steadily since Ellen. I guess I'm guilty of comparing every girl to her and the quality of the relationship we had. A friend who is studying for her doctorate in psychology and knows my history with Ellen would like to see me get into counseling men who physically and sexually abuse women. I can't consider that right now because I still have very violent feelings toward these people and I know that is wrong. Maybe sometime in the future I'll be able to think about it.

Some days I go through mood swings. In the morning I can be the most cheerful optimist and yet come back in the evening seeing red with rage. However, it has been a long time since I've experienced any sort of depression, and I think that is the important thing. I simply write off my mood swings to my Irish temperament. Besides, these mood swings are so minor compared to my former depths of depression that I can joke about them.

Recently I became very ill and spent several days in the hospital confined to a bed and connected to an IV tube. For the next several weeks I was very weak. During this time my speech regressed terribly. It made me realize that my problems had not gone away, but rather I had learned to compensate for them. When I was weak and fatigued I didn't have the concentration necessary to maintain my methods of compensation. I was at first upset and felt once again that I was very different from others. Soon, however, I came to the conclusion that it was a good thing. It would come back every once in a while to make certain that I didn't forget where I came from and how far I've come. I would be reminded from time to time that we all have our strengths and our weaknesses and it is important to accept both from all people. I would be reminded of the simple beauty of a conversation.

Altogether, I have been very fortunate in my life. Some terrible things have happened to me, but then I have also been lucky enough to come into contact with many wonderful people. These people have shown me what it means to be a caring and responsible person. They've allowed me to make all my mistakes without placing any judgments on me. I have learned from them that the way you treat other people really can make a difference for the better. Treat everyone with the dignity and respect they deserve and it will always come back to you. Stand by others when they're in need because when you're in need you'll find you have a lot more friends than you thought you had. But most of all, learn to stand on your own two feet. If you can't help yourself, there is little that others can do for you. Everyone is going to experience pain and hardship at some point in their life, and that is when we learn the depth of both our own strength and of our relationships with others. If we have planted strong roots, we should be able to withstand much of what comes our way. At the library, there was a saying on the bulletin board which I have always liked: *Be optimistic even when you feel desperate.*

16 Forever an Awkward Adolescent

This is the story of a young man born with serious physical disabilities. David describes the tension between his parents over how high their expectations for his autonomy should be. His father's "legendary penchant for interfering" results in his doing everything for him, whereas his mother, having "less patience with incompetence," expects him to learn to do for himself. College becomes a new opportunity for forming close female friendships and for academic achievements, but these are tainted by doubts over whether he is held to the same standards as his peers. And he asks, "What is to become of my sexuality?" and envisions "a 35-year-old with the sexuality of a 14-year-old, and the prospect does not please me." As he plans to begin graduate school for a career in media, he will not accept society's narrow expectation that he should practice his profession as a representative of the disabled because he says "I do not think of myself as a disabled person."

My first clear memory is from nursery school. When I was 3 years old my parents sent me to a small nursery school for three or four hours about twice a week. It was in the basement of a local church, and I distinctly remember being carried down a long corridor past beautifully colored stained-glass windows. Someone was carrying me and pointed out the colored shapes that were on the opposite wall as the sun shone through the windows.

I should note that at this point I had not yet learned to walk. I still think of it as "learning" to walk, but this is not quite accurate. Because I was born with physical disabilities, the first three to five years of my life were interspersed with multiple operations, where the doctors tried to stretch my hamstrings surgically. After each of these operations I was put in a plaster cast—at one point, both legs up to the waist. It was all in an effort to unclub my feet so that I might someday be able to walk. Everyone was very excited when I finally did, spontaneously, while waiting with my father in a doctor's waiting room. My parents and all their good friends were in tears, I guess, because the professionals had been about evenly divided on whether I'd ever walk at all. I don't remember this important occasion, however, which is one of my peculiar tricks of memory—I never seem to understand the full implications of various "remarkable" events in my life.

I don't have a lot of clear early memories of my parents. I always took them for granted, at least until I began to figure out ways that I might lose them. Like when I began to realize that their marriage wasn't that great. They really should have divorced twenty-five years ago. Except then, they wouldn't have had me! Even so, they are very unsuited to each other, and their arguments and periodic leavings and returnings were a bit of a cloud in my childhood.

I am sometimes embarrassed and worried about how little their sour relationship has seemed to affect me. I have had moments of tears and fear during particularly bad patches but, by and large, I have never had those self-blaming feelings that everyone says kids have when their parents have problems. I think it is a testament to my parents that despite their trials, life at our house always had a sense of security and permanence. I don't know if they did it on purpose; more likely it was their conservative view of how one conducted one's life that did it. Breakfast was always there. Dinner was always at 6:30. Everything was predictable. At the time, I came to envy my friends' younger, more adventurous parents (they went to movies—we never did), but now I think that it was better for me to have parents who took refuge in routine. I never really worried that I wouldn't be taken care of, that I wouldn't be loved.

I entered adolescence (and eighth grade) at about the time we made a cross-country move. Thinking back on that period, I am certain that the move was good for me. For one thing, my best friend had moved away the year before, at a time when our relationship was becoming difficult. We first became friends, at age 5, because we shared a disdain for the crowd. We weren't joiners. For me, this trait was determined by my disabilities; I had had to learn how to entertain myself. The fun I had was sedentary: matchbox cars, model planes, books about WWII fliers, and TV—which spent a great deal of time catering to the imaginations of would-be fighter pilots and space travelers. My friend also liked these things, but more by choice. After a while, we reinforced our reclusive tendencies, and as we grew older we grew farther and farther apart from our peers who were either getting into sports or getting into trouble.

Predictably, as puberty struck, my friend and I began to reevaluate (separately) where we stood. I suspect that my friend began to see that others his age were having a lot of physical fun, horsing around in ways that seemed impossible, or at least improbable, for me. Suddenly going over to each other's houses to play with Legos no longer sufficed to sustain our friendship. I, too, began to identify with other peers, people who also stood out, but who seemed to have made the transition from Legos to a kind of makeshift intellectualism. When a group of us began reading *The Lord of the Rings,* my best friend did not join in. Soon after this, he moved away.

For my family, the move across country was very traumatic, though they tried to act as though it was an adventure. My main concern was whether I would be able to survive in the new public school I would be entering. Having spent all my grade school years at an "experimental education" school on a college campus in my hometown, I was not used to a structured school environment. The realm of real schools was a mysterious and sinister one in the lore of this "campus school," and I'm afraid I bought into the horror stories of academic rigor and regimentation, which passed for information on public schools among my 12-year-old schoolmates. I think that entering middle school in the new town, far from any familiar people or places, was the best way for me to get into regular schooling; kind of like being thrown into a pool as a way of learning to swim. As it turned out, it was all right. I gained confidence in my academic abilities by having my intelligence confirmed for the first time by grades. The teachers there were every bit as human as in my other school, and the kids were far more numerous, so I could hide in anonymity. At least, that is what I thought. Actually, because of my disabilities I was almost instantly known, or known of, by everyone in the school. I was also treated with uniform kindness and curiosity from the first day, but even then I wondered, as I do now, how much of that kindness was actually pity for me because of my disability.

Since I have been physically disabled all of my life, I have managed to cope with the purely practical problems arising from this with a minimum of fuss on my part; I felt no loss, because I had no feelings of "normality" to compare with. One of my physical problems is that I am short, about four feet, two inches tall. Until I began growing whiskers on my face and driving a car, I was constantly mistaken by strangers as being a little kid. It's a hell of a pain for a 16-year-old boy to be handed a kiddie's menu every time he enters a restaurant. It is even worse when mere coherent speech is greeted with awe. If explaining to the old lady in church that I am taking five classes in high school provokes an assumption that I must be terribly smart, how am I supposed to know whether I really am or if everyone is just impressed that I don't drool on myself? I have high standards for myself, perhaps not as high as many straight-A college students, but I am always impressed when I witness, say, good writing and intelligent conversation in others and I aspire to such standards of intelligence. During my teen years it was a constant nagging irritation that everyone around me had what I felt were extremely low expectations. I never knew where I stood.

Almost everybody treats me well, whether or not they really know me. In fact, I gained a reputation among some of my high school peers for being really smart, even though plenty of students within my range of ability (such as those with whom I went through an Honors English program) had better grades and study habits than I did. After awhile, I began to realize that people were predisposed to treating disabled people with extra kindness. Perhaps, I thought, my "smart kid" reputation, which I considered to be disproportionate to my actual abilities, was part of this extra kindness. Supporting this notion was my observation that many people who had known me for a long time, even some members of my extended family, tended to express admiration for my accomplishments with an enthusiasm far beyond what I considered to be appropriate. I was able to gauge this by comparing my parents' response with that of my brother and certain close friends, all of whom had gotten used to the fact that, indeed, I had learned to walk and talk and go to school like any normal kid, and hence, responded in a more subdued fashion to what were, after all, fairly minor accomplishments on my part.

My desire to do well academically did not, oddly enough, compel me to become an especially studious student. My parents never really put the pressure on me to get straight As, and when I came home with report cards that were mixed As and Bs, they seemed to feel these were fairly wonderful. Either they were too old to understand grade inflation, or they were falling into the same trap I already explained—being glad that I was still alive and walking and apparently intelligent. I tend to think that it was a little of both, which means that I have been guilty, on occasion, of taking advantage of the very tendency which I despise. I have often allowed myself to rest easy in others' low expectations. This is something that I continue to fight in myself. Still, it was terribly important to me that I never got less than a B. I constructed a sort of artificial line of performance, below which I told myself my parents would be disappointed. For some reason, I was never too concerned about what my teachers or my friends thought of my grades; I looked solely to my parents for approval on that score.

If, as I surmised, peoples' expressed admiration of me was exaggerated by the issue of my disabilities, then how could I be sure exactly how much of that praise and admiration had been earned and how much was phony or misplaced? Naturally, as I moved through adolescence, I cared more and more about where I stood in the grand scheme of things. Since the whole business of looks and sex appeal was entirely outside my league, my only arenas for competition and comparison were in academics and in "being likable." I tended to look to everyone I met for approval and conversation was my weapon. At first, I was just naturally inclined to have an odd sense of humor, and to express both this humor and my interest in history and politics in conversations with adults and with as many interested friends as I could find. After awhile, though, around my senior year in high school, I began to sense that being able to carry on a conversation about a wide range of topics was not just fun but an asset, too.

I have long thought that one of the real handicaps of having congenital disabilities is that one often grows up isolated from all the trivial things that adolescents banter about: music, girls, cars, clothes, films, TV, and magazines—the whole range of popular culture is a special language that the adult world too easily dismisses as unimportant. But for the teenager cut off from this language, relating to peers who are already leery of him or her because of a disability is doubly difficult. The goodwill most people have to "give it a try" with the disabled teen may be there at the beginning, but unless the teen is able to "run with the ball" and "fit in" at least by speaking the same language as his or her peers, the goodwill quickly turns to embarrassment, and then the disabled teen will be ignored. If it were up to me, people who counsel disabled kids and their parents would stress the importance, often denigrated in "normal" kids, of "fitting in."

In retrospect, I think that a lot of what I was doing in high school was constructing a character, a persona, I could live with. Most adolescents do this, but for me, it was doubly important because the character I had, my "default" pigeonhole in the eyes of others, was that of a short, oddly postured, disabled kid. I wasn't sure at the time, and I'm still not positive, just what kind of persona I want to have. This has made constructing myself an ad hoc process. For the most part, however, I think

I have been able to impress others enough with images other than disability. When I get scared, though, when I think about it too much, I wonder if it's all my imagination. Does everybody still think of me as a disability, and not as a person? I don't know. I'll never really know for sure, because I am always suspicious of others' response to me. I guess that I function from day to day on a veneer of faith; I survive with happiness and pride by assuming that other people see me as I see myself.

My parents are two people whose reactions to me I have trusted. From my mother I get a cartload of political convictions, or perhaps prejudices, because at times I think that her convictions are as much prejudice as they are considered opinions. I count among the greatest gifts of my college years the ability to critique and analyze my own political and social beliefs. By and large, I inherit from Mom a respect for what good can be done by government, along with a profound and unquenchable skepticism which prevents me from ever being satisfied with what government or any other authority is doing. I realize, because I have seen it in my mother, that this is a frustrating way to approach the world. Always having to "bitch, bitch, bitch," not because it's right or good or a citizen's responsibility but because I can't contain myself, is a burden—especially in a society that frowns upon excess in expressing one's views.

Having lived for the most part away from my mother for four years, I have found that I still care deeply about what she thinks of my actions. I don't think I could ever pursue a career, for instance, that violated her standards of morality. This cancels out a lot of possibilities, but fortunately, I have no desire to become a stockbroker. Nevertheless, as I pursue graduate studies in mass media and popular culture, I find myself wondering about how she would feel about my being an advertising copywriter, or a television producer or network reporter. I tend to think that as long as I stay true to my own standards, I will not run afoul of hers, but sometimes I am not sure, and that worries me.

One of the peculiar dynamics of my relations with my parents has been growing up in an atmosphere thick with a history of Dad's legendary penchant for interfering. When I was much younger this didn't bother me, because I sought the security he provided. He was always the provider, the caretaker. In fact, he even helped dress me in the mornings right up till I entered high school. He was always looking for ways to make my life easier. Of course, the problem with this is that it retarded the development of my self-sufficiency. Mom was dead set against this. It wasn't that Mom was uncaring, it is just that she had less patience with incompetence.

In the long run, she was right; it was more help to me to force me into doing things myself than to smooth out any remotely rough areas of day-to-day life. As I got older, Mom became increasingly adamant that Dad was now an abnormally doting parent. She felt that perhaps it was more selfishness on his part—his need to feel needed and in charge—than a true concern for my welfare, which kept him so involved in my physical challenges. Eventually, she began to suggest to me that I ought to resent his "interference" as much as she did. In a way, this was good, because it finally caused me to increase and jealously guard my self-sufficiency. At first for Mom's benefit, but eventually for my own, I began to oppose my father's instinctive moves toward helping me dress, get in and out of cars, put on jackets, and so on. He knew that it all was for the best, and I no longer saw him as my guardian for life. Instead, I began to see him as a friend, a father, and sometimes a pain!

Our relationship has since changed for the better. We now have more arguments than we used to, but they are adult-type arguments. And on the whole, we share a mutual interest in each other's lives. I am sure that he harbors more than a little "controlling interest" in my life, but if he does, he at least is honest enough to admit it, and often interrupts himself midsentence, chuckling at his own tendency to criticize and worry the joy out of new adventures.

Other people, too, have influenced me in less vital, but no less enduring ways. I think that I first got a taste of the joys of discussing politics from the high school librarian. He was a balding, middle-aged man with a bit of a paunch, and a wonderfully dry sense of humor. A fan of George McGovern, he introduced me to the blessings of "Norwegian charisma" while we both watched Walter Mondale stumble through the 1984 campaign. I would come in after lunch and wander over to his office, where we would swap political stories we had heard or read about.

Here was a man, as well educated and articulate as my parents, and with similar political stripes, who actually enjoyed watching the "march of folly" that politics provides. It was a liberation for me. There were very few of my peers with whom I could talk about politics, either because they didn't care or because my views were hopelessly out of sync with theirs. For two years, then, I was able to spend at least an hour of every day just yakking away about anything that popped into my head. In fact, from testing my wings with him, I was finally able to spar with my parents on political topics.

I suspect that this kind of jabbering contributed as much as anything else to my interest in editorial journalism. When I approached the journalism advisor about taking the journalism class (thereby becoming a member of the paper staff), I remember that I had a goal in mind of writing a column. My work in his English class impressed him, so he helped me convince the editor that I should have my own column. In retrospect, I am sure that part of his admiration of me was that damnable tendency I mentioned earlier—to see any accomplishments by a disabled person as a miracle—but I guess I didn't really mind it that much if, in the end, I received recognition purely on my own merits.

I am sure that is one reason why I loved writing that column and the one I wrote for four years in college. In college, I began my column before very many people knew who I was. Consequently, when I got favorable comments from strangers, it was all the more special to me. For the first time in my life, I could be sure that I had earned every bit of the praise I got. I am a person who has never been short of expressions of approval from others, but anonymous praise is like gold to me. This is why I look forward to continue writing of this nature and then hopefully, as a career.

There is one incident from my adolescence that has had perhaps the greatest impact on my outlook. During the long drive from the West Coast to what would be my college in the East, I became seriously ill. At this point, the most severe aspect of my disability stemmed from the effects of severe scoliosis on my lung functions. As

I grew, my spine curved even more; the more it curved, the more it applied pressure on my lungs. Hence, my breathing capacity was getting progressively smaller. While a spinal fusion operation at age 10 prevented this from becoming fatal, as it turned out, the procedure left enough room for worsening to make it nearly so.

Knowing that the high altitude we would have to endure on the drive east would make me uncomfortable, my doctors prescribed an oxygen tank that I could use whenever I got too tired by the lack of oxygen. Unfortunately, this did not solve the physical problem of actual breathing, and the result was a potentially deadly spiral; the more oxygen I breathed in, the less my brain was induced to stimulate breathing—the less I breathed, the less I was able to expel carbon dioxide. By the time I had reached my destination I was unable to sleep, because I would stop breathing and wake up.

At one point, I was told that I would never recover fully from this malady—as, in fact, I have not—and that I had about five years to live. The only alternative was to surgically install a permanent tracheostomy so that, in addition to using extra oxygen at night, I could have the help of a respirator in breathing. We waited a few weeks in the vain hope that somehow I would spontaneously pull out of this hole, and during this time I continued to prepare for my first day of classes which was less than two weeks away.

Most of the people around me, my mother and father in particular, saw my entering college as a fantasy. After all, I did look pretty bad, and I could barely cross a room on foot, much less walk to class. Only my older brother seemed to think that they were all overreacting. For all of my life he had lived with the constant and recurrent threat that I would die, that I would never walk, that I could never do thus and such. Every time I had taken a turn for the worse he had been told that "you'd better come and see him, it could be the last time." Every time I had "proved them wrong," as he put it to me. While he was particularly worried with this incident, he still felt that as long as I was certain I would start college on time, there was hope.

To hear him tell it, I am some kind of brave hero for having kept my faith in my ability to recover. From my point of view, it wasn't bravery or faith. I never really realized how serious my condition was. All along, my mind refused to accept the gravity of the situation. Instead, I whiled away these "sick" hours thinking about how I'd decorate my dorm room, and what classes I would take. Finally, it got bad enough that it was decided to do the tracheostomy. Within a week I was going to my first class. To me it seemed natural. It was what I'd planned all along. I was feeling much better, the oxygen with the respirator at night left me quite healthy during the day, and I was doing what I wanted to do.

In a number of ways, this incident is typical of my outlook as I have grown up. First, it shows how I have generally dealt with adversity: I ignore it. I refuse to accept it. I do not think of myself as a disabled person. While this has helped me thus far, it may not continue to do so. Out there in the nonacademic "real" world, disabled people, like any minority group, have to organize and vocally assert their rights. I have always shied away from doing this. For one thing, my relatively privileged family background has to a large extent smoothed my path. I have not had to advocate strongly for myself because money and my father's position as a doctor have advocated for me. Besides that, though, I simply do not want to be labeled. I take no particular "pride" in being disabled, even though I have as much reason to do so as any disabled person. It all comes back to that nagging problem—how can I earn praise and self-esteem without having my disability in the equation?

But as I inch toward a career, perhaps in journalism, certainly in some kind of media, I am finding that I will have to fight society's tendency to view me primarily in terms of my disability. In my chosen field, there is a tendency to pigeonhole people. Blacks report on race issues. Women report on feminism. I don't really want to be a writer or producer of columns or programs about disability. I understand that people see me as a useful tool—articulate, intelligent, and poised disabled people are hard to come by because so many of them have social disabilities that come with their physical problems. Some would say that it is my duty to serve society in the most natural way possible to me, to become an advocate for disabled people. While I accept the logic and morality of this, I simply don't want that!

In addition to calling my attention to this desire in me to be seen in my own terms, my near-death episode also made me more aware than I had ever been before of how important my relationship with my brother is. He was 14 when I was born, and I am pretty sure that he got short shrift because of the all-consuming problems of my infancy. Although he may harbor some resentment toward me, he also has a devotion to me that I always find surprising. Most importantly, he has supported and challenged me consistently throughout my life—from the time he set out to teach me to get up after falling down, to the times he questioned my opinions and forced me to take steps toward independence and maturity that I was unwilling to take. While others let me grow up somewhat spoiled and lazy, he insisted that there was no reason why I couldn't do dishes or cook dinners. During my years at college, the longest time I have ever lived near him, my brother has had a major role in helping me grow up.

By far the richest time in my life has been my four years in college. The intellectual benefits have been enormous, not so much in the amount of stuff I have learned, but in the atmosphere. My college and I were peculiar matches. Traditionally a very athletic campus, it nevertheless fits my personality in that its students have tended to opt for a kind of athleticism that emphasizes the enjoyment of the sport over outright achievement. I, too, get most of my enjoyment out of activities that have no intrinsic value, no tabulation of results.

Socially, college would have been a waste for me had it not been for my fraternity. It is a cliché that fraternity members learn as well as party in the frat, but it really is true in my case. Of course, mine was an atypical one; for fifteen years co-educational, it has for an even longer time been a contradiction, a fraternity for nonjoiners. Because some of the members had the courage to invite me to rush in the spring of my freshman year, I was able to live for two full years in a house with eighteen men and women who considered themselves a true family. We cooked together, studied together, and fought with each other over how to take care of our family and the structure that housed it. Because I lived with these people, they had plenty of time to get to know me.

Far from shutting me up in a closed community, my fraternity experience gave me the confidence to branch out and become better acquainted with others on campus. When people met me, I was identified with my newspaper column and with my fraternity. Thus, I was more than just a disabled student; I had other identities to start me off. I used them as a launching pad from which to make other people understand who I was in a deeper way.

Before writing this meditation on my adolescence, I was asked, among other things, "What makes you want to get up in the morning?" I think that my first answer would be "whatever it is I have to do on that particular day." This illustrates an important tendency of mine. All my life I have done what's been put in front of me to do. Kids go to school, so I went to school. After that, in my family, you go to college, so I went to college. After college, you either get a job or continue your education, so I will attend graduate school. I pay my bills. I do my reading. I grade papers. I cope. I get along. At the same time, however, I am motivated by a need for approval from others.

Some aspects of adolescence are harder to cope with than others. I often wonder what is to become of my sexuality—I cannot envision (except in erotic dreams) a time when a woman would find me attractive enough to spark a long-term love relationship. I have read of other people far more disabled than I am who have found both love and sex with compatible, willing partners. Yet, a paraplegic is, if immobile, still normal in appearance. I am not. I am short, my back curves severely, and because of my rapid metabolism and restricted abdominal cavity, I am skinny to the point of being emaciated. I have had many female friends, but what could possibly provoke them to see me and be sexually attracted to me?

I have tried on two occasions to move closer to two different female friends. In both cases, this consisted of my acting as comforter and patient listener in time of crisis or stress. On both occasions, they appreciated it and the friendships deepened. But in both cases, I suspect, they had no idea that I had any other motive than a friend's concern. And in each instance, I felt like a beast, because I knew that I had ulterior motives. I know something of the dangers of a male/female relationship based on the weak and emotionally distressed woman and the strong "I'll take care of you" man, and I have no desire to become a "co-dependent"— with or without sex.

I look at the future of my sexuality and I see a 35-year-old with the sexuality of a 14-year-old. In this area, I am likely to be forever an awkward adolescent—and the prospect does not please me. At the same time, I hope that the sense of humor, the curiosity, and the weightlessness of carefree adolescence can be preserved, to some extent. I look around me and see many people in both journalism and cultural studies who seem to have retained these characteristics. Perhaps I can, too. I hope, finally, that I do not ever really grow up.

In sum, I have come a long way. Because of me and those who have supported me, I have accomplished many things and done a lot of growing up. I am still an adolescent, though. Only an adolescent has the audacity to hope for what I hope for, which is—everything.

David: Thirteen Years Later

Everyone likes to think of themselves as unique. Nobody likes to admit that they are subject to "textbook" psychology, the courses of their lives determined by recognized trends and phases. Reading what I wrote thirteen years ago, I am struck by how typical I was and how predictable the changes in my life—and lack of changes—since then have been. My disabilities and life history may make me seem different to others, but I know just how common my life experiences have been. This doesn't bother me; in a way, it's even comforting.

In some ways, thirteen years ago, I was at the tale end of adolescence. I had graduated from college and was halfway through graduate school. I had lived on my own for almost five years. I had distinct interests and a good idea of where my talent lay, and had a coherent worldview. I knew (or thought I knew) who I was, what kind of person I was.

Looking back I realize that I was actually in the deep end of adolescence, and that I'm only now really leaving that period behind me. I was still very dependent on my parents, not physically, but emotionally and philosophically. I had little "real world" work experience, and no real leadership experience. I had no sexual experience at all, at least none that involved other people. I had no strong, deep relationships with anyone, platonic or otherwise. I was like what has been called a "functional alcoholic," a person with a definite drinking problem, but one that doesn't interfere with most everyday life activities.

Yet I was a mess. Parts of me were fully developed, but others woefully underdeveloped. I didn't realize it, in fact, because my deficits didn't prevent me from living a seemingly normal life. I was happy and was either unaware of my problems, or, because they hadn't caused anything bad to happen, figured they weren't anything to worry about. Remember my tendency to ignore my medical problems, and therefore be able to survive them? I think that the same held true for my emotional and developmental problems: I felt okay. People seemed to think I was okay, so, I thought, "if it ain't broke, don't fix it."

Before I get into these deeper, more troubling matters, I need to make a list of the ways I have changed in thirteen years:

1. Thirteen years ago, I thought of myself as apolitically radical, or at least a lefty dissenter. Today I am still left of center, but in other ways I am quite conservative, and think maybe I always have been. Growing up during the Reagan administration, I assumed that authority was always wrong, possibly corrupt, definitely stupid. I figured that I'd carry this attitude through all of my life, like my parents, who were never satisfied no matter who was running the country. During the Clinton administration, however, I discovered how restful it could be to sit back and be comfortable with the group in charge. I still enjoyed analyzing and sometimes disagreeing with the finer points of policy, but I quickly got used to feeling that, basically, people in government at all levels were good, smart people who thought mostly like I did about things. If they did stupid things or advocated policies I didn't like, the difference was more like that between Catholics and Episcopalians than between Hindus and Muslims. Lively debate was still possible, but I felt that those in authority and I were heading in the same direction. It was during this time, too, that I began to feel that a lot of what was wrong in the world was due to faulty systems, not faulty people. That's an idea that has played a major part in my professional life, but more about that later.

2.   Thirteen years ago, I had rarely, if ever, experienced open hostility or competition from my peers. An Ivy League education is supposed to be "competitive." In my experience it was difficult, but not competitive in the personal sense. Nobody wanted me to fail so that they could prosper. Also, if people disliked me, they kept it to themselves for the most part. I don't know whether this was because my disability made them feel that it would be inappropriate to oppose me, or because I hadn't yet tried any activities that brought me into real conflict with people. The result is that I was totally unprepared emotionally for open interpersonal conflict. Also, I lacked even the most basic skills for competition and conflict—skills that most 8-year-olds acquire after their first few Little League games. I've come some distance since then, but I still avoid conflict, even when it is necessary, and several times I have missed the signs of serious interpersonal conflict until it was too late.

3.   My parents separated, my father found another love in his life, and my mother died of cancer. These events had their impact, but that impact has been gradual. Even my mother's illness and death had less impact on me as they occurred than her absence has had in the six years since. I have missed her support and guidance greatly. At the same time, I have been able to make my own way in my hometown in a way that I couldn't have if she were still here. I feel bad saying so, but I know that my mother would understand. She was always the one who wanted more than anyone for me to be my own person. Meanwhile, my relationship with my father has improved in some ways and deteriorated in others. We now relate to each other as adults, and Dad has expressed pride in my accomplishments.

4.   After graduate school, I settled in my hometown. I did so because there was a job available there, but my mother, who lived there, and the attractiveness of familiar territory also led me there. I still live there, and probably will for some years to come. While I often think about an alternative career, I have no strong desires to leave my home just for the sake of starting over in a new town.

5.   The most significant change in me over the past thirteen years has been the complete turnaround in my attitude toward my disability and toward working in the disability services field. The job offered to me in 1991 was a position at a new nonprofit organization in my hometown, an organization serving people with disabilities, that was governed and staffed primarily by people with disabilities. I had never heard before of such an organization. Philosophically, it rejected most of the negatives I had come to associate with disabilities: pity, charity, narrow group self-interest, paternalism, and segregation. Instead, this organization was a practical service and advocacy offshoot of the disability rights movement—another thing I knew nothing about even though I had lived with a disability all of my life. I started off doing publicity work for the organization, which wasn't so far from what I thought my career path in writing and media would be. I figured I would spend a year or two gaining work experience, while attempting to do some writing for our local newspaper. I never did write for the paper, not counting letters to the editor and editorials on behalf of the organization for which I worked. One reason was that I didn't have the energy and motivation to pursue journalism while holding down a full-time job. The other reason was that, in the disability rights movement, I found an approach to disability that fits my personality and a mission I am uniquely qualified to serve.

The disability rights movement fits my personality in that it approaches individuals' problems by seeing systemic problems that are at their root. My organization not only helps individuals with disabilities deal with their specific concerns, we also identify ways in which the structures, policies, and practices of ordinary society make life more difficult for people with disabilities. For instance, we typically help an individual with disabilities deal with architectural barriers in a workplace, but we also work to remove such barriers wherever we find them. The disability rights movement has its roots in 1960s activism and political engagement. In other words, it views disability in the same way I view pretty much everything.

Most important, we work in this field not because we feel sorry for people with disabilities, but because we *are* people with disabilities, and because it is just. Previously, I avoided association with any kind of "disability community" because the only ways I'd seen such associations was in the context of charity, and that disgusted me. It also prevented me from truly seeing how my disability gives me a kinship and solidarity with others who have a disability. In a way, I denied myself an important source of support and pride. By working within the field as I do, I have reclaimed my membership in an exciting and vibrant community, rather than joined a sad and depressing begging crew.

The most important qualification for working in the disability rights movement is having a disability. I also bring a superior education and an analytical mind to the movement. I find that I am able to conceptualize disability issues in the abstract, while also emotionally connecting with them. There are many who can do one or the other, but relatively few who can do both. This transforms my choice to work in the field from a mere preference or convenience into a sort of mission. It also led to my taking on local leadership in the movement. I am now the executive director of the organization I joined in 1991.

One thing that hasn't changed in me is my wish to do something with my life that is both personally satisfying and useful. Finding and joining the disability rights movement has been the single most positive development in my life over the last thirteen years.

Although I would have learned more about my strengths and weaknesses no matter what I'd done after graduate school, the fact is that the work I have chosen has brought both my strengths and weaknesses into much sharper focus. I have already mentioned the strengths I have discovered. However, the weaknesses I have discovered may be more important in the long run.

In my original reflection, I wrote about not being sure where I stood in other people's eyes because I felt that they might be taking my disability into account when assessing my personality or performance. I implied that I didn't want or like unearned praise and admiration. I have since discovered that, even though I don't agree with it intellectually, I have become used to people "cutting me some slack," most likely because of my disability. I believe this caused me to be too dependent on being liked, which has led to some of the more serious problems I have had in my working life.

When the executive director's position opened up, I applied for it. As I've said, I was probably the logical choice, based on my resume, life experience, and ability to understand disability issues. However, in retrospect, I see that I was really not prepared for leadership and supervision. I had no previous experience of either and understood them only in the simplest terms. There were one or two people in the organization who, I think, knew this better than I did, and once I became director they made it known in subtle ways that they didn't have much confidence in my abilities. Of course, this was a shock to me. It was the first time I had ever experienced real opposition—not to an idea or opinion, but to my actual abilities and personality. A vicious circle developed in which I was afraid to confront this opposition, which confirmed my weakness and encouraged bad behavior on the part of employees, which I failed to deal with because of my fear of being disliked and creating conflict, and on and on.

Finally, after several years of alternating bad times and good times, I have begun to get a handle on leadership. The biggest hurdle was finding out that if someone doesn't like me or is angry with me, the world doesn't end. My life doesn't collapse. At one point, I even discovered that two of my employees were complaining to the Board of Directors about my "inconsistency." I can't blame them, because, as I've said, I tended to let people get away with things I shouldn't have. This meant that less contentious employees often got better treatment than hard workers. Unfortunately, it took staff plotting and Board intervention to get me to face up to this and other related problems.

Gradually, though, I have changed the way I do my work and the way I relate to people, including those at work. I am more willing to confront people when needed. I procrastinate less. I have learned how to accommodate individuals' needs and strengths, while also holding them to a fair standard of performance.

The best thing about this experience, however, is that it has made me stronger. I always understood the idea that adversity makes you stronger, but never really believed it to be true. I had survived a lot of physical and medical adversity, and didn't see myself as being especially strong. Now that I have experienced the much more difficult forms of adversity found in the workplace and between people, I realize what adversity really is—and that I can survive it. As I said before, the world didn't end just because I screwed up, and this has given me the confidence I need to change myself in ways that will actually improve my performance. So I guess you could say that I had to fail in order to learn how to succeed.

With all of this going on, it's a good thing that I am usually able to put it all aside and enjoy my free time at home.

I still don't feel completely comfortable saying that I like to watch television, but it happens to be true. I don't apologize for it, but I'm certainly aware of the image it presents: a lonely guy letting his mind rot by watching the "idiot box" every night. For me, though, television is not a passive medium. I've always "read" TV. That is, I process it the way serious readers read books. Maybe a better comparison would be to say that I watch TV the way Roger Ebert watches movies. Even the worst shows say something and I'm interested in what TV shows say. It is both a relaxation and intellectual exercise.

Music is one of the few things that instantly reaches me emotionally. It is also one of the areas of my life where I don't mind saying I'm still an adolescent. If anything, I prefer today's music to the music I grew up with. My tastes are fairly broad. I like any genre of music if it is performed with passion and animated with ideas. The ideas don't have to be intellectually sophisticated or even admirable, but if I feel that something genuine is being communicated, then the quality of the musicianship or the sophistication of the composition isn't important to me. Music may be the only form of expression that I enjoy on a completely gut level.

My other spare time obsession is my website and weblog or "blog." I taught myself some of the basics of website design and, using blog software, created my own site on the Internet, which I add to several times a week. The blog has turned into the diary I always told myself I should keep, but never did. It's almost three years old now, and looking through the archives I'm amazed at how much I have written in small, unconnected nuggets, peppered with Web links to news stories, books, music, and other strange things I'm thinking or reading about. I don't get very personal with the blog, which probably makes it less interesting. I guess it's an indication that I am still too shy to share much of my inner self with the world, even though I'm pretty sure only a handful of people ever visit my site. Still, it's fun, and it will be easy to switch to more personal observations and thoughts if I ever resolve to do so.

I often spend hours working to make a single page on my site look the way I want it, but have to force myself to do the more difficult tasks. I know the professional work I do is more important than playing with my website. It helps real people live better lives. It improves my community. It's something I can do that most other people can't. My current work also has the advantage of being the status quo: As difficult as the road ahead may be, at least it's a familiar road. In addition, the idea of doing something for a living that I do for pleasure is very attractive to me.

Lately I've been thinking about picking up my old idea of writing for the local paper. Since I like to watch TV and to write short pieces (as in my blog), I'd like to try to write a television review column. One of the benefits of living in a small city is that it may not be that difficult to achieve. I wouldn't do it for the money or recognition, but as a way to find out if I can combine my two greatest pleasures into something like a job. I like what I'm doing now, but part of me is restless to try something new, something different, something less safe.

I wish I could say that I've solved all of the "intimacy" issues hinted at and referred to directly in my original essay. While I don't feel that I am still an "awkward adolescent," in regard to sexuality and deep interpersonal relationships, I haven't made much progress. Sometimes I feel that I missed out on a window of opportunity—a time when other life concerns were relatively minor, and allowed space to pursue relationships. As a professional, and a single adult among adults with families and careers, I find few opportunities to explore relationships I should have explored when I was younger. I just don't have the time, and neither do most of my peers. Add to that the same old barriers, most of them in my mind, having to do with my disabilities, and I find myself still alone.

For the moment, I'm at peace with that. I have good friends—some of them co-workers, others people I have met through other associations, and still others people I have maintained contact with since college. There are people I can share my ideas and feelings with. It's of little importance to me that I'm not married, that I don't have kids. I miss the intimacy and strong devotion that these bring to my peers. However, I also know peers who, like me, have built their lives of other elements. In fact, I have lived as I do for so long now that I find it hard to imagine any other kind of life. That in itself may be the greatest barrier to forming deeper relationships. Cut through all the noble-sounding words, and it all boils down to what sounds like a sitcom cliché: I'm "afraid of commitment." Whatever. I'm certainly not going to go on some great self-conscious quest for love, connection, commitment. I can't think of any endeavor so dismal and boring. Either another cycle of my life will come about when new opportunities arise, or it won't. I'm keeping my eyes and ears open, but I'm not "holding my breath" for it, as the saying goes.

I'm finally finishing up this adolescence thing. It was delayed. Thirteen years ago, I was just beginning it when I thought I was finishing it. There are still more things to learn, more experiences I haven't had. It's possible that parts of me will always be 19 or 20 years old. I think I can live with that, and happily. On the other hand, I thought thirteen years ago that I knew what my life was going to be like, and have since been surprised in many ways. Thirteen years from now, will I be satisfied with my life? I don't know. But I'm pretty sure that whatever happens, I'll be a better person then than now, just as I think I am a better person now than I was thirteen years ago.

17 Pa Jam Decourajer

This story begins in Haiti and follows Marie's emigration to the United States. She describes the common experience of leaving a relatively comfortable and even privileged existence in a home country, to descend the social and economic ladder as a recent immigrant. At first her family settles in New York City where she attends school and is recognized as exceptionally bright. Through family turmoil and foster home placements, Marie perseveres and excels in school. She finds comfort in the simple mastery of facts and definitions, and escape in her love of reading romance novels. School becomes the primary source of her self-esteem and offers a credible hope of escaping her circumstances. Graduating as high school valedictorian leads to enrollment in a good college, where she is able to create the future she has worked at for so many years. Writing as a senior in college, she describes the emotional damage she has suffered as "layers and layers of protective gear [have grown] over my heart," and worries about her ability to ever "love unconditionally." She also reflects on how her painful experiences have built in her a determination to succeed that will help in facing the challenges of adulthood.

Whenever my sisters and I revisit our past, we have the uncanny ability to laugh at all of the pain and suffering we have undergone. No matter how traumatic the episode or sad the scenario we are able to turn it into a joke. We laugh until we cry, until our bladders feel heavy and we need to relieve ourselves. Though the misfortunes and hard times are not at all mirthful, we are able to appreciate their unconventional humor. Even when I discuss my past with friends, I lighten it up by interjecting a dose of comedy for their amusement.

While I have casually wondered why humor plays such a role in my life, I have never pursued the topic in depth. That is, until I quite innocently came upon a book entitled *Honey Hush!* by Daryl Cumber Dance. This book examines the role that humor plays in the past and present lives of African American women. According to Dance, humor is the one thing that has enabled us to survive all of the misdeeds and misfortunes that have been our lot in this country, and sometimes in our families. She contends that "We laugh to hide our pain, to walk gently around the wound too painful to actually touch. We laugh to shield our shame. We use our humor to speak the unspeakable . . . to get a tricky subject on the table . . . to strike out at enemies and the hateful acts of friends and family . . . to bring about change. Ultimately we recognize, as Toni Morrison has written in *Jazz*, 'that laughter is serious. More complicated, more serious than tears.'"

If the events surrounding my birth are anything to go by, it is no wonder that a good sense of humor and unwavering determination are two of my most cherished traits. When my mother was eight months pregnant, my parents moved to a small town in central Haiti. My mother was quite determined to have the new house in perfect order by the time she went into labor. Thus, even though she was very visibly pregnant, she set about furnishing and decorating the house with the help of the two maids under her employment. About a month and a half later, mother went into labor. The midwife was well known around town as something of a comedienne and had mother in stitches (no pun intended) the entire four or so hours of labor.

At the time of my birth, my parents had two maids and a cook. They were all in their early twenties and from *Ahndeyo*, which means literally *from the outside*, and geographically *from the mountains*. One maid was responsible for washing our clothes and the general upkeep of the house while the other was responsible for watching over the children and tending to the garden. The cook prepared the daily meals.

Mother was well known as the best seamstress in town and had her own shop as well as numerous students under her tutelage. Father was an inspector for the Department of Health. We were relatively well off in those days. Every time someone was born a tree was planted in their honor, livestock was purchased for them, and they were deeded a plot of land. Summers and weekends were spent with relatives in Ahndeyo, where we were free to do as we pleased. Unlike most of our neighbors, we had electricity and a television. It was a good life. However, because most of my mother's family was in the United States, and due to the political turmoil in Haiti, my parents decided to emigrate to America.

In 1982 my parents and brother, Andre, flew to New York leaving my three sisters and me with my eldest sister's godparents in Port-au-Prince, the capital of Haiti. There are six of us in all. Andre is the oldest and only boy. Then there is Sabine, Joanne, Marie (that's me), Pascal, and Samantha, who was born after our stay in Port-au-Prince. Life in the capital left much to be desired. My sister's godmother was very jealous of my family's wealth and ability to move to the United States, so she set about making our lives hell. Whenever our parents sent us food or presents, she would give them to her daughter. We weren't well fed, nor were we allowed to use the indoor toilet. The repulsive outhouse in the woods, however, was at our disposal. She derived intense pleasure from mistreating us. This was quite obvious in the way she forbade me to continue befriending a boy who lived in the neighborhood.

She did not like our relationship, as she thought it inappropriate for boys and girls to be friends. At 5 years old I did not understand her reasoning, nor did

I appreciate her interference in my playtime, so I continued to consort with him. One day while he and I were engaged in a game of tag, she came upon us with a very determined look on her face. She grabbed my left ear and dragged me the several feet separating the field from her chicken coop. She had a brown paper bag in hand.

She pushed me onto the floor and snarled, "Do you want to be a boy!?" By that time I was in tears, and my ear was throbbing in pain. I muttered a watery "no."

"Are you sure," she asked nastily, "because if you do, there's an operation I can perform that will turn you into a boy." She rattled the bag and took a step closer to where I was huddled on the ground.

"No!" I screamed.

She slapped me. "Don't scream! If you want to scream I'll give you something to scream about!" She paused, smiled, looked at the bag for a few moments and then turned her burning gaze in my direction. "Do you know what I have in here? Do you, do you?" I shook my head fearfully and bit my lower lip—hard. She laughed, a loud ringing sound that sent shivers down my spine.

"Well, I'll tell you," she said triumphantly. "I have a great big brown cockroach!" I screamed again and crawled further into the coop until I felt the walls against my ill-clad back. She slapped me again. "Don't scream!" she screeched. She licked her lips and advanced to where I was hunched in the corner. She shook the bag and smiled. "If I ever, ever catch you playing with that boy again I am going to take this cockroach," she paused for dramatic effect "and sew it to your vagina and you will become a boy!" She laughed hysterically.

I placed a hand over my mouth to muffle the scream I felt climbing from my diaphragm. My eyes were swimming with tears of fear, and my heart was pounding an erratic rhythm. She shook the bag again, looked at me, smiled a serene smile and left. I don't remember how long I stayed in that coop, too afraid to move, too afraid to let down my guard. Nevertheless, I did eventually fall asleep only to be awakened by one of my sisters a few hours later. Needless to say, I never played with that boy again! I also became deathly afraid of roaches.

So, when we moved into that roach-infested apartment in Brooklyn, I was petrified, especially at night. The roaches in the apartment were a particular breed. They were flying cockroaches about as wide and long as the four prongs of a fork. At night they had festivals and parades on our ceiling. My younger sister and I shared a bed and we would huddle under the covers and listen to the zooming sound of their flapping wings over our heads. Nothing could have made us come from under the covers, except when one or both of us had to go to the bathroom in the middle of the night. We made a game of having to leave the safety of the covers to go to the bathroom or to the kitchen for a drink of water. We would imagine that we were at war and the cockroaches were missiles being shot at us. Under the thick comforter we would strategize the best route. Because everyone else was sleeping, we could neither speak loudly nor turn on any of the lights, so we invested in a pair of flashlights that we used to light the way to our destination. In the sanctuary of daylight we would trade barbs regarding each other's fear of the cockroaches the night before.

We would continue bantering until one of us said something so outrageous that we would both be reduced to convulsive laughter. Humor gave us the courage to talk about our fright. It gave us a sense of ownership over experiences that were very much out of our control. And nothing was more out of our control than what went on in school.

I started first grade in Brooklyn. Unfortunately, the early 80s were a bad time for Haitians in the United States, especially those in New York. At that time it was believed that the four Hs were the carriers of AIDS: Homosexuals, Heroin Addicts, Hemophiliacs, and Haitians. At six years of age, I was an outcast. Ironically, I was harassed not only by black American students, but also by Haitian students. No one wanted to be Haitian at the time and the best way to prove that you weren't one was to torment those who were.

As the saying goes, "if you can't beat 'em, join 'em, " and that's exactly what I did. I denounced everything that had the slightest possibility of being perceived as Haitian. Out with the accent! Out with the hair ribbons! Out with the name! I was no longer Marie but Mary. While my social life at school was negligible at best, my academic achievements were quite noteworthy. I excelled in many subjects, including reading, math, and social science. My fourth grade teacher would assign a list of twenty words to be defined and all of the students would compete to see who could define all of the terms in the shortest amount of time. Invariably, I would win the title of "fastest definer." After a while, my teacher decided that instead of competing, I should help those students who had trouble with the assignment. I really liked tutoring the other students in the class, so I didn't mind.

The following year, my family and I moved to Miami. My parents had always dreamed of owning a house in Florida, and when I was 10 years old that dream was realized. At the time I was told that because mother had a good paying job as a home health aide, it was decided that she would stay in New York for a couple of years. I took that at face value at the time, but now I wonder if my parents decided on this arrangement because they were in the process of separating. I remember throughout the four years we spent in New York not a day went by without my parents having an argument of some sort. Usually the altercations were verbal, but at times physical force was used, and things were broken.

We had a very nice house in Miami and lived in a good neighborhood. I continued to excel in school, and through the help of a school counselor, I no longer denied my Haitian heritage. My father worked long hours at a hotel as a laundry attendant, so I didn't see him all that much, which was fine with me because it allowed me a great degree of freedom. I spent a lot of time at neighboring homes playing with children my age—something I was unable to do in New York because we were forbidden to play with the black children in the neighborhood. My parents were afraid that they would "contaminate" us with aspects of the black American culture of which they disapproved. Consequently, Pascal and I had no other choice but to play only with each other. So the freedom we had in Miami was a godsend—until the day my entire world turned upside down.

I was walking home from school with Pascal when we saw a parade of police cars and other vehicles parked in front of our house. "Wow, what do you think happened?" asked Pascal. I shrugged my shoulders to convey a nonchalant pose while my heart skipped a beat or two. When we got to the house a woman physically stopped us from entering. We cried and demanded to know the whereabouts of our siblings and father. The woman told us that we were going on a trip but would soon be reunited with our family. She took us in the house and helped us pack a few bags of clothes.

As we walked in the house I noticed that there were people taking pictures of every crevice, from the shower in my father's bathroom to the kitchen refrigerator. And for the first time, I looked at the house as a stranger would—and I was appalled! Father was rarely home, and whenever he was, he slept. Furthermore, my older siblings had no desire to clean—they said that it was Pascal's and my turn to clean now that we were of age. Pascal and I were more interested in playing so we rarely cleaned the house. Consequently, when the people from the Department of Health and Rehabilitative Services (HRS) came in, they saw a dirty, empty refrigerator, a sink full of unwashed dishes, and bedrooms with clothes strewn all over the place.

In addition to the embarrassment, I was afraid of what would happen to us. However, since I was the oldest one there at the time, I knew that I had to protect my little sister. So I asked as many questions as I could in order to find out what was happening. After we had packed the bags the woman took us to collect my 2-year-old sister Samantha at the daycare center she attended.

After what seemed like hours of driving we arrived at a big beige building with a million steps leading to the front door, the official headquarters of HRS. A few minutes after we entered, a man in a white coat came and led me to an adjoining room, where he proceeded to grill me. Over the course of the conversation, I told him about the time when my mother "checked me."

"Well . . . " I paused, thinking, "my mother did once before we moved here. She thought that I was having sex with someone at school or something so she checked me."

"Checked you?" he asked "What do you mean by that?"

"Well, you know," I replied, "She wanted to make sure I was still a virgin."

"Can you tell me what happened?" he urged. "How old were you?"

"I was 9 and one day I came home from school late and my mother was suspicious so she took me to her room, locked the door, and told me to take off my clothes. Then she had me spread my legs and checked to see if I was a virgin. She decided I wasn't and beat me with a wire hanger and a telephone cord . . . what are you writing?"

"Just a few things, go on."

"Well that's it really; she didn't believe me when I said that I didn't do anything, so to stop her from hitting me I lied, and said that she was right. Only, that made her even more angry and she hit me harder—I don't feel like talking about this anymore."

"OK, I'll take you to another room now."

The room he led me to looked similar to a hospital waiting room. I saw my father sitting in a chair. I ran to him and he awkwardly hugged me. Then another man in a white coat came in and ushered us to a room with a desk and a hospital bed. He gave me a gown and asked me to put it on after he and father left. Their return initiated the most uncomfortable ten minutes I had ever spent in my young life. I remember crying as the doctor performed a gynecological exam. My father's back faced me throughout the entire ordeal. He never turned around, not even to look back as he left the room when the doctor finished.

I got dressed and the woman who had brought us to the building came and ushered me downstairs into a large office with many cubicles where my sisters were. She left us with a short Hispanic woman who introduced herself as Ms. Hernandez, our social worker, who informed us that we would be living with some other people for a while, and that she would try her best to keep us together. She took us to a big yellow and white house where we were introduced to Mrs. Price and her husband. They had eleven children already in the house ranging in age from a 4-month-old boy to a 17-year-old girl. We stayed with the Prices for a few months and went to the neighborhood school. Because the house was so crowded we told Ms. Hernandez that we did not wish to remain there and she reassured us that we wouldn't live there for long as it was a boarding house for children waiting to be placed in foster homes. Her desire to keep us together made it difficult to place us.

Eventually she did find someone: Cathy Webster, a single mother of two girls, Sinclair, age 5, and Nicole, age 12. We moved in with the Webster family, but almost immediately I could see that they didn't really like me, though I had no idea why. But as I was determined to stay with my sisters, I tried not to anger them. Pascal was a much more willful and difficult to control child than I was, but they loved her. During our stay with the Websters I behaved beautifully because I realized how well they were treating us, and how much Pascal and Samantha liked Cathy. A couple of months after we moved in with them, Cathy married a widower with two children. A few days later, we moved into a bigger house where Sinclair, Nicole, Pascal, and I shared a room.

One day, Nicole and I got into an argument and had a fight. She bit my nose and I bled. When I told her mother she said don't worry about it, it's only a minor cut. She didn't even punish Nicole. That didn't sit well with me, so I called Ms. Hernandez and told her what had happened. That night she called Cathy to ask for more details. The fact that I called Ms. Hernandez really angered Cathy and she said that she wanted me out of her house. Nothing I said, or promised to do, moved her. She wanted me out.

I went to Pascal expecting her to come with me, but she refused to go. I was shocked and hurt. I felt betrayed and angry. What happened to our pledge to always be together? How could my little sister of all people choose to stay with a stranger rather than with me? I was now all on my own—and promised myself that I would never let anyone else hurt me again. Ms. Hernandez took me to a home that had a similar purpose to that of Ms. Price's house, only instead of housing children who were difficult to place because of special needs, it housed children who were difficult to place because of their temperament.

I really felt that I did not belong in that house and I had no desire to be there. Honoring my vow of autonomy, I kept to myself and spoke only when spoken to. The lady of the house was a God-fearing, heavy-set woman whose husband was half her size. She ran the place with an iron hand and had a very low tolerance for "the workings of the devil." Her favorite phrase was "my way or the highway" and you can be sure she meant every word of it. This was also a disastrous placement. I was ostracized by the other girls just because I was the new girl. I was taunted and falsely accused (later vindicated) and betrayed by the one other girl there I let myself get just a little close to. In my heart of hearts I was hurt, but outwardly I was as cool as a cucumber. My nonchalance undermined their attempts to berate me, so after a while everyone just ignored me—and that was more than okay with me.

I was subsequently reunited in New Jersey with my mother and siblings. Over the course of the following weeks we found out that my sister Joanne was reportedly responsible for our misfortune. I was told she wanted to have a party but father forbade her to as he would not be available to chaperone. Because Joanne was angry, and felt cheated (Sabine was allowed to have a party on her birthday months before), she went to a friend's house and overdosed on a bottle of over-the-counter painkillers. When questioned by officials she told them that we were being abused and mistreated. However, when I questioned her about it a few years ago she denied that is what happened. Nonetheless, that was what I had believed at the time and it shaped how I viewed the following few months with her.

For a long time after the incident, Pascal, Joanne, and I would swap stories about the people we had stayed with. More often than not the stories were funny in nature and we were able to poke fun not only at the people we encountered, but at the entire ordeal as well. "Remember when" and "there was this one time" began many a sentence over the following months. According to Daryl Cumber Dance, whose book I quoted earlier, the formula for laughter is tragedy plus time. This was certainly the case with us, for the stories became funnier and funnier as time progressed. Nonetheless, our intense desire to share our experiences did not supercede the need to be comfortable while doing so. Humor enabled us to relay our anecdotes without causing discontent. There was a lot of anger and guilt under the surface and we were certain to tread lightly. Everyone was angry with Joanne for ruining our lives and mother felt guilty for not having been there to protect us.

For the first few months, we all enjoyed living with mother. Because she hadn't seen us in so long, she spoiled us. Birthdays were never a big deal in our family; however, for my thirteenth birthday she not only baked a coconut cake but also allowed me to go to the movies with Joanne and Pascal. She cooked all our favorite foods, bought us most of what we wanted, and rarely hit us. However, once the novelty wore off, things changed drastically.

All of the special attention and kindness came to an abrupt end with the appearance of mother's peculiar behaviors. She would walk around the house yelling at the walls, the floor, and the kitchen sink. She would clasp her hands behind her back and mutter obscenities at some unknown entity. Whenever there was a knock at the door she would grab a knife, run to the door, open it swiftly, and accost the visitor. After a while, there were no visitors. She spent the few nights she was home from work staring out of the living room window. We came to fear her. She had an untamed quality. Whenever she stayed at home she didn't comb her hair or change out of her housedress. Every little incident set her off, so we learned to tip-toe around her. One night, around midnight, she went outside and started talking to herself—or rather to whomever it was she believed was persecuting her—very loudly. She walked barefoot on the empty streets yelling back at those who told her to be quiet. The words she used those weeks are no longer in my memory bank, but the message was always the same. She believed that someone was out to kill her, or, failing at that, drive her insane. Sometimes that person was father; other times, it was people from her past, of whom we had little or no knowledge.

I have often wondered what happened to mother to trigger her emotional breakdown. And a few weeks ago I learned the answer. Months after we moved in with mother, she was jumped by a group of my older sister Sabine's friends. They beat her so badly that she had to be hospitalized. I have no idea why I do not remember the incident; its significance does not escape me. It is one of the missing pieces to a puzzle that might never be completed.

Mother was never one to spare the rod. However, during the last months of our stay with her, it seemed that her belt was an extension of her right arm. It seemed that I could do no good. I was constantly compared to other more obedient, better-disciplined children. A day didn't go by that I did not feel mother's fist or belt on my back.

The most infuriating part of being beaten came after the fact. Her guilt would take over and she would try to be nice. She'd make my favorite dish or buy me a present to make up for the beating. If I didn't show proper gratitude she would be angry all over again. So I learned to smile through my hatred of her. And I did hate her then. While nursing various wounds, I would make plans to run away from home. All the while, I realized that at 13 I was too young to fend for myself.

However much I wished to be rid of mother, never in my wildest dreams did I think it would come true. But one day it did. I remember the day quite vividly. I came home from school at noon to find the apartment overrun with cops and other uniformed men who had come to evict us from the apartment. For months prior, mother refused to pay rent because the toilet was not working properly. In order to flush it you had to pour a few gallons of water into it. On numerous occasions she told the super that she would not pay until it was fixed. He never fixed it, so she never paid.

When I came in, mother was showing the cops the letters that she had written to the building's superintendent. They were paying scant attention to her words and documents; they were only interested in one thing, and that was her removal from the premises. At one point, one of the cops grabbed mother's arm, so she punched him in the nose. I was immediately pushed out of the way and mother was surrounded by a group of cops who tried to restrain her. They roughly forced her into a straitjacket and took her downstairs to an awaiting ambulance. It occurs to me as I write this that there must have been reports of mother's peculiar behavior for there to have been mental health officials, a straitjacket, and an ambulance in the vicinity. I went with mother to the hospital and filled out all the paperwork that was thrown at me to the best of my ability. I called my sister Sabine, who came to pick me up a few hours later, but mother remained in their custody.

Because I was with her that day, mother still feels beholden to me. She believes that had I not been there, they would have killed her. She calls me her savior. This makes me very uncomfortable. I have never forgiven her for what she did to me when I was 9 years old—the virginity exam and beating—and I don't think I ever will. But I don't hate her anymore—I feel sorry for her. Now, she is a woman all alone. None of her children really interacts with her. All of us, without exception, feel that she has wronged us in some way. She deprived us of our childhood— and now we are depriving her of our company and our love. Has she brought this upon herself or is she just a victim of clashing cultures? I know that many Haitian mothers check their daughters' virginity, just as Haitian parents in general do not believe in sparing the rod. If we were raised in Haiti, would I resent mother as much as I do now or would I just take it in stride? I don't know, but I do know that I will give my children all that I never had: unconditional love, security, and trust. Every child deserves a happy childhood—or failing at that, a childhood. I was deprived of the latter, so the former was just a pipe dream.

Upon mother's eviction, Pascal, Sabine, and I moved in with Pascal's friend Valerie. At that time, Joanne was a student at a small college in New Jersey; my older brother, Andre, was staying with mother's younger sister, and Samantha was with our maternal grandmother. We lived with Valerie for about five months. Sabine was pregnant and was receiving federal aid in the form of food stamps and monthly checks. The same was true of Valerie, who had just given birth to her daughter. Furthermore, Valerie was living in low-income government housing, so the rent was never more than fifty dollars a month. So we were somehow able to manage without parents to support and care for us.

I was in the eighth grade and school was the only stable thing in my life then. While my friends and classmates would complain about schoolwork, I looked forward to it. I relished those times when the most important thing to think about was the spelling of a particular word, or what makes plants grow, or who authored the Declaration of Independence. I graduated with honors from the eighth grade. I had the third highest GPA in the class and was quite proud of that feat, even though no one in my family was able to attend my graduation. That summer I enrolled in a program for college-bound students. I visited many New Jersey colleges that summer. It was then that I knew I wanted to go to college. For the first time, college was a tangible thing. I had always heard it said that it was good to go to college after high school, but it was always just talk to me. Sure, when asked, I would say that I planned on going to college, but only because it seemed the right thing to say. When I visited those campuses I was amazed and excited. Amazed that boys and girls lived on the same floor and excited to experience that myself when the time came.

In November of my ninth grade year, Sabine announced that Pascal, Samantha, and I would be going to Miami to live with father. For some time we lived with him in the single bedroom he occupied in a duplex apartment. This was a very difficult arrangement as father needed to make changes in his lifestyle if he was going to be an adequate parent to us. This was demonstrated by the fact that when he was going to be away for a while he asked a friend of his to stay with us, but this friend molested me by trying to touch me in inappropriate places. I think this man realized how neglectful father was and he tried to take advantage of that. Father, on the other hand, thought that he was protecting us by having his friend in the house while he was away. Unfortunately, it was his friend from whom we needed to be protected. How could father in all good conscience leave us with that dirty old man—a man who tried to molest his friend's youngest daughter, and leer at the two older ones? Father should have known better. He should have been there. Even when he found out about the man's dirty deeds from Samantha, then 9, he elected to discredit her.

I don't hate my father. However, I hate that on more than one occasion he believed strangers over his daughters; I hate that he never once contacted us when we lived with mother in New Jersey; and I hate that he was never around when we needed him most. That is all he is—my father. He is not daddy, he is not papa—he is father.

Upon moving in with my father, I enrolled in Edison High School near our house. After a week of excelling in the "regular" classes, I was rescheduled into AP and Honors classes. There were about twenty-five of us who were considered AP students. I continued to shine academically. However, my mode of dress was very urban, so I acquired the nickname *gangsta-nerd*. Whenever someone called me that name, I outwardly took offense. But secretly, I quite liked it. It meant to me that I was not only viewed as smart, but as tough as well. While I did well in all subjects, English was my favorite. Reading was still my preferred pastime, and I did it at every opportunity. I also loved learning and using new words; I would read the dictionary for fun. I had quite an impressive vocabulary. One day in my AP English class, I was challenged to demonstrate just how extensive my vocabulary was. Armed with dictionaries, the students proceeded to throw out random words for me to define. And I defined every single one of those words correctly. Everyone, including my teacher, was very impressed. Much to my chagrin, everyone began to chant "go gansta-nerd" when I was done. I was quite embarrassed, but proud at the same time.

Because I spent the entire day with those twenty-five students, a few of them became very good friends. Of all of them, Melanie was my closest friend, even though I saw the least of her outside of school. Admittedly, that is not saying much because I rarely hung out with anyone outside of school. When I arrived at Edison, everyone already had their cliques formed and I really did not fit in with the other students. Furthermore, my father did not want me to hang out with the kids from school, so I rarely did. I spent most of my free time at home reading romance novels and baby-sitting my younger siblings.

Mel and I had a lot in common in terms of interests—we both loved Regency romance novels, and would don British accents whenever we spoke to each other; and goals—both of us wanted to go become attorneys. We would spend hours together at the mall talking about our dreams and aspirations, including discussing which colleges we wanted to attend and what we would do when we got there. Sometimes we would pretend that we were both successful lawyers and talk about our exciting lives. We were a great influence on each other. I continued to excel throughout high school and remained determined to go to a good college. I graduated as valedictorian and achieved my goal.

Upon entering college I was greatly excited about making "real" friends for the first time in my life. Consequently, I did not discriminate when it came to befriending others. Freshman year I sought out friends of all races, whites, blacks, Asians, you name it. Unlike my African American roommate, who spent most of her time at the black affinity house, I went everywhere and tried to get to know everyone. However, over the course of these four years it has dawned on me that all of my close friends are women who belong to a minority group, be it Asian, Native, or international; they are all women who are invested in more than one culture. I have found it is easier for me to relate with people who understand what it feels like to be intimately acquainted with more than one mode of thought. They tend to be more receptive to conflicting viewpoints and ideas. They, like me, realize that there is more than one "truth." Sometimes we feel that we are in a foreign land, with very few reminders of home. Consequently, we cling to and magnify things that remind us of home. We play traditional music, we attend cultural nights, and we seek out those who remind us of ourselves.

But no matter how close I feel to my friends, or how much I want to unburden myself, the legacy of independence, or self-imposed isolation, remains. There is a part of me that no one has ever touched. A part of me that I keep safe, secure, and hidden. The 22-year-old me, just like the 12-year-old me, knows that people can only hurt you if you let them in. So, I have been very wary of letting others in, of letting others know who I am. Someone once told me that I am very hard to get to know. I didn't argue with him. I have layers and layers of protective gear over my heart. Very few people have the power to hurt me—and even they are unaware that they have that power. Sometimes I wonder if I will ever give myself totally to someone else. I have been in romantic relationships before, but I have always, always maintained some degree of emotional distance. Sometimes I worry that when the time comes, I won't have the ability to trust and love a man fully and unconditionally.

It is readily apparent that my survival has come at a cost. I am not an emotionally open person. I don't trust easily. I surround myself with an air of nonchalance and outward serenity. I pride myself on being cool, calm, and collected at all times. I talk only when I have something to say, never for the sake of it. I share no more than what I deem necessary and safe. I smile through my tears, and laugh through my pain. I survive. And survival, for me, is the name of the game.

Graduation is but a few days away. And I am ready. I am ready to face whatever challenges life has to offer. I am ready to move forward with sure, steady strides. My past has made me a strong woman; however, that strength came at a dear price—my childhood. Nonetheless, I am very secure in the woman I am today. No matter what went on in my life, I have held tenaciously to the dream of "making it." While nursing various wounds, visible and invisible, I would vow to "show them."

There were many people along the way who believed in me, but more than that, I believed in myself. I knew not to let anyone dissuade me from my hopes and dreams. I knew that in order to "make it," I had to "take it." So I did more than that. I confronted it, laughed at it, and fortified my resolve to triumph. *M'pap jam decourajer!* I will never give up!

18 Proud of the Strength I Had

This writer describes her experience of teenage pregnancy and how she copes with its effects on her emotional and social development. Without the support of her former boyfriend or the knowledge of her parents, Connie decides alone to have an out-of-state abortion soon after her high school graduation. She shares her struggle to find meaning in her actions and to redefine her own identity. In college, Connie finds support from a campus women's group that helps her make sense of her experience and understand herself better. She begins to examine her family life and the impact of those relationships on her feelings about men and the coping styles she has developed. Connie also comes to acknowledge her own strength and courage in dealing with this extremely difficult adolescent experience.

It was a week or so after high school graduation. The air was musty and the cement floor was cold. I played nervously with the phone cord and traced its path to the door with my eyes. The garage was the safest place, but I prayed that no one could hear me. It's funny how you suddenly believe in God when you think something bad might happen.

The woman on the other end of the line finally found my records. "Let's see," she said, "Oh yes, your test came out positive!" She sounded excited. I wasn't. I almost dropped the phone. My stomach felt like lead. I couldn't believe her.

"Are you sure?" I barely managed to utter. "Yes, isn't that what you wanted to hear?" Was she stupid? She had to look up my name for the results, didn't she know I was only 17?

"No," I said. She gave me the name of some abortion clinics and I hung up the phone.

On August 18th I had an abortion. In September I left for college. My grades were never affected; in fact, I got a 4.0 my first semester. Studying kept me from thinking too much. Six months after my abortion I saw a sign for a support group for women who had had abortions. I knew that I needed to go. Shaking, I called the number, and they told me where and when it would be.

In this group I began to let out some of the feelings that I had kept bottled up for months. Listening to the other women taught me that I was not alone, although many told stories and expressed feelings that were different from my own. Sometimes I left the group aching with the pain I felt from reclaiming all those feelings I'd pushed to the back of my mind. Other times I was amazed at how well I connected with these women, how much I learned from them, and how much I looked forward to this meeting every week. In the journal I kept, things came out on paper that I never could have said aloud.

March

My boyfriend and I had just broken up when I found out. He wouldn't even speak to me so that I could tell him, but eventually I cornered him. He didn't care, and he didn't want to help. All he could say was, "Jesus Christ, are you sure?" I reminded him that it was his problem too, and he said he would give me the money, but he wouldn't go with me. He assumed, as I did, that I would have an abortion. My Mom would hate me for it. She had always condemned abortion, saying that it was killing a baby. Maybe it is; maybe I did.

After a few phone calls I found out that you have to be 18 to get an abortion in my state without parental consent. I was just four months too young. Eventually I made an appointment with a clinic in a nearby state. The woman I spoke to was very supportive, but I had to figure out how I would get there. A week went by before I asked a friend to take me. Then a few more weeks of wishing I could tell someone and trying to hide the hurt and tears. I guess I did a good job, because no one noticed. The worst part was when I saw my half-brother, an adorable 3-month-old. I couldn't hold him or look at him without thinking that I might as well be killing him.

April

I live constantly in two worlds. One is where I can talk or write about it and show my real emotion—when I'm alone and cry, when I'm with the few friends who know, or when I'm with the support group, the only people who really understand. The other world is all the other times. Then I have to pretend that I am okay. I have to conceal my feelings. If someone reminds me, I can't share the hurt inside. Nor can I when some guy makes a joke or comment about a girl who had an abortion, when Amy eats a peanut butter and banana sandwich and Jean asks if she's pregnant, or when everyone giggles at the jokes, even me, but they don't know what's going on in my head. The pain is when there is an editorial in the paper about abortion and Mary says, "My friend at home had one—I'll never forgive her. She could have given it up for adoption; I was adopted." If only she knew. The pain is when I walk by a poster advocating reproductive rights that someone has scribbled "Fetus-Bashers" on in red magic marker. I want to scream at the person who did it, but they aren't there. I want to rip the poster down, but I don't. I want to tell the person I'm walking with how upset I am, but she won't understand.

May

Mom,

I know you'd hate me if you knew. To you it's disgusting, it's killing. I'll never be able to tell you. Maybe I'm hurting myself or our relationship by not telling you. I would have liked your support. I needed your help, but I couldn't tell you, and I still can't. I never wanted to hurt you.

Sometimes I wish you had guessed somehow. But you would have wanted me to have the baby; you wouldn't have let me make my own decision. Maybe it was a bad thing to do, maybe it wasn't the "right" thing to do. But I don't want a baby, and I don't want to give birth to one only to give it away. I wanted to go to school and learn and have fun, not be trapped in my own body for nine months. I didn't want to be stared at by mothers who warn their teenager at their side: "She can't be more than 16; I hope you never do a stupid thing like that!" I didn't want my sisters to be ashamed of me. I didn't want my friends and teachers to think I was a bad person. Because as we all know, girls who have sex are bad, and girls who get pregnant are stupid.

When I read these journals over again, I remember feeling so isolated and scared that everyone would hate me if they knew. When I did start telling people, I felt terrified of what they might think or say. But the more people I told the less it hurt to retell and the more confident I felt that I was right. The decision I made was a good one, and it was mine to make. I felt proud of the strength that I had to make it through this crisis on my own and stick to what I really wanted to do.

Experiencing for myself the inaccessibility of abortion for teenagers and going to the support group both pushed me to explore feminism and identify with it. I joined a pro-choice group on campus, went to protests against Operation Rescue, and wrote an article for a women's newspaper. I told my closest friends and even some not so close. My experience with abortion was becoming an integrated part of my life. But I also felt disillusioned by "the feminist movement." The political group I joined talked about "rights," and I didn't feel comfortable talking about my abortion, or talking at all, for that matter. It was hard for me to talk about abortion without including my own experiences. But I continued going because I had to make sure that abortion didn't become illegal, or in my case, more illegal. Being involved politically made me feel like maybe I could make a difference.

The pro-choice group organized rides to Boston for the protest against Operation Rescue, which was trying to close down clinics there. I rode down the night before with Sarah, another woman in the group, and we stayed at my dad's house. I don't remember when exactly I met her, or if we knew before that ride that we'd both had abortions, but for two and a half hours we talked about our experiences. It was amazing how close I felt to her; she made me feel even stronger. We found that we both felt alienated from the political group, and we talked about it a lot. She told me that she was in the support group that I had been in the semester before. I realized how much I missed talking about my abortion with women who understood.

It was an emotional weekend and maybe one of the best ones in my life. Talking with Sarah and being with her at the protest made it seem that much more important to me. I felt so good and real and so passionately involved. This was something I believed in like I never believed in something before. It was an incredible feeling facing, inches away from me, the people who believed I was a murderer and wanted to take away my right to control my own body.

After the protest I saw little of Sarah outside the pro-choice meetings until a later semester. She called and asked if I wanted to help her start a support group, or what we later decided to call a consciousness-raising group, for women who had had abortions. We both missed and needed those discussions. We put signs up and met the people who answered in a café on campus. Soon we were a group of eight, and the first night we met I found myself in tears, realizing how much I still needed to talk about it and how much was still left unresolved. I wanted to piece my life together. Why had all this happened to me? Can I go on hiding it from other people, from my family? At the fourth meeting I decided to tell my whole story. I didn't just talk about my abortion, I talked about my whole life. I was trying to make sense of it all. I began to identify some reasons behind my getting pregnant. One was my family. I told the group; "No one ever talked about anything in my family. My dad left when I was 13 and my mom told us not to tell anyone. My twin sister and I never said a word to each other about it. When my dad told us he was leaving we cried. Actually she cried, I didn't. I went upstairs to my room and closed the door. And that was the end of it, no one ever talked about it again."

The second explanation that I alluded to was my early sexual relationships with men. I described myself during that time as very insecure: "In school I wanted desperately to be liked, and boys actually seemed to like me. When some guy asked me out, I couldn't believe it. I'd say yes. I didn't know what else to say, even if I didn't like him. I dated a few guys and each time one of us got scared off and then avoided each other. Then Rick asked me out." I had difficulty talking about him even with this group of women. I tried to describe him and our relationship. "God, I don't know why I ever went out with him. He was . . . so awful. And we had a nine-month 'relationship.' After the first month I just wanted to break up with him, but I couldn't do it. I didn't want to hurt his feelings and I was afraid of what he'd do. He was always trying to get me to sleep with him. I was only 15. He ended up basically raping me."

Rick said he wanted me to be his girlfriend. There were guys I liked a lot more than him, but no one had asked me out before like that. He was nice and funny and said he loved me. Though I soon found him annoying and pushy, I couldn't break up with him, even after he raped me. I was scared that he might kill himself. I was afraid he might freak out and hurt me. I was attached to him and the attention he gave me. And I didn't even know I had been raped. "I just thought I was a horrible person because I couldn't keep him from touching me. I felt horrible, but I didn't know why. I thought I'd done something wrong. I just cried. I didn't even think of saying anything to anyone; I wouldn't have known what to say. I couldn't believe that I'd just had sex with someone; I couldn't even say the word. My parents never talked about sex either, except my mother's little innuendos about it being bad. So I thought I was the worst person in the world."

I finally broke up with Rick, but I often felt pushed into later sexual experiences as well. I said to the group, "I slept with Chris, too, or he convinced me to sleep with him. That's what it always seemed like. I didn't want to do it, but I would give in. It was always like the guy was trying to convince me and I never really wanted to, but I always would." With Chris, part of me did really want to sleep with him, but I was unsure and I didn't know how to talk about it. I think most of the time I didn't want to was because I was afraid of getting pregnant, and I didn't know how to talk about birth control either.

Chris and I broke up when he went to college, partly because he was going away, and partly because I was interested in someone else. I was 16, almost 17, and a senior in high school. Darren was a junior, but I thought he was the greatest. He drank a lot and did some drugs, and I hated both. But for the first time I really felt comfortable sleeping with someone. To Sarah and the other women I said, "Birth control was just never an issue for us." It was the first time I had admitted it, but it wasn't completely true either. It was an issue, but we never talked about it. I didn't ask him about it and he didn't ask me about it. It was really strange because I was terrified that I was going to get pregnant. I always thought about it, worried about it, but I couldn't do anything about it.

Although we didn't use contraception, and we didn't talk about it, I thought about it constantly, and I was scared. I even wrote a paper about teenage pregnancy for a psychology class. I remember working on it, thinking, "This could be you, you have to do something about this." I remember having this feeling that I HAD to talk to him about it, but I couldn't. It seemed easier not to say anything and put it out of my mind, to try to forget about it.

At one point I thought I was pregnant, and I told him. He couldn't believe it and he said something about me being on the Pill. I said, "No, I'm not, where did you get that idea?" But inside I felt relieved that the subject finally came up. He said that he just figured that I must have been, since I never seemed worried about it. It seems almost funny now, but it wasn't then. How could he have thought that all this time, when for me it hurt so much to pretend it wasn't a problem?

It turned out that I wasn't pregnant. He was so happy and I was relieved. We talked more after all that, we started using condoms "most of the time," and I worried about it less. Then he started to drink more and got more into drugs, and he wanted to be with his friends and not me. He tried to break up with me, but I took a fit. "You can't leave me, Darren," I cried, "I love you, I can't believe you are doing this to me, you said you loved me!" Finally he gave in and said he still did, but he kept away from me and finally he broke it off completely. I was still hurt, but I knew I didn't like the drinking and our disagreements around it, so I didn't argue this time. Two or three weeks later I worried that I was pregnant again. I tried to call him. He was never home, and his brother once just said, "He doesn't want to talk to you." Finally I got in touch with him and told him. He just said, "Jesus Christ, I can't believe this!"

My mother is totally anti-abortion. I knew if I said anything to her, I would be having a kid. I only told one of my girlfriends; she was the only person I thought I could trust. I did one of those home pregnancy tests; I hid it behind the books in my bookcase because you have to let it sit for a couple hours. I totally freaked out when I looked at it and it came out positive. My friend was more clueless about what to do than I was. I turned to another close friend, this time a guy. I asked him to drive me to the hospital so that I could have a real test done. I didn't tell him why I was going, and he drove me, no questions asked. I was convinced that this test was going to be negative, that the first test was wrong. I was sure of it. The next day the woman on the phone told me it was positive.

Meanwhile I started getting involved with someone else. Todd and I started spending a lot of time together. We weren't going out yet, but we were close. One night I told him about it. He said he'd been through it with a girlfriend, but she turned out not to be pregnant. He said he'd take me for the abortion appointment. I was so relieved. I told my mom and my boss that we were going shopping for the day; Mom even let Todd take her car.

When we got there he just dropped me off, he didn't come in with me. At the time it was exactly what I expected, but now it seems strange that I didn't want him there for support. It didn't even occur to me to ask him to come in with me. I think I felt that it wasn't his responsibility and it was something I wanted to do on my own. I am still in awe of the idea that I went through this all by myself.

I walked in alone with my $250 check from Darren. I was nervous, but I felt better once I was inside. The woman on the phone warned me that there might be picketers, but no one bothered me. Most of the people in the waiting room had someone with them, but it didn't bother me too much at the time. I was so relieved to actually be there. I started to get scared waiting, but I still couldn't believe that I had made it there and that I was going to be okay.

The first thing they did was counseling, or at least that's what they called it. It's just when they describe the procedure in detail. I went into this room with the counselor and a 30-year-old woman who was there for the same reason but seemed totally relaxed. The counselor started to explain to the two of us exactly what happens with the doctor and the instruments.

Suddenly I was terrified and I started to cry. I couldn't help it. I was scared of how much it would hurt, of what it would be like. The counselor and the other woman were like, "Oh my goodness, what's wrong?" as if there was no reason whatsoever for me to be the least bit upset.

What bothers me about the whole thing is that no one ever talked about it, I mean really talked about it. They were all robots, just doing their job, describing the procedure, taking blood, giving out pills, acting like it was no big deal. It seems like it wouldn't have been so scary if we could have talked about it more. If someone only said, "I've been through it, too. It's okay to be scared, but you will be okay."

Someone sent me to get changed and directed me to the next waiting room. I was there for two hours in my gown. Or maybe it was just an hour, or only twenty minutes, but it seemed like forever. There were around five other women there, and a woman came in to call a name once in a while. The chairs were arranged in a circle around the room. We sat there facing each other and no one said anything. Everyone seemed scared except the older woman who flipped through a magazine and made comments here and there. But the person who really stuck out in my mind was a girl who looked no older than 13. I felt so terrible for her—she looked so scared. I just wanted to reach out to her, and tell her everything was going to be okay.

Finally they called my name and I followed a woman to another room. Another woman was there to talk to me and to hold my hand during the abortion if I wanted to. The doctor said, "So you are going to college in the fall? So what's your major?" I couldn't believe he was asking me about college; I could barely answer, I was so terrified. But I guess it was better than him not saying anything at all. It was so painful. I remember screaming and crying, literally. Afterward I wondered if anyone heard me. They said it would hurt some, but this was the most painful thing I had ever felt. It hurts to think about it.

Afterward I went into a room with other women who were recovering, lying down with blankets and eating slices of oranges and crackers. After about fifteen minutes I felt a lot better, so they said I could leave even though you're supposed to stay for longer afterward. I started to get cramps after about fifteen minutes driving home. We stopped and bought some pain reliever but it kept getting worse. They said that cramps were normal, so I didn't really worry about it. I didn't realize how bad it was until the next day when I got up and got ready for work. I was still bleeding heavily. I knew I should call the clinic. According to the information sheet they gave me I should have called them if this happened. I thought about it, but I knew they'd want me to see a doctor. I don't know if I was more scared that something was wrong with me or that my mother would find out. For three days I was in agony and then finally it stopped.

My experience with abortion and the support groups I've involved myself in have allowed me to experience a great level of intimacy with other women that I never felt before. But it also seemed to pull me away from my family. It was something I couldn't go talk to any of them about, something I hid from them. I hate that they can't really understand a part of me. The people I'm closest to don't know my deepest secret, my deepest hurts, and the greatest motivation for some of my interests. Sometimes I feel guilty about not sharing it with them. I'm afraid that one of my sisters may have to go through the same thing one day and she wouldn't tell me either. She would have to deal with the same silence I did. But last year I realized that I hadn't hidden everything from them. One day my 17-year-old sister called me at school. She was scared that she was pregnant and didn't know what to do. Even though she didn't know I'd had an abortion, she knew how I felt about it. She said, "I can't have it. School and field hockey, I just couldn't." I told her it was okay and she didn't have to do anything she didn't want to do. I told her where she could go for a test and that she could call me anytime she wanted. If she was pregnant, I told her, "I'd know what to do, it's all right." I was scared for her, but I was happy that I could be there for her. It made me feel good that she wouldn't have to go through it alone.

I know I will never tell my mother, and that's okay now, but sometimes it still makes me sad. We are still very close, though. I'm probably closer to her than any of my sisters. We talk a lot about boyfriends (both of ours), school, jobs, and my dad. I know she's not the best listener in the world, but I like to be there for her. Sometime she really surprises me and gives me good advice, but she has trouble just listening. One of my greatest fears is that she will find out and it will ruin the relationship we have. I think she'd hate me for a while, and she'd feel guilty, too. I'm sure her love for me would overcome it, but I just don't want to put her or myself through it.

I want to tell my twin sister. It is absolutely bizarre to me that she doesn't know this about me. Although we fight and still compete, we've shared a lot more since we've been at school and I feel pretty close to her. I told her about being raped and we talked about that often. But I can't seem to tell her about my abortion. I want to. I'm not afraid of what she will think of me anymore because I've had one, but I'm afraid of what she will think of me for not telling her. I'm afraid that she will really freak out. That she wouldn't believe me anymore or she'd hate me for not telling her. I'm afraid of totally shocking her.

Recently my mom said to me while looking at an old picture of the four of us kids, "You were always so happy as kids, laughing all the time, having fun." I had a really weird feeling when she said it. I never remember being happy as a kid. Scared of my own shadow might be a better description. I couldn't bear to tell her that; I just nodded and smiled.

I remember all of us kids fighting a lot. I remember my mom yelling a lot. I don't remember my dad being home much. I remember him coming home at 1:00 in the morning. I remember them yelling a lot on weekends. We bought a sailboat, but it was mostly just another place to fight. I remember a teacher who I loved in seventh grade. We wrote in journals in her class. Once I wrote about one of our boat trips, only I left out the bad parts, the fighting. When I got the journal back she wrote, "Sounds wonderful!" I felt like she liked me and what I wrote, but I also felt horrified. I had a sick feeling in my stomach, like I knew it wasn't true; it wasn't wonderful.

In the autobiography I wrote my senior year in high school I identified my dad leaving as one of the two events that had the greatest effect on me (the other was being a twin). The hurt was fresher then, and I was angry and jealous. Those feelings certainly haven't gone away, they just aren't so strong. Then it seemed I wanted so badly to believe that my family was perfect before the day he destroyed it all and left. Now I tend to think of the bad times, all of the fights, and I can't remember the good stuff. Now I see that something was very wrong with my family before he left. No one communicated, but everyone fought. I guess my dad just wasn't happy, and he spent less time at home and more at work, and then my mom became unhappy. Or maybe it was the other way around. I don't know how it really happened or whose fault it really was.

To me then it was all my dad's fault; he did everything that hurt me. But sometimes I think my mother's reactions, as well as our own, made things worse for us. No one in the house talked about it, except my mom, who was an emotional wreck. She'd try to pry information out of us after we'd been to my dad's. She told us, begged us, to ask him to come home and to tell him that we loved him. She said he'd come if we did. We couldn't tell him how much it was hurting us; we just went to see him and tried to be "good." But mom telling me this made me feel even more like it was all our fault. She also told us not to tell our friends; she didn't want anyone to know. Until we moved two years later, I told my friends he was on a business trip when they came over.

I don't blame my mother for any of these things, even though they hurt me. I feel thankful that she survived and didn't just give up. As for my dad, I try to see him as much as I can. We can have fun together, but I feel like he can't ever be there for me emotionally. It still makes me sad. For the most part, I'm not bitter anymore. But he still tries to get away with giving my mother as little money as possible and he pays almost nothing toward our college bills. Though they've been divorced for years, the hurt still seems to drag on. Mom still makes comments about his wife and kid. I understand her hurt, but I'm still caught in the middle.

I have tried here to explain my inability to deal appropriately with sexual relationships as being the result of my not having been able to talk about sex and contraception. The feelings from the beginnings of my adolescent sexuality were of being scared, not having control, and not having a choice. I now know that this is related to having grown up in a family that stuffed their feelings and never talked about anything, including sex. My family always avoided subjects that were upsetting, embarrassing, or controversial. So when it came to talking about contraception with my boyfriend, I had no basis to deal with it and felt it was beyond my control. My way of coping with the inevitable crisis of a pregnancy was not to practice contraception, but to put it out of my mind. That was easy; I had practiced that all my life.

19 Seeking the Best of Both Worlds

This is the story of a harrowing emigration from Vietnam to the United States as part of the "boat people" crisis after the war. The author describes his struggle to be both a good son to his very traditional mother and to find a means to belong and succeed in the culture to which his family fled. As he enters adolescence, he begins to feel that his mother's many troubles and unbending ways are harming both him and his siblings. When he discovers that his stepfather is abusing his younger brother and that his mother will not intercede, he experiences a turmoil of shame, guilt, and powerlessness. His mother's insistence on traditional child rearing forces him to live a double life as an increasingly "Americanized" teenager on the outside while playing the role of dutiful son at home in spite of numbing sadness and overwhelming rage toward his mother. Eventually, it is his success in the world outside his family that allows him to gain his mother's respect and thereby influence how she raises his younger siblings.

*C*on *không biết mạ đã trở qua bao nhiêu là nỗi khổ để đem con qua nước Mỹ nay*—You don't know how much I went through to bring you to this country," my mother said in a soft voice as she lay staring at the ceiling. A continuous stream of tears flowed from the outer corner of her eye down into her pillow. At times like this, I would sit next to my mother on our torn carpet while she recounted the tragedies that had happened to her in her previous life of misery, the life she left behind in Vietnam. My older sister Chau, on the other hand, could never stand to listen to our mother's repetitions. She would usually brush her teeth and go to bed or go to our other bedroom, close the door, and delve into the imaginary world of her romance novels. I remember praying at the start of the episodes that I wouldn't end up crying myself (because my mother instilled in me her belief that *"nam nhi đại trượng phu đỗ máu không rơi lệ*—real heroes never show tears even if they are bleeding to death") as these painful stories entered my mind. However, no gods or spirits answered my prayers, and after each occurrence I would feel low and unmanly because I had let tears fall even though I wasn't bleeding to death.

"*Dạ mạ*—Yes, Mom (respectfully)," I said. In Vietnamese a child must always acknowledge his or her parent with a polite "*Dạ*" (pronounced "ya"). It matters not that the parent did not ask the child a question; any less respectful response could very well lead to a beating! I learned this lesson soon after I learned how to talk (being polite was much better than being hit).

"When I was your age living in my village, I never had a full meal to eat," my mother continued. "Most days we would only be given one small bowl of rice and a dab of fish paste for flavor. I wasn't as lucky as you are today. I could never eat meat every day like you can." As far as I can remember, my mother would, without exception, start her stories by establishing that her youth was utterly miserable compared to my life of luxury. To this day I still am not sure whether by stating this she merely wanted me to feel grateful that I had enough food to eat or whether she was actually pitying herself as she realized the vast contrast between her childhood and mine.

"I was cruelly beaten daily by your grandmother and often for no good reason. She had fourteen children, but I was the only one who ever got punished. I don't know why. She'd beat me if I didn't fetch enough firewood for cooking. Or if I didn't cut up enough food to feed the pigs. Or if I stopped fanning her during those scorching summer days because my hands felt like jello." As my mother went on, at this point in her talk I would have a difficult time understanding her because her nose was plugged up from crying so much. Sometimes I tried to pay closer attention so that I could catch everything she said; other times I would not bother since I more or less knew by heart all that she wanted to say.

"The worst period in my life was after I married your father. I had just given birth to your sister when your father disappeared without a trace. I tracked him down finally in Hanoi. I found that he was living with his first wife, a woman that he never told me about. I was more than shocked that the man I loved and trusted lied to me."

After hearing my mother describe my father's deceit, I simultaneously felt resentment, sympathy, guilt, vengefulness, incredible sadness, and, oddly, joy. I resented and even hated my father for ruining my mother's life. The anger I felt inside was so overwhelming that I would often tremble while gasping for air. Sometimes I sat there and wished that he were standing right in front of me so that I could pick him up by the throat and slam him against the wall as hard as I could. I'd scream at him, "You damn asshole! How could you treat your wife like that? Don't you have a conscience? Is this the model that you want your children to follow? I am ashamed to be your son! But don't worry, I won't turn out to be like you, you piece of shit!" At the same time, I felt sympathy for the incredible pain that my mother must have endured since that episode. She did not do anything wrong; her only mistake was falling in love with a lying womanizer. Yet mixed with my negative emotions was a slight ripple of joy. I felt happy to see that my mother was courageous enough to take her children and leave him behind in his poverty-stricken home. I was shamelessly content that he still has to live in filth with his first wife while our family, although poor compared to others in America, has enough to eat everyday.

Throughout my early childhood, occurrences like the one above were commonplace. Almost anything could provoke my mother into telling those stories: seeing happy couples walking together in the park, seeing my sister and me not doing our chores, watching television shows that depicted any aspect of Vietnam, and especially having her children do badly in school (i.e., not getting straight As). Those nights I would cry myself to sleep thinking of how much I should hate my father and how much I should love and respect my mother. I racked my brains wondering how my father could have consciously treated my mother with such inhumanity. "How could he? How could he?" I hollered silently to myself over and over. "There must be some reason for what he did. My mother must be leaving a lot of details out. I should not listen only to her side of the story." I convinced myself that I could not make final judgments about him until I heard what he had to say. Thus, for years I wondered what his story was.

My first memories are of escaping Vietnam and landing in Hong Kong on the way to our final destination, America. I only remember random scenes of our journey; the rest of what happened my mother has filled in through our conversations over the years. Thus, I have a fairly detailed knowledge of what happened in those few days that drastically altered our lives.

In the spring of 1981, my mother, then fairly wealthy thanks to a prospering business, decided that she wanted to give her two children educational opportunities that her country could not offer. I was only 4 years old and my sister just 6 when one ordinary night my mother told us to say good-bye forever to our homeland. . . .

A blinding flash of light snatched me from my restful sleep. Five seconds later the inevitable boom of thunder crashed on our little boat and sent everyone into a state of panic. When I peered out at the darkness, I saw rushing at us some of the largest waves I'd ever seen.

"*Mạ, con sọ' qúa*—Mommy, I'm so scared," I cried. However, the raindrops on my face camouflaged my tears, and the roaring thunder drowned my attempts to communicate with my mother. I finally caught her attention by pulling on her sleeve as hard as I could.

"*Con đừng sọ' nhe*—Don't be afraid, son," my mother comforted, "It's just a little storm. It'll be over real soon." She covered us with a plastic bag, and we huddled so close that I could feel her heart pounding against my cheek.

"*Chị Hong, Chị Hong*—Sister Hong, Sister Hong," my uncle Oanh approached us from out of nowhere and said in a disconcerting tone, "There's too much weight on this end of the boat. We need more people to move to the bow. If we don't do it fast, the waves'll flip us right over."

"What do you want us to do?" my mother answered calmly.

"You put Phuoc on your back and I'll put Chau on mine. Then we'll slowly walk up there."

"Okay, okay," my mother approved. I did not realize what was happening. All I knew was that I wanted to cling to my mother for dear life. "Phuoc," she spoke directly into my ear because at any other distance the thunder would drown out her voice, "We're moving to the front of the boat. I'm gonna give you a piggyback ride, so you grab on as tight as you can, okay?"

"*Dạ,*" I acknowledged and quickly climbed onto her back while the storm blanketed my body with what felt like a thousand pebbles every second. Without thinking, I immediately locked my arms around my mother's neck and grabbed each of my wrists with the opposite hand. Just as instinctively, I wrapped my legs around her waist and also bolted them in place. As we began inching toward our destination just a few meters away, my awareness of the surroundings increased tenfold compared to when I was sitting with my mother. I saw every wave as it crashed on the boat's side, I anticipated the direction of impending thunder, and I felt the blowing raindrops on my skin as if they were needles piercing all parts of my body. Another acute awareness was of my body's position in space. Because I did not budge, it seemed as though I became an extension of my mother's body. When she lifted her left foot to take another step, I felt the entire left half of my frame move accordingly.

"*G`ân tó´i r`ôi con à*—We're almost there, son," my mother said, "Don't worry." When I looked up, I saw the bow just a few steps away. However, I did not feel as though I could breathe a sigh of relief because a few steps is still a few steps. I kept my tight lock around my mother's neck and waist. It turned out that this choice saved my life, because just then a huge wave slammed into the side of our boat with such force that it threw her off her feet and sent us plunging into the freezing water of the South China Sea. I do not recall feeling scared. When I was under water, instinct made me hold onto my mother as tightly as I could, shut my eyes to avoid the stinging seawater, and close my mouth so that no saltwater entered my system. I do not know why I didn't panic. I just didn't. Fortunately, the two of us avoided staying in the water long enough for hypothermia to set in. My uncle, who was following closely behind us with my sister, dived in after us when he saw us fall.

Following our dramatic rescue, the heavens blessed us with sunshine and peaceful waters. The gods also bestowed another miracle on us. Several days after our departure, just when we had almost depleted all of our food supply, we came across a cargo ship headed in the same direction we wished to go: Hong Kong. A year later in April 1982, my mother realized her dreams of raising us in a land where more opportunities and fewer obstacles lay before us. What my mother did not realize was that she herself would become the major obstacle in her children's future.

Throughout my early adolescence, I wished I had a better, more understanding mother. To this day I still believe that most of my "growing pains" could have been alleviated or missed entirely if my mother had also experienced these same "pains" when she was an adolescent. She did not know how best to assist me through my tough times, because she had no understanding of the cultural and social pressures facing teens growing up in America. She was often insensitive and apathetic when I came to her with an adolescent issue such as schoolmates making fun of me.

Puberty started rather simply for me in the sixth grade; there was no big event that announced its arrival. I remember exactly when I knew that I had entered this period of change. One evening while I was showering, I noticed that I had started growing pubic hair. At first I felt confused. "What's this stuff?" I asked myself. Thinking that it was just dirt or something, I tried rubbing it off. After a few unsuccessful attempts, I realized, "Oh, yeah, this is what my sex education class last year taught us. I'm supposed to start this business at my age. Don't worry about it. It's just puberty." I thought about telling my mother to make sure it *was* just puberty, but after some thought I decided against the idea because these topics were not spoken of in our household. Subjects such as sex, love, human genitalia, and rape were taboo in my family because they were supposedly "impure" things to talk about. We were not to adulterate our minds and hearts by bringing them up in conversation. Consequently, many issues that "normal" families in America talk about were never brought up in our household. This lack of discussion forced me to learn about them from other sources, such as television.

At first I did not think that puberty was going to be the time of tremendous psychological change that the sex education videos at school had depicted. I felt like the same little kid I was before, going to class in the morning, coming home to do homework and watch television in the afternoon, talking to my mother before going to bed, and then repeating this same monotonous routine. The only other difference was that my voice started cracking when I spoke, but that did not bother me because I understood that was a natural part of human development.

Although I was only aware of my physical changes, I was also changing mentally. I remember my sudden self-consciousness, low self-esteem, new found interest in girls, and awareness of my lack of peer relationships, all of which started in junior high. Now when I look back, it seems that my experience was nothing out of the ordinary for children of that age. Yet my life then had an additional *extra*ordinary factor. The conditions under which I interacted with others my own age were, culturally, American conditions, while at home I confronted a Vietnamese cultural environment. On the one hand, my mother did not understand American culture and disapproved of the American beliefs (such as gender and racial equality, free speech in the family, etc.) that I had adopted. On the other hand, the children at school who were not Vietnamese did not accept the culturally Vietnamese side of me, probably because they saw it as strange and not "normal." (Back then it was a dream of mine just to be normal like everyone else.) I shall illustrate my point with a few examples.

Before the sixth grade, I never thought about how physically different I looked. I knew that I was Vietnamese, but I never felt that I was an outsider in school because of my skin color. When I began adolescence, however, I became acutely aware of my bodily characteristics. In grade school I was your stereotypical skinny, short, brainy Asian kid with a bowl haircut. When kids made fun of me by calling me "chink" or "nerd," I usually never paid any attention to them. This was true until the day I received a disciplinary referral and was sent home. During music class, a Caucasian classmate of mine, Eugene, was getting upset because Mr. Marmastein told him he was out of tune. The entire class giggled as Eugene squeaked the words to "Yankee Doodle Went to Town." I, being a wiseguy, said loudly, "No more, Eugene, please!" With a frustrated look, Eugene quickly turned to me and yelped, "Shut up, you damn *chink*!" The old me would have just laughed it off without giving it a second thought, but that day a rush of anger swept through me, and I wanted to beat him up right there on the spot. The only thing that restrained me from doing so was my music teacher. I did not want to disrespect him by disrupting the class; I decided to wait till later. When recess time came and we were all let out to the grass field to play kickball, I only had one thing on my mind. As soon as I caught sight of Eugene, I ran over and tackled him onto the ground with all the might that my eighty pound body could conjure up. We wrestled around on the grass throwing blind punches at each other until the recess supervisor pulled us apart and gave us both referrals. The principal sent me home because I was the one who started the fight. Eugene's words somehow triggered a highly reactive area inside me, an area that told me that I was not the same as everyone else, and this made me feel inferior. At the same time, though, the fight made me proud and confident because this time, unlike previous times, I had stood up for myself when others thought I would be weak and passive. However, my raised spirits received a powerful blow from my mother's reaction.

"What? You got in a fight because he said you were Asian? *Sau con ngu qúa vậy*—Why are you so stupid, son?" my mother said, as if she didn't believe that "chink" was a derogatory word. Maybe if I told her again, she would understand.

"But, Mom. That word is racist! He wasn't just saying that I was *Asian*," I repeated, "He had a different meaning."

"Who cares what he meant," she replied. "It's just a word. Those white people are all racist anyway. Next time he says that to you, just ignore him." Ignore him? *What?* How could I do that when Eugene insulted me? And how could my mother say that *all* Caucasians are racist? Didn't the fact that she uttered those words brand *her* a racist? "And they're bigger than you, you know. I don't want you to get hurt again. We're smaller than they are, so we just have to act our size. So next time he makes fun of you, just turn your head and laugh." I did not know how else to persuade her. My mother did not seem to understand that in America, equality is cherished and prejudice is not tolerated. Wasn't that why she decided to risk her life and the lives of her children to come here in the first place? My mother's words directly conflicted with what my teachers had taught me in school all these years. How could I reconcile this? I could not believe what she said nor do as she ordered, because the morals I had acquired in school were too strong. This incident posed yet another problem for me—when should I listen to my mother and when should I not? In the past, she had always taught me how to be a good person, including the dos and don'ts of life and the difference between right and wrong. It was simple— Mother was always right no matter what. Thus, I always listened and took her words to heart. Now that I recognized a flaw in her beliefs, I did not know what to do or who to go to.

Another example of my mother's lack of empathy was how she laughed at me when I told her that other kids made fun of my name. For as long as I can remember, almost everyone I met has mispronounced my name at least twice before getting it right. It was such an embarrassing scene whenever I met anyone new that it made me wish I did not have to meet new people at all. The worst part of it was the name-calling I endured all my life. Through elementary school and beyond high school, my name was the subject of a laundry list of teasings. It may be difficult for others to understand how my name can be so damaging to me psychologically. However, it was not as if I had a name like "Jaime," which everyone pronounced "Himee." People can easily turn my name into vulgar words if they want to (and I believed that everyone around me wanted to). Here are a few of those hurtful teasings: "Fok," "Foo-ok," "Pook," "Fuck," "Phuoc you!," "What the Phuoc!," "Mother-Phuocer." In my high school junior yearbook there is a picture of me playing volleyball (I was on the team). Underneath it the subheading reads, "Phuoc 'U' Nguyen spikes one!" Those kids did not realize that every time they poked fun at me I wanted to crawl into a cave and not come out until everyone was mature enough to accept my name.

The only person who understood my agony was my sister because she too has an uncommon name, but hers had less potential to be the butt of everyone's jokes than mine. On occasion when she and I went somewhere together, we would temporarily change our names to make the experience a lot more pleasant for ourselves. For instance, when I was a sophomore in high school and Chau was a junior, she wanted me to accompany her to a meeting of students interested in applying to college. She was sure that no one we knew would be there, so we decided to become "normal" for the evening. When the hosts asked us to write our names on those "Hello, my name is . . ." stickers, we picked random "American" names. As it turned out, we both found it easier to meet people when we weren't feeling self-conscious.

Whenever I told my mother about people making fun of my name, she would usually laugh and say, "Fuck? Ha, ha . . . isn't that a bad word? Ha, ha . . . That's kinda funny." At times like those I thought my mother was the most insensitive and uncaring person in the world. How could she sit there and laugh at her son when he had just told her that everyone in school was already laughing at him? Did she think that it would make me feel better if she laughed as well? Of course I did not voice those questions. Thinking about it now, I believe that my mother's concept of emotional pain was completely different from mine. The physical pain and agony she endured for most of her life in Vietnam was probably ten times more intolerable than mine. That's probably why she couldn't understand the emotional pain I felt when kids made fun of me.

My mother also hindered my healthy adolescent development by refusing to let me associate with girls. I recall one incident in junior high when a seventh-grade girl wrote me a letter. Minh, a Vietnamese girl who played in the orchestra with me, sent me the first "I like you" letter I ever received; in it she expressed her admiration for me because I was smart and musically talented. Frankly, I did not have the slightest inkling what to think of the situation. No one had ever taught me how to initiate intimate relationships. The guy friends I had at school were all uncool "nerds" like myself who did not have any experience with girls either. I did not even consider asking them for help. I never had an older male role model to turn to with questions; the only older men I was in contact with were my uncles, and they were unlikely candidates because they did not grow up in America.

Asking for my mother's advice about girls would be tantamount to suicide. She always forbade my sister and me to date or see any members of the opposite sex until we were college graduates. One may think that she was just joking—no parent can be that strict, right?—but believe me, she wasn't. She strictly enforced her commands with severe actions. For instance, one day after school when I was waiting for my mother, one of my female acquaintances came up to chat with me. We were talking about how Mrs. Sloboda's world history test was too difficult. But when my mother drove up and saw us standing there together, she thought the subject of our conversation was something less than innocent. She immediately rolled down her window and screamed at the girl, "*Ây, đồ con quỷ sứ kia, mày làm chi với con tao rứa*— Hey, demon, what are you doing with my son?" My friend asked me whether my mother was yelling at her; I told her that she was just telling me to get in the car (this was one of the perks of having a mom who does not speak English). When I stepped into the car, my mother started chastising me for talking to the girl. She did not listen to my explanation and warned me that if she ever saw that scene again, I'd end up in an orphanage. That was the last time I stood next to girls after school.

There I was holding my first love letter in my hand, but I had absolutely no idea what to do with it. I did not understand my role as the male figure: Was I supposed to ask her out first or wait until she made the first move? Should I talk to her just as a friend or try to flirt with her? My mind was filled with confusion at the time. The only places I could think of to turn to for direction were Hong Kong mini-soap operas. These translated productions were usually set in ancient China, where a gentleman was one who followed the Confucian code of conduct and women were innocent and supportive. Honestly, I learned more about relationships from watching those shows than from any other source. They taught me that real men were brave, polite, chivalrous, confident, and independent, while women were caring, sensitive, nurturing, and passive. Of course I am much wiser now, but back then I embraced these ideals. However, even though I knew from those movies how I *should* have acted toward Minh—who I thought was pretty and intelligent—I did not put that knowledge into practice. Instead of initiating any type of conversation, I tried to avoid her. Whenever she walked up to me to talk, I would turn around and walk the other way. Finally, after realizing that I seemed repulsed by her, Minh gave up on me and started seeing someone else. Later on I felt like such an idiot for letting her go. "Why didn't I go for it?" I asked myself repeatedly. "Am I not a guy? She liked me! She really did, and I just let her go." I thought that I did not possess the qualities that a "real" man had, those qualities that the Hong Kong mini-soap operas presented to me. It was not until my last years in high school that I realized what "manly" qualities actually were. It was also then that my self-esteem gradually rose to a level where I was confident enough to look people in the face when I was talking to them. These changes came slowly and originated from an incident that was a milestone in my life. This incident served as the beginning of my long and successful struggle to break free from my mother's emotional influence.

The changes took place shortly after my mother allowed her ex-husband, my stepfather, back into our family. A few months following his return, I learned with horror what kind of man he really was. My half-brother Tai, a vibrant 4-year-old, told me that his father liked to pinch and bite him just for fun; he also liked to fondle Tai's genitals for prolonged stretches of time.

Something like this was not easy to accept or deal with, especially for a 14-year-old. I trembled at the realization that this beast of a man, this perverse monster, sexually abused his own son, my innocent brother. And all of this occurred right beneath our unwitting noses for weeks on end. "This cannot continue," I resolved. "I *will* not allow him to hurt my brother any longer!" Never in my life had I been more sure of what the right thing to do was. Although I knew that this could potentially hurt everyone else in my family, particularly my mother, I did not falter for a moment. I was willing to destroy my mother's happiness to protect Tai.

My method of expressing my frustration was to slam doors. Every time I saw my stepfather touching Tai's genitals, I would walk to my room and slam the door behind me. Our home only had two bedrooms, so Tai's father definitely heard and understood my signal. He understood all right, but he did not change, and the abuse persisted. However, my stubborn-headedness kept me from giving up. I wanted to reach a standoff, a sudden-death situation. That day came about two weeks after my initial resolution to fight. Thoughts of me being courageous or honorable never entered my mind; everything I did was by gut instinct.

It was a windy Saturday afternoon, and everyone was at home except for Chau, who was at work. My mother and stepfather were talking in their room while Tai and I played *Civilization* on my computer. All of a sudden Tai's father summoned him to their room. The inevitable happened, and again a rush of rage crashed into my body. I breathed hard as my heartbeat shot up like a bottle rocket. Shoving my chair behind me, I stepped out into the living room and looked into their room as I walked by. The scene did not differ from the ones I had witnessed over the past few weeks. After standing in the living room for a moment, I went to my room taking loud, heavy steps along the way and, upon reaching my destination, slammed my door with as much force as I could conjure up. I did it! My mother had to say *something*. I wanted to confront him that very moment; I wished that deep inside me there was a courage that would manifest itself now by giving Tai's father the hardest punch on the jaw. I waited for them to come in.

"Phuoc, what the hell are you doing!" my mother screamed as she raced over to my room and gave me a slap on the left side of my cheek. I still vividly remember the physical and emotional pain I felt the instant her hand landed on my face. "He's his father, and he can do whatever he wants with him. It's not like he's killing him or anything, he's just playing. And besides, it's none of your business! Now if you don't want to live here anymore, then I can always put you into an orphanage!" I knew then that my mother cared more about her own selfish needs than about the welfare of her younger son. My respect for her started fading behind a curtain of disappointment. What could I do? Everyone around me could not see what I saw, and after trying fruitlessly to expose the truth to them, this was what I received. Fear and alarm overwhelmed me at that moment, and I did not, could not, fight any longer. I had already drained myself of all the fortitude I possessed, and no matter how deep I searched, my well of courage was dry. At that time, fear—the emotion I detested most and the emotion I constantly encountered—took control of my mind. I didn't want to end up in an orphanage, a ward of the state. I didn't want her to put me in a foster home. No. No. I couldn't let that happen. "It was the wind, Mom," I responded innocently. "The wind slammed the door." And that was that. I was tired. I didn't want to feel any more emotions. I just wanted to lie in bed and pretend that none of it had happened.

I had never been more disappointed with my mother in my life; the time she ignored my pleas for new shoes, the time she made fun of my name, could not begin to compare with this. I wished she was not my mother. I wished that I had never been born into this backward family.

Two months later my mother kicked her ex-husband out. Apparently, he emptied her bank account with his gambling habits. While he had been staying with us, he constantly took her money to play cards at the local casino. Eventually my mother had no money left to pay the bills. This time his leaving was for good, she said. His departure left me with a feeling of relief for my brother because it released him from constant victimization. Yet I knew that what he went through might leave lasting psychological effects.

The problems between my mother and myself did not spontaneously disappear when my stepfather left. I remember not feeling anything at all for her; it was as if my stepfather had taken with him all of my emotions about my mother and left only a void. I did not speak with her for half a year following his separation from us. I constantly asked myself how my mother, whom I regarded so highly—a woman who had risked and sacrificed everything for the sake of her children—could ignore the obvious abuse of her child by her husband. This inner questioning led to my emotional isolation from her. Withdrawing from my mother's world allowed me to step back and reevaluate from a different perspective my perceptions of her and myself. With the help of this new vantage point, I painted a new picture of myself and my relationship with my mother.

"*Thưa mạ con đi học*— (Respectfully) Mother, I am going to school." "*Thưa mạ con đi học về*— (Respectfully) Mother, I am home from school." These eleven words, which tradition forced me to utter every day, were the only words I remember saying to my mother during those silent six months. How did I do it? What did I feel? What did I use to replace my relationship with my mother?

My first few weeks of silence I attribute to hatred. I loathed being in my mother's presence. When we were together in the same room, I never looked at her face or even positioned my body toward hers. At the dinner table, I swallowed my food without tasting it as fast as I could to shorten the torture of sitting near her. When we had company over and she asked me to come out and greet them, I stayed only long enough for them to see my fake smile before returning to my room. I did not think she deserved to be a mother, thus I did not treat her like one. I regarded her like a distant relative—with respect, but with no warmth or emotion. At night when my mother slept with Tai in her arms, so much anger welled up inside me that one time I released my rage by biting on a pillow with all my strength. "How could she go on like nothing happened?" I asked myself. "How could she not feel guilty?" Those nights I stayed up until two or three in the morning feeling sorry for my brother, furious at my mother, and disappointed in myself. I did not talk to anyone about my problems. Chau had isolated herself from the rest of our family, so she and I did not communicate, and I did not feel close enough to any of my friends at school to share with them my inner emotions. I also felt too ashamed to tell anyone about the unhappy circumstances in my family. Consequently, I existed for weeks like a walking balloon full of negative emotions just waiting to burst when I could no longer contain them. But I did not burst. I needed to appear strong, stolid (like the heroes in the Hong Kong movies). I needed to show my mother and myself that I did not depend on her for my emotions. The way I subdued these feelings is similar to what happens when a chemist immerses a helium-filled balloon into a vat of liquid nitrogen. Like the helium in the balloon, my emotions underwent a condensation into a colder, less active state.

For the remaining months of my silence, hatred and anger no longer played a large role in my reluctance to communicate with my mother. I figured, "Why should I torture myself with all these bad feelings? They don't do any good. I can't go on living so miserably." Convinced that emotions only hurt rather than benefited me, I gradually suppressed them. Soon I replaced those gut-wrenching feelings of guilt, sadness, and animosity with apathy and insensitivity. I no longer felt uncomfortable sitting next to my mother, because I had no feelings for her. Although I still remembered the events that occurred several weeks prior, it ceased to cause pain and anguish. My indifference made it easier for me to sleep at night, increased my ability to concentrate in school, and lifted the midnight clouds that hovered over me. In retrospect, I can understand the attraction of this defense mechanism; it was an easy escape from emotional pain and dependence on my mother. The side effect of my remedy, however, was that I lost the ability to feel other types of emotions as well, such as sympathy, sadness, and joy. I felt like a machine. When I watched inspirational movies, I did not have warm, fuzzy sensations. When I was elected president of the sophomore class, my only reaction was, "Good, this'll look good on my college applications." When my friend Vu made a full recovery after undergoing chemotherapy for lymphatic cancer, I never felt ecstatic, just relieved for him. Now I realize the price of indifference, and I have been trying hard to gain back— with little success—my ability to feel deep emotions.

In the months following my isolation from my mother, I found numerous ways to convince myself that she had absolutely no influence on me and that I had completely and irreversibly broken away from her. I guess this was the rebellious stage of my adolescence. However, I did not rebel in the typical demonstrative fashion, like screaming "I hate you" to my mom or getting drunk. Instead, I rebelled in a passive way so that only *I* knew I rebelled, while everyone, including her, still thought I was the perfect son. One of my defiance strategies was to achieve top grades in my classes without putting in any effort. I cheated in almost every subject. After school, when my mother asked me if I had any homework, I always replied, "No, Mom, I'm already done." She never asked me to show her my completed work because she could not read a word of it. I also started lying a lot to my mother. One time I told her that my friends and I went to the library to study, but actually we drove to San Francisco and spent the day playing volleyball on the beach. I cannot count all the times that I lied to her and she never found out the truth. I felt much satisfaction knowing that I had some control over her; it raised my self-confidence and esteem and felt like sweet revenge for her dominance over me when I was younger. I simply wanted to believe that my mother had no part in my success in both academics and life. Yet I allowed her to continue assuming that I was the model son and that without her I would have been nothing. I figured she deserved at least that much because of the sacrifices she made in bringing me to America and raising me in a strange land.

What did I use to replace my mother's absence from my life? Certainly not other relationships! I found it difficult to make close friendships in high school for several reasons: my school environment, my inability to share feelings (mostly because I had no emotions), and the fact that I thought close friends were unessential for my well-being. The school I attended had the lowest SAT score averages in the country. Fifty percent of the student body was black, while about 90 percent of the faculty was white; the remaining students consisted mainly of Hispanics and Asians, with a few token white students. Almost everyone came from poor households; I once read an article about our school that revealed that over 70 percent of the students' families depended on welfare as their sole source of income. I witnessed gang fights almost every week, mostly between black gangs—the Bloods versus the Crips. But sometimes I also saw some action from the smaller Asian gangs like the Oriental Boyz. The extraordinarily high incidence of violence and drug abuse in my school forced the government to establish a gun- and drug-free zone around the school and the nearby housing complexes. Fortunately, I participated in the school's magnet program, called the Academy of Math, Science, and Engineering, that better prepared me for college. I limited the group of friends I hung out with mainly to other Vietnamese students from the Academy, and I stayed away from most of the black students because I was afraid of being associated with any of the gangs. My friends and I had lunch together, copied homework from one another, and joined the same clubs. However, outside of school we did not go out on a regular basis or call each other to have heart-to-heart conversations. Even when my friends did call me, we never discussed my family problems or feelings, probably because I didn't want to admit that I had any troubles at home. I also never developed strong companionships in high school because I did not feel that I needed them to make me content. I felt satisfied that I had friends to turn to when I wanted to copy homework from someone; other than that I had no burning desire to have best friends.

Relationships with girls also did not fill the void left by my mother's absence. In my high school years, a number of girls wrote me love letters, asked me out to proms, or tried to get to know me, but not once did I take the initiative to pursue a relationship with any of them. Sure, I went to their proms, but I only did it because I did not want to turn them down. It wasn't that I didn't find women attractive or that I didn't want a steady relationship; rather, I think that the combination of my mother's strict rules and a lack of male role models contributed to my nonaggressive behavior. As I stated before, my mother adamantly forbade me to have girlfriends, and although I wanted to establish my independence from her, I still needed to abide by her rules because I was living under her roof. The other reason I wasn't able to tell girls that I liked them was because I didn't know how. No one ever taught me the correct procedures for getting to know women, and what I saw on TV seemed too straightforward for my tastes. My closest male friend in high school, Vu, never had any experience with girls either. Thus, even if I wanted to go out with someone, I did not know how to approach her and ask.

I do not believe anything replaced my relationship with my mother. Her dominant presence simply disappeared as a result of my ability to suppress my emotions. How she felt no longer dictated how I felt. When she cried, I no longer cried; when she laughed, I no longer laughed with her; and when she told her disturbing childhood stories, they no longer affected me emotionally. It may seem heartless, but that was how I felt. I did not need anyone to take her place; what I *did* need, however, was to fill up the free time I had now that I wasn't spending it with my mother. I kept myself busy in high school by joining numerous clubs, volunteering at nursing homes and hospitals, playing on the tennis team, participating in math and science competitions, working, attending Vietnamese school on the weekends, and enrolling in night courses at the closest community college. I occupied my days with so many activities that on a typical day, I would not return home until eight or nine in the evening, and by that time my mother would be in bed.

In other ways, I came to understand my mother at a deeper level. In junior year I had a history class in which we learned about ancient China; we discussed Confucius's philosophy and how his ideals still permeate East Asian culture. One of the most important aspects of Confucian theory is its emphasis on role-playing in the family and in society. I remember writing a report on Confucian influence on contemporary Vietnamese society and realizing that my family performed the parts that he outlined centuries ago. Observing my family as a source for my essay, I learned that Confucius dictated our use of verbal and physical affection.

To this day I cannot say "I love you" to my mother, older sister, or younger brother. The only person whom I *do* verbally acknowledge my love for is Carol, my 4-year-old half-sister. It may seem strange, but Carol is also the only one that I hug, kiss, or show any other form of affection to. The same is true for my mother, Chau, and Tai—from an outsider's perspective it may seem as though all of us love only Carol. I also hear Chau verbalizing her love for Vinh, her fiancé, and it seems perfectly natural. What would be completely *unnatural* and unprecedented is if she said "I love you" to me, my mother, or my brother.

During elementary school my mother nurtured and cared for me as if I had just learned how to walk. One of the ways she made me state that I loved her was by asking, "Phuoc, where do you put your love for me?" My rehearsed answer was, "Mom, I put my love for you on my head!" (She considers the head the most important part of the body, so putting my love there meant that it was the most important love.) We kissed and hugged one another all the time and without reservation. By the time I started junior high school, however, we suddenly yet intuitively stopped being physically affectionate. Even though I missed my mother's touch, especially when I witnessed her affection for Carol, I knew that its cessation was appropriate for my age. Thinking back, the start of my adolescence and newfound need to break away from the nest, particularly when kids at school filled my head with the notion that kissing your mom was "sissy" and "gay," influenced the shift in our relationship. A change in my mother's attitude also contributed; she no longer asked me where I put my love for her. Instead, she asked Tai, who was 2 at the time, this question, which I thought she had reserved just for me. It was as if the game had age limits, and I had already passed them. My mother now expected me to show my love for her by obeying her and bringing home the As. Accordingly, she showed her love by feeding and clothing me.

"*Con không cha như nhà không nóc*—Children without a father are like houses without rooftops." My mother never failed to remind me of this Vietnamese proverb whenever she wanted to show off how she had disproved the old saying. She was correct in her claim, because we never grew up with a father, yet our house definitely has a "rooftop." My mother played the roles of breadwinner and caring mother at the same time. She disciplined us while bandaging our wounds, taught us how to ride a bike and then cleaned our scrapes and bruises, encouraged us to succeed in the real world while wishing we would never leave her side. In December of my last year before entering college, I unwittingly replaced my mother as the rooftop and the foundation of my home.

The news jumped at me out of the blue. "I'm going to Vietnam next month to visit Grandpa and Grandma," was all my mother said. "I'll leave some money for you while I'm gone. I'll be there for a month." She never discussed with me the possibility that I did not want to take care of 1-year-old Carol and 8-year-old Tai for an entire month, especially December, when I had so many things to do in my senior year. She never taught me how to cook dinner, potty train Carol, comfort her when she cried, and keep the house clean all in one day. Yet I never raised a single objection to her vacation plans. The only thing I recall telling her while we said good-bye at the airport was, "Have a safe trip, Mom. Don't let anyone con you over there, okay? Let me know when you want me to pick you up." For the next thirty-one days I enrolled in a crash course in parenting in which the teacher and student were one—me.

The most difficult part of the day came after Tai got home from school. During those few hours before bedtime, I ran around my two-bedroom home like a madman in nerve-racking attempts to prevent my hyperactive sister from hurting herself while also trying to complete multiple tasks. Within a two-hour stretch, I made dinner, did the laundry, mopped the floors, took out the garbage, changed Carol's diaper when I forgot to remind her about the mini-toilet, helped Tai with his fractions and long division, answered phone calls from friends seeking advice on how to fill out college applications, and played with Carol to keep her from wrecking the floors I had just mopped!

Every night I longed for nine o'clock to come around so that I could put the two children to sleep and actually attend to my own affairs. This was the time during my senior year when the college application deadlines loomed. In addition to completing seven or eight college applications, I worked on finishing nearly a dozen scholarship applications, all of which kept me up late every night. Luckily, I did not have trouble finding a topic for my personal essays; it was easy to write about my experiences performing the duties of a parent and how much I learned from them. This topic proved productive; the following spring I was accepted to a prestigious college and also won a full scholarship to the school of my choice.

Looking back on that month, I recognize now the richness of my experience and just how much it contributed to me as a person. During that time I learned what qualities an ideal man and woman should possess. My firsthand knowledge replaced my archaic notions of men as chivalrous protectors of passive, caring women. Another new concept I developed was that there weren't any obvious differences between the required traits of a man and a woman. I no longer divided the genders and designated specific attributes each should acquire. It was as if I took my culture's gender role assignments and synthesized them into one person, and that was who I became. Whether it was hugging Carol to sleep when she cried in the middle of the night, explaining fractions to Tai, cooking, cleaning, or fixing the door handle, I did not feel as though I switched roles when I performed them. I never thought to myself, "No, I can't do this because I'm a man. That's not what I'm supposed to do. But, since Mom's not here, I *have* to do the woman's work." Those thoughts didn't cross my mind. What I did think, however, was, "Of course I'll do this. I'll do it because I love my sister and brother. No other reason."

Ever since my sister went away to college, my role and responsibility in my family has changed dramatically. I have much more say in household affairs than before. Now whenever I am at home I take care of all the bills and paperwork that my mother has accumulated over the months while I was in college. If there is a decision to be made, I usually make it and then tell my mother why I did so. I think she finally realized that I was old enough to make the right choices for our family. Along with my added responsibility, the weight of my word has increased markedly since high school. Again, I think my mother takes my opinion more seriously because I am old enough now to play the role of an influential person in our family. Knowing that what I say has a more profound influence on her than ever before, I have not wasted an opportunity to help my little brother and sister. Whenever I have a chance, I persuade her to change her ways toward Tai and little Carol so that they can have a smoother childhood than I did. By this I mean that I encourage her to allow them to make friends within and outside of the Vietnamese ethnicity, let Tai talk to girls his age because he can benefit from them and vice versa, and most importantly discipline them with words instead of whips. I believe my words have not gone unheard, especially those dealing with punishment, because since I started college I cannot recall ever hearing about her spanking Tai or Carol.

My years in college have allowed me to develop a new, more equal relationship with my mother. I think the time I spent at school three thousand miles away has made us both appreciate and respect one another (although she would never admit that she respects or appreciates me). She now sees me as an independent individual, and I see her as both a mother and a friend. I know that she takes much pride in seeing me succeed in my academic life, but even though I want to make her proud of me and hope that she gains the proper admiration she deserves from those in Vietnam, I do not base my goals and aspirations on pleasing her. If in the process of attaining my goals I also make her happy, then I will have lived up to both my American and Vietnamese ideals—doing things for myself and doing things to show respect for my parents. I praise my mother when I see the improvements in the way she is raising Tai and Carol compared to her raising of Chau and me. I think she knows that she cannot apply every aspect of Vietnamese culture to children she is raising in America. When I go home for vacations, I still function as the man in the house, the person who takes care of the bills, fixes doorknobs, and attends the parent–teacher conferences. At the same time, I am also the only male figure for my brother, which puts pressure on me to be the best role model I can. I play these roles willingly and with satisfaction.

As for my search for the culture that suits me best, I have come to the decision that neither Vietnamese nor American culture alone can fulfill my needs. Thus, I chose to pick out the best aspects of each culture and synthesize them into one. For instance, while I believe in the American ideal that every person is equal, I also disapprove of children not treating their elders with respect and proper manners. I do not consider myself Americanized or Vietnamized; rather, I'm enjoying the best of both worlds.

What are the issues that I am still struggling with? As I enter my senior year, I'm still trying to inflate the emotional balloon that I've suppressed for so long. Recently, my girlfriend Jennifer has been helping me recover my ability to feel strong emotions again. Last month she and I cried together, something I haven't done since my sophomore year in high school! However, I find it much more difficult to bring back the emotions than to tuck them away, and so far I haven't made much progress.

From the academic success my sister and I have earned, it may seem that our family is living out the American dream. We escaped from a war-scarred country that offered us few opportunities and arrived in a land we knew nothing about. My mother worked hard all her life to provide her children with a home that was conducive to learning. She created such an atmosphere by using the whip, along with guilt-provoking stories to encourage us to learn. Now that two of her children are excelling in their respective postsecondary institutions, my mother feels that she has done an admirable job of raising us. However, her feelings of pride come at a high cost to the relationships in our family. Maybe she did not know any other way to raise us than by using her native culture's means. She did not realize that most families who bring up successful children do not use the switch as their tool of support. I believe that practicing Confucian ideals in the family will lead to decreased communication and ultimately to feelings of isolation similar to those that Chau and I felt and are still experiencing. Fortunately, after seeing her family structure crumble because of her, my mother realized that her rearing methods needed improvement. She knows now that her children will inevitably become "Americanized" to some degree. Accordingly, she now allows Tai and Carol more freedom; hopefully, they will also live up to her ideals. I can sense that the relationships in my family are becoming more intimate. We all can hug and kiss each other now, and I am optimistic that in the near future my mother and I will be able to say "I love you" to one another.

CONTRIBUTORS

Andrew Garrod is Professor of Education and Director of Teacher Education at Dartmouth College, where he teaches courses in adolescence, moral development, and contemporary issues in U.S. education. His recent publications include two co-authored articles, "Forgiveness After Genocide?: Perspectives from Bosnian Youth" and "Culture, Ethnic Conflict, and Moral Orientation in Bosnian Children"; and the co-edited books, *Crossing Customs: International Students Write on U.S. College Life and Culture* and *Learning Disabilities and Life Stories.* In 1991 he was awarded Dartmouth College's Distinguished Teaching Award.

Robert Kilkenny is Clinical Instructor in Psychology, Department of Psychiatry, at Harvard Medical School and Research Child Psychologist at McLean Hospital. He is co-editor of *Souls Looking Back: Life Stories of Growing Up Black* (with Andrew Garrod, Janie Ward, and Tracy Robinson). He is Executive Director of the Alliance for Inclusion and Prevention, a public–private partnership providing mental health and special education services to at-risk students in the Boston Public Schools.

Sally Powers is Professor and Head of the Clinical Division in the Department of Psychology, and Director of the Center for Interdisciplinary Research on Families at the University of Massachusetts, Amherst. In addition to teaching courses in adolescent and adult psychopathology, she is principal investigator of a study, funded by the National Institute of Mental Health, that investigates a bio-psychosocial model of gender differences in adolescent depression.

Lisa Smulyan is Professor of Education and Chair of the department at Swarthmore College, Swarthmore, Pennsylvania, where she teaches courses in educational foundations, adolescence, women and education, and school and society. Her publications include *Balancing Acts: Women Principals at Work, Collaborative Action Research: A Developmental Process,* and several articles. Her research focuses on classroom-based research with teachers, life/case history as a basis for understanding school practice, and investigations into the role of gender in teachers' and administrators' work experience.

BIBLIOGRAPHY

Adelson, J., & Douvan, E. (1975). "Adolescent friendships." In J. Conger, P. Mussen, & J. Kagan, *Basic and Contemporary Issues in Developmental Psychology*, 277–90. New York: Harper and Row Publishers.

Adelson, J., & O'Neil, R. (1975). "Growth of political ideas in adolescence: The sense of community." in J. Conger, P. Mussen, & J. Kagan, *Basic and Contemporary Issues in Developmental Psychology*, 53–70. New York: Harper and Row.

Adler, N. (1975). "Emotional responses of women following therapeutic abortion." *American Journal of Orthopsychiatry* 45:446–56.

Allen, J. P., Hausen, S. T., Bell, K. L., & O'Conner, T. G. (1994). "Longitudinal assessment of autonomy and relatedness in adolescent-family interactions as predicators of adolescent ego development and self-esteem." *Child Development* 65:179–94.

American Psychological Association: Interdivisional Committee on Adolescent Abortion. (1987). "Adolescent abortion: Psychological and legal issues." *American Psychologist* 42(1):763–78.

Ames, N., & Miller, E. (1994). *Changing Middle Schools: How to Make Schools Work for Young Adolescents*. San Francisco: Jossey-Bass.

Aristotle. (1941). *Rhetorica*. New York: Random House.

Bakan, D. (1972). "Adolescence in America: From idea to social fact." In K. Kagan and R. Coles (eds.), *Twelve to Sixteen: Early Adolescence*, 73–89. New York: W. W. Norton.

Bardige, B. (1988). "Things so finely human: Moral sensibilities at risk in adolescence." In C. Gilligan, J. V. Ward, J. M. Taylor, & B. Bardige (eds.), *Mapping the Moral Domain*, 87–110. Cambridge, MA: Harvard University Press.

Baumrind, D. (1989). "Rearing competent children." In W. Damon (ed.), *Child Development Today and Tomorrow*. San Francisco: Jossey-Bass.

———. (1987). "Development perspectives on adolescent risk-taking in contemporary America." In C. E. Irwin (ed.), *Adolescent Social Behavior and Health*, 93–125. San Francisco: Jossey-Bass.

Beardslee, W. R. (1981). "Self-understanding and coping with cancer." In J. E. Koocher and G. P. O'Malley (eds.), *The Damocles Syndrome: Psy-chosocial Consequences of Surviving Childhood Cancer*. New York: McGraw-Hill.

———. (1989). "The role of self understanding in resilient individuals: The development of a perspective." *American Journal of Orthopsychiatry* 59(2):266–78.

Benedict, R. (1950). *Patterns of Culture*. New York: New American Library.

Berndt, T. (1981). "Relations between social cognition, non-social cognition, and social behavior: The case of friendship." In J. Flavell and L. Ross (eds.), *Social Cognitive Development: Frontiers and Possible Futures*. Cambridge, MA: Cambridge University Press.

———. (1982). "The features and effects of friendship in early adolescence." *Child Development* 55:151–62.

Berndt, T. J., & Ladd, G. W. (1989). *Peer Relationships in Child Development*. New York: Wiley.

Berndt, T. J., & Perry, T. B. (1990). "Distinctive features and effects of early adolescent friendships." In R. Montemayor (ed.), *Advances in Adolescent Research*. Greenwich, CT: JAI Press.

Berry, Gordon L., & Asamen, Joy Keiko (eds.). (1989). *Black Students: Psychosocial Issues and Academic Achievement*. Beverly Hills: Sage Focus.

Blos, P. (1962). *On Adolescence: A Psychoanalytic Interpretation*. New York: Free Press.

———. (1972). "The child analyst looks at the young adolescent." In K. Kagan and R. Coles (eds.), *Twelve to Sixteen: Early Adolescence*. New York: W. W. Norton.

Blyth, D., Hill, J., & Thiel, K. (1982). "Early adolescents' significant others: Grade and gender differences in perceived relationships with familial and non-familial adults and young people." *Journal of Youth and Adolescence* 11:425–50.

Bracken, M., Hachamovitch, M., & Grossman, A. (1974). "The decision to abort and psychological sequelae." *Journal of Nervous and Mental Disorders* 15:155–61.

Bracken, M., Klerman, L., & Bracken, M. (1978). "Coping with pregnancy resolution among never-married women." *American Journal of Orthopsychiatry* 48:320–33.

Brown, L. M. (1991). "Telling a Girl's Life." In C. Gilligan (ed.), *Women, Girls, and Psychotherapy*, 71–86. New York: Harrington Park.

Brown, L. M., & Gilligan, C. (1992). *Meeting at the Crossroads*. Cambridge, MA: Harvard University Press.

Buhrmester, D., & Furman, W. (1987). "The development of companionship and intimacy." *Child Development* 58:1101–13.

Bukowski, W., Newcomb, A., & Hartup, W. (eds.). (1996). *The Company They Keep: Friendship in Childhood and Adolescence*. Cambridge, MA: Cambridge University Press.

Burleson, B. (1982). "The development of comforting communication skills in childhood and adolescence." *Child Development* 53:1578–88.

Chodorow, N. (1974). "Family structure and feminine personality." In M. Rosaldo and L. Lamphere (eds.), *Women, Culture, and Society*, 43–66. Stanford, CA: Stanford University Press.

———. (1989). *Feminism and Psychoanalysis*. New Haven, CT: Yale University Press.

Clark, R. (1983). *Family Life and School Achievement: Why Poor Black Children Succeed or Fail*. Chicago: University of Chicago Press.

Coleman, J. C. (1987). "Friendship and the peer group in adolescence." In J. Adelson (ed.), *Handbook of Adolescent Psychology*, 408–31. New York: Wiley.

Cooley, C. H. (1902). *Human Nature and the Social Order*. New York: Scribners.

Côté, J., & Levine, C. (1987). "A formulation of Erikson's theory of ego identity formation." *Developmental Review* 7:273–325.

Cottle, T. J. (1972). "The connections of adolescence." In J. Kagan and R. Coles (eds.), *Twelve to Sixteen: Early Adolescence*, 294–336. New York: Norton.

Crockett, L., Losoff, M., & Peterson, A. C. (1984). "Perceptions of the peer group and friendship in early adolescence." *Journal of Early Adolescence* 4(2):155–81.

Cross, W. (1991). *Shades of Black: Diversity in African-American Identity*. Philadelphia: Temple University Press.

Csikszentmihalyi, M., & Larson, R. (1984). *Being Adolescent*. New York: Basic Books.

Cvejic, H., Lipper, I., Kinch, R. A., & Benjamin, P. (1977). "Follow-up of 50 adolescent girls two years after abortion." *Canadian Medical Association Journal* 116:44–46.

Diaz, R., & Berndt, T. (1982). "Children's knowledge of a best friend: Fact or fantasy?" *Developmental Psychology* 18:787–94.

Dickinson, E. (1960). *Complete Poems*. Boston: Little, Brown.

Elder, G. (1980). "Adolescence in historical perspective." In J. Adelson (ed.), *Handbook of Adolescent Psychology*, 3–46. New York: John Wiley and Sons.

Erikson, E. H. (1959). "Identity and the life cycle." *Psychological Issues* 1:1–171.

———. (1964). *Insight and Responsibility*. New York: W. W. Norton.

———. (1966). *The Challenge of Youth*. New York: Anchor Paperback.

———. (1968). *Identity: Youth and Crisis*. New York: Norton.

———. (1975). *Life History and the Historical Moment*. New York: W. W. Norton.

———. (1980). *Identity and the Life Cycle: A Reissue*. New York: W. W. Norton.

Ewing, J. A., & Rouse, B. A. (1973). "Therapeutic abortion and a prior psychiatric history." *American Journal of Psychiatry* 130:37–40.

Feldman, S., & Elliott, G. (1990). *At the Threshold: The Developing Adolescent*. Cambridge, MA: Harvard University Press.

Finkelhor, D. (1984). *Child Sexual Abuse: New Theory and Research*. New York: Free Press.

Ford, C., Castelnuovo-Tedesco, P., & Long, K. (1971). "Abortion: Is it a therapeutic procedure in psychiatry?" *Journal of the American Medical Association* 218:1173.

Fordham, S. (1988). "Racelessness as a factor in Black students' school success: Pragmatic strategy or pyrrhic victory?" *Harvard Educational Review* 58(1):54–84.

Fordham, S., & Ogbu, J. (1986). "Black students' school success: Coping with the burden of acting white." *The Urban Review* 18(3):176–206.

Fowler, J. W. (1981). "Adolescence." In *Stages of Faith: The Psychology of Human Development and the Quest for Meaning*, 69–77. San Francisco: Harper and Row Publishers.

Freud, A. (1946). *The Ego and Mechanisms of Defense*. (C. Baines, trans.). New York: International Universities Press.

———. (1958). "Adolescence." In *Psychoanalytic Study of the Child*. New York: International Universities Press.

Freud, S. (1962). "The transformations of puberty." In *Three Essays on the Theory of Sexuality*, 73–74, 85–96. New York: Basic Books.

Fritz, G. K., Williams, J. R., & Amylon, M. (1988). "After treatment ends: Psychosocial sequelae on pediatric cancer survivors." *American Journal of Orthopsychiatry* 58(4):552–61.

Garmezy, N. (1985). "Stress-resistant children: The search for protective factors." In J. E. Stevenson (ed.), *Recent Research in Developmental Psychopathology*. Oxford: Pergamon Press.

———. (1987). "Stress, competence, and development: Continuities in the study of schizophrenic adults, children vulnerable to psychopathology, and the search for stress-resistant children." *American Journal of Orthopsychiatry* 57(2):159–74.

Garrod, A., & Larimore C. (1997). *First Person First Peoples: Native American Graduates Tell Their Life Stories*. Ithaca, NY: Cornell University Press.

Garrod, A., Ward, J., Robinson, T., & Kilkenny, R. (1999). *Souls Looking Back: Life Stories of Growing up Black*. New York: Routledge.

Gibbs, J. T. (1984). "Black adolescents and youth: An endangered species." *American Journal of Orthopsychiatry* 54(1):6–23.

Gilligan, C. (1977). "In a different voice: Women's conceptions of self and morality." *Harvard Educational Review* 47(4):481–516.

———. (1982). *In a Different Voice*. Cambridge, MA: Harvard University Press.

———. (1987). "Adolescent development reconsidered." In C. Irwin (ed.), *Adolescent Social Behavior and Health*, 63–92. San Francisco: Jossey-Bass.

———. (1989). "Teaching Shakespeare's sister." In C. Gilligan, N. Lyons, & T. Hanmer (eds.), *Making Connections*. Cambridge, MA: Harvard University Press.

———. (1990). "Joining the resistance: Psychology, politics, girls and women." *Michigan Quarterly Review* 19(Fall).

Gilligan, C., & Brown, L. M. (1990) "Psyche embedded: A place for body, relationships and culture in personality theory." In A. Rabin (ed.), *Studying Persons and Lives*. New York: Springer.

Gilligan, C., Lyons, N., & Hanmer, T. (eds.). (1989). *Making Connections: The Relational Worlds of Adolescent Girls at Emma Willard School*. Troy, NY: Emma Willard School.

Gilligan, C., & Murphy, J. (1979). "Development from adolescence to adulthood: The philosopher and the dilemma of the fact." In D. Kuhn (ed.), *Intellectual Development Beyond Childhood*, 85–99. San Francisco: Jossey-Bass.

Goethals, G. W., & Klos, D. S. (1976). *Experiencing Youth: First Person Accounts*. Boston: Little Brown.

Gold, M., & Yanof, D. (1985). "Mothers, daughters and girlfriends." *Journal of Personality and Social Psychology* 49:654–89.

Goldberger, N., Tarule, J., Clincy, B., & Belenky, M. (eds.). (1996). *Knowledge, Difference and Power*. New York: Basic Books.

Gonzales, Nancy, & Cauce, Ana Mari. (1995). "Ethnic identity and multicultural competence: Dilemmas and challenges for minority youth." In W. D. Hawley & A. W. Jackson (eds.), *Toward a Common Destiny*, 131–62. San Francisco, CA: Jossey-Bass.

Gordon, S., & Gilgun, J. F. (1987). "Adolescent sexuality." In V. B. Van Hasselt & M. Hersen (eds.), *Handbook of Adolescent Psychology*, 147–67. New York: Wiley.

Gottman, J. M., & Parker, J. G. (eds.). (1987). *Conversations with Friends*. New York: Cambridge University Press.

Grotevant, H. D., & Cooper, C. R. (1986). "Individuation in family relationships." *Human Development* 29:82–100.

Hall, C., & Lindzey, G. (1978). *Theories of Personality*. New York: John Wiley and Sons.

Hall, G. S. (1904). *Adolescence: Its Psychology and Its Relations to Physiology, Anthropology, Sociology, Sex, Crime, Religion, and Education*. New York: Appleton-Century-Crofts.

Hatcher, S. (1976). "Understanding adolescent pregnancy and abortion." *Primary Care* 3:407–25.

Hauser, S. T., & Bowlds, M. K. (1990). "Stress, coping, and adaptation." In S. S. Feldman and G. R. Elliott (eds.), *At the Threshold: The Developing Adolescent*, 388–413. Cambridge, MA: Harvard University Press.

Hauser, S. T., Houlihan, J., Powers, S. I., Jacobson, A. M., Noam, G., Weiss-Perry, B., & Follansbee, D. (1987). "Interaction sequences in families of psychiatrically hospitalized and non-patient adolescents." *Psychiatry* 50:308–19.

Hauser, S. T., Powers, S. I., Noam, G., Jacobson, A. M., Weiss, B., & Follansbee, D. (1984). "Familial contexts of adolescent ego development." *Child Development* 55:195–213.

Havighurst, R. J., Bosman, P. H., Liddle, G., Mathews, C. V., & Pierce, J. V. (1962). *Growing up in River City*. New York: Wiley.

Hill, J. P. (1987). "Research on adolescents and their families: Past and prospect." In C. E. Irwin (ed.), *Adolescent Social Behavior and Health*, 13–31. San Francisco: Jossey-Bass.

Hollingshead, A. B. (1949). *Elmstown's Youth*. New York: Wiley.

Jackson, J. S., McCullough, W. R., & Gurin, G. (1981). "Group identity development within black families." In H. McAdoo (ed.), *Black Families*, 252–63. Beverly Hills, CA: Sage.

Jordan, D. (1971). "Parental antecedents and personality characteristics of ego identity statuses." Unpublished doctoral dissertation. State University of New York at Buffalo.

Josselson, R. (1987). *Finding Herself: Pathways to Identity Development in Women.* San Francisco: Jossey-Bass.

Kohlberg, L., & Gilligan, C. (1972). "The adolescent as philosopher: The discovery of the self in a postconventional world." In J. Kagan & R. Coles (eds.), *Twelve to Sixteen: Early Adolescence.* New York: Norton.

Koocher, G., & O'Malley, J. (1981). *The Damocles Syndrome: Psychosocial Consequences of Surviving Childhood Cancer.* New York: McGraw-Hill.

LaFromboise, T., Coleman, H., & Gerton, J. (1993). "Psychology impact of biculturalism: Evidence and theory." *Psychology Bulletin* 114(3):395–412.

Leadbeater, B., & Way, N. (1996). *Urban Girls: Resisting Stereotypes, Creating Identities.* New York: NYU Press.

Lewin, K. (1939). "Field theory and experiment in social psychology: Concepts and methods." *The American Journal of Sociology* 44:868–97.

Lewis, C. C. (1987). "Minors' competence to consent to abortion." *American Psychologist* 42(1): 84–88.

Lyons, N. (1983). "Two perspectives: On self, relationships, and morality." *Harvard Educational Review* 53(2):125–36.

Manaster, G. J. (1989). *Adolescent Development: A Psychological Interpretation.* Itasca, IL: F. E. Peacock.

Marcia, J. (1966). "Development and validation of ego—Identity status." *Journal of Personality and Social Psychology* 3:551–58.

———. (1967). "Ego identity status: Relationship to change in self-esteem." *Journal of Personality* 35:118–33.

———. (1980). "Identity in Adolescence." In J. Adelson (ed.), *Handbook of Adolescent Psychology.* New York: Wiley.

Margolis, A. J., Davidson, L. A., Hanson, D. H., Loos, S. A., & Mikelson, C. A. (1971). "Therapeutic abortion: Follow-up study." *American Journal of Obstetrical Gynecology* 110:243–49.

Martin, J. R. (1981). "Sophie and Emile: A case study of sex bias in the history of educational thought." *Harvard Educational Review* 51(3):357–72.

Martin, K. (1996). *Puberty, Sexuality and the Self: Girls and Boys at Adolescence.* New York: Routledge.

Masten, A. S., & Garmezy, N. (1985). "Risk, vulnerability and protective factors in developmental psychopathology." In B. B. Lahey & A. E. Kazdin (eds.), *Advances in Clinical Child Psychology* (vol. 8). New York: Plenum.

McAdoo, H. P., & McAdoo, J. (1985). *Black Children: Social, Educational and Parental Environments.* Beverly Hills, CA: Sage Focus.

McLaughlin, M., & Heath, S. (eds.). (1993). *Inner City Youth: Beyond Ethnicity and Gender.* New York: Teachers College Press.

Mead, G. H. (1934). *Mind, Self and Society.* Chicago: University of Chicago Press.

Mead, M. (1958). "Adolescence in primitive and modern society." In E. Maccoby, T. Newcomb & E. Hartley (eds.), *Readings in Social Psychology.* New York: Norton.

Miller, A. (1983). *The Drama of the Gifted Child.* New York: Basic Books.

Miller, J. B. (1976). *Toward a New Psychology of Women.* Boston: Beacon Press.

———. (1991). "The Development of Women's Sense of Self." In J. V. Jordan et al. (eds.), *Women's Growth in Connection,* 11–26. New York: Guilford Press.

Modell, J., & Goodman, M. (1990). "Historical perspectives." In S. S. Feldman and G. R. Elliott (eds.), *At the Threshold,* 93–122. Cambridge, MA: Harvard University Press.

Monosour, K., & Stewart, B. (1973). "Abortion and sexual behavior in college women." *American Journal of Orthopsychiatry* 43:803–14.

Montemayor, R. (1983). "Parents and adolescents in conflict: All families some of the time and some families most of the time." *Journal of Early Adolescence* 3:83–103.

Montemayor, R., & Hanson, E. (1985). "A naturalistic view of conflict between adolescents and their parents and siblings." *Journal of Early Adolescence* 5:23–30.

Mosley, D. T., Follingshead, D. R., Harley, H., & Heckel, R. V. (1981). "Psychological factors that predict reaction to abortion." *Journal of Clinical Psychology* 37:276–79.

Muuss, R. (1996). *Theories of Adolescence,* 6th ed. New York: McGraw-Hill.

Noam, G. (1988). "The theory of biography and transformation: Foundation for clinical-developmental therapy." In Shirk (ed.), *Cognitive-Developmental Approaches to Child Therapy.* New York: Plenum.

Noam, G., Powers, S., Kilkenny, R., & Beedy, J. (1990). "The interpersonal self in life-span developmental perspective: Theory, measurement and longitudinal case analysis." In M. Perlmutter, D. L. Featherman, & R. M. Learner (eds.),

Life-span Development and Behavior (vol. 10). Hillsdale, NJ: Lawrence Erlbaum Associates.

Olson, L. (1980). "Social and psychological correlates of pregnancy resolution among adolescent women: A review." *American Journal of Orthopsychiatry* 50:432–45.

Parker, J. G., & Gottman, J. M. (1989). "Social and emotional development in a relational context: Friendship interaction from early childhood to adolescence." In T. J. Berndt & G. W. Ladd (eds.), *Peer Relations in Child Development*. New York: Wiley.

Payne, E. C., Kravitz, A. R., Notman, M. T., & Anderson, J. V. (1976). "Outcome following therapeutic abortion." *Archives of General Psychiatry* 33:725–33.

Perry, W. A. (1970). *Forms of Intellectual and Ethical Development in the College Years: A Scheme*. New York: Holt, Rinehart and Winston. 45–56.

Peterson, L. (1989). "Coping by children undergoing stressful medical procedures: Some conceptual, methodological, and therapeutic issues." *Journal of Consulting and Clinical Psychology* 57(3):380–87.

Piaget, J. (1972). "Intellectual evolution from adolescence to adulthood." *Human Development* 15:1–12.

Plato. (1921). *Republic*. Oxford: Clarendon Press.

Ponterotto, J., & Pederson, P. (1993). *Preventing Prejudice: A Guide for Counselors and Educators*. Newbury Park, CA: Sage.

Powers, S. I. (1988). "Moral judgment in the family." *Journal of Moral Education* 17:209–19.

Powers, S. I., Hauser, S. T., Schwartz, J., Noam, G., & Jacobson, A. M. (1983). "Adolescent ego development and family interaction: A structural-developmental perspective." In H. D. Grotevant, & C. R. Cooper (eds.), *Adolescent Development within the Family*. San Francisco: Jossey-Bass.

Pritchett, V. S. (1971). *Midnight Oil*. London: Chatto and Windus Ltd.

Rogers, A. (1991). "A feminist poetics of psychotherapy." In C. Gilligan (ed.), *Women, Girls, and Psychotherapy*, 33–53. New York: Harrington Park.

Rogler, L. H., Cortes, D. E., & Malgady, R. G. (1991). "Acculturation and mental health status among Hispanics: Convergence and new directions for research." *American Psychologist* 46:585–97.

Root, M. (ed.). (1996). *The Multiracial Experience: Racial Borders as the New Frontier*. Thousand Oaks, CA: Sage.

Rosen, R. H. (1980). "Adolescent pregnancy decision-making: Are parents important?" *Adolescence* 15:43–54.

Ruddick, S. (1989). *Maternal Thinking*. Boston: Beacon.

Rutter, M. (1975). "Attainment and adjustment in two geographical areas. I: The prevalence of psychiatric disorder." *British Journal of Psychiatry* 126:493–509.

———. (1979). "Protective factors in children's responses to stress and disadvantage." In M. W. Kent and J. Rolf (eds.), *Primary Prevention of Psychopathology: III: Social Competence in Children*. Hanover, NH: University Press of New England.

———. (1987). "Psychosocial resilience and protective mechanisms." *American Journal of Orthopsychiatry* 57(3):316–31.

Rutter, M., & Quinton, D. (1984). "Long-term follow-up of women institutionalized in childhood: Factors promoting good functioning in adult life." *British Journal of Developmental Psychology* 18:225–34.

Rutter, M., Graham, P., Chadwick, O., & Yule, W. (1976). "Adolescent turmoil: Fact or fiction?" *Journal of Child Psychology and Psychiatry* 17:35–56.

Santrock, J. W. (1990). *Adolescence*, 4th ed. Dubuque, IA: William C. Brown.

Sears, J. (1996). "Black-Gay or Gay-Black? Choosing identities and identifying choices." In G. Unks, (ed.), *The Gay Teen*. New York: Routledge, 135–57.

Selman, R. (1980). *The Growth of Interpersonal Understanding*. New York: Academic Press.

———. (1979). "A structural-developmental model of social cognition: Implications for intervention research." In Mosher, R. L. (ed.), *Adolescents' Development and Education*, 123–32. Berkeley, CA: McCutchan.

Sharabany, R., Gershoni, R., & Hoffman, J. (1981). "Girl-friend, boy-friend: Age and sex differences in intimate friendship." *Developmental Psychology* 17:800–08.

Sisson, L., Hersen, M., & Van Hasselt, V. (1987). "Historical perspectives." In V. Van Hasselt & M. Hersen (eds.), *Handbook of Adolescent Psychology*, 3–10. New York: Pergamon Press.

Slater, E. J., Stewart, K. J., & Linn, M. W. (1983). "The effects of family disruption on adolescent males and females." *Adolescence* 17(72):203–14.

Slaughter, D. (1972). "Becoming an African-American woman." *School Review* 299-318.

Smith, E. M. (1973). "A follow-up study of women who request abortion." *American Journal of Orthopsychiatry* 43:574–85.

Spaulding, J. G., & Cavenar, J. O. (1978). "Psychoses following therapeutic abortion." *American Journal of Psychiatry* 135:364–65.

Sullivan, H. S. (1953). *The Interpersonal Theory of Psychiatry*. New York: W. W. Norton.

Surrey, J. (1984). "The self-in-relation." In *Work in Progress*. Wellesley, MA: Stone Center for Developmental Services and Studies.

Taylor, R. (1976). "Psychosocial development among black children and youth: A reexamination." *American Journal of Orthopsychiatry* 46(1):4–19.

———. (1989). "Black youth, role models and the social construction of identity." In R. Jones (ed.), *Black Adolescents*. Berkeley, CA: Cobbs and Henry.

Unks, G. (ed.). (1996). *The Gay Teen*. New York: Routledge.

Van der Kolk, B. A. (1987). *Psychological Trauma*. Washington, DC: American Psychiatric Press.

Ward, J. (1989). "Racial identity formation and transformation." In C. Gilligan, N. Lyons, & T. Hanmer (eds.), *Making Connections: The Relational Worlds of Adolescent Girls at Emma Willard School*. Troy, NY: Emma Willard School.

Weiss, L., & Fine, M. (1993). *Beyond Silenced Voices: Class, Race and Gender in U.S. Schools*. Albany: SUNY.

Werner, E. (1989). "High-risk children in young adulthood: A longitudinal study from birth to 32 years. *American Journal of Orthopsychiatry* 59(1):72–81.

Wilson, A. (1996). "How we find ourselves: Identity development and two-spirit people." *Harvard Educational Review* 66(2):303–17.

Youniss, J., & Smollar, J. (1985). *Adolescent Relations with Mothers, Fathers, and Friends*. Chicago: University of Chicago Press.

Zeldin, R., Small, S., & Savin-Williams, R. (1982). "Prosocial interactions in two mixed-sex adolescent groups. *Child Development* 53:1492–98.